THE REAGAN LEGACY

THE REAGAN LEGACY

Promise and Performance

Edited by

CHARLES O. JONES
University of Wisconsin-Madison

CHATHAM HOUSE PUBLISHERS, INC.
Chatham, New Jersey

THE REAGAN LEGACY
Promise and Performance

CHATHAM HOUSE PUBLISHERS, INC.
Post Office Box One
Chatham, New Jersey 07928

PUBLISHER: Edward Artinian
ILLUSTRATIONS: Adrienne Shubert
JACKET AND COVER DESIGN: Lawrence Ratzkin
COMPOSITION: Chatham Composer
PRINTING AND BINDING: BookCrafters

LIBRARY OF CONGRESS CATALOGING-IN-PUBLICATION DATA

The Reagan legacy.

Includes index.
1. United States--Politics and government--
1981-   .   I. Jones. Charles O.
JK271.R3317   1988   973.927   88-18137
ISBN 0-934540-71-3
ISBN 0-934540-70-5 (pbk.)

Manufactured in the United States of America
10 9 8 7 6 5 4 3 2 1

Contents

Introduction

CHARLES O. JONES

The Presidency of Ronald Reagan will be the subject of scores of books. He remains personally popular, and the style and substance of his administration are fascinating. It is not too soon to begin an analysis, understanding that perspectives on him and his performance will change over time. This volume treats major topics regarding this extraordinary administration, providing a review and early assessment of the political, institutional, organizational, electoral, and policy record.

President Reagan closed the gap between the public and its leader. The public has come to feel personally about him, so much so that even his critics feel bad when he is not doing well. We even observe a tendency to blame others for not serving the President well when things go wrong. Oh, there are Reagan haters, but there is an enormous amount of goodwill toward this President. Indeed, were it not for the Twenty-Second Amendment, it is very likely that Ronald Reagan would win reelection to a third term.

In part, the profile of Ronald Reagan that emerges here is, in the words of Anthony King and David Sanders, "one of puzzlement." Possibly no knowledgeable person would recommend an "ex-actor" and "ex-professional after-dinner speaker" as President, or as governor of California for that matter. Thus what King and Sanders report as a view from Europe has credence here too. It should be said, however, that many Reagan watchers create the conditions under which they are assured of being puzzled by the President's performance. For example, they expect little from this actor/President, thus setting themselves up to be overly impressed even with ordinary accomplishments. In predicting and evaluating Reagan's performance, analysts are wont to rely more on his acting career than his political career. He was, after all, the governor of our

most populous state. And a great deal of his after-dinner speaking was at political party fund-raising dinners.

The judgment by many of his critics is that the President is popular enough
to win office but not smart enough to manage it well. Some have convinced
themselves that the popularity is purely a surface phenomenon—attributable
to the actor's winning ways, even perhaps to sympathy for a midwestern kid
who made it in Hollywood and now finds himself in the White House.

The chapters in this volume acknowledge this image of popularity without
substance, management without intelligence. Yet in seeking to identify Reagan's
legacy, the authors are moved to account for significant policy and political
developments during his years in office. No President is responsible for all that
takes place during his tenure. But he deserves at least as much credit for the
good as blame for the bad.

The chapters are organized into four broad parts. Part 1 treats the major
policy-making institutions—the Presidency, Congress, the courts, and the bureaucracy. In the lead chapter, Bert A. Rockman points out that Ronald Reagan,
like all Presidents, had to solve the problem of controlling that for which he
is held responsible. Not surprisingly, therefore, he created an organization designed to shape "basic policy parameters." Rockman also sensibly places Reagan
in the context of historical developments, urging the reader to comprehend both
the man and the time in which he served—not a simple exercise, to be sure.

The next chapter in this part is by me. It focuses on the relationships with
Congress, stressing Reagan's 1980 victory and how it was used to great advantage in getting his program enacted. Reagan's success in 1981 shaped subsequent congressional relationships. The four Congresses, the 97th to 100th, were
very different politically. Following the successes of 1981, the three subsequent
patterns identified are those of avoidance of hard policy choices, assertiveness
by Congress, and survival efforts by the President. Reference is made to a "policy trap" for the successful President—that is, a commitment to early policy
goals that restricts subsequent choices.

In his chapter on the White House, Rockman makes the point that organization there is a "nondurable," since it is tailored to the incumbent. In the
third chapter in this section on institutions, David O'Brien describes a most
durable legacy, that of federal court appointments. He points out that by the
time he leaves office, Reagan will have appointed nearly half the lower-court
judges, "more than any other President." Media attention was naturally directed
to his U.S. Supreme Court appointments, and Reagan's choices there will un-
questionably have future impact. But both the number of lower-court appointments and their tested conservatism suggest a far broader effect, justifying the
concern of many liberals during earlier campaigns.

The last chapter in part 1 examines President Reagan's impact on the bureaucracy. Peter Benda and Charles Levine identify the President's rather bold intentions: political control of policy formulation and implementation, debureaucratization through devolution and privatization, and administrative cost cutting. They describe how the White House sought to achieve these goals, emphasizing the use of appointments and other controls designed to enforce Reagan's agenda. They also treat the effects of these actions on bureaucrats themselves, most notably on senior civil servants. Among the many lessons learned from this chapter is that redirecting government is no simple task, even for a popular President.

Part 2 treats President Reagan's effect on politics outside the institutions—specifically on political parties, elections, and public opinion. In the first chapter in this part, Paul Allen Beck describes Reagan's role in the revival of the Republican party. Following Watergate, most analysts quite sensibly predicted that it would take the Republican party a very long time to recover. Beck demonstrates that Republicans now are well organized and financed. In fact, he judges that they seem "better positioned than at any time since the New Deal years to become the leading party." That they did not become the majority party during the Reagan years, however, suggests a lost opportunity.

James Ceaser considers a topic of major interest in any study of Ronald Reagan: public reaction to the man and his message. For the "great communicator," tests of public approval are naturally of great interest. Ceaser identifies six periods in the President's standing in public opinion polls: takeoff, decline, restoration, anointment, debacle, and equilibrium. Ceaser stresses not only the approval ratings but the interpretations placed on them. He emphasizes how the President's relationship with the public enabled him to achieve his goals and concludes that since approval is a lag indicator, Presidents are advised to sacrifice a high score today for a positive assessment in the future.

Part 3 deals with public policy. Paul E. Peterson and Mark Rom tackle the domestic scene, logically focusing on fiscal matters. They provide the details on which so many other conclusions in this book are based. Beginning with the deficit, Peterson and Rom outline the major tax and spending policies and their effects on selected groups. They are sensitive to the manifold political implications of these policies throughout the Reagan years and as they affect future administrations. Here, then, is an analysis of the profound effects of the Reagan administration on the domestic agenda.

Foreign policy is the subject of the next chapter in this part. In treating this topic, I.M. Destler finds that he cannot escape "Reaganomics and the legacy of debt." For the impact of the deficit was not confined to our borders. The theme of Destler's chapter is what might be labeled *pragmatic stubbornness* on the part of Reagan. The President demonstrates impressive persistence in pursuing certain policy goals and yet is willing to cut a deal at some point. As examples, Destler uses the debt, the Strategic Defense Initiative, aid to the *contras,* and the release of the hostages (leading to the Iran-*contra* affair). While Destler acknowledges certain gains from Reagan's style, his judgment on balance is negative.

The final section of the book offers two contrasting perspectives on the Reagan Presidency. The first is a "view from Europe," written by Anthony King and David Sanders. They report an unflattering evaluation of the President from across the Atlantic, yet an acknowledgment that the government and Reagan's policies appear to have worked. "The European view of Reagan was thus somewhat schizoid." King and Sanders provide a most useful review of available poll data regarding Reagan and a comparative analysis with Margaret Thatcher that contributes to an understanding of both leaders. They test Reagan's foreign policy more in terms of whether it led to disaster than whether opportunities were realized. Their conclusion? "World war did not break out. NATO did not disintegrate."

Aaron Wildavsky has written the final chapter. He stresses Ronald Reagan's strategic abilities, questioning whether the President's accomplishments are the result of dumb luck. Wildavsky asks that we consider the status of the Democrats in judging Reagan's political savvy. In 1984 the Democrats were forced to campaign on Republican issues. In Wildavsky's judgment, "Ronald Reagan . . . integrated public policy with political support so as to provide creative policy leadership." He asks that this accomplishment be considered in the context of what he describes as an "antileadership system."

Although this book directs attention to the President, the reader will discover a great deal in each chapter about the politics of the time. President watching is simply a means for keeping track of major national and international issues. All Presidents leave something of themselves behind, to be sure, but whatever that legacy may be, it is fitted into larger, ongoing political developments. No President is forgotten. But all leave town when it is over.

PART ONE

The Political Institutions

1

The Style and Organization
of the Reagan Presidency

BERT A. ROCKMAN

Presidents and the Problem of Organization

In contrast to the streamlined and spartan operations that prevail in the offices of central leaders elsewhere, the U.S. Presidency is a portrait in complexity and gigantism. This condition is born of the unique match between the constitutional independence of the office and the demands of modern government. Whereas prime ministers and their ministerial colleagues rely upon civil servants in the ministries, their party in parliament, and a cabinet to mediate between them, U.S. Presidents are compelled to organize both politics and policy through the White House.

Glancing through any outline of functions performed by the White House and the Executive Office of the Presidency (EOP) suggests a wide variety of activities. Three very obvious ones are (1) those of central clearance, monitoring, and organization; (2) those of political advice, campaigning, and liaison; and (3) those of policy advice, analysis, and review. In reality, there is necessarily a good bit of seepage across White House and EOP roles designed to deal primarily with one or another of these functions. The key, obviously, to a President's organizational success and, therefore, to an important element of a President's political success is to get these functions to mesh together, not only within the White House and EOP but throughout the executive branch. This is no easy task. The competitive nature of American government, a product of the separation of powers and the equally competitive effort on the part of the media, interest groups, and opinion leaders to gain and exploit information about executive decision making, multiplies the effects of diversity.

All governments, of course, are faced with problems of coordination and integration. But these problems are particularly daunting in the United States because in our system there is no regularized apparatus for collectively bargaining a governmental course. A President, simply put, is not a prime minister. He has no government as such, only himself and his associates. The White House, therefore, is virtually driven to be the central political operation for Presidents attempting to advance their political prospects, their political leverage, and their policy goals. Consequently, a President can listen to anyone he pleases or to no one. The ghosts of Washington past—Clark Clifford, Abe Fortas, Bryce Harlow, among others—played important informal as well as formal roles, and even presidential friends such as Charles Kirbo appear to have influenced President Carter, even though they were physically removed from the precincts of Washington.

Presidents themselves rarely rise to the top as team players. Instead, they tend to be entrepreneurs. And, like most entrepreneurs, they have developed a sense of what they think they want, a dulled sense of empathy for what others might want, and frequently have acquired a set of retainers with skills honed chiefly in political salesmanship.

The problems of organization and operating style that a President (indeed, any chief executive in any organization) faces are to be able to find a balance between *what he wants to do* and *what he needs to know.* An implicit assumption here is that if a President knew what he needed to know, he often would not want what he wants. The implication is that a President's real interests can be other than his expressed preferences.[1] This, to be sure, is tricky territory.

Whether any particular system of White House organization can help a President know what he must know is certainly a question that cannot be easily resolved. Richard Neustadt, for instance, sees Presidents as soloists.[2] If, in his view, they do not already know what they need to know or how to intervene in order to get it, no system of organization will suffice. Above all, presidential dependencies on others can heighten the leverage of others over the President. A President who lacks the prudence and instincts to help himself soon will be in need of help from his help.

When a President feels very strongly about what he wants to do and feels relatively unencumbered by what he needs to know, the resulting organizational style is likely to be one of command. But commands go through a chain, and at each level they become subject to increased distortion and operational puzzlement as to what they might conceivably mean. When the puzzlement becomes deep enough and the quest for operational meaning unavailing, implementers tend to sit on their hands and continue doing what it was they had been doing until clarification arises, if it ever does. In other words, even in order to command *effectively,* a President also needs to know someting about what he wants to do operationally and how he wants to do it organizationally. Yet a President consumed mainly with a need to know ironically will appear to be ad hoc in direction and even paralyzed. To be successful, a President must be a chief— but he also must be a chief executive.[3]

It is evident that Presidents vary a great deal in what they want to do and in their rate of learning about what it is they can do, but they also vary in their need to know and what it is they already do know. Lyndon Johnson, for example, knew a great deal about Congress and legislative strategy but little about policy management or even party politics. Nixon, in contrast, had great diplomatic visions and a taste for the dramatic but little concern for legislative strategy.

In brief, every President comes to office with unique virtues and deficiencies. Like any chief executive officer (CEO), he knows some things and has a talent for finding out about others. But any given President also does not know a lot of things and is dependent on the organizational apparatus around him, the people who fill relevant advisory and organizational roles, and his own sense of curiosity and ideas about what he believes is important to know. Unlike a corporate CEO, a President, by definition, is inevitably an outsider, even when he has had Washington experience or even prior cabinet-level appointment. There is little permanence surrounding him. And that which appears to be permanent—the civil service and subgovernments—often is distrusted.

The role of an organizational system is to compensate for the deficiencies and complement the strengths of the leader at the top. That, ideally, is a system of organization that informs Presidents of what they need to know to help them get what it is they truly want to get. Precisely because what Presidents want to do varies, and because Presidents rarely get to the Presidency without extolling their own unique qualities and desires for change, Presidents typically want a system that is responsive to their command. At the same time, there is a strong tendency for observers detached from the fate of any given President to focus on the organizational problems of Presidents and the Presidency and to look for institutionalized solutions to provide the "help" that the Brownlow Report claimed Presidents needed.[4] The underlying assumption behind enthusiasms for institutionalization is that Presidents are interchangeable or, if they are not, that they more or less ought to be. The tacit premise is that presidential needs have a remarkable continuity, even though Presidents themselves are unlikely to acknowledge that.

From a President's perspective, therefore, institutionalization appears as a constraint in an environment that seems to him already vastly constrained.

Typically, then, Presidents want responsive coordination but not necessarily institutionalization. Not always but often, they also want a form of democratic centrism. They want to have policy and political debates about presidential decision making channeled and immune from public scrutiny, which they perceive as forcing their hand. In the extreme case of Lyndon Johnson, inferences drawn from leaks frequently resulted in decisions that seemed to be perversely taken so as to result in outcomes opposite those inferred by the leak. The assumption that presumably lay behind this was that if the leaker or the press could be rendered less credible, the incentive for leaking would decline.

Whatever the virtues of institutionalization, its liabilities are clear for most Presidents. Presidents want to steer. They do not want to be anchored with the weight of the past. Moreover, each President usually has developed a characteristic style of operation by the time he arrives at the White House. Accordingly, each is remarkably free to make use of the apparatus as he wishes, to reformulate what he desires to do, and to generate for himself a system that is comfortable for him to work through. The last especially does not come easily. Some Presidents go through several iterations until they find a system they think works for them. Of course, a President is freer to do all these things with his entourage inside the west wing of the White House than he is with the departments "out there." That, no doubt, is a source of presidential mistrust of the executive agencies. Whether he would wish it or not, however, he cannot live without them. Congress has mandated their existence and a great deal of their operating law. The linkage between the White House and the operating departments of the executive branch thus becomes one of the central challenges to a President's organizational strategy. Can he optimize what he wants and equally gain what he needs to know?

Although the EOP now contains a variety of organized shops (some, such as the Office of Management and Budget [OMB], are at least medium-size businesses), many change character quickly with presidential transitions.[5] Still, there is, as Sam Kernell points out, remarkable persistency in the creed of presidential organization. The creed, as Kernell notes, emphasizes the value of small staffs and coordination.[6] Sooner or later, according to his argument, Presidents adapt to this idea.

Other organizational creeds are equally powerful. One of them is the value of cabinet government, of delegation, and of interdepartmental coordination at high levels. These aspirations usually are voiced at the outset of an administration, duly recorded, and, after a decent interval, most often duly dismissed in fact if not always in form or rhetoric. Yet, not all the elements disappear. And, in some respects, the Reagan Presidency clearly gave more than lip service to these elements of the organizational creed—a necessity, indeed, for a

President who, more than most, has seen his role as a *chief* rather than as an *executive.*

The Man and the Machinery

Ronald Reagan came to the Presidency as its oldest incumbent. Although his political career as an officeholder was a relatively brief eight years as governor of California, there was little mystery about him. This certainly was in vivid contrast to his immediate predecessor, Jimmy Carter, the former governor of Georgia, about whom little was known or, for that matter, to even a political veteran such as Richard Nixon, the former vice-president, whose transfigurations of style and character were astonishingly frequent, even if never complete. Instead, Ronald Reagan was a political figure of stunning transparency in terms of his core political beliefs and his work habits.

Simply stated, Ronald Reagan believes in a few things with great passion and holds to them uncompromisingly. In presentation of his public self, Ronald Reagan has brought more personal presence to the office than any President at least since John F. Kennedy. Reagan's acting career and speechmaking in behalf of General Electric were excellent preparation, but not every actor has been so at ease with his script. At least during the early stages of his administration when Reagan needed to sell his program of tax and budget reductions, the ability to project the need for change in an environment receptive to change was a helpful quality.

Reagan's projection of self, however, has at least two threads. One is the ability to handle small talk, to provide the disarming one-liner, and to give mellifluently the set speech that portrays the ideas he is firmly attached to. The other thread is the President's vulnerability to facts and the consequent need to distance him from settings in which probing of his knowledge can occur, particularly news conferences. Whatever the cause of Reagan's fragile hold on facts—whether it derives from the firmness of his ideological commitments, from work habits that charitably can be characterized as laid-back, or, probably, from both—these conditions provide unusual challenges to organizing a system that would highlight the President's obvious strengths while compensating for his equally obvious deficiencies.

No system, of course, is safe from failures, even when it is working well. As Paul Anderson suggests, sound processes can have "normal failures."[7] Moreover, it has become increasingly clear that no system of organization is appropriate for all seasons, and certainly not for all Presidents. Presidencies run through cycles, and the problems of both politics and policy they face will change. A major problem, therefore, is whether a style of operation and a system of organization appropriate to one phase can adapt to another one in which the political and policy demands will be different.

In spite of these inevitable adaptations required in presidential organization, the Reagan White House could be organized around the basic and well-known characteristics of the President's political and policy objectives and his work style. To an extent that is, I believe, remarkable, there has been fundamental constancy to the President's objectives throughout his administration, to the rhetorical instruments he seeks to apply, and to the operative style he employs in decision making. Insofar as objectives are concerned, President Reagan has been committed to a fairly fundamental shift toward a smaller and less extractive government on the domestic side, to a high-spending military apparatus, to reversing established yet fragile toeholds of Marxist regimes in the Third World, and to a political realignment inside and outside of Washington that involves electoral politics but also the planting of committed partisans throughout the federal judiciary and the executive establishment. It is fair, then, to characterize President Reagan in much the same ways one can characterize candidate Reagan: deep ideological commitment to a path that, by the norms of American politics, promises radical change. The commitment to radical change is masked by two features of the Reagan personality, one being the dulcet tones in which the President propounds his vision of change, the other being the remarkably detached style through which the President pursues his goals.

Across the sea, in the United Kingdom, Margaret Thatcher's most untraditional and un-Tory-like style of leadership gives every indication that she means business, that she knows exactly what she is saying and means very well to follow it up. Mrs. Thatcher is every bit as committed as Mr. Reagan, but far more involved in the operative elements of her agenda, and in developing the means necessary to get it to work. Much like Neustadt's ideal President, Mrs. Thatcher seems endlessly curious and concerned with consequences. Reagan, to the contrary, most often appears more mellow than manic, at least until recent times when things have gone less well for him.

The problem of managing the Reagan Presidency, therefore, can be stated as follows: How can organizational structures, systems, and strategies be developed for a committed Presidency and a detached President?

Even with notable exceptions, it is fair to say that the management of the Reagan Presidency, in the first term particularly, was a success. Of course, organizational success basks in the glow of more generalized political success, and organizational failures are perceived to result in, rather than be the result of, broader political failures. Like football quarterbacks, presidential organization often bears excessive responsibility for outcomes. Yet, presidential organization is often a key element in the ability of a President to achieve his goals, as well as in calculating his Washington repute. What, then, becomes most especially interesting about the organization of the Reagan Presidency is the fact that it requires organizing around two seemingly contradictory elements: the Reagan style and the Reagan agenda. One (the style) mostly appears as soft and comforting, the other (the agenda) mostly appears as clear and polarizing.[8]

In the next section of this chapter, I want to focus principally on what mechanisms would presumably best serve a President whose style and agenda, unlike those of the much bolder Margaret Thatcher, are so nonreinforcing. I then want to proceed with an examination of the apparatus that was set up during various crossroads of the Reagan Presidency.

The Operational Style of a President

PURPOSE AND DELEGATION

The particular contribution that Ronald Reagan brought to his Presidency was clarity of purpose and a straightforward vision of his objectives. Clarity, however, often has been greater in rhetoric than in operations. The key to the Reagan Presidency was to have the President fuel the policy agenda—to enunciate his goals and sell them rather than watch over operations or intervene obtrusively in the process of decision making and policy formulation at lower levels. Reagan's style has been distinctly that of a "hands-off" President.

What does such a President need in the organization of his Presidency? Ironically, for one thing, a President as distanced from detail as Reagan typically has been needs to have the strongly articulated commitments that he has. For his key role vis-à-vis those who work for him and act in his name is to emit strong and clear signals about directions. Nevertheless, such a President necessarily will delegate; indeed, he will be almost asymmetrically dependent on those to whom he delegates. This makes it very important for a President such as Reagan to have an administration of like minds—those who can enthusiastically support the President's agenda and will speak in behalf of his goals.

There is certainly strong evidence to suggest that the Reagan administration's appointments within the White House and in the departments reflected this desire to put a strong ideological stamp on the executive. An analysis of three White House staffs—Nixon's, Carter's, and Reagan's—indicates that Reagan's was by far the most ideologically homogeneous.[9] Placing lieutenants in the White House with deep loyalties to the President's ideas was an essential element to a strategy of delegation.

Equally important to a strategy of delegation, though, was to ensure that loyalists to Reagan's ideas also permeated the departments through the careful use of discretionary appointments. In some instances, the Reagan administration pushed the limits of discretionary appointments allowed by law. The Civil Service Reform Act of 1978, which was a pet project of Jimmy Carter's, established a Senior Executive Service (SES) to replace the previous supergrade positions. As stipulated by law, 10 percent of the total SES appointments could be held by noncareer personnel, and in any given department this figure could rise to 25 percent. Between 1980 and 1986, the total percentage of career SES officials declined by 5.3 percent, whereas the total percentage of noncareer SES officials increased by 13.1 percent. In addition, discretionary Schedule C appointments also rose by 12.8 percent.[10]

In addition, the executive agencies experiencing the sharpest increases in noncareer executives and decreases in career executives included the core central management agencies such as the Office of Personnel Management (OPM) and the Office of Management and Budget (OMB). Line departments that were especially important to the President's program or of great political importance to the President's support constituencies also exhibited drops in senior career staffing and increases in noncareer staffing. Among these especially noticeable agencies were those of Justice, Housing and Urban Development (HUD), and Education. In all these agencies, senior career employment dipped, while noncareer employment rose in significant proportions. In another target department, Health and Human Services (HHS), a general decline in the number of executives suggests a tendency to eliminate jobs throughout this most costly and complex of domestic departments.[11] This also seems to have been the case with regulatory agencies whose budgets were drastically cut. Among these was the controversial Environmental Protection Agency (EPA), which took considerable personnel losses.[12]

Such efforts, along with other tactics, constitute what Richard Nathan has called "the administrative Presidency."[13] The idea of the administrative Presidency is to plant White House loyalists in the departments—persons who can be relied on to act as the White House would wish them to. Although actual application of the concept could well have preceded the Presidency of Richard Nixon, it was the Nixon Presidency, particularly in its aborted second term, that became celebrated for its deployment of this strategy. The Reagan Presidency intended to perfect the strategy and to do that from the beginning, so as "to hit the ground running." The right-wing think tank, the Heritage Foundation, which was particularly influential in the first term, emphasized the importance of deploying an administrative Presidency strategy, arguing that civil servants could not be trusted to carry forth the President's "mandate."[14]

The principal point here, though, is that it was very important for a President of Ronald Reagan's style and work habits to be able to delegate. Thus he needed people with whom he was comfortable and who enjoyed his confidence. It is, therefore, understandable that old associates such as Michael Deaver and Edwin Meese formed two-thirds of his White House triumvirate. Deaver essentially provided public relations and help in political logistics while Meese tried to ensure ideological purity. But beyond the White House, Reagan needed a bureaucracy responsive to his ideals, essentially a bureaucracy without bureaucrats. Unlike Nixon, however, whose ideological tendencies were more pragmatically attuned to what he perceived as his personal political interests and stakes, Reagan wanted responsiveness to an agenda that would transform both the existing repertoire of public policies (within the bounds of political survival, of course) and the political landscape. Nixon's interests were largely in Richard Nixon; Reagan's were in broad-scale policy and political change.

Consequently, for Richard Nixon the administrative Presidency was a mechanism designed to ensure responsiveness to him personally. For Ronald Reagan, the administrative Presidency was a mechanism to ensure responsiveness to a political agenda that Reagan, and certainly his followers, hoped would outlast his own tenure in office. One of the potential drawbacks of pursuing the latter objective is that the enthusiasts stationed to man the operations of the departments can outrun the political realities faced by the White House. They can complicate the President's choices by forcing the President to confront problems within the executive posed by conflict between his more rabid political constituents in the agencies and those seeking to maintain broader support for the President. This problem was not new to Reagan, although he often was faced with such choices by the "social issues" agenda to which he gave both lip service and some appointments, and in foreign policy where he was faced with mediating between that part of his constituency that was rabidly anticommunist and the pragmatics of conducting a foreign policy. In fact, these same generic issues frequently arose during the Carter administration, some of whose political appointments came from left-wing equivalents of the Heritage Foundation and were imbued with contempt for what they saw as a status quo bureaucracy.

In sum, Reagan's style required delegation. His politics required an unusual degree of responsiveness from the executive, particularly because Congress, not atypically among recent Presidents, was viewed as an impediment to his plans. Thus, much governing would be done through executive means. Despite the fact that operational complications inevitably will arise from even the best-laid plans, the effort of the Reagan White House to create an executive more in tune with its purposes than that which confronted Nixon must be judged largely but not unqualifiedly as a success. Recently collected data show, for instance, that by the sixth and seventh years of the Reagan administration, its appointees to the executive agencies were almost uniformly Republican and conservative. Further, the added flexibility in deploying career officials in the general SES list also seems to have enabled the Reagan administration to fill top posts with careerists, when they had to, who were considerably more Republican and conservative (but not nearly so much so as the appointees) than those the Nixon administration had to deal with. It appears further that the Reagan administration carefully deployed in the sensitive social service departments top career executives (again, only when they had to) whose political and policy sympathies were less out of line with those of the Republican administration they were serving than was the case during the Nixon administration.[15] In other words, while the administrative Presidency was Nixon's proposed solution to his problem of executive responsiveness, it came to be Reagan's achievement.

FUNNELING UPWARD

Delegation is important to a President of Reagan's operating style. So also are clarity and regularity in funneling options to the Oval Office. While all Presidents, by the definition of their jobs, are high-level decision makers, President Reagan, more than most, has seen his role principally in terms of providing the impetus for direction, selling his agenda, and making decisions only on matters clearly necessitating presidential attention.

What requires presidential attention and decision, however, is a variable, not a constant. The degree of presidential intervention is influenced greatly by the nature of the President himself and, of course, by the nature of the problems that the country is faced with at any given time. Anything labeled a crisis requires the appearance of presidential action. Some Presidents want to get involved in most everything. Carter and Johnson, despite their greatly different styles and temperaments, were inclined to think that nearly all decisions were (or should be) *their* decisions. Dwight Eisenhower and Ronald Reagan seemed to define a narrower band of decisions as ones requiring them to make choices. As noted, in Reagan's case, this feature of his temperament, in conjunction with his agenda, also required an "administrative Presidency" through which he could safely assume that his will was being carried out across the executive.

The style, then, required not only a high degree of delegation but, especially, a high degree of cooperation and coordination among the President's emissaries within the executive. Because both the processes of funneling upward and monitoring downward are of special significance to the Reagan Presidency, I first describe some aspects of the delegation-coordination strategy to funnel options up to the President and then look at some of the strategies for enforcing White House perspectives on the departments.

Although Presidents, usually while introducing their newly appointed cabinet members to the press, like to talk about cabinet government as their goal, cabinet government is an impossibility in the American system. Still, it is possible to try to develop mechanisms to push upward options that have been reviewed in the departments and to use such mechanisms to broker differences.

Colin Campbell's excellent analysis of organizational structures and processes in the Reagan Presidency suggests that Reagan indeed did wish to develop such coordinating mechanisms that could both reconcile and funnel up options.[16] The President, in fact, hoped to reconstitute something similar to the Ash Commission proposals that President Nixon put forth in 1971—a series of supersecretaries to develop coordinated functional policy options and oversee implementation of the President's agenda.

Nonetheless, such efforts were not completely, or perhaps even largely, successful. Despite developing a highly structured system of cabinet-level consultation,[17] one of the problems that arose to prevent the system from achieving its brokerage function was the clash that naturally emerges from the pragmatic purposes of brokerage and the ideological missions that key policy makers in the departments and sometimes in the White House felt fervently committed to pursue. Such clashes are inevitable in cabinet governments, as well as in ours, but as an astute observer has put it, "in a parliamentary system the Cabinet *does* have to come down and produce a single story [whereas] in the United States . . . this is not necessary."[18]

In this regard, the intermediary functions of the cabinet-level councils could meet only with uncertain success. This probably would be so in any administration, if for no other reason than that Washington simply is not, and cannot be, Whitehall or Bonn. Freelancing is always possible in our system, and strongly committed individuals (especially if they believe that they speak for the President's true beliefs) can find numerous ways to head off their adversaries. They also can limit a President's policy options by altering his political options. A useful tactic in this regard is to appeal to key presidential constituencies by suggesting that other executive actors are lacking in commitment to the President's convictions.

The areas of greatest disarray have been those of foreign policy and economic policy. During his abbreviated tenure as secretary of state, Alexander Haig came into conflict with numerous others, especially Defense Secretary Caspar Weinberger, United Nations Ambassador Jeane Kirkpatrick, Central Intelligence Agency Director William Casey, and the national security assistant to the President. These clashes were fueled by problems of personal chemistry, to be sure, but they also reflected differences of organizational view and policy operations. In economic policy, also, there remained a number of deep-seated and unresolved differences between supply-siders and monetarists. Of course, these were by no means the only policy areas that were affected by these problems.

Yet it is important to recognize that policy confusion is not an abnormal phenomenon in any American presidential administration because every one contains people strongly committed to their understanding of its objectives, who claim to speak for what the President really wants (or would want if they were able to deal directly with him). No administration, however, has the opportunity of a forum through which these diversities *must* be reconciled. Viewed in this way, the Reagan administration has achieved only a mixed success in being able to speak and act with unity. Viewed from the standpoint of our system, however, and also of recent presidencies, a mixed success is not the same as failure.

Efforts to provide for a brokered funneling up of options to the President also have to be seen from what Reagan's style of engagement permitted. President Reagan has been disinclined to reach down for details. His preference has been to have *comprehensible* options funnel up to him. That the cabinet council system that prevailed in Reagan's first term did not meet all the hopes placed in it has to be juxtaposed to what the prospects of an even less structured system would be for a President of Reagan's operating style.

MONITORING DOWNWARD

Although no single rule applies to how the Reagan White House monitored the agencies—and, obviously, the administrative Presidency itself is a prophylactic form of monitoring—it was important to the Reagan agenda to ensure administrative compliance with its rather straightforward objectives. In this effort, OMB assumed a position of centrality. A great deal of the Reagan agenda focused on deregulating or at least lightening the regulatory load on business by easing standards, reinterpreting their meaning, or subjecting proposed regulations to stringent cost-benefit tests. The administration's motives stemmed from a combination of ideology and interests; the ideology emphasized "the magic of the marketplace," while the Reagan administration's clienteles were businesses and producers who stood to gain immediate relief by moving the burden of proof from those being regulated on to the regulators.

In addition, Reagan's interests in decreasing domestic spending also could be implemented, to a degree, from the top. The emphasis on lowered spending in domestic programs elevated the already potent role of OMB while inundating it with yet more responsibility. Because of this addition to the OMB workload, its former (and most formidable) director, David Stockman, had requested increased funding for OMB while targeting other expenditures for sharp reductions. Congress, not very pleased with Stockman's high-handed methods, proceeded to cut the budget for OMB with considerable glee.

Nevertheless, OMB was involved increasingly also in reviewing administrative practices in the agencies—an exercise, it is fair to say, that did not go down well either in the agencies or in Congress. Thus, from the standpoint of the bureaucrats in the departments, OMB not only proposed drastic budget reductions but also proceeded to micromanage their functions to accord with the President's agenda as OMB interpreted it. This micromanagement by OMB, especially when its intention seems to have been to bring legislative intent into compliance with the White House point of view, has not gone unchallenged by Congress. One result is that Congress also has been micromanaging, by writing increasingly restrictive amendments onto the legislation covering administrative practices. For the bureaucrats in the departments, caught in the middle of this squeeze play, their discretion has been significantly reduced—a consequence of the administrative Presidency running into the rights that Congress legally has to influence bureaucratic practice and gain compliance with the laws it passes.

As had the Nixon administration in its latter stages, the Reagan administration from the outset tried to run the government through administrative means when it did not otherwise need legislation. Its assumption, like that of the Nixon White House, was that the administrative apparatus was its sole property and that it held exclusive rights to interpret legislative intent and often reinterpret legislative guidelines. In following this strategy, the Reagan administration was immediately effective until political sentiment and congressional reaction could catch up to it.

The tactics of the administrative Presidency required a heavy role (and perhaps also a heavy's role) for the key management and overhead units of the executive. Not only were the central clearance functions of OMB enhanced, if not equally its capabilities, so also were those of OPM. In neither case were these functions politically neutral. The process of politicization at OMB has been profound since the days of the Nixon Presidency; indeed, its creation from the old Bureau of the Budget (BOB) was a part of that process. Because of the Reagan agenda, it was inevitable that politicization would grow, especially as the government agenda itself became more and more a budget-driven one, and as the Reagan Presidency sought to govern as much as possible through administrative means.

David Stockman also had an unrelenting and principled agenda that he wished to pursue, one that brought him into conflict with cabinet officials whose relations with the President were very close and who were in especially close touch with the President's thinking. Donald Regan, then secretary of the trea-

sury, and Caspar Weinberger, then secretary of defense, were Stockman's major antagonists. Although Stockman's budget-cutting and antiregulatory attitudes were very much in accord with Reagan's, his desires to bring the budget
into balance through tax increases and by cutting the dramatically increased
defense budgets flew directly in the face of key elements of the Reagan agenda.
Stockman sought to take the so-called voodoo out of Reaganomics by bringing the budget into balance. When he made his case public to a reporter, William Greider, who proceeded to publish "Stockman's Complaint" in the *Atlantic
Monthly*, Stockman's credibility inside the Reagan administration plummeted.
Still, given the administration's agenda, Stockman's role and that of OMB remained a powerful one.

The OPM role was a new one, since the agency itself was relatively new.
The Reagan administration placed a great premium on having personnel in
key posts committed to its outlook. To this end, E. Pendleton James and later
John Herrington, as personnel directors inside the Reagan White House, and
Donald Devine, the first OPM director in the Reagan administration, played
key roles. The vetting of appointee positions was done with great thoroughness
in the White House, even to the point where positions were left vacant for long
periods of time lest they be filled by someone less than fully trustworthy. The
manipulation of positions within the agencies, made possible by the Civil Service Reform Act passed under Carter and from which the OPM itself derived,
was assisted by Devine and his associates at OPM. The key in regard to the
latter, of course, was first to politicize OPM. The evidence in this regard is
formidable.[19]

Governments are composed of many elements. But three of the most critical
are budgets, laws, and people. The Reagan administration strategy to ensure
compliance with its far-reaching agenda for change was to control each of these
three elements. After the first year, the administration did lose control of the
budgetary process, but the cuts it achieved then and the subsequent budgetary
pressures arising from the growing deficits virtually assured that the inertia de-
riving from the first year would be powerful. To that extent at least, the Reagan administration did maintain control over the approximate allocation of
expenditures. It might not be fully able to spend what it would like to on defense, for example, but during a time of strong budgetary pressure, it was difficult, though not always impossible, for the opposition to restore spending
levels that the White House most wanted to cut. As for people, while there
are some natural limits imposed by any career service system, the Reagan personnel operation took advantage of all the opportunities the system would allow to provide it with maximum flexibility and, for the administration, maximum advantage. Finally, insofar as laws are concerned, by placing its people

in the right positions, the administration also helped to interpret existing law to fit its pleasure.

In monitoring downward, therefore, exuberant leadership of the overhead agencies in behalf of the goals of the administrative Presidency was vital to the Reagan Presidency. Up to a point, this system worked very well, but strong actions tend to beget strong counterreactions. The inability of Donald Devine to regain his post as OPM director after taking temporary leave was eloquent testimony to the power of this reaction.

REACHING OUTWARD

To this point, the focus of the chapter has been on how the system created to generate choices for the President worked and how the politics of policy management worked. Both President Reagan's style of operation and his agenda are critical features to this story. There is yet a third organizational element for which the Reagan White House gained early plaudits, especially in contrast to the perceived incompetencies of the early Carter White House. This element is that of managing the administration's politics in regard to its congressional and public liaison functions and with respect to political and party organization.

In many respects, Reagan began with a set of natural resources that Carter lacked. Reagan was a party politician and Carter was not. Reagan had an ability to communicate well in front of a camera or microphone, which Carter lacked. Reagan had a set of clearly demarcated priorities to push, and for which there was broadly responsive middle-class support. Whatever Carter's vision, it became bogged down in competing yet equally urgent priorities, some of which were his and others those of important party constituencies.

Aside from the natural resource represented by President Reagan himself, the Reagan White House approached its political and public outreach functions with great care and professionalism, in marked contrast to the rocky beginning of the Carter administration. Although it remains the instant reflex in Washington to associate the experienced Washington insider with being an inveterate Democrat, while Republican administrations bring in short-term temporary help from Newport Beach and other sun-kissed spots, the fact is that the procession of Republican administrations in Washington has produced a considerable number of experienced operators with a feel for various elements of the Washington community. Thus, while Carter brought in his fellow and equally inexperienced Georgians to man key liaison posts in his White House, Reagan has generally relied on people with experience and good marks from prior administrations. To a considerable degree, his Presidency also has relied on the Republican political party apparatus to help mobilize support and propaganda.

Thus, Reagan began his Presidency with veterans in key posts. James Baker as the pivotal figure in the early White House triumvirate, Max Friedersdorf as head of legislative liaison, and David Gergen as director of communications were all figures with experience in previous Republican administrations and ones largely knowledgeable of, and respected by, key elements of the Washington community. Their presence, of course, was not the key to the early Reagan success, but the presence of respected veterans in key outreach posts added to the aura of an administration that appeared to be politically invincible.

One of the outstanding successes of the public liaison operation was its orchestration of favorable interest groups and party activists in mobilizing support in 1981 for the President's budget cuts in the Democratic-controlled House. The culmination of these efforts to gain support for the Reconciliation resolution produced a sufficient switch of votes in the House to keep, if by a narrow margin, the President's program on target.[20] In this, Reagan's own personal speechmaking in behalf of his economic program also was seen as a vital element in the concerted effort to bring influence to bear on Congress. From the Reagan administration's great success on the Reconciliation resolution, legends and reputations were made. The glow of success further embellished the professional reputations of key Reagan operatives and that of the President personally as "the great communicator."

While political forces in the environment are more powerful determinants of outcomes than are the machinations of an administration's political operatives, ineffective outreach can be harmful to a President's prospects more than effective outreach can help them.[21] From this standpoint, the Reagan White House at its inception inevitably would be contrasted with the Carter White House that immediately preceded it. The Carter political operation started off with two left feet, uncomprehending of some of the most basic elements of political tact, as well as tactics. The early days were reputation building (or ruining), despite later improvement in some of the Carter administration's political operations. Its repute in this regard was almost fatally sealed by its inept beginnings. The barometer of that fate was not in relative legislative success—that is determined by more powerful forces—but in the administation's reputation among the political cognoscenti. Carter failed to recover from that.

The Reagan operation got it right from the start, and that surely helped the President's reputation as a political whiz. They would later get it wrong in the middle when Donald Regan replaced James Baker, when Pat Buchanan replaced Gergen, and Friedersdorf, and later Ken Duberstein, his able successsor, left their liaison functions. Friedersdorf and Duberstein later would return in other roles; Howard Baker, of course, replaced Regan after the Iran-*contra* scandal broke. Pat Buchanan also returned to throwing bombs from the sidelines rather than from within the White House. But by this time, Reagan had lost his "touch" and was widely viewed as being out of touch with new political realities that cut against the grain of his agenda for political and policy change.

In the early days, Reagan's instincts, the country's willingness to accept change (in part because of the deteriorating economic conditions and the seeming helplessness of the United States in world affairs), and the effectiveness of a highly professional political apparatus in the White House to see through a clear-cut and simple policy agenda in the first year all converged to the advantage of the Reagan Presidency.

Later, the President's instincts to push other aspects of his agenda, and to ignore the policy consequences of his earlier successes (the massive tax cuts without any greater net reductions in spending), played well to the Republican right wing but lacked resonance elsewhere. While Donald Regan's management of the White House and Buchanan's inflammatory rhetoric played to many of Reagan's own instincts, such operations also reduced Reagan's chances for persuading other elites, particularly Congress.

After Reagan's stock suffered from the fallout of the Iran-*contra* affair and the Democratic capture of the Senate in the 1986 elections, the apparatus improved and was again well regarded on Capitol Hill. But now different problems emerged. One was that Reagan the President and the Reagan Presidency seemed detached from one another, if not at odds. The reconstituted White House seemed better equipped to deal with Congress overall and, especially, the Democratic majority. But Reagan the President did not always seem to be in accord with its strategies nor with its tendencies for compromise and reconciliation. The Republican Right now claims that the White House has been captured by moderates in some kind of palace coup. Although the slogan "Let Reagan be Reagan" has not recently been voiced, the sentiment remains. Thus the circumstance of an ideologically inspired President facing an opposition Congress with diminished reluctance to oppose him is the problem of the Reagan White House in its sunset. The White House apparatus under Howard Baker is clearly in a position of tryng to get the best obtainable bargain for the President's goals while mediating the politically unfavorable realities those goals face. Baker's position is one of great vulnerability; Reagan's is one of political, though not ideological or rhetorical, exhaustion.

THE ADVISORY APPARATUS

Like any President, Ronald Reagan took advice from whom he wished and ignored those whom he felt did not have his best interests at heart. No process can compel a President to do otherwise. Presidents, of course, vary in their willingness to tolerate diversity, but, typically, they are more kindly disposed to letting "a hundred flowers bloom" earlier in their administrations, before they discover that some of the flowers turn into weeds. At some point, usually by midterm, they know whom they want to listen to and whom they don't.

Presidents typically are inclined to listen to those who reinforce their instincts rather than contradict them. Unlike prime ministers, they are not compelled to listen to anyone. They can, therefore, and frequently do, choose to find reinforcements unless the political situation dictates otherwise. There also are sound political reasons for Presidents being alerted to potential opposition within their administrations. Among these is the leaky Washington environment. Advice that cannot get to the top or get backing from the top often will be propelled toward the press or Congress.

As noted, foreign policy and economic policy were areas of considerable controversy within the Reagan administration despite a broad, but not very operational, ideological consensus. The controversies regarding economic policy were (and are) many, but their point of focus has been the problem of the budget deficit produced by the first-year legislative success of the Reagan tax program, the greatly increased defense expenditures, and the only modestly decreased nondefense expenditures. To some degree, the tax-reform legislation also exacerbated the deficit problem because the final legislative product was not completely revenue neutral.

In the first Reagan administration, Treasury Secretary Donald Regan was an ardent partisan of the President's program and minimized the effects of the budget deficits despite an assortment of views among appointees within the department. In fact, the most ardent supply-side advocates who accepted large budget deficits as a necessary, if temporary, evil were coaxed to leave their posts within the Treasury relatively early in the first term. Yet the most vigorous sources of opposition to supply-side doctrine were in OMB, the Federal Reserve, and the Council of Economic Advisers. Although Reagan depended on OMB director David Stockman for his knowledge of the federal budget and his willingness to go after spending cuts and regulations with great zeal, Stockman consistently lost his battles with Regan, whose posture of advocating tax cuts over deficit reduction was a curious one for a Treasury secretary. But Regan spoke Ronald Reagan's convictions most deeply, and that enabled him to wield considerable influence with the President.

In accordance with Stockman's agenda, Paul Volcker, as chairman of the Federal Reserve Board, exercised the sizable powers of the Federal Reserve toward a sometimes painful deflationary course. Volcker was a strong advocate of deficit reduction, of tax increases, of higher interest rates, and of the sort of fiscal and monetary austerity that bankers often welcome and politicians always dread. The independent status of the Federal Reserve and the fixed-term appointments of the board members give it considerable leverage with the White House when the chairman has a lot of discretion, which Volcker tended to have.

Volcker's term expired midway into the Reagan Presidency. Although there was much sentiment in the White House to replace him with someone more pliable, his stature within the domestic and international banking and finance communities was such that it limited the administration's discretion in this regard. Over time, however, attrition gave the administration the opportunity to appoint members of the Federal Reserve Board who were less likely to accept Volcker's penchant for austerity and high interest rates. This change made his own internal situation on the board more politically precarious. Eventually, in 1987, Volcker tendered his resignation to a President who was more than grateful to accept it. Alan Greenspan replaced him. Greenspan's views were thought to be more in line with the White House. His views about the deregulation of the banking industry, for example, were more in tune with those of the administration than the views held by Volcker. In any event, Volcker's views were known and his stature sizable. Of Greenspan, less was known.

Whatever views Greenspan held of the economy and a proper monetary course for it more generally, became irrelevant in the face of the stock market losses of October 1987. The condition of the securities markets dictated doing something. In the absence of any clear diagnosis, "doing something" has since come to mean making gestures toward budget deficit reduction.

Another sore spot for the Reagan administration was the Council of Economic Advisers (CEA). Murray Weidenbaum, a highly respected economist who also served in the Treasury during the Nixon administration, was the first chairman of the CEA under the Reagan administration. Weidenbaum, it appears, had strong misgivings over the supply-side policies that Reagan had grown quite fond of. Despite these concerns, Weidenbaum mostly kept them from public display until he left his post at about the midpoint of the first Reagan administration. His replacement, Martin Feldstein, also an eminent economist, was less reticent about keeping his sentiments from public expression. Hostilities between Feldstein and Treasury Secretary Regan grew especially strong, and Larry Speakes, the President's spokesman, engaged in public ridicule of Feldstein during a briefing of the press. Feldstein's criticism of the budget deficits and the failure to accept tax increases made him clearly persona non grata within the Reagan administration, and the volume of his criticism seemed to increase as the election season grew nearer.

After Feldstein left, the post of CEA chairman remained open for an exceedingly long time. In fact, at one point only one member of the Council remained in place. Speculation arose that the White House found the attrition in the CEA a desirable situation and that the best replacements would be named "vacant." Indeed, there was much discussion about the possibility of an administrative abolition of the CEA. But, unfortunately for the White House, the existence of the CEA was mandated by the Full Employment Act of 1946.

Obviously, the administration wanted to avoid another Feldstein fiasco, and so embarked on a search for reliability rather than eminence as the chief criterion for the chairmanship of the CEA. Eventually, after a long interregnum, Beryl Sprinkel, a monetarist and former Treasury official earlier in the administration, was chosen to head a CEA whose role in the Reagan White House had been greatly diminished.

Although the Reagan administration itself, within a given range, had a diversity of perspectives, especially about macroeconomic issues, Reagan the President had very clear ideas as to what he wanted and what he wanted to resist. Unlike President Carter, whose mind never seemed fully closed, and who was consequently overly susceptible to being influenced by the last good argument in his ear, President Reagan knew firmly what he wanted and, above all, what he wanted was lower taxes or at least no retreat from the accomplishments of 1981. The mission was pursued with rare singlemindedness and, inevitably, it limited what Reagan wished to hear. Certainly, it limited what the President was willing to sign off on, no matter how delicately a deal had been prearranged. A careful proposal to cut some expenditures and raise some revenues had been arranged in 1983 between James Baker in the White House, the then Senate Republican leader Howard Baker, the Senate Finance and Budget chairmen Bob Dole and Pete Domenici, and their Democratic counterparts in the House. It was an impressive display of interparty and interbranch bargaining, except for one thing—it lacked the President's consent. The firmness of Reagan's ideas made analysis irrelevant. But it also made bargaining irrelevant, until external conditions—the stock market bust of October 1987 and the Gramm-Rudman spending reduction deadline—virtually forced the President to bargain on the issue of increasing revenues somewhat.

On matters of foreign policy, Reagan also had some firmly fixed ideas. These consisted of vastly increasing defense expenditures, especially for the navy and, later for the Strategic Defense Initiative (SDI), a space-based antiballistic missile system that clearly fascinated Reagan well beyond any operational capabilities it might have. (See Destler, chap. 8). Equally, although never formally articulated, Reagan was firmly committed to the support of selected insurrections against Marxist-governed states at the periphery, such as Nicaragua, Angola, and Afghanistan. This came to be called the Reagan doctrine.

By contrast to these concerns, until 1985 and the emergence of Mikhail Gorbachev as the Soviet leader, which followed a succession of elderly, infirm, and mortally stricken predecessors, relatively little high-level (White House) attention was being paid to relations between the Soviet Union and the United States, "evil empire" speeches aside.

These circumstances also fit well the Reagan style of operations and organization. There being little need to make policy directly out of the White House—a matter that would later change at the operational but not conceptual level—the role of the President's national security assistant could be downgraded and the NSC staff itself drawn more from military officers on secondment and less from academicians than had previously been the case. The "twin towers" of the Reagan administration foreign policy thus became guns and covert operations. Guns were delegated to the Defense Department (DOD) and, particularly, to Caspar Weinberger, who was the President's ardent advocate for more of them, and Richard Perle, an exceedingly influential assistant secretary at DOD, who argued for less restraint on their deployment. Covert operations were delegated to CIA Director William Casey and, ultimately, to the National Security Council in the White House through the irrepressible Colonel Oliver North.

As with his views on taxes, President Reagan held firm to his fundamental ideas on foreign policy. For the most part, policy making was decentralized, and frequently stridently competitive and conflictual. Reagan's views nevertheless provided powerful guides. In the end, some of these powerful guides (for instance, aid to the *contras* in Nicaragua) exposed him to great political risks and served to weaken his Presidency. On matters that Reagan held firmly to, counter streams of advice were hard to find.

Despite their assertions, Presidents are rarely on the lookout for contrary streams of advice when they themselves hold sharply defined views. As between what they want to do and what they need to know, when Presidents know what they want to do (or at least what they do not want to do), they rarely find compelling the argument that they might need to know more. What distinguishes the Reagan Presidency in this respect from others is that, far more than most, it knew with great conviction what it wanted to do. For Americans, the Reagan Presidency was a rare presidential breed, one strongly committed to a political ideology that, until it came toward the end of the road, was held powerfully enough to fend off efforts to adjust course.

From the Dawn to Middle Age to Twilight

Although the points cannot always be definitely charted, every presidential administration tends to engender a certain rhythm of activity. Each begins with ideas as to what it wants to do, some being clearer than others, and, over time, finds itself reacting more than initiating. Over time also, every administration goes through a certain organizational shake-out (sometimes several), replacing the square pegs in the round holes with ones that fit better. That there has not been a full two-term administration since Eisenhower's Presidency does not mean the absence of a rhythmic pattern of activity and organization. It only means that the precise timing of these junctures will differ somewhat.

New presidential administrations, perhaps new regimes everywhere,[22] begin their tenure fueled with vital enthusiasms to produce change, especially when they succeed the opposition party. During the so-called honeymoon period, the opportunities for change typically are greatest. Clearly the Reagan administration arrived on the scene with a clear head as to its goals and what it wished to achieve, and went quickly about the business of doing so. The OMB director-designate, David Stockman, was photographed during the transition period poring over detailed analyses of the budget so as to be prepared to recommend drastic cuts and program abolishments as soon as the new President was inaugurated. (See Peterson and Rom, chap. 7.) Similarly, presidential transition teams, many of them manned or influenced by ardent ideological enthusiasts from the right-wing Heritage Foundation, readied the ground for Reagan's appointees and sometimes were seen by the incumbent Carter administration as beginning the Reagan Presidency before inauguration. All in all, the Reagan administration came in "hitting the ground running."[23]

More than any recent Presidency, the Reagan administration not only had clear goals but also had a clear strategic concept. It knew what it wanted. It also knew who it wanted to help it get what it wanted. Many of those it wanted were ideologically zealous. As in any administration, a number of people were loyal to the President as an individual, and some were loyal to the party of the President, and would be so inclined regardless of the incumbent. More than any other administration, however, many individuals who composed this one were loyal to the ideas for which Ronald Reagan stood. Much of this zealotry was summed up in the now famous slogan "Let Reagan be Reagan." It is hard to imagine a similar catch phrase being conjured up for any other American President.

Many of the administraton's early appointees were especially notable for their ideological robustness. Some—James Watt at Interior, Anne Gorsuch Burford and Rita Lavelle at EPA—later got themselves into fatal political or legal trouble. Yet, during this time, the White House staff was running at peak efficiency with round pegs mostly fitting into round holes. The triumvirate of James Baker, Meese, and Deaver soon developed specialization and an implicit hierarchy with Baker as chief of staff, Deaver handling public liaison and outreach, and Meese offering ideological spin to a President well versed on the spin he wished to give to issues.

The triumvirate that worked well during the first Reagan administration ended by the beginning of the second. The President nominated Meese to become attorney general, a nomination that hung in limbo for some time. In the year after the second Reagan administration was installed, Deaver also left the White House. Baker switched jobs with Regan, in a deal that apparently was hatched without informing the President until it came to him for approval. In addition, the able communications director of the Reagan White House, David Gergen, departed.

The shift of Baker to Treasury, and with him, Richard Darman, left the White House devoid of mediators and brokers. The movement of Regan to the position of chief of staff changed the role of the chief as well. Baker had performed the brokerage functions of the role especially well. Regan saw his responsibilities differently. Regan apparently saw himself as the chief operating officer in an administration where the President played a hands-off role. Baker's tendencies toward mediation gave way to Regan's more imperious manner. The shift had significant consequences for the style of White House operations.

Replacing Gergen with the provocative ideologue Pat Buchanan also stiffened the backs of the anti-Reagan forces. Gergen's low profile was gone. Buchanan was everywhere, ranging widely over issues dear to the heart of the Republican Right, provoking Democrats in Congress, and probably adding to their willingness to resist Reagan initiatives, especially on the controversial issue of aid to the Nicaraguan *contras*.

After the first year's successes, the Reagan administration mostly struggled to stay in place and resist any "givebacks" from the first-year agenda. Beginning in the first quarter of 1983, however, the Reagan administration and the country began to experience the longest sustained period of economic growth in this century. As a result, except to Reagan and his ardent supporters, it made little political difference from a reelection standpoint as to how much more of their policy agenda the administration could achieve. Its electoral and public approval situation was immensely favorable. There was an economic environment of high growth and low inflation. Whether all this was a result of his policies or not, Reagan could claim that it was—and be credited for that claim. Still, the large debt remained troubling and brought forth sporadic efforts in Congress and from within some quarters of the administration to repair it. Reagan's adamancy on this matter characterized his resistance to giving back any first-year victories.

There would be at least one more major legislative success for the Reagan Presidency. This was the tax reform act passed in 1986, after occupying prime time on the presidential agenda throughout 1985. Thus, in middle age the Reagan administration largely settled into a pattern of defending its hard-won gains from the first year; it also had to make adjustments in the bureaucracy when its most zealous advocates got the administration into political trouble or embarrassing situations. Although leadership in many departments and agencies became more conciliatory (although not uniformly, of course, as William Bennett replaced Terrel Bell in Education), the White House itself became less politically adept, especially at building coalitions.

With the revelations of the Iran-*contra* affair, Regan was soon forced out of the White House. So too was John Poindexter, the President's national security assistant—a man of obviously limited political sensitivity.

After the crisis, President Reagan brought in as his chief of staff the former Senate Republican leader Howard Baker, who brought with him others with whom he had previously worked. In addition, Frank Carlucci, who since has become secretary of defense, replaced Poindexter as national security assistant. In contrast to Regan and Poindexter, Baker and Carlucci are men of exquisite political sensitivity and substantial governmental experience.

The style of reconciliation and compromise and political tact had come to the White House, but it did not seep through the doorway to the Oval Office. Ironically, although perhaps not so surprisingly, as the President's political situation became more difficult, his posture became more adamant and uncompromising, leading him to compound these difficulties. After the Democratic takeover of the Senate, the Iran-*contra* scandal, two defeats of ideologically inspired Supreme Court nominees, and the stock market crash, the President's repute was tattered and his latitude limited. It remains to be seen whether in the last year of the Reagan administration, it will be able to function as the lead in a grand coalition government of congressional Democrats and a Republican White House. Although there are signs of adjustment, these tend to reflect Baker's instincts while robbing Reagan of his.

Organization and Style—Can There Be a Legacy?

All Presidents leave some legacy, even when it is negative. In his wake, Carter's legacy, for better or worse, was that an American President should not be like Jimmy Carter. Whatever Carter's virtues, and arguably there were many, his inability or unwillingness to be the flag carrier for his party's traditions, rapidly disintegrating as they were, made his most basic source of support a questionable one. One conclusion to be reached from the Carter Presidency is that a President must have a strong base within his party, although, paradoxically, for the present that often will consign most potential Democratic candidates for the Presidency to electoral doom. The lessons derived are not always the right ones.

Reagan's legacy largely comes in the form of shaping some basic policy parameters for a longer time frame than most Presidents have the opportunity to do.[24] Politicians have been, and will be, struggling with the consequences of Reagan's first-year political victories. The Reagan legacy also has been institutionally powerful. The care taken to scrutinize judicial nominees for ideological conformity (if not necessarily for their recreational habits) has also helped remold the federal bench—not as much as the Reagan enthusiasts would have liked, but more than their opponents feared. (See O'Brien, chap. 3.)

To a considerable degree, however, a President's style and mode of operations are uniquely his. Sooner or later, a President will disown or work around an organization that fails to satisfy him. In short, because every President is who he is, and every Presidency is largely about who the President is, we are dealing here mostly in nondurables.

Nevertheless, Presidents recently have been driven to certain compulsions. One of them is the politicization of the bureaucracy[25] and the growing visibility in mid-level appointments and sometimes high-level ones of activists whose contempt for the bureaucracy and bureaucrats is legion. (See Benda and Levine, chap. 4.) The Carter administration, if for somewhat more speckled reasons, was as inclined as the Reagan administration to impose professional bureaucracy haters on operating agencies. This is not a Reagan legacy. Rather, Reagan powerfully reinforced a preexistent legacy.

Presidents, too, likely will feel stronger urges to *do* than to *know*. Because of that, much will depend on the architects of White House organization in any administration. The staff, especially the chief of staff, will need to develop mechanisms and procedures for getting to Presidents what they need to know while clarifying, as well as seeking to facilitate, what Presidents want. But there are strong limits here, and chiefs of staff in particular have taken more abuse than is rightfully theirs. It was H.R. Haldeman, after all, who asked Nixon about the condition of the Italian lira; Nixon responded that his daughter's hairdo while disembarking from an aircraft was the more important matter. So there is a "catch-22." No system or organization ultimately can save a President from himself when he is inclined to self-destruct. And no system that a President is uncomfortable with will last.

In our system, but probably in almost any system, the political leader at the center—in our case, the President—is held accountable for things that cannot be influenced immediately and directly, the state of the economy, for instance. Nevertheless, in recent times an argument has developed that what goes on in the President's own house is not his doing but that of an incompetent or even nefarious staff. Since in our system it is difficult to throw out Presidents, others are expected to sacrifice their careers, their reputations, and possibly even their freedom for him. This is a disreputable doctrine. It is true that the President is a chief, and he is not merely an executive. But he is the chief executive. What goes wrong is his responsibility as surely as if he himself had carried out the operations. The management legacy of the Reagan Presidency— which I do not expect to last for long—may be exactly the idea that Presidents need to know a lot more than they claim they do and, above all, that they should be held to account for what they know or *should* know.

In the end, then, Neustadt is right. The Presidency *is* the President's. The question is whether anything can be done to make that observation a source of confidence rather than of trepidation. But that, as the saying goes, is another matter.

Notes

ACKNOWLEDGMENT: I am grateful to Stephen Hess for his careful reading of this chapter and for his helpful comments.

1. For this argument, see Joel D. Aberbach and Bert A. Rockman, "Mandates or Mandarins: Control and Discretion in the Modern Administrative State," *Public Administration Review* 48 (March/April 1988): 606-12.

2. Richard E. Neustadt, *Presidential Power* (New York: Wiley, 1960).

3. Richard Rose, however, emphasizes the "chief" rather than the "executive" role of the President. See his "The President: A Chief but Not an Executive," *Presidential Studies Quarterly* 7 (Winter 1977): 5-20.

4. A particularly thorough analysis of issues of presidential staffing and organization derived from the Carter and Reagan Presidencies is Colin Campbell, *Managing the Presidency: Carter, Reagan and the Search for Executive Harmony* (Pittsburgh: University of Pittsburgh Press, 1986).

5. See, in this regard, Carey Covington, "Organizational Memory in Presidential Agencies," *Administration & Society* 17 (August 1985): 171-96.

6. Samuel Kernell, "The Creed and Reality of Modern White House Management," in *Chief of Staff: Twenty-Five Years of Managing the Presidency,* ed. Samuel Kernell and Samuel L. Popkin (Berkeley: University of California Press, 1986).

7. Paul A. Anderson, "Normal Failures and the Foreign Policy Advisory Process," *World Affairs* 146 (1983): 148-75.

8. This distinction was earlier suggested to me in oral commentary by Charles O. Jones.

9. See John H. Kessel, "The Structures of the Reagan White House," *American Journal of Political Science* 28 (May 1984): 231-58; see also John H. Kessel, "The Structures of the Carter White House," *American Journal of Political Science* 27 (August 1983): 431-63.

10. U.S. General Accounting Office (GAO), "Federal Employees: Trends in Career and Noncareer Employee Appointments in the Executive Branch," Fact Sheet for the Chairman, Committee on Governmental Affairs, U.S. Senate, July 1987, Appendix 2, 9.

11. Ibid.

12. Ibid.

13. Richard P. Nathan, *The Administrative Presidency* (New York: Wiley, 1983).

14. For example, see Michael Sanera, "Implementing the Agenda," in *Mandate for Leadership II,* ed. Stuart Butler, Michael Sanera, and Bruce Weinrod (Washington: Heritage Foundation, 1984).

15. For evidence of this, see Joel D. Aberbach and Bert A. Rockman, "From Nixon's Problem to Reagan's *Achievement*—The Federal Executive Reexamined" (paper delivered at the Hofstra Conference on the Presidency of Richard M. Nixon, Hofstra University, Hempstead, N.Y. 19-21 November 1987).

16. Campbell, *Managing the Presidency.*

17. Ibid., 43.

18. Richard Rose, in private correspondence, 3 November 1987.

19. GAO, "Trends in Career and Noncareer Employee Apointments," Appendix 2, 9.

20. See Darrell M. West, *Congress and Economic Policymaking* (Pittsburgh: University of Pittsburgh Press, 1987).

21. See John F. Manley, "Presidential Power and White House Lobbying," *Political Science Quarterly* 93 (Summer 1978): 255-75.

22. See Valerie Bunce, "Changing Leaders and Changing Policies: The Impact of Elite Succession on Budgetary Priorities in Democratic Countries," *American Journal of Political Science* 24 (August 1980): 373-95.

23. James P. Pfiffner, *The Strategic Presidency: Hitting the Ground Running* (Chicago: Dorsey Press, 1988).

24. Bert A. Rockman, "Conclusions: An Imprint but Not a Revolution," in *The Reagan Revolution?* ed. B.B. Kymlicka and Jean V. Matthews (Chicago: Dorsey Press, 1988), 191-206.

25. Terry Moe, "The Politicized Presidency," in *The New Direction in American Politics,* ed. John E. Chubb and Paul E. Peterson (Washington, D.C.: Brookings Institution, 1985), 235-72.

2

Ronald Reagan and the U.S. Congress: Visible-Hand Politics

CHARLES O. JONES

This chapter examines President Reagan's method of, and success in, dealing with Congress. There is perhaps no better indicator of a President's political style than his working relationship with those on Capitol Hill. Ronald Reagan's style contrasts sharply with that of the last President to serve two full terms, Dwight D. Eisenhower. In his account of Eisenhower's leadership, Fred I. Greenstein describes a "hidden-hand" method born of the President's image of himself. "Eisenhower . . . concealed his involvement in conventional politicking that would not have been controversial if he had been prepared to be viewed as a political professional." Greenstein describes the President's endorsement of a plan for managing congressional relations, a plan outlined in a letter to Robert Anderson, Eisenhower's secretary of the treasury.

> This not very novel codification of ways to influence Congress would have elicited only modest interest had it leaked from the Kennedy or Johnson White House. In the Jimmy Carter years its release might even have been a reassuring sign that the President was learning the rules of the Washington game. But such directives were inappropriate for a President who avoided being linked with political operations. Consequently, in sending the . . . memorandum along with a comment on it by General Persons [chief of congressional liaison] Eisenhower instructed Anderson to study the documents carefully, and after doing so, "I request that you personally destroy them both. I am particularly anxious that no word of any concerted effort along this line ever reach the outside because a leak would tend to destroy the value of the effort."[1]

At this writing, Ronald Reagan's Presidency is the third longest since 1945 (Truman served nearly seven and three-quarter years), and prospects are that he will serve out a second term. The Eisenhower and Reagan Presidencies operated under similar political conditions (i.e., a personally popular President and Democratic strength in Congress), but the two men differ in striking ways. There has been nothing hidden about Reagan's hand in politics, his penchant for relaxation to the contrary notwithstanding. Ronald Reagan's principal legacy in regard to working with Congress is a visibly political, often partisan, one. In fact, if we are to believe currently available accounts for each President, they are opposites. Eisenhower was politically active behind the scenes, but eschewed public display of this involvement. Reagan has promoted public perceptions of his political sagacity, but has allowed others to orchestrate activity behind the scenes. Maybe it does help in understanding their respective approaches to politics that one was a general, the other an actor.

In developing this chapter on Reagan's legislative record, I turn first to the remarkable 1980 election and the advantages it bestowed on Ronald Reagan for dealing with Congress. Then I discuss how the President organized his congressional relations so as to realize the benefits of his election. The next two sections direct attention first to the astounding success President Reagan had in 1981 and then to how it was that subsequent Congresses coped with what I call the "1981 legacy." A brief analysis of voting scores is followed by final remarks emphasizing a Reagan style that will surely be his legacy in working with Congress.

This actor liked playing the President. He understood the role better than most, possibly because his occupational training prepared him to do so. The distinction between becoming President and playing the President is an interesting and important one. Reagan himself appeared to make it in an interview in 1986: "Some people become President. I've never thought of it that way. I think the Presidency is an institution over which you have temporary custody and it has to be treated that way. . . . I don't think the Presidency belongs to the individual."[2] Perhaps one starting point in the exercise of power is knowing who you are and where you are.

The 1980 Election: Advantage Reagan

Mandates are inherently implausible. For one thing, many people vote for their party's candidate almost reflexively. . . . Others base their votes on the candidates' apparent personal qualities. . . .

People who believe in mandates usually say that those who voted for a candidate did so because they favored the policies he advocated. The search for the mandate becomes a textual analysis of the winner's campaign utterances. The problem here, of course, is that candidates say a great many things. . . . Not all these promises can be important. As Chairman Mao might have said, "Many issues, one vote."[3]

Raymond E. Wolfinger is surely correct, and yet as he himself points out in discussing the 1984 election: " 'Mandate' was one of the favorite nouns on the election night television coverage. . . ."[4] Those who interpret elections search for the message. If a President wins 91 percent of the Electoral College vote, and his party returns with a majority in the Senate for the first time in twenty-six years, it is virtually guaranteed that a "mandate" will be declared to exist. This will occur regardless of the implausibility of the concept in American national elections or solid evidence that, for example, many voters were expressing dissatisfaction with President Carter, not approval of candidate Reagan.[5]

Reading a mandate into the 1980 election outcomes established policy expectations of President Reagan and provided him with significant political advantages in working with Congress. As it happened, Reagan conveyed a rather strong policy message during the campaign—"an unusually coherent social philosophy," as one analyst put it.[6] Thus, those anxious to declare a mandate did not have to search long and hard for a policy message. During the campaign, Reagan offered a prescription for change and promised to put it into effect once in office. There was none of the ambiguity that came to be identified with the Carter approach. When the pundits declared a mandate to exist, they could then follow that announcement with a clear exposition of what to expect.

Meanwhile, at the other end of Pennsylvania Avenue, House and Senate Republicans returned triumphantly to Washington after the election. In the House, the net increase of thirty-three Republicans was the greatest in a presidential election since 1920. But it was the Senate results that stunned observers. No one called that one in advance. Even the respected *Congressional Quarterly* predicted on 1 November that "although the GOP may narrow the 59–41 margin Democrats now enjoy, it is very unlikely Republicans can take control of the Senate in 1981. To do so, they would need to win all of the close races, plus two of the seven that are currently leaning toward the Democratic candidate."[7]

As it happened, Republican candidates won eight of the nine races that were too close to call, five of the seven that were leaning Democratic, and one of eight that were declared safe for the Democrats. The net gain of twelve seats was the second greatest in this century for the Republicans. The fact that the Democratic senatorial candidates as a whole actually outpolled the Republicans was lost, or not discovered, in the short-term rush to declare a Reagan mandate.

Comparison of these results with those of previous Republican landslides in the post-World War II period shows why observers were encouraged to declare a Reagan mandate. In 1952 Eisenhower won impressively, to be sure, but by a lesser percentage in the Electoral College (83 percent). Further, the 1952 race was between nonincumbents; Reagan defeated an incumbent Democratic President (the first to lose since 1888). The Republicans did gain House and Senate majorities in 1952, but the actual gains were less impressive than in 1980: a net increase of twenty-two House seats (33 in 1980) and just one Senate seat (12 in 1980). In his second term, Eisenhower did slightly better in the Electoral College (86 percent) but House Republicans had a net loss of two seats; the number of Senate Republicans did not change. The third landslide for Republicans belonged to Richard Nixon in 1972. His Electoral College margin (97 percent) surpassed that of Reagan in 1980, but the net gain of House seats gained was small (12), and there was a net loss of two Senate seats. The 1972 election was widely interpreted as a triumph for Nixon, but not for his political party in Congress—in this regard similar to Reagan's 1984 reelection.

Also relevant is the fact that Ronald Reagan ran with his party in 1980, not alongside it. Eisenhower was judged to be above party politics, and publicly he sought to preserve that image. In 1972 Nixon ran more for himself than for his party. Reagan worked at unifying the party at the nominating convention and after. He integrated his campaign effort with that of the national party organization, and he never shied away from appearing with or aiding other candidates. Further, for those who pay attention to such matters (as do most members of Congress), Reagan ran ahead of thirty of thirty-four Senate Republican candidates (counting just the two-party vote). And although he ran behind most successful House Republican candidates in their districts (most presidential candidates do these days), still he did better than President Ford in 1976 in most districts.[8]

The point is that there was more reason than usual in 1980 to interpret the presidential and congressional elections as representing a package deal. The victory for Reagan was decisive, there seemed to be "nontrivial coattail effects,"[9] and the policy message was unambiguous. Even the Democrats and liberals detected a conservative tide in the nation. Defeated incumbent Senator Frank Church of Idaho concluded that "the conservatives are in charge now. This is what they wanted and the people have given it to them."[10] The liberal columnist Anthony Lewis agreed: "What happened in the 1980 election reflected a profound and general turn to conservatism in this country."[11] There was a receptive mood for giving the President a chance, even though to do so was to invite dramatic change.

Remarkably enough, this attitude even carried forward to the partisan Speaker of the House of Representatives, Thomas P. O'Neill, Jr., of Massachusetts. In his book O'Neill discusses the politics of the situation. After the 1980 election, he received "more letters than I had seen in my entire career—asking me to give the President's program a chance." He met with House Republican leaders and agreed to expedite consideration of the program, understanding the advantage he was providing to the administration. As O'Neill explains it:

> . . . Despite my strong opposition to the President's program, I decided to give it a chance to be voted on by the nation's elected representatives.
> For one thing, that's how our democracy is supposed to work. For another, I was afraid that the voters would repudiate the Democrats if we didn't give the President a chance to pass his program. After all, the nation was still in an economic crisis and people wanted immediate action. . . .
> I was less concerned about losing the legislative battle in the spring and summer of 1981 than I was with losing at the polls in the fall of 1982. I was convinced that if the Democrats were perceived as stalling in the midst of a national economic crisis, there would be hell to pay in the midterm elections.[12]

Specifically in regard to the tax cut, O'Neill was quoted as stating that "we will ultimately send a bill to the President that he will be satisfied with."[13] Speaker O'Neill proved himself correct, and as a consequence unwittingly provided an early announcement of what was to become a major part of the Reagan legacy—unimagined deficits.

Organizing to Take Advantage

President Lyndon B. Johnson observed that "you've got just one year when they [members of Congress] treat you right, and before they start worrying about themselves."[14] He acted on this knowledge and had one of the most productive first years of any President. Ronald Reagan intended to be an activist President too, although in the opposite direction from the one that Johnson took. Therefore, Reagan wanted to act fast, to "hit the ground running," as the phrase has it.

As has been emphasized, the 1980 election and how it was interpreted offered many advantages to the new Reagan administration. As an additional plus, it seemed that members of Congress from both parties were ready for somewhat better treatment by the White House. Presidents Nixon and Carter, in particular, preferred the full length of Pennsylvania Avenue in distancing themselves from Congress. Neither had very flattering views about the institution or its members.

The Reagan style was very different. Although not from Capitol Hill, Ronald Reagan demonstrated respect for the politics practiced there. Whereas he was unlikely to be as close to the members as either Presidents Johnson or Ford, still he would not make the mistake of distancing himself from Congress in either thought or deed. And as the "great communicator," he understood the need to sell his program to those who would vote on it. James P. Pfiffner describes how it went in those months between election and inauguration:

The President-elect held a series of dinners to which he invited members of Congress. With the realization that Democratic votes would be necessary for his legislative agenda he announced that he would retain ex-Senator Mike Mansfield as ambassador to Japan. He took particular care to court House [Speaker] Tip O'Neill who had chafed at perceived slights from the Carter White House. He and his wife were invited to a private dinner at the White House, and he was also invited to the President's small 70th birthday party. Republican members of Congress were invited to advise the transition teams in the departments. And the President-elect sought the advice of Senators Robert Dole, John Tower, and Strom Thurmond in making his cabinet choices.[15]

Members of Congress loved this attention. As Speaker O'Neill explained:

Reagan had tremendous powers of friendly persuasion. . . . The President was continually calling members of the House. He didn't always get his way, but his calls were never wasted. . . .
The members adored it when he called, even when they had no intention of changing their vote. The men and women in Congress love nothing better than to hear from the head guy, so they can go back to their districts and say, "I was talking to the President the other day." The constituents love it too. . . .[16]

Senator Paul Laxalt (R-Nevada), one of the President's closest friends and most loyal supporters, advised him in regard to establishing connections with Congress. Laxalt, since retired, was respected by senior members on both sides of the aisle. Following his advice was bound to help the President. The Laxalt-Reagan association has few parallels in the history of presidential-congressional relations.

The President also acted quickly in establishing a congressional liaison team and in preparing his program for submission to Congress. A veteran Capitol Hill staff person, Tom Korologos, was called on to assist the President-elect in his preinaugural congressional contacts and to build a White House liaison team that would take over after the inauguration.

Korologos himself did not stay on to manage the team. That task fell to another Hill veteran, Max Friedersdorf. It would be hard to imagine a better choice, given the circumstances. Friedersdorf served on the liaison team for both the Nixon and Ford administrations, and before that he worked for a House member from Indiana for ten years. He also served as chairman of the Federal Election Commission, an agency with many congressional contacts. The executive director of the House Democratic Steering and Policy Committee, S. Ariel Weiss, a seasoned and tough partisan, reacted to Friedersdorf's appointment as follows: "With Max running the show, they are experienced. . . . Initially, their moves have clearly been good."[17] Whether or not they agreed with Reagan's policy preferences, those on Capitol Hill were reassured that they would be dealing with, in Speaker O'Neill's characterization, "an experienced and savvy team." In fact, O'Neill was impressed with the whole White House staff: "All in all, the Reagan team in 1981 was probably the best-run political operating unit I've ever seen."[18] No doubt this was in part because the Speaker himself got quite good service, even as a Democrat: "Reagan's aides were never parochial, and despite our many disagreements, they never showed any animosity toward me. On a few occasions, when lower-echelon people tried to block programs for my district, I would call the White House, where Mike Deaver or Jim Baker or somebody else on the President's team would always straighten things out."[19] Later in the Reagan administration, O'Neill's relationship with Donald Regan was not so amiable.

All Presidents must depend heavily on their staffs, but Reagan's style made him more dependent than most. His has been a very public Presidency, yet, compared to other recent Presidents, he has a low tolerance for detail. Further, he proposed a difficult, even contentious, agenda for Congress. Thus he needed an able and experienced liaison staff. Friedersdorf was just the person to provide it. He selected "young-old" people. "I wanted people youthful enough to put up with the long hours and physical demands, yet old enough to be patient and mature."[20] It was an impressive group. The average age was thirty-seven. All the principal lobbyists had experience on Capitol Hill—four in the Senate, four in the House, one in both. In addition, several either had experience as interest-group lobbyists or, like Friedersdorf himself, in executive liaison offices.

Given the credentials of those beneath him, it was possible along the way for Friedersdorf to step down and be replaced by another "pro." In fact, turnover in the liaison office was rather high. Kenneth Duberstein, initially chief House lobbyist, took over the top position in 1982. Then M.B. Oglesby, Duberstein's replacement as head of the House liaison team, took over for Duberstein in managing the whole office in 1982. Following the 1984 election, Friedersdorf returned so as to get the second administration off to a good start. Oglesby stayed on with his close friend, so the liaison office more or less had two chiefs. While a suitable arrangement for Friedersdorf and Oglesby, it did not work well on Capitol Hill, and in the fall of 1985 Friedersdorf left once again. Then Oglesby left in early 1986, and William L. Ball III took over. Ball had been managing congressional relations for the Department of State—again, an experienced hand to guide the White House liaison office. In late February 1988, Ball was chosen secretary of the navy. His replacement was Alan M. Kranowitz, who had been directing White House lobbying efforts in the House.

Dick Kirschten observed that "if the attrition rate of the White House staff is any indicator, proximity to the power of the Oval Office is somewhat akin to the moth's attraction to the flame. There is a high burnout rate."[21] That would seem to be the case with the congressional liaison office. Yet the liaison operation itself appeared to serve well as a feeder system for leadership, and two of the most talented directors were willing to return to the White House staff— Friedersdorf in his old job and Kenneth Duberstein as deputy chief of staff for Howard Baker when he took over for Donald Regan early in 1987.

No liaison staff can expect smooth sailing throughout. Staff members act as "point persons" for the President on the Hill, and when it comes to difficult issues, members are unlikely to be cooperative just because the White House lobbyists are experienced and talented. Once the Democrats recaptured control of the Senate and the Iran-*contra* matter broke, the liaison team had its hands full. Fashioning majorities for budgets, domestic priorities, even treaties, and certainly appointments to the Supreme Court would be very difficult. What can be said here is that no more problems were added because of liaison personnel themselves. Apart from the confusion caused by Friedersdorf's returning in 1985, the liaison staff performed ably in coping with deteriorating political conditions.

Finally, the President himself was a tremendous asset for the liaison team. "We had to lasso him to keep him off the Hill" during the first year, according to one close adviser.[22] Members of Congress naturally make comparisons with the immediately preceding occupant of the White House. They found Reagan to be approachable; a willing participant in support of his legislation (if seldom conversant with the details). Relationships with President Carter, even for Democrats, were much more uncertain and distant.

Establishing the Legacy in 1981

Very few Presidents can claim legislative triumphs that are truly turning points in domestic policy. In this century, Franklin D. Roosevelt and Lyndon B. Johnson can legitimately make that case. The New Deal and Great Society programs constituted quantum increases in the role of the federal government in social and economic life. In both cases the President and Congress acted quickly to effect a policy shift that was so dramatic as to dominate future agendas. The politics of incrementalism, so characteristic of the American system, was suspended for a short time. We experienced unprecedented policy breakthroughs, unchecked by the normal restraints of separated institutions and intergovernmental divisions.

Ronald Reagan could claim such a breakthrough in 1981. By employing "speed and focus," the White House produced breathtaking legislative successes.[23] Friedersdorf was quoted as saying that "we knew we had to get our bills enacted before the Labor Day recess" and that "the President was determined not to clutter up the landscape with extraneous legislation."[24] The Carter legacy of distressingly high interest rates and inflation contributed mightily to determining the policy focus.

The economy became the first, second, and third objective and Reagan staked his reputation on it. By choosing the economy, he added simplicity to both policy making and the policy process. All social and domestic issues were discussed not in terms of need, equity, or values, but in budget recommendations—how much can be cut back without causing an uproar.[25]

Alongside the maxim "Establish a focus" is the advisory "Don't come up with other mischiefs."[26] This important lesson was also a product of the recent Carter administration. For in addition to overloading the legislative circuits, President Carter induced ill will on Capitol Hill by asking members to eliminate public works projects from their states and districts. Such "mischiefs" were highly diverting from his other priorities. For Reagan, certain far-right causes could easily cause mischief. As Chief of Staff James Baker noted: "Abortion cuts both ways hard. If you come down one way or the other, you lose some people. Most of the social issues are polarizing."[27]

One learns much about the Reagan legacy from this avoidance of mischiefs. The politician uses ideology, but does not lose because of it. Ideology provides policy direction, but not to the exclusion of political success. Presidents who try to satisfy the fringes of their support, whether it be to the right or left, sacrifice support in the middle, where the majority normally resides. The trick is to press policy preferences to a limit beyond which you would lose support, then compromise and declare victory, saving ideological purity for another day.

What was won in 1981, and with what impact? Allen Schick points out that "Ronald Reagan won the battles but lost the budget."

On four issues he challenged congressional Democrats and obtained the legislation he demanded. The first budget resolution was crafted according to his specifications, as was the reconciliation bill it triggered. The President also emerged victorious in a bidding war over tax legislation. His final triumph came in the closing days of the session when Congress approved a continuing appropriation that satisfied most of his demands.[28]

Schick concedes that winning the battles may have been more important to President Reagan than losing the budget. "Perhaps the budget was only a cover for his real objectives."[29] Whether that was the case or not (and Reagan's then budget director, David Stockman, seems to believe that it was),[30] the effects were clear enough. First, winning most of the battles in 1981 focused attention on the budget and growing deficits. Those favoring additional government welfare programs were literally made speechless. Those supporting current programs were forced to justify them as never before. Many Republicans, including Stockman, wanted to go much further in dismantling the welfare state. Some such advocates felt betrayed by Reagan. Regardless, the 1981 victories produced a significant agenda shift that altered policy politics in Washington.

Second, the effects of 1981 were not limited to one year. Tax cuts went into effect over a three-year period. Defense expenditures were to increase over several years. And although cuts were made in certain domestic programs, Reagan's 1981 plan for social security adjustments was defeated. This combination of less revenue and a significant boost in defense spending, without fully compensatory reductions in entitlement programs, assured mind-boggling deficits through a first and into a second Reagan term. Subsequent policy conversation would be dominated by the legacy of 1981. Democrats too drew from Reagan's thesaurus in preparing for the 1984, even the 1988, election.

A third effect was simply that it was difficult to judge who had won when the President lost, as he did with increasing frequency after 1981. The game was being played on his field, with his ball—that was the effect of 1981. The Democrats prevented him from scoring, but it is hard to win any game by playing defense only. Further, if the Democrats mounted an offensive (typically in cooperation with congressional Republicans), they might find that the President joined them at the goal line to take the ball across (e.g., as with the 1982 tax increase).

The details of the 1981 triumph on Capitol Hill are as follows:

1. Passage of the Economic Recovery Tax Act, a multiyear package that projected a reduction of nearly $750 billion.

2. Enactment of a budget reconciliation resolution designed to reduce domestic spending by over $35 billion.

3. Approval of a defense plan of nearly $200 billion for 1982, less than the President wanted originally but more than President Carter had proposed.

4. Significant reductions in the Aid to Families with Dependent Children (AFDC) benefits, food stamps, certain antipoverty programs, and other minor welfare benefits.

5. Savings in Medicaid and Medicare programs, but postponement of an overhauling of the social security retirement system.

The first session of the 97th Congress was described as "a great personal triumph for Reagan. Congressional approval of his plan was due largely to his own efforts and strength."[31] Certainly the President played the central role, but his "personal triumph" was accounted for by an extraordinarily effective White House political operation. A strategy was developed and executed for taking advantage of the favorable political conditions.

Since so much of the strategy was centered in the budget, it was understandable that David Stockman, as OMB director, played a key role. A Legislative Strategy Group (LSG), made up of "the inner circle of White House aides," met frequently in Chief of Staff James Baker's corner office in the west wing of the White House. The LSG "wasn't even on the White House organizational chart," but it played a key role in formulating an approach to Congress and, in the process, communicating political signals and policy information among the key players in the White House and on Capitol Hill.[32]

Essentially the strategy was designed to capitalize on advantages and be ever attentive to the political situation. How this was done in the first months of the new administration is itself an important part of the Reagan legacy. No doubt other Presidents in similar situations will seek to emulate the Reagan strategy. First and foremost, the LSG sought to concentrate congressional and media attention on the budget. The Reagan White House got high marks for setting priorities and for not dissipating its energies. Yet, making the budget a priority is not exactly an oversimplification of the policy world. The budget is very nearly everything. Therefore, the Reagan strategists had the double advantage of a seemingly simple agenda and yet one that was bound to have a significant and comprehensive policy impact.

Second, Congress itself facilitated this concentration by its budget reform of 1974. It would have been very difficult for the President to keep all eyes fixed on the budget had it not been for the new organization and procedures on Capitol Hill. The Congress provided itself with budget committees, a budget office (as a counterpart to the Office of Management and Budget), and a budget resolution (as a counterpart to the executive budget). The media could now follow the action. Further, a so-called budget reconciliation was tried for the first time by the Carter administration in 1980, thus providing a sort of test run for Reagan. The reconciliation process is designed to enforce the budget resolution within congressional committees. Thus it was a perfect tool for the Reagan strategists in forcing Congress to meet its own budget targets.

Third, the LSG knew by instinct and recent experience that mandates are short lived, particularly those that are illusory to begin with. Thus it was important to act fast. Among other things, members returning to their states and districts after the first six months of a new administration get a decent reading of constituents' attitudes. It was unlikely that the domestic budget-cutting portion of the Reagan mandate would hold up well back home.

Fourth, it was essential that the administration display strong unity behind the President's program. This required White House control throughout the departments and agencies; the appearance of agreement and cooperation within the White House itself; and few, if any, leaks from those unhappy with policy decisions. Such unity is always desirable, but it is essential if the President is to command support on Capitol Hill. Coalition building there naturally started with the Republicans. If Reagan could keep his troops in line, then he needed only a few House Democratic votes to get his program enacted. In this crucial first year, overall congressional Republican support was high, and it was phenomenal in regard to votes on major budgetary and economic proposals. House Republicans averaged nearly 98 percent support on seven key votes; Senate Republicans averaged 97 percent support on nine key votes.[33]

In 1981 the Reagan administration created a legacy for itself. "Politics had triumphed," according to Stockman.[34] We experienced one of those rare policy breakthroughs, and its effects reverberated throughout the subsequent years of the President's term. Speaker O'Neill conceded that "I . . . wasn't prepared for what happened in 1981."[35]

Managing the Legacy—The Subsequent Years

Having directed congressional and media attention to the budget, the White House now had to produce its own plan for reducing the deficit. But the President had conflicting goals. Having just cut taxes, he did not want to turn around and raise them. So that option for deficit reduction was out. He favored further increases in defense expenditures, thus obviating another possible source of deficit reduction. And he was not about to stand alone on social security adjustments, especially with the upcoming 1982 elections. David Stockman even indicates that the President failed to support OMB's effort to make significant cuts in other domestic programs (e.g., farm supports).

As proposed by the administration, the fiscal year (FY) 1983 budget did speak of a deficit reduction plan of $239 billion over three years. The reductions were primarily in what might have been spent if certain cuts were not made. In other words, savings were counted where there was a decrease in the rate of growth. No amount of rhetorical or statistical manipulation could cover up the stark reality of huge imbalances, however. The bottom line was a projected $92 billion deficit for the new fiscal year and abandonment of the plan for a balanced budget in 1984.

For their part, members of Congress were unlikely in an election year to be receptive to President Reagan's proposals. Nor were they anxious to go it alone in cutting domestic programs further or in raising taxes. Yet much of the FY 1983 budget was rewritten on Capitol Hill, and the President was even convinced to approve a tax bill—one primarily designed to close loopholes and prevent tax evasion. Democrats used the deficit to frighten voters about the future of social security, noting that the President's plan for increased defense expenditures and reduced taxes would lead eventually to drastic cuts in retirement and other social welfare programs.

Presidential-congressional politics, as practiced in 1982, essentially became the basic pattern for the remainder of Reagan's term in office. His budget success in 1981 created the conditions for unpleasant confrontations. The President's personal popularity was his principal resource in the struggle to cope with mounting deficits. Meanwhile, congressional Democrats were emboldened by midterm election successes in 1982 to assert their independence. Unfortunately, they did not have the leadership or the organization to prepare credible alternative proposals. At times, in fact, it seemed that the Senate Republicans were offering the only options to the President's proposals.

Table 2.1 shows how political conditions changed for each of the four Reagan Congresses. Clearly no two were alike, and changes in the 98th, 99th, and 100th naturally contributed to different policy responses to the 1981 legacy. Each deserves brief review.

THE 98TH CONGRESS—THE POLITICS OF AVOIDANCE

Representative Bill Gradison (R-Ohio) was quoted in 1983 as saying: "I don't remember a presidential election starting so early."[36] Political conditions changed rather dramatically following the 1982 congressional elections, for several reasons. First, of course, was the significant increase in the number of House Democrats—from 243 to 269. This change meant that 52 Democrats would now have to defect for the Republicans to win a vote—double the number required in the 97th Congress. Effectively then, the House Democratic leadership was able to resume control over its membership.

Actually the Republican losses in 1982 were somewhat smaller than predicted for the average midterm election. But following the 1980 elections, Democrats were fearful that a realignment might be under way—that, as happened in 1934 for Roosevelt's Democrats, Reagan's Republicans might actually increase their numbers. Therefore the twenty-six-seat increase reassured Democratic leaders that the President's popularity was not fully transferable to congressional Republicans. They were bound to be less deferential to Reagan and more optimistic about recapturing the Senate and the White House in 1984.

Second, the President's own popularity was declining. His Gallup poll rating slipped into the 40s during 1982 and declined further to 35 percent in January 1983.[37] Reagan's economic program was not working in the short run. Although inflation had been cut, unemployment and interest rates remained high, and the national debt continued to soar. Doubt was expressed that the President would even seek reelection.

Third was the inevitable media reaction to any exposed failing of the President. Dick Kirschten reflected the views of many commentators when he stated:

> The mood in Washington has changed vastly since the heady first months of the Reagan administration, when the President adroitly pulled off a series of startling coups. One no longer hears of a Reagan Revolution or of an emerging Republican

TABLE 2.1
POLITICAL CONDITIONS, 97TH–100TH CONGRESSES

	House				Senate			
	Party		Leadership[a]		Party		Leadership[a]	
Congress	D	R	D	R	D	R	D	R
97th	243	192 (+33)	O'Neill[b] Wright Foley Long	Michel Lott Kemp	47	53 (+12)	Byrd Cranston Byrd	Baker[b] Stevens McClure
98th	269 (+26)	166	Same[b]	Same	46	54 (+1)	Same	Same[b]
99th	253	182 (+14)[c]	O'Neill[b] Wright Foley Gephardt	Same	47 (+2)[c]	53	Same	Dole[b] Simpson Chaffee
100th	258 (+5)	177	Wright[b] Foley Cohelo Gephardt	Same[d]	55 (+8)	45	Same[b]	Same

a. Includes the Speaker, floor leader, whip, and caucus chairman for the House Democrats; the floor leader, whip, and conference or caucus chairmen for the rest.

b. Majority leadership.

c. Republicans won interim elections to increase their numbers to 168 in the House and 55 in the Senate.

d. Jack Kemp resigned as conference chairman in 1987; Dick Cheney was elected in his place.

majority. Democratic gains in the 1982 elections, while not shattering, nonetheless indicated disenchantment with Reagan's leadership.[38]

The one encouraging result from the 1982 election was that the Republicans retained their Senate majority status for the first time since 1930. Thus the Reagan White House continued to enjoy the advantage of sequence—gaining Senate approval first, then pressuring the House for action.

With one major exception, these political conditions led to a politics of avoidance throughout the 98th Congress. The exception was passage of social security reform. Acting on a bipartisan basis, Congress accepted the recommendations of a National Commission on Social Security Reform. Referred to as "artful work" by Representative Barber B. Conable, Jr. (R-New York and a member of the National Commission), passage of this legislation removed a major negative issue for Reagan in 1984.[39] Democrats pounded away on Republican candidates in 1982 on social security. They would not be able to do so again.

Otherwise, major issues were more or less postponed. Neither the White House nor Congress had the solution to the budget impasse. Deficits continued to mount. The end-of-session reviews in 1983 and 1984 highlighted the separation between the two branches and its consequences.

> 1983: Congress and President Reagan generally kept to their own turf in 1983—each branch going about its business with little involvement from the other side.[40]

> 1984: A year of politics and procrastination on Capitol Hill left many members of the 98th Congress disappointed with their track record and a long list of unsolved problems for the new Congress to address.[41]

Whether resolved or not, however, the 1981 legacy dominated presidential-congressional policy politics in the 98th Congress. The hard facts were that the Reagan agenda would carry through into the 1984 election, forcing Democrats to discuss budget deficits and taxes. Meanwhile, the economy improved steadily during the 98th Congress, and with it the chances that Ronald Reagan would seek a second term.

THE 99TH CONGRESS: THE POLITICS OF ASSERTIVENESS

Elsewhere I have labeled the 1984 contest an "approval election," that is, one in which the voters said yes to an existing government of split-party control (Republicans controlling the White House and Senate, Democrats the House of Representatives).[42] Ronald Reagan won a huge landslide, winning the electoral count of every state but Minnesota (and the District of Columbia). Meanwhile, a large proportion of incumbent representatives and senators were also reelected—95 and 90 percent respectively. Obviously a high return rate of congressional incumbents means relatively little shift in the partisan balance there. In 1984 the Republicans had a net gain of fourteen House seats and a net loss of two Senate seats. In this respect, the 1984 election was not very different from two previous landslide reelections by Republicans in recent decades—those by Eisenhower in 1956 and Nixon in 1972. In neither case was there a major change in the partisan balance within Congress. Both were approval elections too.

Nevertheless, if "mandates are inherently implausible" under circumstances where it is logical to assume that the voters were sending a policy message (as in 1980), they are doubly so where voters are affirming a split-party Congress and reelecting a minority-party President by one of the greatest landslides in history. How is one to interpret such behavior in policy terms? One common explanation was simply that Ronald Reagan's popularity exceeded that of his political party, that the voters approved of him more than they approved of his policies. Yet no President is a personality only. He holds the most important policy and partisan position in Washington. Thus, who he is mixes with what he favors. And he may be expected to interpret reelection as approval of his behavior in office.

Given the mixed signals of an approval election of this type, it is not surprising that the 99th Congress was more assertive. House Democratic leaders acknowledged the President's popularity but were bound to take more initiative than before. The Republicans were still in the majority in the Senate, but Howard Baker (R-Tennessee) did not seek reelection and the new majority leader, Robert Dole (R-Kansas), was selected in part because of his greater independence from the administration. Then, of course, however popular the President might be, he could not run again.

It was also the case that the second term brought changes in the management of the White House. Donald Regan took over as chief of staff, with James Baker assuming Regan's previous position as secretary of the treasury. Regan's style was better suited to the boardroom than the White House. He had limited tolerance for members of Congress, and would have less with each passing month.[43] Having an antipolitical chief of staff was strangely inapt for a political President. It raised questions about how attentive he was in regard to his own staff operations, questions that resurfaced during the Iran-*contra* hearings.

Finally, the agenda itself encouraged a more assertive posture for Congress. The 1981 legacy continued. There was no escaping the heavy burden of the deficits. Congressional anxiety increased during the 98th Congress and was bound to result in greater initiative in the 99th. The President's budgets were deemed "dead on arrival" by congressional Democrats—a declaration suggesting that they were prepared to provide an alternative. Then foreign and defense policy issues became more and more contentious—for example, sanctions on South Africa, aid to the *contras,* the strategic defense initiative, arms control, the MX missile.

To declare that Congress was more assertive is not to say that Reagan was helpless or that the legislative branch somehow took charge of the government. One of the most sweeping tax-reform bills in history was passed. Other Presidents—most recently Carter—campaigned for changes in the tax laws, but Reagan made it a priority for his second term, and presidential-congressional cooperation was achieved beyond the expectation of the most seasoned political observers. Congress publicly announced its limitations in coping with the budget by enacting the Gramm-Rudman-Hollings measure, a procedure for establishing automatic budget cuts should Congress fail to meet designated targets. The procedure did have the effect of focusing even greater attention on deficits, but it turned out not to be a substitute for the hard choices that had to be made.

The 99th Congress closed to very mixed reviews. Yet, under the circumstances, it is hard to imagine what more one could have expected from either end of Pennsylvania Avenue. For his part, despite his overwhelming victory, Reagan was unable to match the accomplishments of his first two years. But he was far from being an incapacitated lame duck. For its part, Congress demonstrated a capacity to produce major legislation despite split-party control between the two chambers. Leadership in both chambers received high marks for their efforts. "The record of the 99th Congress belies early predictions that it would dissolve in partisan rancor."[44] Yet no one believed that we could govern only with Congress. In other words, it all went about as well as could be expected, given what the voters had done in 1984.

THE 100TH CONGRESS: THE POLITICS OF SURVIVAL

Presidents who serve two terms are understandably anxious about the second midterm election. There is talk about the "six-year itch," that is, voter dissatisfaction with the President and his party in the sixth year. And there is talk about lame-duck status as a President enters the final two years. Neither phenomenon is an immutable law, but talk is reality too, and it can be unsettling to the President and his advisers.

In 1986 Ronald Reagan accepted the electoral challenge of his status and campaigned heavily for Republican Senate incumbents and challengers. He did so in spite of the conventional wisdom that presidential coattails are threadbare in midterm elections. The results were close to being a disaster. The Democrats recaptured their majority status in the Senate with a net gain of eight seats. Seven Republican incumbents were defeated, and Democrats won two seats held by retiring Senate Republicans. One Republican won a seat previous-ly held by a Democrat.

Presidential success in campaigning is typically measured by wins and losses. Thus President Reagan lost in his gamble to defy the odds in 1986. Closer ex-amination of the Senate results reveals some interesting developments for under-standing future elections, however. The average Democratic percentage in the seven races in which Republican incumbents were defeated was less than 52 percent. The percentage of the two-party vote garnered by all Republican candi-dates was greater in 1986 than it was in 1980 *when the Republicans had a net gain of twelve Senate seats.* What these results suggest for the longer run is that Senate contests are now highly competitive across the nation. It is entirely possible that the Republicans may recapture control of the Senate again in fu-ture elections—a prospect that reflects the growing strength of the party and, possibly, the nationalization of Senate elections.

There was no discernible six-year itch in voting for the House of Represen-tatives. Incumbents were returned at an exceptionally high rate—98.5 percent. The net loss of five House Republicans was the second smallest loss for the President's party in a midterm election in this century and the smallest by far for a minority-party President.

Comparisons with the two most recent Republican Presidents to win re-election are instructive. In 1958, the second midterm election for Eisenhower, Republicans had a net loss of forty-seven House seats and thirteen Senate seats. Even with the loss of a Republican majority in the Senate, President Reagan was in a better position than Eisenhower or Ford. Most commentators do not engage in historical comparisons in evaluating Presidents. They tend to com-pare a President only with himself: Can he repeat his successes of the first term? The comparative party splits for each chamber are shown in table 2.2.

TABLE 2.2

HOUSE AND SENATE PARTY SPLITS FOR THE FINAL CONGRESS:
EISENHOWER, NIXON-FORD, REAGAN

	House		Senate	
	D	R	D	R
Eisenhower	283	154	66	34
	(65%)	(35%)		
Nixon-Ford	291	144	62	38
	(67%)	(33%)		
Reagan	258	177	55	45[a]
	(59%)	(41%)		

a. Changed in 1987 to 54 Democrats, 46 Republicans, with the death of a Democratic senator and the subsequent appointment of a Republican.

Loss of the Senate forced a change in White House strategy. Appointments requiring confirmation were in jeopardy, majority building for treaties was altered, and the advantage of playing one chamber off against the other was lessened, if not lost altogether. There was also a change in House leadership. Thomas P. O'Neill, Jr., of Massachusetts retired, and a more aggressive Jim Wright of Texas assumed the chair. Determined to establish his own leadership style, as distinct from that of O'Neill, Wright was unlikely to cooperate very often with the administration.

These political developments encouraged a more defensive posture by the White House regardless of what else might occur. In other words, managing the government as a lame-duck minority-party President while working with a Congress controlled by the other party is something less than an ideal formula for success. But there was more. Analysts barely had time to ponder the 1986 election results when it was revealed that the administration had been dealing with Iran in a complicated maneuver involving the release of hostages, arms shipments, and the diversion of profits to the *contras* in Nicaragua. The following summary judgment reflected the dominant perception of the President's condition as he entered the last two years of his administration.

> Ronald Reagan is heading into the final two years of his Presidency with his credibility damaged, the competency of his administration questioned and investigations under way into the conduct of his foreign policy. . . .
>
> Although supporters rallied to him, and critics said they did not want to see a crippled Presidency, many in Washington agreed that Reagan's ability to govern has been severely damaged and that the next few months will test his mettle more than anything in his tenure so far.[45]

No doubt having the Watergate debacle in mind, the President acted quickly to manage the Iran-*contra* affair. National Security Council personnel were fired, an independent counsel was requested, an investigating commission was appointed, and a Department of Justice probe was launched. Later Donald Regan, White House chief of staff, was replaced by Howard W. Baker, the former Senate majority leader.

No amount of initiative from the White House was likely to interfere with congressional investigations. Several were announced, and eventually a committee from each house was appointed. These committees agreed on joint hearings to be conducted during the summer. The President was determined to prevent the Iran-*contra* affair from interfering with his agenda. Although he made several moves to control matters, he could not manage it all. It was not an auspicious start for the last two years of his Presidency.

In looking ahead to the 100th Congress the forecasters predicted distractions due to the Iran-*contra* imbroglio and confrontations over the budget. In his response to the State of the Union Message, the new Speaker of the House, Jim Wright, stressed an equal partnership between the President and Congress. He then proceeded to outline important areas of disagreement:

> The basic disagreement is not over how much we spend. It's where we spend it—what we get for it—and who pays the bill, ourselves or our children.
> The President's newest budget would cut $5.5 billion from the education of our young—and spend that same amount on research just for one new weapon.
> It asks more for the Pentagon, more for foreign aid, more for space, more for "star wars," more for the war in Latin America.
> But it would cut education, cut the clean water program, cut Medicare and Medicaid, cut what we do for the disadvantaged, and—are your ready for this?—the President's budget would make deep cuts in our commitment to drug enforcement.[46]

The direct confrontations were not long in coming. The President had pocket-vetoed a water-pollution-control bill at the end of the 99th Congress. The bill was quickly passed again by large margins in the House and Senate at the start of the 100th Congress. Reagan vetoed it directly this time, and his action was overridden in both chambers (401–26 in the House, 86–14 in the Senate). In late March, Congress presented him with a highway bill that he opposed. Again he accepted the challenge and vetoed it. And again the veto was overridden—this time by the very narrowest of margins in the Senate (67–33), following active lobbying by the President to sustain his veto.

Although he lost both battles, the President established his own combative posture in the face of the Iran-*contra* distraction. This aggressiveness probably benefited him later in the year when the impact of the hearings had abated. Even at the time, Senator George Mitchell (D-Maine) observed in regard to the highway bill defeat: "I don't think it's a total loss for the President. This was an opportunity for the President to demonstrate aggressive, personal involvement in government. . . ."[47] His action certainly suited Reagan's determination not to suspend politics as a result of the Iran-*contra* affair or become too protective or defensive.

The events of 1987 consistently threatened presidential leadership. A brief review of some of the more dramatic presidential-congressional conflicts illustrates what a remarkable year it was.

☐ The joint hearings of the House and Senate Select Committees to investigate the Iran-*contra* affair took place throughout the summer, from 5 May to 6 August. There were forty days of public hearings, four days of closed meetings, thirty-two witnesses, and nearly 10,000 pages of transcripts. Lieutenant Colonel Oliver North was the star witness; his testimony and questioning took up approximately 14 percent of the transcript pages. A highly critical report was issued on 18 November, signed by all fifteen Democrats and three Republicans. Six Republicans issued a minority report.

☐ Supreme Court Justice Lewis F. Powell retired on 26 June, providing President Reagan with an opportunity to appoint a conservative who would then tip the political balance on certain crucial cases. The President nominated Robert H. Bork on 1 July. Confirmation hearings before the Senate Committee on the Judiciary did not begin until 15 September, thus allowing ample time for those for and against Bork to mount their campaigns. The two weeks of hearings were very nearly as riveting as those of the Iran-*contra* committees. The Bork nomination was then rejected by the Senate. The President's next nominee, Douglas Ginsburg, withdrew following revelations regarding his personal life.

☐ The stock market took a record tumble on 19 October, followed by demands for presidential-congressional cooperation to reduce the deficits. This major event drew the attention of everyone in official Washington, but revealed again the differences between the President and congressional Democrats for resolving the budget issue. A White House-congressional summit was begun on 27 October, and an accord was finally reached on 20 November. The President was forced by circumstances to accept tax increases.

☐ Mikhail S. Gorbachev visited the United States 8–10 December to sign a treaty banning intermediate-range nuclear-force missiles (INF) and to discuss outstanding issues between the two nations. Senate approval of the INF treaty was an issue where the President could expect cooperation from the Democrats and criticism from the far-right wing of his own party.

There were many other extraordinary developments that led to conflict between the branches—for example, the involvement of Speaker Wright in seeking to bring peace to Central America, passage of a revised Gramm-Rudman-Hollings procedure, a reinterpretation by the Reagan administration of an agreement with the Soviet Union regarding the testing of antiballistic missile (ABM) weapons, the reflagging and protection of Kuwaiti ships in the Persian Gulf (without the invocation of the War Powers Act). And through it all was the continuing battle over the budget.

By late summer, it was generally conceded that Ronald Reagan was weaker even than previous lame-duck Presidents. "Out of steam," "paralyzed," "impotent," "aging," were a few of the judgments made in newspaper headlines. "The

Reagan Presidency Fades into Its Twilight: Congress Becomes the Dominant Force" expressed a common sentiment by the fall.[48] The argument was made that Reagan had lost control of the agenda, in part because he had not sufficiently reset the issues in the 1984 campaign. "In 1984 he ran on fluff and feel-good advertising" is the way one Democratic political consultant put it.[49]

Once again, however, one has to raise the question whether the President's loss of control led to an advantage for the Democrats. Among other things, the 1988 presidential election was in full flower during much of 1987, with a variety of Democrats seeking to win the nomination. Along the way, the front-runner, Gary Hart, withdrew for rather embarrassing reasons. Leadership for the Democrats was something less than well focused.

Regarding domestic affairs, Democratic leaders were still struggling with the 1981 legacy. They found it very difficult to form a new program in the traditional Democratic cast. And where they did take initiatives, as with trade legislation and welfare reform, there was the threat of presidential veto. In foreign policy, it is inherently difficult for Congress to assume leadership if the President fails. Thus, the President was crippled by the Iran-*contra* affair more than congressional Democrats were advantaged. And, in the end, the President recouped much of his status through the summit meeting with Gorbachev and his leadership in arms control.

The end-of-the-year evaluations of Reagan were much more positive. He actually won more *contra* aid and forced Democrats to withdraw certain broadcast regulations in the final appropriations measure.

> On the heels of his December arms-control summit with Soviet leader Mikhail S. Gorbachev, some Democrats grudgingly conceded that Reagan ended 1987 on a roll.
>
> "The President did come on strong in the last month of the year," said Rep. Dennis E. Eckart (D-Ohio). "It was like old times."[50]

Prospects for the second session of the 100th Congress were for continued conflict between the two branches. Many of the divisive issues carried over into the election year. Helen Dewar's description of the end of the first session is a decent portrait for 1988: "Like two muscle-bound wrestlers, Reagan and the Democrats held each other in a clumsy hammerlock to the end. . . ."[51]

President Reagan survived in 1987. It is interesting now to read *New York Times* reporter R.W. Apple, Jr.'s, introduction to the Tower Commission report. Having reviewed "five Presidencies prematurely terminated," Apple speculated about the effects of the Iran-*contra* affair on Reagan's.

> For almost six years, Ronald Wilson Reagan seemed destined to break the string, seemed, indeed, to be one of those rare politicians blessed with the ability, so admired by Machiavelli, to identify himself with the national purpose. But then came

the series of events for which no one has been able to devise a more euphonious name than the Iran-*contra* affair. Their revelation shook the President's grip on the nation and shook the President himself. . . .

Iran-*contra* is not Watergate, and it seems highly unlikely, as this is written, that it will force Ronald Reagan from office. But it has profoundly affected relations between the United States and its friends as well as its foes. It has crippled the Reagan Presidency, perhaps paralyzed it. It has changed the way that the American public and the world look at this President, perhaps forever.[52]

As analysts, we do not have the advantage of rerunning Presidencies to see how they might have turned out plus or minus this or that event. Thus, much of what we say is relative. Even so, it seems fair to state that President Reagan sustained the events of 1987 about as well as could be expected by a lame-duck Republican President working with a Democratic Congress. He was seriously wounded, if not totally crippled, by several events, but he ended the year fully ambulatory and perhaps even politically strengthened for his final year in office.

Scoring the Reagan Administration

It is common to review how the President scored on Capitol Hill and compare his record with that of other Presidents. Figure 2.1 shows the percentage of votes won by the President—that is, votes on which he took a position. The scores are calculated by the *Congressional Quarterly.* Note that President Reagan's scores decline steadily after 1981. President Eisenhower, the only other President to serve two full terms during the period, did better in two ways: He had a more successful first term (79 percent compared to 72 percent), and he scored high in the second year of his second term (76 percent compared to 57 percent for Reagan).

I have combined two other administrations so as to make comparisons— Kennedy with Johnson, Nixon with Ford. The first of these shows a very high average score (84 percent) and defies the third-, fourth-, and fifth-year losses exhibited by the other three (Eisenhower, Nixon-Ford, and Reagan). Johnson had phenomenal success in getting his way with Congress in the final month of 1963 and in 1964 and 1965. The average score during this period was nearly 90 percent. And Johnson asked for a lot compared to Eisenhower, who in 1953 had a high score but few legislative requests.

Nixon and Ford, like Eisenhower, had a decent increase in the sixth year, despite the fact that Nixon was forced to resign the Presidency. Their overall average for the second term, however, was low: 56 percent.

Jimmy Carter had an average but steady record in support scores. Remarkably, however, it is closest to that of Nixon in his first term (76 percent average

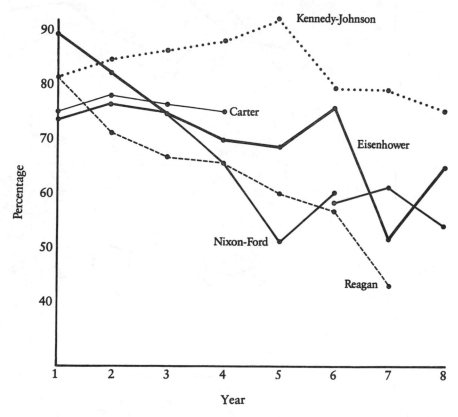

FIGURE 2.1

PRESIDENTIAL SUPPORT SCORES, EISENHOWER TO REAGAN

AVERAGES: Eisenhower = 72%; Kennedy-Johnson = 84%; Nixon-Ford = 65%; Carter (4 years) = 76%; Reagan (7 years) = 64%.

SOURCES: Various volumes of *Congressional Quarterly Almanac* and issues of *Congressional Quarterly Weekly Report.*

compared to 73 percent) in spite of the fact that Carter had strong Democratic majorities in both the House and Senate and Nixon's party was a minority in both chambers.

The steady decline in Reagan's support scores fits the basic pattern of his association with Congress. That is, he had phenomenal success in his first year with a set of proposals bound to dominate the subsequent agenda. He indeed "struck while the iron was hot," so to speak. What he won in 1981 was likely to increase Democratic opposition to his subsequent requests as they struggled to regain an identifiable program of their own. Republicans too were left

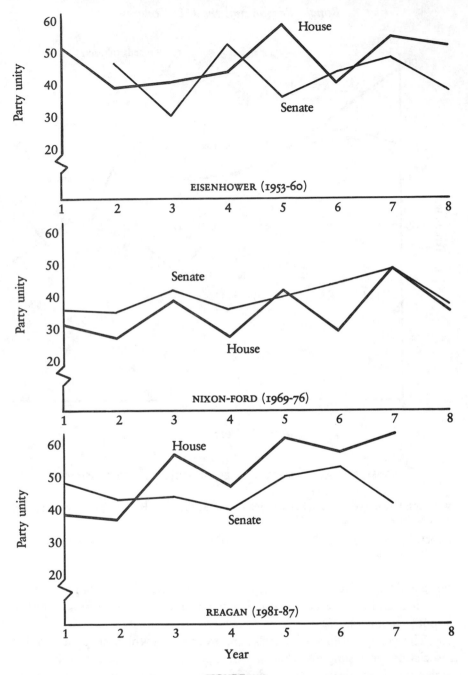

FIGURE 2.2

HOUSE AND SENATE PARTY UNITY, EISENHOWER, NIXON-FORD, REAGAN

SOURCES: Various volumes of *Congressional Quarterly Almanac* and issues of *Congressional Quarterly Weekly Report.*

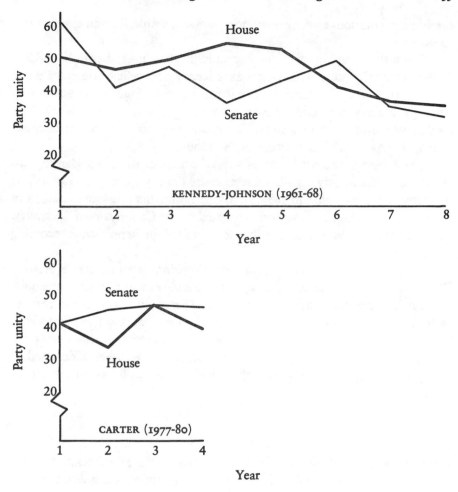

FIGURE 2.3

HOUSE AND SENATE PARTY UNITY, KENNEDY-JOHNSON, CARTER

SOURCES: Various volumes of *Congressional Quarterly Almanac* and issues of *Congressional Quarterly Weekly Report*.

to struggle with the unpopular choices of cutting popular programs or raising taxes.

Reagan's support score for 1987 (43 percent) was the lowest recorded for a President by the *Congressional Quarterly*. His average for the first seven years was the lowest of any President in this set, even Nixon-Ford. Yet it is uncertain whether these scores are the best measure of the success or failure of the Reagan Presidency. In an era of budget-deficit politics, Congress is unlikely to prefer

presidential solutions to their own; nor, perhaps, would Reagan expect them
to do so.

Given this scenario, one may expect high party unity beyond President
Reagan's first Congress. That is, the 1981 legacy of a deficit-oriented agenda
encouraged greater partisanship once it was in place. Figures 2.2 and 2.3 on
pages 54–55 show this to be the case. Party unity scores, the percentage of recorded votes on which a majority of Democrats opposed a majority of Republicans, show a significant increase in the House.

The Senate scores are lower, possibly because of the bipartisanship encouraged by close party divisions (never more than 55–45 for either party). It
is interesting to note that in 1987, partisanship by this measure increased in
the House to the highest figure ever recorded by the *Congressional Quarterly*.
Yet it decreased in the Senate, possibly as a result of the Republicans becoming
a minority.

Again, comparisons with other administrations are instructive. Among
Republicans, the House scores during the Eisenhower administration were quite
high on the average, but rather steadily so. The Senate scores were lower. Scores
in both the House and Senate were markedly lower during the Nixon-Ford
administration. Among Democrats, party unity was rather steady during the
Kennedy-Johnson administration until the last two years, when it declined. It
was quite high and steady in the Senate and somewhat lower and erratic in
the House during the Carter years.

Conclusions

In the words of the British scholar Nigel Bowles, "Reagan successfully fused
policy prescription with politics."[53] He took advantage of favorable conditions
in 1981 to produce "quick and profound policy change." It was the nature of
this initial success, however, that he could not expect to realize anything like
it again. That is not to say he lacked other triumphs. Enactment of a tax-reform
program was a significant and unexpected achievement. Instead, it directs attention to the scope and effects of what occurred in 1981, which were akin to the
policy breakthroughs of the Great Society. Ronald Reagan did not reduce government to nearly the same extent as Lyndon Johnson expanded it. But he created the policy conditions for a contractive politics that had never been played
before.

Thus, President Reagan leaves a policy and political legacy for Congress
and the next President. His 1984 opponent, Walter Mondale, describes the policy
legacy for the Democrats this way:

> Democrats are in a real box. Reagan has practiced the politics of subtraction. He knows the public wants to spend money on the old folks, protecting the environment and aiding education. And he's figured out the only way to stop it is to deny the revenues. No matter how powerful the arguments the Democrats make for the use of government to serve some purpose, the answer must be no.[54]

Of course, the "politics of subtraction" can produce discomfort for legislators of both parties. No elected representative is anxious to cut back programs affecting constituents. Democrats, then, are denied their traditional platform, even as voters appear to support more spending. Republicans are pressured to support their President even when it hurts. Meanwhile, the President's popularity remains relatively high, declining only as an effect of an affair of his own making—Iran-*contra*—and not of the economic and budgetary legacy left for Congress and the nation.

The next President and Congress cannot easily escape the Reagan legacy. They may be able to manage it better without him, however. Presidents who achieve policy breakthroughs are not the best ones to control the subsequent effects. There seems to be a policy trap for the successful President. Being identified with, and committed to, programs for which they receive political credit, they are then ill prepared to propose solutions to the problems these programs create. Perhaps Presidents of achievement should be limited to one term!

The campaign rhetoric in 1987 and 1988 continues to be dominated by the Reagan legacy. Presumably, however, the victor will be free to meet the policy demands of a postcontractive era, possibly even to the extent of raising taxes. Whether the new President can do so with Reagan's style is highly problematic. As one account has it: "Ronald Reagan is going to be a tough act to follow."[55]

Notes

1. Fred I. Greenstein, *The Hidden-Hand Presidency: Eisenhower as Leader* (New York: Basic Books, 1982), 60, 61.

2. *Time*, 7 April 1986, 27.

3. Raymond E. Wolfinger, "Dealignment, Realignment, and Mandates in the 1984 Election," in *The American Elections of 1984*, ed. Austin Ranney (Durham, N.C.: Duke University Press, 1985), 293.

4. Ibid., 292.

5. See, for example, Gregory B. Markus, "Political Attitudes during an Election Year: A Report on the 1980 NES Panel Study," *American Political Science Review* 76 (September 1982): 560.

6. A. James Reichley, "A Change in Direction," in *Setting National Priorities: The 1982 Budget*, ed. J.A. Pechman (Washington, D.C.: Brookings Institution, 1981), 229.

7. Christopher Buchanan, "Modest GOP Congressional Gains Expected," *Congressional Quarterly Weekly Report*, 1 November 1980, 3242.

8. Charles O. Jones, "A New President, a Different Congress, a Maturing Agenda," in *The Reagan Presidency and the Governing of America,* ed. Lester M. Salamon and Michael S. Lund (Washington, D.C.: Urban Institute, 1985), 266-69.

9. Gary Jacobson, *The Politics of Congressional Elections* (Boston: Little, Brown, 1983), 136.

10. *New York Times,* 6 November 1980, A-29.

11. Ibid., A-35.

12. Thomas P. O'Neill, Jr. (with William Novak), *Man of the House: The Life and Political Memoirs of Speaker Tip O'Neill* (New York: Random House, 1987), 344.

13. Quoted in Gail Gregg, "Reagan Proposes Dramatic Reduction in Federal Role," *Congressional Quarterly Weekly Report,* 14 March 1981, 445.

14. Quoted in Harry McPherson, *A Political Education* (Boston: Little, Brown, 1972), 268.

15. James Pfiffner, "The Carter-Reagan Transition: Hitting the Ground Running," *Presidential Studies Quarterly* 13 (Fall 1983): 627.

16. O'Neill, *Man of the House,* 341-42.

17. Quoted in Dick Kirschten, "The Pennsylvania Avenue Connection—Making Peace on Capitol Hill," *National Journal,* 7 March 1981, 384.

18. O'Neill, *Man of the House,* 345.

19. Ibid., 342.

20. Kirschten, "The Pennsylvania Avenue Connection," 385.

21. Dick Kirschten, "Governors Get the Red Carpet . . . the Message Is Pure Reagan," *National Journal,* 1 March 1986, 519.

22. Stephen J. Wayne, "Congressional Liaison in the Reagan White House: A Preliminary Assessment of the First Year," in *President and Congress: Assessing Reagan's First Year,* ed. Norman J. Ornstein (Washington, D.C.: American Enterprise Institute, 1982), 50.

23. Pfiffner, "The Carter-Reagan Transition," 627.

24. Wayne, "Congressional Liaison," 56-57.

25. Wallace Earl Walker and Michael R. Reopel, "Strategies for Governance: Transitions and Domestic Policymaking," *Presidential Studies Quarterly* 16 (Fall 1986): 747.

26. Ibid., 746.

27. Quoted in ibid., 747.

28. Allen Schick, "How the Budget Was Won and Lost," in Ornstein, *President and Congress,* 14.

29. Ibid., 43.

30. David Stockman, *The Triumph of Politics: Why the Reagan Revolution Failed* (New York: Harper & Row, 1986), 376.

31. Irwin Arieff et al., "The Year in Congress," *Congressional Quarterly Weekly Report,* 19 December 1981, 2505.

32. Stockman, *Triumph of Politics,* 4 and passim.

33. See Jones, "A New President," 276-77.

34. Stockman, *Triumph of Politics,* 376.

35. O'Neill, *Man of the House,* 345.

36. Quoted in Diane Granat et al., "Partisanship Dominated Congressional Year," *Congressional Quarterly Weekly Report,* 26 November 1983.

37. "Opinion Roundup," *Public Opinion* 7 (February-March 1984): 34.

38. Dick Kirschten, "President Reagan After Two Years—Bold Actions but Uncertain Results," *National Journal*, 1 January 1983, 4.

39. Quoted in Paul Light, *Artful Work: The Politics of Social Security Reform* (New York: Random House, 1985), vii.

40. Granat et al., "Partisanship Dominated Congressional Year," 2467.

41. Diane Granat et al., "98th Congress Leaves Thorny Legacy for 99th," *Congressional Quarterly Weekly Report*, 20 October 1984, 2699.

42. Charles O. Jones, "The Voters Say Yes: The 1984 Congressional Elections," in *Election 84: Landslide Without a Mandate?* ed. Ellis Sandoz and Cecil V. Crabb, Jr. (New York: New American Library, 1985), chap. 4.

43. Diane Granat et al., "On Balance, a Year of Taking the Initiative," *Congressional Quarterly Weekly Report*, 28 December 1985, 2727.

44. Jacqueline Calmes, "The 99th Congress: A Mixed Record of Success," *Congresessional Quarterly Weekly Report*, 25 October 1986, 2648.

45. John Felton, "Iran Arms and 'Contras': A Reagan Bombshell," *Congressional Quarterly Weekly Report*, 29 November 1986, 2971.

46. The speech is reprinted in *Congressional Quarterly Weekly Report*, 31 January 1987, 203-5.

47. Quoted in Paul Starobin, "Highway Bill Veto Overridden After Close Call in the Senate," *Congressional Quarterly Weekly Report*, 4 April 1987, 604.

48. Article by Ronald D. Elving and Janet Hook, *Congressional Quarterly Weekly Report*, 17 October 1987, 2499-2503.

49. Quoted in ibid., 2501.

50. Janet Hook, "Budget Deal Enacted at Last, Congress Adjourns," *Congressional Quarterly Weekly Report*, 26 December 1987, 3183.

51. Helen Dewar, "Full Plate of Leftovers Awaits Hill, Reagan in 1988," *Washington Post*, 23 December 1987, A6.

52. *The Tower Commission Report* (New York: Bantam Books, 1987), x-xi.

53. Nigel Bowles, *The White House and Capitol Hill: The Politics of Presidential Persuasion* (Oxford: Clarendon Press, 1987), 217.

54. James M. Perry and David Shribman, "Reagan Era Restored Faith in Government Until Recent Slippage," *Wall Street Journal*, 30 November 1987, 1.

55. Ibid., 13.

3

The Reagan Judges:
His Most Enduring Legacy?

DAVID M. O'BRIEN

Federal judges are "Ronald Reagan's best legacy." This view, expressed by former presidential counselor Fred Fielding, is widely shared by those who served in the Justice Department.[1] Even the administration's critics agree that Reagan's judicial appointments have had a profound impact on the composition of the federal judiciary with major consequences for the direction of legal policy making into the next century.[2]

Before he leaves the Oval Office, Reagan will have appointed close to half of all lower-court judges, more than any other President. Nor has any, other than Dwight Eisenhower, appointed a greater percentage of the federal bench since Franklin Roosevelt's record of filling 80 percent of a much smaller federal judiciary. (See table 3.1.) Indeed, Reagan named more judges in his first six years than FDR did in twice as many years (from 1933 to 1945). In addition, Reagan elevated William H. Rehnquist to chief justice of the U.S. Supreme Court and appointed three justices to the Court.

Numbers are only part of the story. Judgeships, at all levels, have never had greater political symbolism or higher priority for an administration than in the Reagan years.

Federal judgeships were campaign issues for the Republican party in the 1980 and 1984 presidential elections. Candidate Reagan promised to abide by his party's platforms pledging the appointment of only those supportive of "traditional family values" and opposed to abortion and past judicial activism. And in 1986 he proudly offered this assessment of his efforts to remake the federal courts:

TABLE 3.1

NUMBER OF JUDICIAL APPOINTMENTS FROM EISENHOWER TO REAGAN

	Eisenhower	Kennedy	Johnson	Nixon	Ford	Carter	Reagan
U.S. Supreme Court	5	2	2	4	1	0	4
Circuit courts	45	20	41	45	12	56	76
District courts	127	102	125	179	52	202	258
Special courts[a]	10	2	13	7	1	3	6
TOTAL	187	126	181	235	66	261	344

a. Includes the defunct Courts of Customs and Customs and Patent Appeals, and the Court of International Trade. Data for Reagan appointees are for those confirmed through 1987. As of 1 January 1988, there were an additional 58 nominees or vacancies remaining to be acted on and another 30 to 40 expected before the expiration of Reagan's term.

In many areas—abortion, crime, pornography, and others—progress will take place when the federal judiciary is made up of judges who believe in law and order and a strict interpretation of the Constitution. I am pleased to be able to tell you that I've already appointed 284 federal judges, men and women who share the fundamental values that you and I so cherish, and that by the time we leave office, our administration will have appointed some 45 percent of all federal judges.[3]

Behind the campaign rhetoric and political symbolism, Reagan's administration had a more coherent and ambitious agenda for legal reform and judicial selection than any previous administration. Indeed, judges were viewed as instruments of presidential power and a way to ensure the President's legacy. Through the appointment of judges, as Attorney General Edwin Meese III put it, the administration aimed "to institutionalize the Reagan revolution so it can't be set aside no matter what happens in future presidential elections."[4]

The key to Reagan's judicial legacy lies in his Department of Justice's agenda for legal reform and how it structured the process of judicial recruitment. The selection of federal judges, of course, is always political. Every administration weighs differently political patronage, professional considerations, and its own legal policy goals when recruiting judicial nominees. All administrations favor party faithfuls when recruiting judges, and the Reagan administration is no exception (see table 3.2). In addition, Reagan's Justice Department put in place the most rigorous and decidedly ideological screening process ever.

TABLE 3.2

PARTY AFFILIATION OF JUDGES APPOINTED BY PRESIDENTS
FROM FDR TO REAGAN

President	Party	Appointees from Same Party (in percent)
Roosevelt	Democrat	97
Truman	Democrat	92
Eisenhower	Republican	95
Kennedy	Democrat	92
Johnson	Democrat	94
Nixon	Republican	93
Ford	Republican	81
Carter	Democrat	90
Reagan	Republican	97

The ways in which the Justice Department has pressed its agenda for judicial reform and has challenged political norms governing the appointment of judges are likely to have a lasting impact independent of the actual performance of those appointed to the bench. For the process of judicial selection has changed in such fundamental ways that future administrations, whether Democratic or Republican, are sure to follow Reagan's lead in vigorously pursuing their legal policy goals when picking judges. Beyond that, a profile of Reagan's lower-court judges and Supreme Court justices provides a basis for a preliminary assessment (later in the chapter) of their impact on the direction of judicial policy making and some of the anticipated and unanticipated consequences of Reagan's judicial legacy.

The Politics of Law and Judicial Reform

One of Ronald Reagan's great strengths is his ability to forge a broad coalition among traditional conservatives, moderate Republicans, and the New Right or "movement conservatives." Like other Presidents who had to deal with special-interest groups, once in office Reagan sought in symbolic and tangible ways to satisfy his New Right supporters. Remarkably, though, it was the New Right's agenda, rather than traditional conservative concerns with judicial self-restraint and "law and order," that defined Reagan justice and his administration's politics of law. This led to some intraparty fighting over the appointment of a few lower-court judges and badly divided the conservative legal establishment in the unsuccessful battle for Senate confirmation of Judge Robert H. Bork to the U.S. Supreme Court in 1987.

AN AMBITIOUS AGENDA FOR LEGAL REFORM

"No administration has thought longer and more deeply about law since that of FDR, and we have thought more deeply than that administration."[5] That was no immodest boast on the part of Terry Eastland, the Justice Department's director of public affairs. From the outset, the department developed a coherent and ambitious agenda for judicial and legal reform.

The Justice Department's agenda reflected both staffing and political strategy. Young "movement conservatives" were attracted to the department, particularly under the leadership of Meese, who served as counselor to the President during Reagan's first term and as attorney general in the second, and the assistant attorney general, William Bradford Reynolds. Attorneys were recruited from senatorial staff and the ranks of former law clerks of leading conservative jurists, such as Chief Justice Rehnquist, and law professors such as Bork and Antonin Scalia, who were elevated by Reagan to the federal bench. In addition, many were associated with the Federalist Society, a conservative legal fraternity founded in the early 1980s at the University of Chicago and several other law schools.

What they shared was a sense of being in the vanguard of a new conservative legal movement—a movement that went beyond older conservatives' opposition to the "liberal jurisprudence" of the Warren Court (1953-69).[6] They defined the department's social policy agenda largely in terms of the New Right's opposition to rulings of the Burger Court (1969-86) on abortion, affirmative action, busing, school prayer, and the like. Its economic legal policies, in the enforcement of antitrust and government regulation, were grounded in the University of Chicago School of Law's economic approach to law, which teaches that legal questions should turn on economic theories and techniques such as cost-benefit analysis.[7]

As a result, not since the Kennedy and Johnson administrations, when department attorneys identified with the civil rights movement, has the Justice Department had as politicized a view of courts, judges, and law. For underlying its agenda was a renewed appreciation for the fact that judges make law and that law is an instrument for political control and change.[8]

The department's promotion of the New Right's social and civil rights positions and a free-market economic analysis of law were also politically strategic. During his first term, Reagan lent presidential prestige to proposals for constitutional amendments that would overturn the Supreme Court's 1973 abortion ruling in Roe v. Wade and curb the jurisdiction of lower federal courts in other controversial areas.[9] But within a couple of years it was clear that Congress would not go along.[10] Thereafter, the President offered politically symbolic support, but the White House assigned low legislative priority and never really pushed the New Right's agenda in Congress. Instead, the Justice Department pursued it in litigation and judicial selection.[11] So too, after the deregulation movement that began during Gerald Ford's Presidency had largely run its course in Congress by the end of Reagan's first term, the department continued to push for reforms in antitrust and government regulation through its enforcement policies.

Four other factors contributed to the department's pursuit of its substantive agenda in judicial selection. First, there was a greater appreciation than in earlier administrations of the significance of the expanding number of judgeships and the changing role of courts in American politics.

The fact is that with fifty or more judicial vacancies becoming annually available (as a result of the creation of new judgeships to keep abreast with rising caseloads and more judges taking senior status), the federal bench may quickly come to bear the imprint of a particular President. Because judgeships enjoy a new economy of scale and, unlike other political appointees, are basically guaranteed lifetime tenure, they are attractive vehicles for achieving a President's legal policy goals. This was not lost on Reagan's Justice Department, fiercely opposed to past "judicial activism" in the area of civil liberties-civil rights, yet keenly aware that in our "litigious society" judges will continue to pass on major questions of public policy.[12] As Bruce Fein, the former associate deputy attorney general who helped set up Reagan's judicial selection process, observed, "The judiciary is a primary player in the formulation of public policy," and hence "it would be silly for an administration not to try to affect the direction of legal policy" when filling vacancies on the federal bench.[13]

Second, the judges appointed by previous Republican administrations were viewed by the Justice Department as disappointing and representing lost opportunities. Quite simply, earlier administrations failed to take judgeships seriously. They let political patronage and professional considerations overshadow their own legal policy goals in judicial selection. As a result, the judicial trend in the last two to three decades was perceived to be in the liberal-to-moderate direction; the Supreme Court led the way, even though no justice has been appointed by a Democratic President since 1967.

Eisenhower's appointments of Chief Justice Earl Warren and Justice William J. Brennan, Jr., two of the Court's most liberal members, were the worst from the perspective of Reagan's Justice Department. But even judges named by Richard M. Nixon and Gerald Ford were deemed disappointing. In 1968 Nixon campaigned on the theme of returning "law and order" and appointing only "strict constructionists" to the bench. Yet his administration failed to bring these legal policy goals to bear on judicial selection. Stephen Markman, the assistant attorney general overseeing judicial selection in Reagan's second term, offered this critical assessment: "While many of the Nixon appointees were more conservative judicially than judges selected under earlier administrations, the ability of the Nixon Administration to affect the overall philosophy of the federal bench was ultimately frustrated by the concessions the Administration was forced (or chose) to make."

Judges picked during the Ford Presidency were even more disappointing than Nixon's. In Markman's words, "The Ford Administration did not make significant changes in the judicial selection process" and "the weakness of the Ford Administration may be seen in the statistic that a record 21 percent of its district court appointments went to members of the opposing party." Both administrations, to be sure, were constrained by Democratic-controlled Congresses, and the Watergate scandal further eroded their bargaining power with the Senate. Still, in the view of Markman and others, these administrations failed to "view the philosophical grounding of [judicial] candidates to be as important" as did those in Reagan's Justice Department.[14]

Third, President Jimmy Carter's "affirmative action" program for selecting judges inspired a reaction. Carter forged historic changes in the federal bench by seeking a more "representative judiciary" through the recruitment of blacks, women, and other minorities. For those in Reagan's Justice Department, Jimmy Carter's "affirmative action" program was irrelevant and sacrificed "judicial merit" for the political symbolism of a more "representative" federal bench.[15]

The judicial recruitment policies of the Carter and Reagan administrations could not have diverged more in this regard. Carter named 28 blacks out of 206, or 13.5 percent, of his district court judges; and 16 percent of his appellate court judges were black. By comparison, Reagan filled only 5 vacancies with black judges, for less than 2 percent. A similar pattern appears with the appointment of women. Almost 20 percent of Carter's appointees to appellate courts were women, whereas less than 10 percent of Reagan's judges are women. At the district level, women amounted to almost 15 percent of Carter's judges, but only 8 percent of Reagan's.[16]

At the same time, however, those in Reagan's Justice Department justified pursuing their substantive agenda on the ground that Carter had refashioned the federal bench in light of his "affirmative action" policy.

Finally, during Reagan's Presidency, the Justice Department became more aggressive in defining and pushing its agenda in litigation, arguments before the Supreme Court, and judicial selection. This reflected changes in the staffing and strategies of the department during Reagan's two terms, along with a perceived mandate to reform the federal courts.

During Reagan's first term, under Attorney General William French Smith, the department basically sought to establish what it was *against*. It wanted to overturn the Court's expansive protection of the rights of the accused, especially its enforcement of the exclusionary rule and *Miranda* warnings. And it opposed judicial decisions permitting abortions and affirmative action, as well as those requiring a rigid separation of church and state.

In Reagan's second term, under Attorney General Meese, the department aimed broadly to establish what Reagan justice stood *for*. Nothing symbolized this more (nor captured wider public attention) than Meese's call for a "return to a jurisprudence of original intention," and Judge Bork's defense of that view during his confirmation hearings.[17] Beyond the jurisprudential debate, it meant returning power to the states over a range of issues—abortion, school prayer, regulation of free speech, and criminal justice. It also included cutting back on the law of standing, which governs access to the courts. In particular, the emergence of congressional standing—allowing congressmen to challenge decisions of the executive branch in the courts—was strongly opposed. More generally, the department sought to establish precedents supporting presidential power over congressional claims with regard to executive privilege, controlling administrative agencies and independent regulatory commissions, and the conduct of foreign affairs.

REFORMING THE JUDICIAL SELECTION PROCESS

"The Reagan administration," in the words of Stephen Markman, "has in place what is probably the most thorough and comprehensive system for recruiting and screening federal judicial candidates of any administration ever. This Administration has, moreover, attempted to assert the President's prerogatives over judicial selection more consistently than many of its predecessors."[18]

Democrats and even moderate Republican senators countered that Reagan had imposed an "ideological litmus test" on the selection of federal judges. One long-time critic of the Warren Court, University of Chicago law school professor Philip B. Kurland, charged that "judges are being appointed in the expectation that they will rewrite laws and the Constitution to the administration's liking. Reagan's judges are activists in support of conservative dogma—what some people would call hanging judges in criminal law and antiregulation judges in civil law."[19]

Yet even the sharpest critics conceded Reagan's prerogative to pursue his legal policy goals through judicial selection. What disturbed them most, perhaps, was that the administration proved so successful in winning Senate confirmation of its judicial nominees.

Indisputably, Reagan's Justice Department systematically and effectively infused its legal policy goals into the judicial selection process. From the outset, according to Bruce Fein, it was clear that greater presidential control over judicial selection was necessary if the department was to reverse what it saw as a trend toward appointing moderate-to-liberal judges. One of the first steps was the elimination of Carter's nominating commissions for appellate court judges. And Reagan, with somewhat greater success than Carter, also requested senators to submit three to five names for each district court vacancy in their states. This gave the department more flexibility and bargaining power over the nomination of lower-court judges.

Presidential control over the judicial selection also was enhanced by abandoning Jimmy Carter's policy of working with the National Bar Association, which represents the country's black lawyers, and various women's organizations. These groups no longer had input into the Justice Department's judicial selection process. In addition, the department's relationship with the American Bar Association (ABA) changed, particularly after some of Reagan's nominees ran into trouble. The attitude within the Justice Department toward the ABA was often hostile; in Fein's words, "We didn't think one second about ABA ratings."

Even more crucial was the reorganization of the judicial screening and selection process within the department. Primary responsibility shifted and became a larger staff operation, subject to greater White House supervision. The attorney general no longer had total responsibility or solely relied on his deputy attorney general for assistance. Instead, the assistant attorney general for the Office of Legal Policy was put in charge of screening candidates. A White House Judicial Selection Committee was created to decide who the President should nominate. It met weekly and included the attorney general; the deputy attorney general; the counselor to the President; and the assistant attorneys general for the Office of Legal Policy, personnel, and legislative affairs; as well as other White House advisers, including the chief of staff.

This reorganization concentrated power, institutionalized the role of the White House, and better positioned the Reagan administration to combat senatorial patronage when filling lower-court vacancies. Also, as the political scientist Sheldon Goldman noted, it enabled "consistent ideological or policy orientation screening."[20] Fred Fielding agreed that it helped in choosing "people of a certain judicial philosophy."[21]

In addition, a rigorous screening process for potential nominees was introduced. The White House Judicial Selection Committee considered judicial candidates only after they had undergone day-long interviews with department officials. In selecting some 300 judges, Markman estimated, "over 1000 individuals [were] interviewed." And the interviews took place after candidates' records—containing speeches, articles, and opinions—had been compared with hundreds of others in the department's computer databank.

The interviews were unprecedented and controversial. Among those criticizing the practice were Eisenhower's attorney general, Herbert Brownell, and Carter's attorney general, Griffin Bell. Brownell termed the questioning of judicial candidates "shocking." In Bell's words, "It politicized the process badly. I don't believe that you should ask a judge his views [on specific issues] because he is likely to have to rule on that."[22]

No less controversial were some of the questions asked of candidates for judgeships. Some who made it to the bench (and others who did not) told of being asked about their views on abortion, affirmative action, and criminal justice. The National Public Radio correspondent Nina Totenberg reported that several contenders said "they were asked directly about their views on abortion." "One female state court judge said she was asked repeatedly how she would rule on an abortion case if it came before her." Another observed, "I guess most of us have accepted that we're not going to get these judgeships unless we're willing to commit to a particular position which we think would be improper."[23]

Two well-publicized candidates turned down for judgeships were Judith Whittaker and Andrew Frey. Whittaker is associate general counsel of Hallmark Cards, first in her law school class, and highly rated by the ABA. Yet the Justice Department refused to nominate her because she once supported the Equal Rights Amendment and was viewed as antibusiness and proabortion. Frey was a deputy solicitor general within the Reagan administration. But New Right Senators John East (R-North Carolina) and Jeremiah Denton (R-Alabama) pressed him for his views on abortion, religion, school desegregation, and affirmative action. Subsequently, they discovered that he had made donations to Planned Parenthood and the National Coalition to Ban Handguns. Along with Utah's Senator Orrin Hatch and ten others, they prevailed on the department to withdraw his nomination.

This screening of judicial nominees drew criticism, not surprisingly, from liberal senators and groups like the Alliance for Justice, created to monitor judicial nominations for a number of liberal organizations. Even some officials in past Republican administrations and leading conservative law professors, like Philip Kurland, were critical. Philip Lacovara, a former official in Nixon's Justice Department, resigned as Reagan's representative on the judicial nominating commission for the District of Columbia courts. He claimed that officials told him that he was "too liberal," "not politically reliable," and failed the "litmus test for philosophical orthodoxy." He was denied a judgeship because, in his words: "Ideology is *the* primary qualification, and it is a candidate's demonstrated orthodoxy that brings his name before the President and ultimately before the Senate. Unique in our nation's history, the current Justice Department has been processing any judicial candidate through a series of officials whose primary duty is to assess the candidate's ideological purity."[24]

Justice Department officials denied having a "litmus test;" in Fielding's words, "no one factor was considered." Candidates, they explained, were asked about past rulings and hypothetical cases—dealing, admittedly, with heated issues like abortion—but that was to "see how they think through a case" and where they stood on the role of the courts. As Attorney General Meese further explained:

> We *do* discuss the law with judicial candidates. . . . In discussing the law with lawyers there is really no way *not* to bring up cases—past cases—and engage in a dialogue over the reasoning and merits of particular decisions. But even here, our primary interest is how someone's mind works, whether they have powers of discernment and the scholarly grounding required of a good judge.[25]

Others in the administration defended their screening process on the obvious political ground that "a President who fails to scrutinize the legal philosophy of federal judicial nominees courts frustration of his own policy agenda."[26]

Such explanations satisfied few critics and troubled moderate Republican senators. Indeed, the latter had the toughest time with the Justice Department. That, perhaps, is one of the best measures of the extent to which the department placed its own legal policy goals above partisan patronage and at times even the professional qualifications of nominees.

Earlier administrations usually deferred to senators in their own party when filling lower-court vacancies. This meant occasionally bargaining and sacrificing their own legal policy goals. But Reagan's Justice Department was less willing to do so. This led to delays in filling judgeships and to some rather bitter fighting within the Republican party. In Pennsylvania, for example, six vacancies remained open for almost two years because of the department's refusal to nominate James R. McGregor, a respected trial court judge supported by Pennsylvania's two Republican senators, Arlen Specter and John Heinz. McGregor was deemed too lenient on criminal justice matters and only after Democrats regained the Senate in 1987 did the department finally agree to his nomination.

There were some other occasions when the Justice Department was forced into hard horse-trading in order to win confirmation for its nominees. Daniel Manion's controversial nomination for the Court of Appeals of the Seventh Circuit showed how far the administration at times pressed its legal policy goals and took a hard line when dealing with moderate Republicans. Manion was narrowly confirmed, by a vote of 48 to 46, but only after the Justice Department was forced to trade other judgeships for the votes of moderate Republican senators. Minnesota's Republican Senator Dave Durenberger withdrew his opposition to Manion after the department relented on a year-long veto of the nomination to a district court of his friend and past president of Minnesota's state bar association, David Doty. Then Washington's Republican Senator Slade Gorton shifted positions on Manion, casting a crucial vote for confirmation despite widespread criticism of the nominee by the legal profession and a sitting judge on the Seventh Circuit. Gorton did so because the Justice Department finally approved, after nearly a year, William Dwyer for a district judgeship in Gorton's home state. That well-publicized incident, however, became a campaign issue that contributed to his defeat for reelection.

The Reagan administration's meticulous screening of judicial nominees and hard-line positions with moderate Republicans challenged the norms of senatorial patronage. It nevertheless strengthened presidential control over judicial selection. The administration, to be sure, faced a few tough battles and some setbacks. The nomination of Jefferson B. Sessions III to a district court in Alabama was narrowly defeated by the Senate Judiciary Committee; this had happened only once before in the last fifty years. Sherman Unger, the only Reagan nominee rated "not qualified" by the ABA, confronted stiff opposition but died before his confirmation. A few others also ran into trouble: Sidney Fitzwater, Alex Kozinski, former Senator James Buckley, and in 1988 conservative law professor Bernard Seigan and former Louisiana governor David Treen. Reagan was also forced into withdrawing from consideration law school professors William Harvey and Lino Graglia, because of unfavorable ABA reports and strong political opposition. Still, considering the unrivaled number of appointments, Reagan achieved remarkable success and suffered only one major defeat, his nomination of Judge Bork to the Supreme Court in 1987.

WINNING SENATE CONFIRMATION

For Reagan, as for any President, the main obstacle to appointing judges was the Senate's power to reject nominees. Yet it rarely posed a major threat and remained a function of the level of judgeships, fluctuations in presidential strength, the chairman of the Senate Judiciary Committee, and the composition of the Senate. This is because there are few institutional incentives for the Senate to do more than pass on the vast majority of judicial nominees. Supreme Court nominees are the exception; one of every four nominees has been rejected or forced to withdraw from consideration. Lower-court judges, although more numerous, are routinely approved by the Judiciary Committee and confirmed by the Senate without debate, reflecting the norms of senatorial courtesy and political patronage. It costs senators if they have to battle with colleagues, and it gains them little or nothing with their constituents. Besides, the chairman of the Judiciary Committee is especially powerful in determining when nominees have hearings and, usually, whether and how much opposition they face. Whether the Senate "rubber stamps" or challenges nominees largely depends on whether the chairman is of the President's party (which turns on whose party holds a Senate majority), and on how willing the chairman is to push the President's nominees. These factors certainly weighed in Reagan's winning confirmation for his judges when the Republicans were in the majority, just as they did in the processing of judicial appointments when the Democrats regained control of the Senate after the 1986 elections.

During the first six years of Reagan's Presidency, the chairman of the Judiciary Committee, South Carolina's Senator Strom Thurmond, proved an influential ally. In the words of one Democratic committee staffer, he "was willing to swallow and push the most controversial of Reagan's nominees." Under Thurmond, most nominees were quickly approved. By comparison with the committee under Massachusetts's Democratic Senator Edward Kennedy (1979-80), which passed on appellate court nominees after an average of sixty-six days and district court nominees after fifty-five days, Thurmond's committee referred nominees to the full Senate within twenty days of their nomination.[27] There was little or no independent inquiry into their backgrounds and only brief hearings before a subcommmittee of one or two senators.

Thurmond's handling of Reagan judges during the 99th Congress (1985-86) remains illustrative. The Judiciary Committee considered 136 nominees, yet only 6 had more than one pro forma hearing. Only one, Jefferson Sessions, failed to make it out of the committee. Of those who had more than one hearing, two district judges—Stanley Sporkin and George Revercomb—were later confirmed without a record vote. The four others—Alex Kozinski and Manion for the appellate bench, and Sessions and Sidney Fitzwater for district courts—encountered heated confirmation fights. None was rejected, however. Besides Kozinski, Manion, and Fitzwater, the Senate had roll-call votes on only three others: Chief Justice Rehnquist, Justice Scalia, and the appointment of former Senator James Buckley to the appellate bench. In only two cases, Manion and Rehnquist, did the committee bother to file reports to the full Senate. For the vast majority, a transcript of their hearings was not even available before the Senate's confirmation vote.

The rubber stamping of nominees by Thurmond's committee drew criticism on the Senate floor in two instances. Michigan's Democratic Senator Carl Levin led a fight against Kozinski's narrow confirmation (by a vote of 54 to 43). Levin cited evidence he claimed was not fully considered by the Judiciary Committee, bearing on Kozinski's temperament and allegations of mishandling cases and misrepresenting his record as special counsel for the Merit Systems Protections Board. Subsequently, Fitzwater was barely confirmed (by a vote of 52 to 42), although five members of the Judiciary Committee voted against him and the Senate had no report on his qualifications or allegations of his insensitivity to black voting rights. During the floor debate, Maryland's Democratic Senator Paul Sarbanes voiced concerns about the rubber stamping of nominees:

> Far be it for me really to intrude into the procedures of the Judiciary Committee, but it does seem to me that if we are going to have controversial nominations on the floor of the Senate—and this obviously is such a nomination, with a fairly close cloture vote, and I assume a fairly close vote on confirmation—we ought to have a report, or at a minimum that the hearings of the Committee should be printed so that the members of the Senate can have the opportunity to at least have the printed hearing record before them and be in a position to review it.[28]

The unsuccessful nomination of Sessions underscores the extent to which Thurmond stood by the Justice Department in pushing Reagan's nominees. The department, the ABA, and Thurmond knew that Sessions would encounter severe opposition. As a United States attorney he had made racially insensitive remarks and unsuccessfully prosecuted black leaders for ballot tampering. A number of attorneys described him as "petty, vindictive and not having the proper temperament to serve as a federal judge."[29] During the committee's hearings, he angered senators by changing positions and claiming his earlier statements were taken out of context. As a result, a bipartisan group within the committee turned against Thurmond when voting 10 to 8 to reject Sessions, and on a 9–9 vote, thwarted sending his name to the full Senate. The most dramatic moment came when home state Senator Howell Heflin (D-Alabama) cast a negative vote. "There are admissions, explanations, partial admissions, statements about jokes," the former judge explained when concluding, "a person should not be confirmed for a lifetime appointment as a district judge if there are reasonable doubts about his ability to be fair and impartial."

Thurmond's promotion of Reagan judges created some bitter feelings and fights within the committee. Initially, this was because Thurmond sided with New Right members in pushing controversial nominees and attacking those deemed too moderate. Senators Denton, East, and Hatch took the unprecedented step of sending nominees questionnaires seeking views on abortion, the death penalty, the exclusionary rule, affirmative action, and freedom of religion. That further eroded the tradition of not asking nominees about specific rulings. Thurmond was eventually forced by Democrats and moderate Republicans to put a stop to their questionnaires.

There were other sources of conflict as well. Most troubling was Thurmond's processing a larger number of nominees in a shorter period of time than had been done when Kennedy chaired the committee. In late 1985, Thurmond and ranking Democrats finally reached agreement on waiting at least three weeks before holding hearings on nominees and allowing as long as two weeks before voting on them. The accord also limited the number to be considered at any point to six, and permitted unlimited time for considering those singled out as controversial. In addition, the committee's questionnaire was revised to include more questions about nominees' legal experience and to provide for the release of financial disclosure statements (which had been available until 1984 when Thurmond bowed to pressure from the Justice Department to withhold that information).

Thurmond's alliance with Justice Department officials was nonetheless instrumental to Reagan's winning confirmation for judicial nominees. During Thurmond's chairmanship, and after Meese took over as head of the department, the administration made most of its controversial lower-court appointments. One measure of this is the degree to which the ABA's fifteen-member Committee on Federal Judiciary, which reviews nominees' legal qualifications, became increasingly split when rating Reagan's appellate judges "qualified." Table 3.3 compares the ABA's rating of Carter and Reagan appellate judges

TABLE 3.3

ABA SPLIT VOTES IN RATING CARTER AND REAGAN APPEALS JUDGES

ABA Rating	Carter Judges		Reagan Judges[a]		Attorney General Smith		Attorney General Meese	
	Total	(%)	Total	(%)	Total	(%)	Total	(%)
Exceptionally well qualified	8	(14.0)	10	(15.2)	7	(21.2)	3	(9.0)
Well qualified	35	(61.4)	25	(37.9)	13	(39.4)	12	(36.6)
Qualified	11	(19.3)	15	(22.7)	8	(24.2)	7	(21.2)
Qualified/not qualified	3	(5.3)	16	(24.2)	5	(15.1)	11	(33.3)
Not qualified	—	—	—	—	—	—	—	—

a. Data for those appointed through 1986. Based on data supplied to author by the ABA.

and shows that more Reagan judges were rated "qualified" by a split vote. Notably, half of those named under Meese during 1985-86 were given the lowest rating of "qualified," and a third of them received a split vote by the ABA committee. By contrast, after the Senate changed hands in 1987, fewer controversial conservatives were named to the lower courts, and only one was rated "qualified" by a split vote; the rest unanimously rated "qualified" or "well qualified."

The importance of Thurmond's chairmanship and a Republican-controlled Senate was even clearer after Democrats regained a senatorial majority and Joseph Biden (D-Delaware) became chairman of the Judiciary Committee in 1987. The committee was no longer disposed to pass quickly on Reagan's judges. Democrats immediately sought to ensure that by reducing the committee's size from eighteen to fourteen, thereby excluding North Carolina Senator Jesse Helms. Biden also created a four-member panel, headed by Vermont's Democratic Senator Patrick Leahy, to screen nominees and acquired additional investigatory staff. The administration in turn was slow to fill vacancies and named fewer controversial conservatives. Officials in the Justice Department perceived that the kinds of conservatives approved by Thurmond's committee were not as likely to win confirmation, hence not always worth the trouble of nominating. Those, like Bernard Seigan, were forced to wait almost a year before the committee held hearings and then had to battle for confirmation.

The most dramatic consequence of the change in the Senate came with the rejection of Supreme Court nominee Judge Bork, a leading conservative intellectual identified with the legal policies of the Justice Department and the New Right. In 1986 Reagan again made judgeships an issue of campaign politics. When campaigning for Republicans in ten Senate races, including five in the South, he asked voters to elect Republicans so that his judicial nominees would continue to win Senate confirmation. But all ten races were lost to Democrats. The conservative Southern Democrats elected (who received 90 percent of the black vote in their states) were especially not inclined to be counted as allies in a confirmation battle raising the issue of race and civil rights. Along with six moderate Republicans, they cast the crucial votes defeating Bork's confirmation.

A Profile of Reagan's Lower-Court Judges

The striking feature about Reagan's lower-court judges is that they are predominantly young white upper-middle-class males, with prior judicial or prosecutorial experience and reputations for legal conservatism established on the bench, in law schools, or in politics.

Simply put, the oldest President appointed some of the youngest judges in our history. Compared with Carter's appellate judges, who on average were fifty-two years old at the time of their appointments, the average age for those

TABLE 3.4

NUMBER OF WOMEN APPOINTED TO THE FEDERAL BENCH

Court	Number of Judges	Appointing President
Supreme Court	1	Reagan
Courts of appeals	1	Roosevelt
	1	Johnson
	11	Carter
	6	Reagan
District courts	1	Truman
	1	Kennedy
	2	Johnson
	1	Nixon
	1	Ford
	29	Carter
	22	Reagan
Special courts	1	Coolidge
	1	Eisenhower
	1	Carter
	1	Reagan
TOTAL	81	

SOURCE: Based on data supplied by the Department of Justice for judges appointed through 1987. Note that Reagan appointed two women to district courts and subsequently elevated them to the appellate bench. They are counted here only as appointments to the courts of appeals.

TABLE 3.5

NUMBER OF BLACK JUDGES APPOINTED TO THE FEDERAL BENCH

Court	Number of Judges	Appointing President
Supreme Court	1	Johnson
Courts of appeals	1	Truman
	1	Kennedy
	2	Johnson
	9	Carter
	1	Reagan
District courts	3	Kennedy
	5	Johnson
	6	Nixon
	3	Ford
	28	Carter
	4	Reagan
Special courts	1	Johnson
	1	Eisenhower
TOTAL	66	

SOURCE: Based on figures supplied by the Justice Department. Note that several black judges were also women. One of them was appointed by Johnson, seven by Carter, and one by Reagan.

named under Attorneys General Smith and Meese was, respectively, fifty-three and forty-seven.[30] Moreover, almost 10 percent of Reagan's appellate judges were under forty at the time their appointments. By contrast, less than 2 percent of those named by Eisenhower, Johnson, and Kennedy were under forty, and only 3 percent of Carter's judges. So, too, Reagan's district court judges tended to be younger than those named by earlier administrations. The average age of those appointed in the first term was 49.6 years and dropped to 48.2 years in the second term.[31] This registers the Justice Department's strategy for ensuring the President's judicial legacy by picking judges who will ostensibly stay on the bench longer.

Reagan, as noted, appointed few women, blacks, and other minorities. Yet, in historical perspective (see tables 3.4 and 3.5), his record in appointing women was second to that of Carter's; it was the worst record for blacks since the Ford and Eisenhower administrations, when the pool of qualified blacks was much smaller than it is today. Twelve Hispanics and two Asians also were named.

Reagan judges generally came from wealthy upper-class backgrounds and medium-to-large legal practices, the judiciary, or government. Close to half had a net worth exceeding $500,000, compared to barely a quarter of Carter's judges

TABLE 3.6

NET WORTH OF REAGAN JUDGES COMPARED WITH CARTER JUDGES

| | Reagan (1981-86) | | Carter (1979-80) | |
	District N (%)	Appeals N (%)	District N (%)	Appeals N (%)
Under $100,000	15 (6.6)	4 (6.4)	19 (12.8)	2 (5.1)
$100,000-199,999	28 (12.5)	4 (6.4)	24 (22.9)	11 (28.2)
$200,000-499,999	83 (37.0)	24 (38.7)	61 (41.2)	15 (38.4)
$500,000-999,999	48 (21.4)	29 (30.6)	28 (18.9)	7 (17.9)
Over $1 million	50 (22.3)	11 (17.7)	6 (4.0)	4 (10.2)
TOTAL	224	62	148	39

SOURCE: Based on data reported by Sheldon Goldman, "Reagan's Second-Term Judicial Appointments: The Battle at Midway," *Judicature* 70 (1987).

(see table 3.6). Notably, one in five of Reagan's district court judges was a millionaire at the time of appointment.

Approximately 90 percent of Reagan's judges had prior judicial or prosecutorial experience, a slight drop from the 91.4 percent for Carter's judges and lower than the 94 percent record for Ford's judges. During Reagan's first term, law professors with conservative publication records were also favored. Somewhat of a change occurred during the second term. Under Meese, the department looked less to those with prior judicial track records when naming appellate court judges. Instead, it relied more on personal associations and knowledge of the judge's legal orientations. This was reflected in the elevation of more assistant attorneys general from within the department (e.g., Douglas H. Ginsburg, Lowell Jensen, and Stephen Trott), as well as the appointment of slightly more party activists (e.g., Danny J. Boggs, James Buckley, and Roger J. Miner). Table 3.7 on page 78 compares the prior occupations of Reagan judges with those appointed by Nixon, Ford, and Carter.

The Justice Department claimed to pay no attention to the religious orientation and background of its nominees (and stopped keeping records on religious affiliations). Nevertheless, a comparison of lower-court judges appointed by Presidents from FDR to Reagan (in table 3.8) is revealing. Not since the Kennedy and Johnson administrations has a greater percentage of Catholics been appointed. In Reagan's second term, moreover, almost 40 percent of the appellate judgeships went to Catholics. In addition, Reagan was the first President to name two Catholics to the Supreme Court, Justices Scalia and Anthony M. Kennedy. (Out of the 104 to serve on our highest court, only 6 others have been Catholics, and there have been 5 Jewish justices.) Whether coincidentally or because of the Justice Department's search for opponents of abortion and

TABLE 3.7

PRIOR OCCUPATIONS OF JUDGES APPOINTED BY PRESIDENTS
NIXON THROUGH REAGAN

	District Judges							
	Nixon		Ford		Carter		Reagan	
Occupation	N	(%)	N	(%)	N	(%)	N	(%)
Politics/government	19	(10.6)	11	(21.1)	9	(4.4)	28	(12.5)
Judiciary	51	(28.4)	18	(34.6)	90	(44.5)	84	(37.5)
Private legal practice								
Large firms (100+)	1	(0.5)	1	(1.9)	4	(1.9)	7	(3.1)
Medium size (25-99)	19	(10.6)	4	(7.6)	24	(11.8)	25	(11.1)
Moderate (5-24)	50	(27.9)	13	(25.0)	40	(19.8)	45	(20.0)
Small or solo (1-4)	34	(18.9)	5	(9.6)	28	(13.8)	27	(12.0)
Professor of law	5	(2.7)	6	(2.9)	6	(2.6)		
Other					1	(0.4)	1	(0.4)
TOTAL	179		52		202		224	

	Appeals Judges							
	Nixon		Ford		Carter		Reagan	
Occupation	N	(%)	N	(%)	N	(%)	N	(%)
Politics/government	2	(4.4)	1	(8.3)	3	(5.3)	3	(4.6)
Judiciary	24	(53.3)	9	(75.0)	26	(46.4)	32	(50.0)
Private legal practive								
Large firms (100+)					1	(1.7)	2	(3.1)
Medium size (25-99)	2	(4.4)	1	(8.3)	5	(8.9)	7	(10.9)
Moderate (5-24)	10	(22.2)	1	(8.3)	9	(16.0)	7	(10.9)
Small or solo (1-4)	3	(6.6)	3	(5.3)	1	(1.5)		
Professor of law	1	(2.2)			8	(14.2)	10	(15.6)
Other	3	(6.6)			1	(1.7)	1	(1.5)
TOTAL	45		12		56		64	

SOURCE: See table 3.6.

a growing conservativism among Catholics, Reagan set a record in appointing more Catholics than any other President since FDR, who had a policy of rewarding Catholics with lower-court judgeships because of their part in the New Deal coalition.

Finally, in terms of the ABA's ratings of professional qualifications, Reagan's judges on balance compare favorably with those appointed by earlier administrations. This is so despite the fact that in the first half of his second term, Reagan's judges generally received low ABA ratings and, especially during 1985-86, the ABA was sharply split on rating a large number "qualified." The ABA's split

TABLE 3.8

RELIGIOUS AFFILIATION OF LOWER-COURT JUDGES APPOINTED BY
PRESIDENTS FROM FDR TO REAGAN (IN PERCENT)

Religion	FDR	Truman	Eisenhower	Kennedy	Johnson	Nixon	Ford	Carter	Reagan
Protestant	70.9	59.1	78.2	58.9	58.0	72.8	70.3	59.3	59.9
Catholic	24.5	29.9	15.8	30.7	39.2	18.3	29.3	26.7	30.6
Jewish	4.5	9.4	5.8	10.4	11.7	8.9	4.4	14.0	9.4
TOTAL	99.9	98.4	99.8	100.0	99.9	95.0	100.0	100.0	99.9

SOURCES: On Roosevelt appointees, "Comparative List Showing Religion of Judges," Francis Biddle Papers, Box 2, Franklin Roosevelt Presidential Library, Hyde Park, N.Y. For other Presidents, Sheldon Goldman and Thomas Jahnige, *The Federal Courts as a Political System*, 3d ed. (New York: Harper & Row, 1985). See also table 3.6.

ratings, discussed earlier, partially reflected the Justice Department's recruitment of younger nominees from law schools and from within its own ranks.
Because of their age, they lacked extensive legal experience and occasionally
ran afoul of the ABA's requirement of twelve years of prior legal experience
for a "qualified" rating. There were also some, such as Judge Manion and Supreme Court nominee Judge Bork, on whom the ABA committee split because
of disagreements over their "judicial temperament." This angered New Right
senators and Justice Department officials, who tended to have an ambivalent
attitude toward the ABA anyway. Nonetheless, for whatever the ABA's ratings
are worth, Reagan's judges as a whole stand up well next to those named by
earlier administrations. Table 3.9 compares the ABA's rating of district and appellate judges appointed by Presidents from Johnson through Reagan.

The Performance of Reagan Judges: Toward a More Conservative Evolution Rather Than a Judicial Revolution

Beyond the demographic changes in the federal judiciary brought by the Reagan
era, the Justice Department's legal policy goals and rigorous screening of ju-

TABLE 3.9

ABA RATINGS OF JUDICIAL APPOINTEES FROM JOHNSON THROUGH REAGAN
(IN PERCENT)

District Court Judges

ABA Ratings	Johnson (N = 122)	Nixon (N = 179)	Ford (N = 52)	Carter (N = 202)	Reagan (1981-86) (N = 225)
Exceptionally well qualified	7.4	4.8	0	4.0	5.3
Well qualified	40.9	40.4	46.1	47.0	45.8
Qualified	49.2	54.8	53.8	47.5	48.8
Not qualified	2.5	—	—	1.5	—

Appeals Court Judges

ABA Ratings	Johnson (N = 40)	Nixon (N = 45)	Ford (N = 12)	Carter (N = 57)	Reagan (N = 66)
Exceptionally well qualified	27.5	15.7	16.7	14.0	15.2
Well qualified	47.5	57.8	41.7	61.4	37.9
Qualified	20.0	26.7	33.3	24.6	46.0
Not qualified	2.5	—	—	—	—

SOURCES: For Johnson, Nixon, and Ford, Sheldon Goldman, "Carter's Judicial Appointments: A
Lasting Legacy," *Judicature* 64 (1981): 344. Data on Carter and Reagan appointees provided by ABA.

dicial nominees generated a major controversy over whether the courts were being packed with those who would forge a counterrevolution in developing law and "rewrite the Constitution."

This charge was made by a number of liberal organizations, such as the People for the American Way, the NAACP Legal Defense Fund, and the Alliance for Justice. In the words of one critic, American University law professor Herman Schwartz, the administration was bent on "turning the federal courts away from their historic role of protecting individual rights . . . [and] this effort will politicize the courts and deprive them of both the substance and appearance of that fairness on which so much of their legitimacy depends."[32]

Judicial performance concerned Reagan's supporters no less than his critics. They and organizations identified with the New Right, such as the Center for Judicial Studies, the Heritage Foundation, and the Washington Legal Foundation, also fueled the controversy. They not only applauded the Justice Department's endeavor to redefine the role of the judiciary but, while monitoring judicial nominations, pressured it to remain faithful to the President's "pledge to appoint men and women to the bench who exercise restraint."[33]

In an early study of judicial opinions by Reagan's first-term judges, Craig Stern of the Center for Judicial Studies observed:

> Of the sixty-two judges evaluated in this study under the standards specified [i.e., adherence to the 1980 Republican Party Platform] . . . thirty-one judges exercised restraint in all of their significant cases without exception . . . sixteen exercised restraint in nearly all their significant opinions . . . nine . . . exercised restraint in no more than half of their significant cases . . . and six published no [pertinent] opinions. . . . The conclusion is inescapable that the Reagan judiciary, so far, has lived up to expectations.[34]

This view was shared by, among others, the Center's founder, James McClellan, a former aide to Senators Hatch and Helms. In his words, "The President has done exceedingly well at the appellate level and fairly well at the district level."[35]

Toward the end of Reagan's administration, some "movement conservatives" began voicing disappointment with the performance of the Reagan judges.[36] They had not gone far enough and had followed precedents too closely. To be sure, Reagan judges, such as Tennessee District Judge Thomas Hull, offered some hope when ruling that Christian fundamentalists could teach their children at home because they were offended by the textbooks used in public schools. Others readily embraced the Supreme Court's approval of "good faith" exceptions to the exclusionary rule and expansion of the "harmless error" doctrine, which permits criminal convictions even when procedural rules and constitutional rights have been violated by police and the prosecution. And in a number of emerging areas of law, dealing with sexual harassment, homosexual rights, and nonracial discrimination, there was retrenchment as well.[37] Still, no sweeping judicial counterrevolution emerged in the areas of abortion, affirmative action, criminal justice, or the law of free speech dealing with pornography, libel, fighting words, and the like.

In retrospect, the expectations of the Far Left and Far Right of the political spectrum never appeared nor seemed likely to be fully borne out by Reagan judges. This is partially because the Far Left and Far Right were united in mistakenly associating all of the Reagan lower-court judges with the New Right's agenda and brand of conservative judicial activism.[38] Both inflated the impact of the Reagan judges by overestimating their ideological conformity and miscalculating the weight of judicial norms respecting precedent and the operation of a decentralized federal judiciary.

Drawing firm conclusions now about the impact of Reagan's lower-court judges on the development of law, of course, would be premature. But some tentative observations are possible. There is no doubt that they will make a difference, though not with the sweeping changes anticipated by many. Studies of judicial behavior generally find that judicial ideology appears significant in less than one case out of six; partisan considerations, such as the party affiliation of judges, account for only a fraction of all rulings.[39] Appellate court decisions are overwhelmingly unanimous. Differences between the Reagan judges and those appointed by other Presidents may thus prove narrower or wider than expected, vary according to areas of law, and develop more or less sharply over time and with future changes in the composition and direction of the entire federal judiciary.

A preliminary study of the voting behavior of appeals court judges during 1982-83, by the political scientist Jon Gottschall, found differences between Reagan judges and others, particularly those appointed by Carter. Reagan and Carter appointees agreed in 74 percent of the cases in which they participated together. When they disagreed, as expected, their differences were pronounced. Carter's judges voted for what Gottschall "defined as the liberal outcome 95 percent of the time, as compared to 5 percent for Reagan appointees." Still, contrary to claims by both the Far Left and Far Right, Reagan judges proved no more ideological than their peers appointed by earlier Republican administrations. In nonunanimous cases involving civil rights and liberties "appointees of the Carter and the Kennedy/Johnson administrations cast, respectively, 63 percent and 61 percent of their votes for the liberal result, whereas Reagan and Nixon/Ford appointees both cast only 26 percent of their votes in favor of what has been defined as the liberal outcome."[40]

Focusing on criminal justice rulings in a more comprehensive study of district and appellate court judges during Reagan's first term, the political scientists

Pete Rowland, Donald Songer, and Robert Carp revealed a sharper divergence between the Reagan judges and those named by previous administrations. The differences were statisically significant for district judges, even greater for appellate judges, and they cut along party lines. Carter's district judges were 64 percent more supportive of claims made by criminal defendants than were Reagan's judges. Carter's appellate judges were "almost 90 percent more likely than Reagan appointees to support the criminal defendant." When the voting of Reagan's appellate judges was compared with that of the remaining Nixon appointees, the latter's were more moderate and less aligned than indicated by Gottschall. As these political scientists concluded, "Nixon appointees actually were somewhat more supportive of criminal defendants, while Carter's appointees become dramatically more supportive and Reagan appointees slightly less supportive."[41] That divergence may further widen as Reagan's second-term appointees make their mark. But, as other studies indicate, the Reagan judges on the whole do not differ markedly from others appointed by prior Republican Presidents.[42]

Rather than forge a "judicial revolution," Reagan's legacy in the lower federal courts reinforces the trend toward greater judicial conservatism that has been building during the last twenty years. Almost 60 percent of those sitting on the appellate bench in 1986-87 were appointed by Republican Presidents, with Reagan naming 38 percent of them. Likewise, a majority of all district court judges identify with the Republican party, and for the same reason: Over 57 percent owe their judgeships to Republican Presidents (64 percent of them to Reagan alone).[43]

Reagan's lower-court judges reinvigorate traditional notions of judicial self-restraint, as much heralded by pre-1930s liberals as by the Warren Court's critics. They have not overturned (and are unlikely, in the near future at least, to overturn) landmark rulings on civil liberties/civil rights, or uniformly infused the New Right's social policy goals into law. This is so for a number of reasons. For one thing, lower-court judges are not self-starters and legal change occurs incrementally. The roulette of litigation brings mostly routine cases (for which a decision is frequently more important than which way the ruling goes). And it rarely affords judges opportunities, even if so inclined, to strike out on their own. Institutional norms respecting precedents set by the Supreme Court are strong. Lower-court judges put their reputations at risk by straying too far and invite reversal of their decisions by higher courts. Developments in law percolate, and shifts are moderated by the rotation of three-judge panels and the nature of collegial decision making in the thirteen appellate courts around the country.

"You won't see Reagan's appointees taking over school systems and jails or ordering forced busing," observed University of Virginia Law School professor

A.E. Dick Howard.[44] But there is more to it than their temperament, legal orientation, and deference to landmark rulings. The federal judiciary is part of the
political system. It registers changes in litigation, federal legislation, and governmental policies no less than shifts in electoral politics and social movements.[45]
Hotly contested and once widely litigated disputes over social policy, such as
school desegregation, have largely been settled, political consensus has been
reached, and states and localities have proven responsive. The kinds of judicial
intervention witnessed in the last twenty years become less likely as legal developments run their course, pressures for federal court action decline or shift
to new areas and toward state courts and other political institutions. It is thus
in emerging areas of law—dealing, for instance, with sexual harassment, the
developing law of personal privacy, and governmental taking of private property "without just compensation"—as well as others still on the legal horizon
that the Reagan judges may initially have their major impact.

Where and how far Reagan's lower-court judges go in the long run remains
impossible to gauge or predict precisely. But movement toward a more passive,
conservative judiciary should appear more in what the Reagan judges *do not
do*, rather than in terms of what the Far Left and Far Right claimed they *would
do*. Curtailing further expansion of law in certain directions (as under the Four-
eenth Amendment's Equal Protection Clause), refusing to recognize some new
claims (such as those by homosexuals), along with more fine-tuning and retrenchment in other areas (notably in those involving the rights of the accused
and criminal justice), appears more likely than any sweeping judicial revolution or counterrevolution. Much depends, however, on the future directions
of the Supreme Court and its guidance for the lower federal courts.

Reagan's Justices

While hugely successful in appointing close to half the judges in the lower federal
courts, Reagan failed to turn the Supreme Court around or to win a majority
over to the Justice Department's positions on abortion, affirmative action, and
other hotly contested issues.[46] This was so in spite of naming three associate
justices to the Court and elevating Justice William H. Rehnquist to the chief
justiceship. A chance to turn the Court around, however, did not come until
Justice Lewis F. Powell, Jr., stepped down on 28 June 1987. Then the administration suffered its major setback. Judge Bork, the first nominee for Powell's seat,
was defeated after an extraordinary and bitter confirmation battle. The second
nominee, Judge Douglas H. Ginsburg, was forced to withdraw from consideration after controversies over his personal affairs led the New Right to turn
against him. Reagan's third nominee, Judge Anthony M. Kennedy, won easy

confirmation, mainly because of his reputation for being open-minded and his distance from the administration's hard-line legal policy positions. Although Reagan's successful nominee disappointed many in the administration and was not the kind of justice that officials in the Justice Department hoped would "lock in the Reagan Revolution," collectively Reagan's appointees represent a new conservativism that may well have far-ranging consequences for public law and the Court's role in American politics.

JUSTICE SANDRA DAY O'CONNOR

Justice Sandra Day O'Connor was chosen more for symbolic than for ideological reasons. During the 1980 election, Reagan promised to name the first woman to the Court. Less than a year later, in May 1981, Justice Potter Stewart privately told the President that he would retire after twenty-three years on the bench at the end of the term that summer. An Eisenhower appointee, Stewart had a reputation as "a swing voter" because he occasionally cast the crucial vote and increasingly sided with the Court's conservative members—notably, in cases involving affirmative action and the death penalty—while voting with the liberals on abortion, obscenity, and some criminal procedure cases. With his departure, the Court was certain to shift in a slightly more conservative direction. A two-month search concluded with a woman Reagan said shared his view "that the role of the courts is to interpret the law, not to enact new law by judicial fiat." Although conservative, Judge O'Connor was not doctrinaire and had practical experience in state courts and politics.

Not yet widely known in legal circles at the time of her nomination, Judge O'Connor had risen through the ranks of Republican politics in her home state of Arizona. She had served as an assistant attorney general and in the state legislature, where she was majority leader, as well as on a municipal court, before former Democratic governor Bruce Babbitt appointed her to a state appellate court. Her nomination was endorsed by both senators from Arizona and supported, privately, by Chief Justice Warren E. Burger (who had met her years earlier) and Justice Rehnquist (a classmate at Stanford Law School). Even the president of the National Organization for Women, Eleanor Smeal, greeted Judge O'Connor's nomination, proclaiming "a major victory for women's rights."

Judge O'Connor's confirmation hearings (the first ever to be televised and carried by the Public Broadcasting System) generated only minor controversy. The Moral Majority and the National Right to Life Committee, among others, attacked her once it was discovered that as a state legislator she had supported a "family planning" bill that would have repealed existing state statutes prohibiting abortions, and had favored the Equal Rights Amendment. During the Judiciary Committee hearings, Republican Senators Charles E. Grassley and

Roger W. Jepsen (both from Iowa) tried to extract concessions on how she might vote on those and other heated issues. But Judge O'Connor, as all earlier nominees, refused to give detailed answers or say little more than that she would uphold and apply settled law.[47] Her refusal to do so and her vague answers to other questions disturbed some in the Justice Department and the New Right, but the Senate voted unanimously (99 to 0) for confirmation.[48]

On the Court, Justice O'Connor quickly earned respect for her graciousness, dedication, and tough-minded independence. She takes oral arguments before the Court very seriously and engages attorneys with probing questions. And, as anticipated, she has bolstered the conservative wing of the Court with her deference to federalism and governmental interests, especially in law enforcement, and a corresponding concern about thwarting legislative powers.[49]

In her first six terms, Justice O'Connor voted on average almost 87 percent of the time with Rehnquist, and barely more than 50 percent of the time with Brennan. While generally advocating judicial self-restraint, she does not uncritically embrace the corollary view that prior rulings should always govern or stand immune from reconsideration and even reversal.[50] As a result, like Rehnquist and Scalia, Justice O'Connor has been criticized for bringing to the Court a new judicial conservativism that borders on "judicial activism."[51] However, she has broken with Rehnquist, and disappointed the Reagan administration and the New Right, in a number of important cases — for example, striking down statutes requiring school prayer[52] and approving affirmative action for women (though not for blacks).[53] Based on her opinions and insistence on reconsidering, yet not necessarily overturning, the landmark abortion ruling, *Roe* v. *Wade* (1973), Justice O'Connor may continue to move toward a more centrist, though still conservative, position on the Rehnquist Court.[54]

CHIEF JUSTICE WILLIAM H. REHNQUIST

Reagan was handed a major opportunity to make an imprint on the Court in June 1986, when Chief Justice Burger announced that he would step down to head full-time the Commission on the Bicentennial of the Constitution. And the President shrewdly maximized it when filling the center chair on the high bench.

The decision to elevate Rehnquist from associate to chief justice, and to appoint Judge Antonin Scalia to Rehnquist's seat, could not have been more politically symbolic or strategic. Both are not just sympathetic to the administration's legal policy goals; they could claim to be intellectual architects of its agenda. Through their writings and judicial opinions, they had largely defined the administration's positions on separation of powers, federalism, and the role of the judiciary in balancing competing claims between majority rule and minority rights. A number of their law clerks had come from, or been sent back to, top positions within Reagan's Justice Department. In addition, the White House knew that Rehnquist would prove controversial because of his long-standing, often extremely conservative views. But naming him chief justice would symbolize Reagan's judicial legacy, and Rehnquist's elevation as a sitting justice made it even harder for the Senate to deny confirmation.

Rehnquist came to the Court in 1971 from Nixon's Department of Justice, where he served as an assistant attorney general. He had established his conservative credentials years earlier, initially as a law clerk for Justice Robert H. Jackson (1952-53) and then as an Arizona attorney and supporter of Arizona Senator Barry Goldwater's presidential candidacy. Like others in the 1950s and 1960s, he attacked the "liberal jurisprudence" of the Warren Court (1953-69) for revolutionizing constitutional law and American society.

During the Burger Court years (1969-86) there was no "constitutional counterrevolution," as some predicted based on Nixon's four appointments. This was because the Burger Court was fragmented and increasingly polarized, divided 6 to 3 or 5 to 4, and pulled in different directions by either its most liberal or most conservative members. As chief justice, Burger was a disappointment for conservatives. For one thing, although a devoted Republican, he came from the liberal wing of the party, in the mold of fellow Minnesotan Harold Stassen. For another, he could not lead the Court intellectually, and his personal style created tensions among the justices. Justice Harry Blackmun, after initially voting with Burger almost 90 percent of the time, now sides over 70 percent of the time with the liberal wing of the Court. Powell gradually emerged as "the conscience of the Court," often casting the crucial fifth vote and siding with conservatives on criminal justice matters but with liberals on issues like abortion, affirmative action, and some First Amendment issues. As a result, there were only modest "adjustments," as Burger noted when announcing his retirement, in the jurisprudential house built by the Warren Court (although there were a few new additions, as with rulings on abortion, affirmative action, busing, and expanding the application of the Equal Protection Clause).

Within the Burger Court, it largely fell to Rehnquist to stake out a conservative philosophy. In holding his own ground, he articulated a well-developed view of the power of judicial review. Less willing than others to compromise, Rehnquist appeared extreme, writing more solo dissents (54) than any of his colleagues in his fifteen years as an associate justice.

Rehnquist's nomination as the sixteenth chief justice thus sparked a major controversy. Senator Kennedy led the attack, as he had when Rehnquist was first named to the Court, calling him "too extreme on race, too extreme on women's rights, too extreme on freedom of speech, too extreme on separation of church and state, too extreme to be Chief Justice." The confirmation hearings, Senator Hatch countered, threatened to become a "Rehnquisition."

The Judiciary Committee's televised hearings, however, were less enlightening than an occasion for speeches by supporters and attackers. Rehnquist was repeatedly asked about earlier judicial opinions. He refused to discuss them or how he might handle major issues in the future, saying correctly that would impinge on judicial independence. He also confronted charges, aimed at tarnishing his integrity and veracity, that as a law clerk in 1953 he supported segregated schools and later had harassed minority voters at polling places.

About all that the committee accomplished was a reassertion of its power to consider judicial philosophy when confirming appointees, no less than the President does when nominating them. Rehnquist was approved, with 5 Democrats voting against him and 2 joining Republicans in a 13 to 5 vote. He was subsequently confirmed by a vote of 65 to 33, based on Southern Democrats voting with Republicans and 2 Republicans siding with 31 Democrats in opposition.

As chief justice, Rehnquist quickly proved an improvement over his predecessor. Even liberal justices agree that he is "splendid." This is because he has the temperamental and intellectual wherewithal to be a social and task leader. He is self-confident, relaxed, and has the sense of humor of a practical joker (apparent even during oral arguments). His no-nonsense approach to conducting the Court's business was evident in his first term as chief: The justices' September conference (during which fewer than 50 cases from more than 1000 are granted review) took half the time that it did under Burger, and the Court finished its term before the end of June (something it had not done in years).

When presiding over the justices' weekly private conferences (at which they vote on cases), Rehnquist also wins praise. His summaries of cases are crisp and cogent, and he does not compromise his views simply to be in the majority or cast his vote (as Burger was accused of doing) in order to manipulate the assignment of opinions. This meant that, in his first term as chief justice and Powell's last, Brennan wrote or assigned (as senior associate justice) a larger number of majority opinions, notably on affirmative action and the death penalty.[55] But Rehnquist remains an intellectual force with strong task and social skills that make for, in Justice Thurgood Marshall's words, "a great chief justice." How often Rehnquist masses a majority in the future may depend more on how the Court's composition changes than his leadership abilities.

JUSTICE ANTONIN SCALIA
In contrast to the intense scrutiny of Chief Justice Rehnquist, the Senate Judiciary Committee's staff spent little time on Judge Scalia, and his hearings were

quick and amicable. The differences are reflected in the committee's final reports on each: Rehnquist's runs 114 pages; Scalia's consists of 76 words. Scalia was also unanimously recommended, and the full Senate, after barely five minutes of debate, voted (98 to 0) for confirmation.

Next to Justice Rehnquist and Judge Bork, however, no other jurist was closer to Reagan's Justice Department.[56] In the 1970s, Scalia became connected with many who would assume positions of power in the Reagan administration. After graduating from Harvard Law School, he practiced for six years before joining the University of Virginia Law School. Then, in 1971-72, he took a one-year leave to work as general counsel in the Nixon administration. Two years later, he was tapped by Ford's attorney general, Edward H. Levi, to head the Office of Legal Counsel in the Justice Department. When Ford left office, Levi returned to the University of Chicago Law School and persuaded Scalia to come along.

Before going to Chicago, Scalia spent perhaps the most crucial year of his early career at the American Enterprise Institute (AEI), then the largest conservative think tank in Washington. It was a Republican refuge, a stronghold from which to attack the Carter administration and formulate what would become much of the Reagan agenda. Along with Bork and Laurence H. Silberman, also Reagan appointees to the District of Columbia Circuit Court of Appeals, Scalia joined James C. Miller III, later Reagan's director of the Office of Management and Budget; Jeane J. Kirkpatrick, who served as Reagan's ambassador to the United Nations; Irving Kristol, the influential neoconservative; and Jude T. Wanniski, architect of supply-side economics. Later, at Chicago, Scalia maintained his association with AEI, serving as editor of its magazine, *Regulation,* as well as helping found the Federalist Society, from which the Reagan administration drew its ranks of lawyers.

In 1982 Reagan placed Scalia on the appellate court in Washington. On the bench, Scalia continued to make his mark. He remained a prolific writer: almost two dozen articles and, in four years on the appellate court, more than eighty majority opinions and dozens of concurring and dissenting opinions. And his law clerks went into the administration or on to clerk at the Supreme Court.

Scalia consistently developed a trenchant judicial philosophy based on a limited view of freedom of expression, and a deep antagonism toward affirmative action, abortion, and the "liberal jurisprudence" that undergirded past judicial activism. In addition, he is a forceful proponent of broad presidential power, a rigid separation of powers, and limited government intervention in the economy based on free-market capitalism.[57]

On the Court, Scalia is an influential ally of Chief Justice Rehnquist and Justice O'Connor, voting with them, respectively, over 85 and 74 percent of the time. He pays less deference than they do to states' rights, however, and disappointed some conservatives by adhering to precedents in the area of criminal justice.[58] Still, Scalia's style is closely matched to that of Brennan—the old consensus builder who knows how to sway and yield so as to consolidate power—and that makes him formidable. Though one is a conservative Italian Catholic and the other a liberal Irish Catholic, both are sons of immigrants, students of the art of politics who know how to work well with others and shape opinions and forge coalitions. The challenge for Scalia will be to master Brennan's style and approach without sacrificing his own agenda in forging a solid conservative majority on the Court.

THE NOMINATIONS OF ROBERT H. BORK AND DOUGLAS H. GINSBURG

The controversy over the nominations of Judges Bork and Ginsburg remains extraordinary. Instead of becoming the 104th justice, they became the 27th and 28th nominees to be rejected or forced to withdraw due to Senate opposition.* Bork was opposed by the widest margin ever (58 to 42). Revelations about Ginsburg's private life—notably that he had smoked marijuana as a Harvard Law School professor—forced him to withdraw after New Right senators turned against him. The controversy nevertheless underscores the extent to which judgeships were perceived as symbols and a way to ensure Reagan's legacy.

A political battle was virtually assured by the selection of Bork to replace Justice Powell. Powell was not just the pivotal vote on the Court; in his last two terms, the justices ruled 5 to 4 in eighty-one cases, and Powell had the controlling vote over 75 percent of the time. He repeatedly cast the crucial vote in cases rejecting the administration's positions on abortion, affirmative action, the death penalty, and some other issues. With his departure, the balance on the Court would shift.[59] Over more moderate Republicans and conservative jurists, the President chose one of the most outspoken critics of the Warren and Burger Courts.[60] He did so despite the Democrats having regained control of the Senate, which meant a battle over any nominee closely aligned with the New Right. In addition, Reagan made clear that Bork's confirmation was top priority in the final days of his administration; this appeared as one of the most visible ways of reasserting presidential strength, badly damaged by the Iran-*contra* affair.

*In this century, one out of eight nominees confronted this fate, and all for political reasons. In 1930 President Herbert Hoover's nominee, Judge John J. Parker, went down by a vote of 39 to 41. Two of Nixon's successive nominees in 1969 and 1970 were likewise defeated, Judges Clement Haynesworth and G. Harrold Carswell. In 1968, Justice Abe Fortas was forced to withdraw from consideration to replace Chief Justice Earl Warren, after mustering a 45 to 43 favorable vote but failing to get the two-thirds vote needed to cut off a filibuster led by Republicans and conservative Southern Democrats.

The administration also underestimated the opposition. Yet Bork had been passed over three times before, by Ford in 1975 and by Reagan in 1981 and 1986. Shortly after Scalia's appointment, the White House had rumored that the next vacancy would go to Bork, who Reagan had earlier named to the District of Columbia Circuit Court of Appeals. Liberal interest groups therefore had studied Bork's record and were prepared to fight his confirmation.

Senator Kennedy immediately denounced Bork. More than eighty-three organizations followed. Calling him "unfit" to serve on the high bench, the American Civil Liberties Union (ACLU) abandoned its practice of not opposing nominees. The ACLU had only once before taken such a position; it opposed Rehnquist's nomination in 1971 but took no position on his elevation to chief justice. Promising a "no-holds-barred battle," the AFL-CIO also came out in opposition, something it had not done since joining the coalitions that defeated Judges Haynesworth and Carswell.

New Right organizations were no less active, although they were initially discouraged by White House Chief of Staff Howard Baker from strident support. Over the objections of Meese and others in the Justice Department, the White House advanced the strategy of recasting Bork's conservative record in order to make opponents appear shrill and partisan. In a 29 July speech, the President equated his nominee with Powell, despite Bork's past attacks on that justice's opinions. A 70-page White House briefing book was prepared, followed by a 240-page report released by the Justice Department, aimed at portraying Bork as a "mainstream" jurist.[61]

The publicity was extraordinary. Numerous reports, analyzing Bork's record, were distributed to editorial boards around the country. The staff of the Democratically controlled Judiciary Committee issued its own 72-page study refuting the administration's "centrist" depiction of Bork. For political consultants and fund-raisers, Bork was a "bonanza." People for the American Way launched a $2 million media campaign opposing the nomination, while the National Conservative Political Action Committee (NCPAC) committed over $1 million to lobbying for confirmation.[62]

What had far greater impact, however, was Bork's own role in the preconfirmation fray and in the confirmation proceedings. Even before the hearings began, Bork took the unusual step of granting an unrivaled number of newspaper interviews. Like Louis Brandeis in 1911, Bork faced charges of being a "radical." Unlike Brandeis and all prior nominees, who let their records speak for themselves, Bork sought to explain, clarify, and amend his twenty-five-year record as a Yale Law School professor, as a solicitor general, and as a judge. That broke with tradition and gave the appearance of a public relations campaign.[63]

During his five days of nationally televised testimony before the Judiciary Committee, Bork continued to give the appearance of refashioning himself into a moderate, even "centrist," jurist. A key consideration thus became, in Senator Leahy's words, one of "confirmation conversion"—whether Bork was "born again."

Besides deserting much of his past record, Bork's lengthy explanations were unprecedented in other ways. Since 1925, when Harlan F. Stone first appeared as a witness during his confirmation hearings, down to Reagan's previous appointees, all nominees have refused to talk about their views on specific cases, let alone discuss how they might vote on issues likely to come before the Court. But Bork gave unusual assurances on how he might vote, if confirmed.[64]

Republican Senator Arlen Specter and Arizona's Democratic Senator Dennis DeConcini extracted promises (or concessions) on the First Amendment, the Fourteenth Amendment, the commerce clause, and issues like abortion and gender-based discrimination. Although still finding fault with the reasoning in *Bolling* v. *Sharpe* (1954), which desegregated the schools in the District of Columbia, for instance, Bork said he "would never dream" of overturning it. As much as anything else, Bork strove to assure all that he had "no ideological agenda" and had "great respect for precedent." That proved difficult because of his history of assailing so many watershed rulings and his repeated declarations that "in the field of constitutional law, precedent is not all that important."

By the time Bork finished his thirty hours of testifying, he had contradicted much of what he had stood for and for which he was nominated. Noting the "considerable difference between what Judge Bork has written and what he has testified he will do if confirmed," Specter observed, "I think that what many of us are looking for is some assurance of where you are." Even Bork seemed troubled and at the end of his testimony sought to assure the Senate that "it really would be preposterous to say things I said to you and then get on the Court and do the opposite. I would be disgraced in history."

Bork's testimony weighed far more than that of the 110 witness assembled for and against him in the following two weeks. They, to be sure, contributed to the atmosphere of campaign politics that surrounded the hearings. For the first time, a former President, Gerald Ford, introduced a nominee to the committee. And Carter subsequently sent a letter expressing his opposition. Nor have justices, especially sitting justices, ever before come out as allies of a President or his nominee. Yet retired Chief Justice Burger testified and Justices John Paul Stevens and Byron White publicly endorsed Bork.

The strategies of members of the Judiciary Committee were also important. Bork's staunchest defenders, Senators Orrin Hatch and Alan K. Simpson (R-Wyoming), repeatedly decried the "campaign of distortion." Chairman Biden was measured and meticulously fair; he even won praise from Senators Hatch, Simpson, and Thurmond. Biden was also well advised by conservative law professor Philip Kurland, among others, to frame the debate broadly in terms of the Court's role in protecting individual rights—such as the right of privacy—rather than focus on narrower, more divisive issues such as abortion and affirmative action. The debate, in Biden's words, was "not about Judge Bork but about the Constitution." This was tactical and timely, since the hearings began two days before the Bicentennial of the Constitution (on 17 September).

In spite of the publicity and pressure-group activities, the hearings were remarkably illuminating, particularly in Bork's exchanges with Biden, DeConcini, and Specter. They focused on the nature of the Constitution: Is it "the Founders' Constitution," as identified with Meese's call for "a jurisprudence of original intention" and defended by Bork? Or, is the Constitution a "living document," one that amendments and the Court's rulings have made more democratic and afforded greater protection for civil rights?[65] Put this way, the hearings came closer than any before to a national debate; in Biden's words, "a referendum on the past progress of the Supreme Court and a referendum on the future."

The fundamental issue remained, after all, the constitutional views shared by Bork and the administration. That is what had already sown divisions with the legal establishment over some lower-court judges and broke open with the battle over Bork. It was reflected in the ABA's rating of Bork "well qualified," but with a third of its committee opposed, and the broad opposition of the legal profession; 1925 law professors (40 percent of the academic legal profession) signed letters opposing Bork, more than five times the number (300) that had opposed Carswell.

What captured attention at the end of three weeks of hearings, however, were public opinion polls. A Washington Post/ABC News poll found that 52 percent of the public opposed confirmation. An *Atlanta Constitution* poll of twelve Southern states found that 51 percent of its respondents were against Bork, including white conservatives. Bork and his supporters, not surprisingly, decried the influence of public opinion on the outcome.

But to attribute Bork's defeat entirely to public opinion polls is wrong. Most senators and their staffs spent an entire summer examining Bork's record, reputation, and judicial philosophy. The committee's hearings were more exhaustive, perhaps, than any before. It is no less wrong solely to credit or blame the pressure of civil rights groups for Bork's defeat. There was also a campaign for Bork by the New Right. That is why some senators delayed the Senate's final vote for two weeks, over the objections of Majority Leader Robert Byrd (D-West Virginia) and Minority Leader Robert Dole (R-Kansas), so that more money could be raised and certain senators targeted with letter-writing campaigns.[66]

The publicity and pressure-group activities, to be sure, figured into the outcome. Within a couple of days of the Judiciary Committee's vote, seven conservative Southern Democrats, led by Louisiana's Senator J. Bennett Johnston, announced their opposition. This, along with similar announcements by Senators Specter and DeConcini, prodded the two remaining Democrats on the committee, Senators Byrd and Howell Heflin, to abandon their view that the committee ought not make any recommendation to the full Senate. As a result, the vote was 9 to 5.

Ultimately, though, Bork was defeated because of his views and his association with the Justice Department's and the New Right's legal policy goals. That was what the debate over the Constitution during the committee's hearings was about. It is what turned conservative Southern Democrats and six moderate Republicans against him in the final vote on the Senate floor.

The defeat was a major setback for the Justice Department and the administration. Bork, Meese, and others in the department were bitter, and blamed White House staff for not pushing hard enough for confirmation. They were also vindictive and persuaded Reagan to nominate Judge Ginsburg rather than Ninth Circuit Court of Appeals Judge Anthony M. Kennedy, a less controversial conservative.[67]

Ginsburg shared more with Bork than a nomination and a seat on the same appellate court. He was Bork's protégé, twenty-years younger but tracking a similar path back to law school days at the University of Chicago. After graduating, Ginsburg followed Bork in specializing in antitrust and in an academic career. In 1983 Ginsburg joined the Justice Department as an assistant attorney general in the antitrust division. There he became known for moving it in the direction long advocated by Bork and others of the Chicago school of thought. In 1985 Ginsburg was promoted to chief of the division and a year later to the appellate bench.

In its haste to find a suitable successor to Bork, the Justice Department failed to investigate Ginsburg's background fully. Instead, it expected him not to provoke the kind of scrutiny or outcry that had dogged Bork, since he had written virtually nothing outside of a few articles on antitrust and only twenty opinions since becoming a judge. Besides Ginsburg's being relatively unknown, the department also figured that his youth (age forty-one) and the fact that he is Jewish would deflect opposition.

Within ten days after his nomination, however, Ginsburg was forced to withdraw, amid disclosures about his personal life and growing concerns about his ethical conduct as an attorney in the Justice Department, as well as his lack of judicial experience.[68] A few days later, Reagan nominated Judge Kennedy for the seat vacated by Justice Powell almost five months earlier.

JUSTICE ANTHONY M. KENNEDY

The nomination of Judge Kennedy met with immediate and generally bipartisan praise. New Right senators and supporters remained disappointed (and initially considered a challenge), but the Democratic-controlled Senate was in no mood for another battle. And this was reflected in his confirmation hearings in mid-December. They were reminiscent of most hearings in the past; few reporters showed up; none of the commercial television networks broadcast them (as they had Bork's); and only PBS, C-SPAN, and CNN offered coverage.

At the Judiciary Committee's hearings, Kennedy's testimony was subdued and routine. His answers were reserved and straightforward, often descriptive discourses on developing constitutional law. When pressed on heated issues, such as abortion, by Senators Hatch, Grassley, and Gordon Humphrey (R-New Hampshire), he claimed that he had "no fixed view." Judge Kennedy also clearly distanced himself from some of the administration's and Bork's controversial positions. For instance, he accepted the constitutional status of a right of privacy and expressly rejected the view that "a jurisprudence of original intention" provides a sure guide for constitutional interpretation. The latter, in Kennedy's words, is a "necessary starting point," rather than a "methodology," and "doesn't tell us how to decide a case." Although such responses troubled New Right senators, the Judiciary Committee unanimously recommended confirmation.[69]

Kennedy's confirmation sparked no major controversy and little opposition (except from groups like the National Organization for Women) because he is a seasoned and well-respected jurist who comes about as close to Justice Powell in his legal orientation as could be expected. Appointed to the Ninth Circuit by Ford in 1975, he had for more than a decade before practiced commercial and constitutional law, after graduating from Harvard Law School. In the 1960s and 1970s, he was modestly active in Republican state politics, meeting then-governor Reagan and helping in 1973 to draft a state tax-cutting measure. During those years and while on the appellate bench, he also taught constitutional law at McGeorge School of Law in Sacramento.

In his twelve years on the court of appeals, Kennedy established a reputation as an old-time conservative jurist, taking each case on its merits, adhering to precedents and High Court rulings, and narrowly tailoring his opinions. He wrote some 335 majority opinions and, remarkably, in over 90 percent there were no dissents—a higher rate of unanimity than found among most of his colleagues.[70] His record is that of a conservative, but nonconfrontational or doctrinaire. As with Powell, notes Bruce Fein, Kennedy is "a technician rather than a judicial philosopher" like Bork.[71]

It remains to be seen what kind of mark Justice Kennedy (at fifty-one) makes on the Supreme Court. Based on his previous record, he is likely to pay considerable deference to precedent, generally siding with conservatives on such matters as criminal justice[72] and presidential claims over those of Congress in separation-of-powers disputes,[73] while proving less supportive of states' rights and, like Powell, remaining concerned with delicately balancing competing societal and individual claims in areas that touch on matters of personal privacy.[74] In the near term, the Rehnquist Court is thus not likely to make any major sweeping changes but to continue in the directions that it has been going in recent years.

Reagan's Judicial Legacy

Reagan indubitably has had a major, lasting impact on the federal judiciary, both in terms of his unrivaled number of appointments and in reinvigorating judicial conservatism on the bench. Although encountering a few setbacks and failing to achieve as much as some in the Justice Department and the New Right sought, on balance Reagan's judges reflect the consensus of the dominant national political coalition on the role of the federal courts in American politics.

The Rehnquist Court is likely to continue (in the near future at least) as it has, in a more conservative direction but without sweeping changes. Much depends, though, on further changes in its composition and on the next presidential election. For because of the ages of the Court's most liberal and centrist members, Reagan's successor is likely to fill two or more vacancies.

The direction of the lower federal courts will also be affected by how the Court's composition changes and whether the next President is a Republican or a Democrat. In addition, Reagan's legacy in the lower courts may be put in some jeopardy because of low judicial salaries and the appointment of younger judges. They may find it necessary (for financial reasons, unless salaries are increased) to leave the bench sooner than older appointees, for more lucrative legal practices.[75]

A new judicial federalism may be another unanticipated consequence of Reagan's judicial legacy. As the Rehnquist Court and the lower federal courts continue to move in more conservative directions—in the areas of criminal justice, freedom of expression, privacy, and equal protection, for example—state courts are likely to go in a more liberal direction when interpreting individual rights based on their own state constitutions. This has been a developing trend since the early years of the Burger Court, and there is now a steadily growing body of state constitutional law vindicating rights broader than, or left unprotected by, the Supreme Court.[76]

Federal judgeships are nevertheless certain to have greater political symbolism and priority in presidential politics after the Reagan era. And that is no small part of Reagan's legacy.

Notes

1. Quoted and further discussed by the author in his background paper appearing in *Judicial Roulette: The Report of the Twentieth Century Fund Task Force on the Appointment of Federal Judges* (New York: Twentieth Century Fund, 1988). For further background and more extensive discussion, readers should consult that report. The author also acknowledges the benefit of discussing Reagan's appointment of federal judges with Task Force members Walter Berns, Hugh Carey, Lloyd Cutler, Philip Kurland, Jack Peltason, Nick Spaeth, Michael Uhlmann, and Robert F. Wagner.

2. See, e.g., Herman Schwartz, *Packing the Court* (New York: Scribner's, 1988).

3. Ronald Reagan, Message to the National Convention of the Knights of Columbus, 5 August 1986.

4. Quoted by David M. O'Brien, "Meese's Agenda for Ensuring the Reagan Legacy," *Los Angeles Times, Opinion,* 28 September 1986, 1.

5. Stephen Markman, "Memorandum for Attorney General Meese: A Comparison of Judicial Selection Procedures" (manuscript made available to the author, 8 September 1986).

6. See also David M. O'Brien, "The Supreme Court: From Warren to Burger to Rehnquist," 20 *PS* (1987): 12.

7. For a further discussion, see David M. O'Brien, "Ginsburg and the Chicago School of Thought," *Los Angeles Times, Opinion,* 8 November 1987, 1.

8. See, e.g., Richard Posner, "What Am I, a Potted Plant?" *New Republic,* 14 October 1987, 26.

9. Further discussed in David M. O'Brien, *Storm Center: The Supreme Court in American Politics* (New York: Norton, 1986), 41.

10. However, in 1977 Congress passed the so-called Hyde Amendment, limiting federal funding of abortions.

11. The Justice Department's litigation strategies are examined in Lincoln Caplin, *The Tenth Justice: The Solicitor General and the Rule of Law* (New York: Knopf, 1987).

12. See also David M. O'Brien, " 'The Imperial Judiciary': Of Paper Tigers and Socio-Legal Indicators," *Journal of Law and Politics* 2 (1985): 1.

13. Quoted in O'Brien, *Judicial Roulette.*

14. Markman, "Memorandum for Meese."

15. For studies of Carter's and Reagan's judicial appointments, see Larry Berkson and Susan Carbon, *The United States Circuit Judge Nominating Commission* (Chicago: American Judicature Society, 1980); Elliot Slotnick, "Lowering the Bench or Raising It Higher?: Affirmative Action during the Carter Administration," *Yale Law and Policy Review* 1 (1983): 270; Sheldon Goldman, "Reaganizing the Judiciary: The First Term Appointments," *Judicature* 68 (1985): 315.

16. See also Elaine Martin, "Gender and Judicial Selection: A Comparison of the Reagan and Carter Administrations," *Judicature* 71 (1987): 136.

17. See Edwin Meese, "The Attorney General's View of the Supreme Court: Toward a Jurisprudence of Original Intention," in *Law and Public Affairs, Special Issue,* ed. Charles Wise and David M. O'Brien, *Public Administration Review* 45 (1985): 701.

18. Markman, "Memorandum for Meese."

19. Quoted in "Justice Under Reagan," *U.S. News and World Report,* 14 October 1985, 65.

20. Goldman, "Reorganizing the Judiciary," 315.

21. Quoted on National Public Radio, "All Things Considered," 28 August 1985.

22. Based on interviews quoted and discussed in O'Brien, *Judicial Roulette.*

23. Quoted in U.S. Congress, Senate, *Confirmation Hearings on Federal Appointments: Hearings before the Committee on the Judiciary,* 95th Cong., 1st sess. (Washington, D.C.: Government Printing Office, 1986), part 2, 430.

24. Based on author's interviews discussed in O'Brien, *Judicial Roulette;* and Philip Lacovara, "The Wrong Way to Pick Judges," *New York Times,* 3 October 1986, A35.

25. Edwin Meese, Address Before the Palm Beach County Bar Association, 10 February 1986, 6.

26. Based on author's interviews, discussed in O'Brien, *Judicial Roulette.*

27. Based on data supplied to the author by the Senate Judiciary Committee and further discussed in ibid.

28. Quoted in Judicial Selection Project, *Year End Report* (Washington, D.C.: Alliance for Justice, October 1986).

29. Quoted in *Report on the National Bar Association on Jefferson Beauregard Sessions, III, for Appointment to the Federal District Court for the Southern District of Alabama.* Copy made available to the author.

30. Based on data supplied by the American Bar Association.

31. See Sheldon Goldman, "Reagan's Second Term Judicial Appointments: The Battle at Midway," *Judicature* 70 (1987): 324, 328.

32. Testimony of Herman Schwartz, U.S. Congress, Senate, *Confirmation Hearings on Federal Appointments: Hearings before the Committee on the Judiciary,* 99th Cong., 1st sess., pt. 2 (Washington, D.C.: Government Printing Office, 1985), 449.

33. Craig Stern, "Judging the Judges: The First Two Years of the Reagan Bench," *Benchmark* 1 (1984): 1.

34. Ibid., 5.

35. Quoted by Grover Rees, "Dr. James McClellan," *Review of the News,* 1985, 31, 37.

36. See, e.g., "Reagan's Revolution Comes Up Short," *U.S. News and World Report,* 2 February 1987, 27.

37. This discussion draws on David M. O'Brien, "Reagan's Legacy for U.S. Courts," *Los Angeles Times, Opinion,* 23 August 1987, 1.

38. For a discussion of this view, see Lincoln Caplin, "Judicial Restraint Means Activism on the Right," *Washington Post, Outlook,* 19 January 1986, G1; and Howard Kurtz, "Amid Many Failures, Meese Makes a Mark," *Washington Post,* 13 July 1987, A1.

39. See Donald Songer, "Consensual and Nonconsensual Decisions in Unanimous Opinions of the United States Courts of Appeals," *American Journal of Political Science* 26 (1982): 238; and Sheldon Goldman, "Voting Behavior on the United States Courts of Appeals Revisited," *American Political Science Review* 60 (1975): 491.

40. Jon Gottschall, "Reagan's Appointments to the U.S. Courts of Appeals: The Continuation of a Judicial Revolution," *Judicature* 70 (1986): 49.

41. C.K. Rowland, Donald Songer, and Pete Carp, "Presidential Effects on Criminal Justice Policy in the Lower Federal Courts: The Reagan Judges" (paper, 1985, supplied to the author and for which he expresses appreciation). The study was based on a random sample of 1222 district court opinions and 1500 appellate court opinions.

42. See, e.g., Note, "All the President's Men? A Study of Ronald Reagan's Appointments to the U.S. Courts of Appeals," *Columbia Law Review* 87 (1987): 101.

43. For further discussion, see O'Brien, *Judicial Roulette*.

44. Quoted by David Whitman, "Are Reagan's New Judges Really Closet Moderates?" *Washington Post*, 9 August 1987, C1.

45. See O'Brien, "Imperial Judiciary."

46. For further discussion of the Justice Department's and the Solicitor General's unsuccessful attempts to win the Court over to the Reagan administration's positions in these areas, see Caplin, *Tenth Justice;* and David M. O'Brien, "The Solicitor General: Assessing the Influence of the U.S. Top Lawyer," *Philadelphia Inquirer*, 8 November 1987, S1.

47. See U.S. Congress, Senate, *Nomination of Sandra O'Connor: Hearings Before the Senate Committee on the Judiciary on the Nomination of Judge Sandra Day O'Connor of Arizona to Serve as an Associate Justice of the Supreme Court of the United States*, 97th Cong., 1st sess. (Washington, D.C.: Government Printing Office, 1981), 57-58.

48. For a critical discussion of Justice O'Connor's confirmation hearings, see Grover Rees III, "Questions for Supreme Court Nominees at Confirmation Hearings: Excluding the Constitution," *Georgia Law Review* 17 (1983): 913. (In Reagan's second term, Rees served in the Justice Department and oversaw the judicial selection process before becoming a territorial judge.)

49. Justice O'Connor has discussed some of her jurisprudential views in several speeches and articles. See, for example, "Our Judicial Federalism," *Case Western Reserve Law Review* 35 (1985): 1; and "Trends in the Relationship between the Federal and State Courts," in *Views From The Bench: The Judiciary and Constitutional Politics*, ed. Mark W. Cannon and David M. O'Brien (Chatham, N.J.: Chatham House, 1985), 244.

50. See, e.g., *New York v. Quarles*, 104 S.Ct. 2626 (1984) (con. and dis. op.); and *United States v. Place*, 103 S.Ct. 2637 (1984).

51. See, e.g., Comment, "The Emerging Jurisprudence of Justice O'Connor," *University of Chicago Law Review* 52 (1985): 389.

52. See *Wallace v. Jaffree*, 472 U.S. 38 (1985) (con. op.).

53. See and compare Justice O'Connor's opinions in *Johnson v. Transportation Agency*, 107 S.Ct. 1442 (1987) (con. op.); and *United States v. Paradise*, 107 S.Ct. 1053 (1987) (dis. op.).

54. *Roe v. Wade*, 410 U.S. 113 (1973). For Justice O'Connor's views, see *Thornburgh v. American College of Obstetricians*, 106 S.Ct. 2169 (1987), and *Akron Center for Reproductive Heath v. Akron*, 462 U.S. 416 (1984).

55. See, e.g., *United States v. Paradise*, 107 S.Ct. 1053 (1987); *Johnson v. Transportation Agency*, 107 S.Ct. 1442 (1987); and *Booth v. Maryland*, 107 S.Ct. 2529 (1987).

56. This discussion draws on David M. O'Brien, "Scalia and the Court: Pulling Consensus to the Right," *Los Angeles Times, Opinion*, 29 June 1986, 1.

57. See, e.g., *Arizona v. Hicks*, 107 S.Ct. 1149 (1987).

58. See, besides Justice Scalia's opinions, his articles, "The Disease as Cure," *Washington University Law Quarterly* (1979): 147; "The Doctrine of Standing as an Element of Separation of Powers," in Cannon and O'Brien, eds., *Views from the Bench,* 200; and "Historical Anomalies in Adminstrative Law," *Yearbook of the Supreme Court Historical Society* (1985): 200.

59. For a further discussion of Justice Powell's role on the Court, see David M. O'Brien, "For the Majority" (an interview with Justice Powell), *Los Angeles Times, Opinion,* 3 May 1987, 1; and "Reagan Gets His Shot at Tipping Court's Scales: The Powell Resignation," *Newsday,* 1 July 1987, 77.

60. See also David M. O'Brien and Ronald Collins, "Picking a Supreme Court Justice to Perpetuate the Reagan Legacy," *Los Angeles Times, Opinion,* 27 June 1987, 1.

61. These and other reports are reprinted in *Cardozo Law Review* 9 (1987): 187-508.

62. See Richard L. Berke, "Bork as a Bonanza," *New York Times,* 11 September 1987, 32.

63. Much of the following discussion draws on the more extensive discussion cited in O'Brien, *Judicial Roulette*; and Ronald Collins and David M. O'Brien, "Just Where Does Judge Bork Stand?" *National Law Journal,* 7 September 1987, 13.

64. See also O'Brien, *Judicial Roulette*; and David M. O'Brien and Ronald Collins, "Bork's Shifts Made Credibility an Issue," *Baltimore Sun,* 11 October 1987, K1.

65. For further discussion, see Meese, "Attorney General's View"; Rehnquist, "The Notion of a Living Constitution," in Cannon and O'Brien, eds., *Views from the Bench,* 127; Bork, "Tradition and Morality in Constitutional Law," in Cannon and O'Brien, eds., *Views from the Bench,* 166; Andrea Neal, "Robert Bork: Advocate of Judicial Restraint," *American Bar Association Journal,* 1 September 1987, 82; and David M. O'Brien, "Toward a More Perfect Union," *Philadelphia Inquirer, Bicentennial Supplement,* 15 September 1987, 3.

66. For further discussion, see Elizabeth Drew, "Letter from Washington," *New Yorker,* 2 November 1987, 150.

67. Much of the following discussion draws on O'Brien, "Ginsburg and the Chicago School."

68. For further discussion, see Kenneth Karpay, "Questions Linger as Ginsburg Returns to Circuit," *Legal Times,* 16 November 1987, 8; Aaron Freiwald, "Ginsburg Inflated Legal Experience," *Legal Times,* 9 November 1987, 1; and Kenneth Karpay, "In Search of Judge Ginsburg," *Legal Times,* 2 November 1987, 1.

69. For further discussion, see Terence Moran, "Conservatives Set to Challenge Kennedy," *Legal Times,* 14 December 1987, 6; Al Kamen, "Kennedy: No 'Fixed View' on Abortion," *Washington Post,* 14 December 1987, 1; Linda Greenhouse, "Judge Kennedy Says Rights Are Not Always Spelled Out," *New York Times,* 15 December 1987, B16; Ronald Collins and David M. O'Brien, "Kennedy Hearings as Bad as Bork Hearings—In Different Way," *Baltimore Sun,* 20 December 1987, E1; and Terence Moran, "Privacy, Partiality, and Pugnacity," *Legal Times,* 21 December 1987, 4.

70. See Gerald F. Uelman, "A Jurist to Fit Powell's Shoes," *Los Angeles Times,* 22 November 1987, pt. 2, p. 23.

71. Quoted by Paul Marcotte, "Bork to Ginsburg to Kennedy," *American Bar Association Journal,* 1 January 1988, 15.

72. But see Bruce A. Green, "Criminal Law: Judge Kennedy Might Not Meet Expectations of Administration," *National Law Journal,* 21 December 1987, 20.

73. See *Chadha* v. *Immigration and Naturalization Service,* 634 F.2d 408 (1980). The Supreme Court subsequently upheld Judge Kennedy's opinion in *Immigration and Naturalization Service* v. *Chadha,* 462 U.S. 919 (1983).

74. Compare Judge Kennedy's opinion in *Beller* v. *Middendorf,* 632 F.2d 788 (1980), with Justice Powell's opinion in *Bowers* v. *Harwick,* 106 S.Ct. 2841 (1986) (both involving claims to a right of privacy by homosexuals).

75. See Sheldon Goldman, "The Age of Judges: Reagan's Second-Term Appointees," *American Bar Association Journal,* 1 October 1987, 94; and Chief Justice William H. Rehnquist, *1987 Year-End Report.*

76. For a further discussion, see Justice William J. Brennan, "Guardians of Our Liberties—State Courts No Less Than Federal," in Cannon and O'Brien, eds., *Views from the Bench,* 229; Ronald Collins, Peter Galie, and John Kincaid, "State High Courts, State Constitutions, and Individual Rights Litigation Since 1980: A Judicial Survey," *Publius* 16 (1986): 141; and Ronald Collins and Peter Galie, "Upholding Rights Left Unprotected By U.S. Supreme Court Decisions," *National Law Journal,* 9 November 1987, 32.

4

Reagan and the Bureaucracy: The Bequest, the Promise, and the Legacy

Peter M. Benda
and
Charles H. Levine

When Ronald Reagan took office on 20 January 1981, he was taking control of a damaged institution. The Presidency had been rocked by the Watergate scandal, the Iran hostage crisis, and a decade of economic "stagflation." The Carter administration had left office discredited—unable in the minds of the electorate to manage the nation's affairs in matters big or small. Some of President Carter's difficulties were directly traceable to the widespread perception that he had failed to deliver on one of his major promises in the campaign of 1976, that is, to make the government and its principal agent, the bureaucracy, more "manageable."

The 1980 Reagan campaign made similar promises. To avoid the problems that had undermined the Carter Presidency, the Reagan White House formulated a plan that was at once more limited and yet considerably more ambitious than its predecessor. In fact, from the outset, the Reagan administration pursued a campaign to maximize presidential control over the federal bureaucracy that was more *self-conscious* in design and execution, and more *comprehensive* in scope, than that of any other administration of the modern era. The plan revolved around a few clearly articulated policies supported by a variety of administrative strategies. Each policy goal that was central to the administration's domestic agenda—decreasing the size and cost of the federal government and its role in the nation's economic affairs—would be pursued through a two-pronged administrative strategy that would strengthen presidential control over the bureaucracy *and* cut the administrative costs of conducting government programs.

Near the end of President Reagan's second term, the neat logic tying together the administration's policy goals, administrative strategies, and overall institutional objectives for a strong Presidency no longer seems to retain its original coherence. Although some policy goals have been achieved in whole or in part and some management strategies have worked as planned, the administration's hope for a strong Presidency based on tight control over an effective and efficient bureaucracy has only partially materialized.

In searching for an explanation as to why the Reagan administration's management strategy has only partly succeeded, one is drawn to contradictions inherent in the logic of the original plan and to counterproductive administrative tactics that came to light as the plan unfolded over the President's two terms in office. Historians are likely to point to the Iran-*contra* scandal in late 1984 as the signal turning point of the Reagan Presidency. But smaller and less noticed administrative breakdowns and developments have contributed to the mixed record of success.

To understand why and how these problems arose, it is necessary to understand that the Reagan administration's objectives for managing the executive branch have remained consistent over the years, but its tactics have changed, especially in the President's second term. Thus, while the White House continues to espouse three central goals for the administrative arm of government — the political control and coordination of policy formulation *and* implementation; "debureaucratization" through devolution and privatization; and administrative cost cutting through systems modernization, productivity improvement, and the tight control of personnel costs — it has several times changed directions in attempting to achieve them.

This chapter reviews these developments in order to assess their effects on the Reagan administration's ability to achieve its goals as well as their longer-term implications for the relationship between the Presidency and the bureaucracy. We address five important and related questions:

1. What did Reagan inherit from Carter?
2. What control and coordination devices did Reagan add?
3. What "debureaucratization" (i.e., devolution and privatization) strategies were found workable?
4. What management initiatives served to modernize government, enhance productivity, and cut administrative costs?
5. What short- and long-term effects did these initiatives have on the institutional capacity of the federal government and its workforce?

What Reagan Inherited

Looking back on the Carter administration with several years of hindsight, some initiatives launched then appear to have influenced the Reagan administration's management strategy. They are important to an understanding of the Reagan years because some of Carter's initiatives proved more costly in terms of time, energy, and political capital than they were worth; some provided a foundation on which the Reagan administration could build; and some provided insight into how it could more effectively achieve its goals. Among the important Carter initiatives that ultimately failed, two in particular deserve brief mention: (1) the President's Reorganization Project (known as PRP, or "the Project"); and (2) zero-based budgeting (ZBB). The PRP, established shortly after Carter assumed office, was charged to develop reorganization proposals for submission to Congress. The PRP became a centerpiece of the Carter administration's approach to executive branch management because the President had entered office promising to reorganize and "streamline" the government by reducing the number of federal agencies. However, most of the PRP's more ambitious proposals were never implemented. In fact, by the end of Carter's term, there were actually more, rather than fewer, federal agencies.

The zero-based budget initiative also proved to be a major disappointment. Primarily intended to create more rational budgeting processes than those in use at the time, ZBB was also considered to be a management tool to improve program effectiveness. Although announced with considerable fanfare and high expectations, ZBB had many unhappy parallels with the Johnson-era's Planning, Program and Budgeting System (PPBS) and the Nixon administration's Management-By-Objectives (MBO) efforts. "What happened," Ronald Randall observes, "is clear. Just as Johnson and Nixon could not sustain an interest in management techniques, so Carter's interest in ZBB quickly waned."[1] In the end, ZBB proved to be just another technique designed to create an image of management leadership, rather than a serious effort to exercise direction and control.

A more enduring Carter-era reform was the Inspectors General Act of 1978, which established inspectors general in twelve federal agencies responsible for investigating allegations of fraud, waste, and abuse in the federal government. This legislation gave agents of the President new powers to "ferret out" misdeeds of career employees and promote greater economy, efficiency, and effectiveness in agency operations.

Three other Carter-era initiatives left Reagan with institutional devices and models that were to prove useful in pursuing his management agenda: (1) regulatory reform and regulatory review; (2) civil service reform; and (3) a government-wide management improvement council. In January 1978, Carter established the Regulatory Analysis Review Group (RARG), composed of members of major executive agencies as well as presidential economic advisers, to review selected federal regulations (most costing industry over $100 million a year). And in March 1978, Carter issued Executive Order 12044, which strengthened existing "regulatory analysis" requirements by demanding that proposed regulations be assessed in the light of their overall economic impact (rather than simply their possible inflationary impact) and that agencies consider lower-cost alternatives for achieving regulatory objectives. Yet individual agencies retained the authority to determine which of their regulations were subject to economic-impact analysis, and the order was unclear about who had final responsibility for resolving conflicts between presidential advisory bodies and the affected agencies. These problems were exacerbated by internal disagreements among Carter appointees about regulatory policy.

Perhaps the most important step taken by the Carter administration in the area of regulatory reform was to promote the passage of the Paperwork Reduction Act of 1980. The act established an Office of Information and Regulatory Affairs (OIRA) in the Office of Management and Budget (OMB), charged with responsibility to reduce the volume of information required of citizens and businesses by establishing a government-wide "paperwork budget" and by clearing (approving) agency information-collection requests. At first a little noticed deregulation initiative, the Paperwork Reduction Act turned out to be one of Carter's most significant bequests to Reagan.

The Civil Service Reform Act of 1978 (CSRA) was intended to address some long-standing issues surrounding the federal personnel system. Among the more important changes introduced with the enactment of CSRA were (1) the division of the Civil Service Commission (CSC) into the Office of Personnel Management (OPM), the Merit Systems Protection Board (MSPB), and the Federal Labor Relations Authority (FLRA); and (2) the establishment of the Senior Executive Service (SES), which was intended to replace most of the "supergrade" (GS-16 through GS-18) positions that made up the top management corps of the federal civil service.

Finally, the President's Management Improvement Council, which was established late in Carter's term and co-chaired by the directors of the Office of Management and Budget and the Office of Personnel Management, was intended to bring the expertise of the private sector, as well as the talent within federal agencies, to bear on specific management problems. The Management Improvement Council focused on a number of problems, such as the abuse of travel by federal employees and the need to improve the government's debt-collection efforts, that would receive even greater emphasis during the Reagan years.

What Carter Left to Reagan

The Reagan administration received three legacies from the Carter experience: (1) some lessons about what *not* to do; (2) some lessons about what *to* do; and (3) some mechanisms for better controlling the executive branch. In the first category, Reagan administration strategists concluded that President Reagan should not be drawn into the political quagmire that surrounds large-scale executive branch reorganization efforts. Unlike Carter, who entered the reorganization process with only vague notions of "streamlining" the executive branch, President Reagan had a vision for changing government that minimized the value of redesigning the formal administrative structure of the executive branch. Moreover, Carter's attempt to rationalize the budget process taught Reagan strategists that attempting to reform budgeting through changes in the format and processes of budgeting would yield more paper than product. The control and reduction of government spending would eventually have to be accomplished through political control of the appropriations process, not changes in budgetary techniques. Finally, Carter's experience with deregulation underscored the importance of having a unified team to implement reform.

On the positive side, Carter's experience taught Reagan that special councils like the President's Management Improvement Council could spotlight ideas for the modernization and improvement of administrative processes. Carter's effort to attack instances of fraud, waste, and abuse in the bureaucracy by using inspectors general also proved to be a popular idea that Reagan would later expand upon. Finally, Carter's civil service reform, in addition to reforming the federal personnel system's institutional structure, also introduced the notion of "pay for performance" to parts of the federal workforce—an idea that would be encompassed in a major pay-reform package proposed by the Reagan administration in 1986.

The third cluster of bequests that Carter left Reagan concerned the machinery for managing the federal government. Most of these tools, like the creation of the inspectors general, regulatory review, and civil service reform, enhanced the ability of the President to gain greater control over the bureaucracy. Thus, although the Carter administration never fully succeeded in making the bureaucracy "manageable," it did contribute significantly in providing ideas and structures that strengthened President Reagan's hand in 1981.

The Reagan Managerial Strategy

Questions about the administrative legacies of the Reagan era are important because the effort to reshape the organization and administrative apparatus used to carry out government's role has been an integral component of the so-called Reagan revolution. Such questions are not easily answered because in its approach to management the Reagan administration has pursued a threefold strategy of centralization, devolution and privatization, and administrative modernization and cost control, whose long-term implications are difficult to gauge.

Part of the difficulty in assessing the Reagan administration's approach to executive branch management lies in the fact that the various elements of its managerial strategy did not emerge fully blown when President Reagan assumed office in 1981, but came to light only gradually or in phases. Thus, the administration's agenda for management improvement and reform, which initially betrayed a strong centralizing impulse, was later offset by an increased emphasis on decentralization and devolution—shifting in accordance with a changed political environment. But while combining tactics of centralization and decentralization in one overall management strategy may be ultimately compatible, the attempt to move in both directions at once can give rise to distinctive problems, tensions, and mixed results.

Centralizing Control

PERSONNEL SELECTION

The Reagan administration assumed office with a keen awareness of the need to ensure that the politics that won President Reagan the 1980 election would not be forgotten in managing the government. In particular, Reagan and his key advisers recognized that making effective use of the President's appointment power would be an essential ingredient in translating Reagan's electoral mandate into a successful managerial strategy.

In fact, efforts to recruit a loyal team of supporters began as early as April 1980 when long-time Reagan adviser Edwin Meese III asked Pendleton James, a former White House official, to set up a personnel operation. Using five criteria as their guide—compatibility with the President's philosophy, integrity, toughness, competence, and being a team player[2]—James and his staff set about the daunting task of identifying candidates for 3000-plus "political" appointments Reagan would be authorized to fill on entering office. Following the election, these efforts were intensified. With James at the helm, the Reagan administration "undertook transition personnel selection with more forethought, with a larger commitment of resources, and with more attention to detail than any other administration in the postwar period, perhaps more than any administration ever."[3]

The high priority President-elect Reagan and his key advisers attached to the careful screening of potential appointees was born of one overriding concern. Essentially, they sought to avoid repeating what all concerned regarded as a crucial mistake committed by incoming Presidents Nixon and Carter. Each of these Presidents had initially allowed department heads considerable leeway in selecting their principal subordinates and assembling their own management teams—a decision both came to regret. President Reagan and his aides were determined not to fall into this trap. Hence, even while the new President was publicly extolling the virtues of cabinet government, steps were being taken to ensure that ultimate control over subcabinet appointments—indeed, over *all* lower-level political appointments—would remain firmly in the hands of the White House.

The task of ensuring tight control over appointments fell principally to the White House Office of Presidential Personnel (OPP) under the leadership of Pendleton James. Generally regarded as something of a "stepchild" in the ranks of White House offices, the OPP emerged from the shadows during the early stages of the Reagan Presidency to become a key force in mobilizing the support that would be necessary to carry out the Reagan agenda. James himself was accorded the rank of assistant to the President and given an office in the West Wing of the White House. With a staff of over a hundred, the OPP not only assumed principal responsibility for recruiting and selecting appointees for all cabinet-level and agency-head positions but carefully screened candidates for vacancies at the assistant, deputy, and undersecretary levels, as well as directorships of major agency subunits. Indeed, the OPP was "directly involved in recruiting and approving persons for all political positions at levels below the cabinet right down to private secretaries."[4]

Even with a large staff and the help of a new computerized tracking system, the OPP could not have handled a personnel operation of this magnitude without some input from the departments and agencies concerned, nor did it always have the clout to dictate appointments at the subcabinet level. There can be no question, however, that the OPP played an instrumental role in the entire recruitment and selection effort. It successfully discharged its responsiblity to ensure careful White House scrutiny of and control over a vast array of personnel decisions, thereby laying the groundwork for the implementation of the Reagan managerial strategy. As James put it, "We handled all the appointments: boards, commissions, Schedule Cs, ambassadorships. . . . [I]f you are going to run the government, you've got to control the people that come into it."[5]

CABINET COUNCILS

By refusing to delegate the appointment authority to members of the cabinet, and by insisting on demonstrated ideological compatibility with and personal loyalty to the President as necessary conditions for employment, the Reagan

White House clearly sought to offset the likelihood that the administration's appointees would end up becoming more responsive to their own bureaucracies, interest groups, or Congress than to the Reagan agenda. Needless to say, the Reagan approach was not immune to criticism. Some observers argued that the administration leaned too far in the direction of White House control, that undue emphasis was placed on ideological purity at the expense of other considerations (especially prior government experience and/or managerial competence), and that the comparatively slow pace at which lower-level appointments were made "did little to facilitate the transition in the administration of the executive branch."[6] Several of the administration's early major appointments, notably of Anne Gorsuch Burford and James Watt, to head the Environmental Protection Agency (EPA) and the Department of the Interior, proved politically costly. In addition, the number of administration appointees who have faced or may yet face prosecution for alleged transgression of federal conflict-of-interest and related statutes clearly has been a major source of embarrassment.

These criticisms notwithstanding, the administration clearly succeeded in bringing about an unprecedented depth of loyalty and activism among its appointees through the careful and systematic use of the appointment power. As Elizabeth Sanders recently observed, the result of the high priority the President and his aides assigned to White House control of personnel is that "Reagan has achieved a degree of loyalty and coherence in the bureaucracy that other Presidents have longed for. . . . His practices [in this respect] differ from those of his predecessors in their effectiveness, not their intent."[7]

The use of appointment power may have contributed importantly to the "triumph of Reagan management,"[8] but it was far from the only factor. Nor was it the only device utilized by the administration in its effort to ensure bureaucratic "responsiveness" to the Reagan agenda. Despite the care taken in appointing the cabinet and filling key executive posts, the President and his key aides remained extremely wary of the possibility that these officials might "marry the natives" (i.e., end up functioning as departmental advocates to the White House rather than as a team of White House emissaries to the departments).

To prevent this scenario from coming to pass, the Reagan White House was convinced that additional steps were needed to keep those in cabinet and subcabinet positions at a safe distance from the career civil servants who comprise the "permanent government." This promised to become more difficult with the passage of time, once the departments and agencies were operating at full strength and the "cycle of accommodation" between political appointees and the career civil service had set in. The President and his aides had to devise a way to counteract the potential threat such an "accommodation" might pose to vigorous and unified pursuit of the Reagan agenda—without, however, allowing relations between the White House and the departments to degenerate into a we/they confrontation.

It would seem to present no small challenge to devise a scheme that would serve these potentially conflicting objectives. Within months after the administration came to office, however, the groundwork had been laid for a set of institutional arrangements that proved (for a time at least) remarkably well adapted to this purpose. At the heart of this set of arrangements was a system of "cabinet councils," established in February 1981 at the recommendation of Presidential Counselor Edwin Meese III. Originally, there were five councils —the Cabinet Councils on Economic Affairs (CCEA), Commerce and Trade (CCCT), Human Resources (CCHR), Natural Resources and Energy (CCNRE), and Food and Agriculture (CCFA)—"consisting of from six to ten cabinet Secretaries and the heads of EOP cabinet-level offices as principal members, including a departmental secretary as chairman *pro tempore*."[9] Two additional cabinet councils, one on Legal Policy (CCLP), the other on Management and Administration (CCMA), were established in January and September 1982.

In general terms, cabinet councils operated at the second or third tier in the Reagan White House policy apparatus. Their primary function was to serve as focal points to pull together executive branch and White House resources and facilitate coordinated action on a number of important but decidedly second-level policy issues that affected the interests of more than one department or agency (ranging from coal exports [CCCT] and dairy price supports [CCFA] to outer continental shelf leases [CCNRE] and family planning regulations [CCHR]). Some of the councils (notably the CCEA) were quite active, and each played a useful role in providing a forum, under the overall supervision of the White House Office of Policy Development (OPD), for cabinet deliberation on issues of common concern. Despite their affiliation with the OPD, however, these councils dealt with what one commentator has characterized as "a host of matters that scarcely fit the term *policy development*; they [were] more concerned with facilitating implementation of agendas."[10] In the end, Hugh Heclo has suggested, the cabinet councils served to underscore the primacy of a few key actors in domestic policy affairs by "forcing departmental policy development into a system of strategic decision making closely held at the White House."[11]

That the cabinet council system was designed to keep political executives focused on the Reagan agenda while insulating them from the permanent departmental bureaucracies is apparent in the "rules of the game" on which the system's operation was predicated. The primary rule, as James P. Pfiffner has observed, was that "issues were not to be brought up to the President on a bilateral basis, but that all issues [were] to be 'roundtabled' by discussing them at a cabinet meeting."[12] Obviously, the requirement that all issues be "round-tabled" made it that much harder for individual cabinet secretaries to act as effective advocates or brokers for particular policy proposals impressed on them by the career bureaucracy. Any such proposal would have to survive "the scrutiny and criticism of cabinet peers and White House staff members"[13] before making its way higher up the chain of command.

Of course, an individual cabinet secretary might still try to end-run the councils and lobby the President on his or her own, but White House staffers were continually on guard against this possibility, and Reagan himself appears to have been generally unreceptive to special appeals of this kind. According to Edwin Meese, who devised the entire scheme, the President appreciated the important function served by the cabinet councils: "The difference is that Reagan has used his system so that cabinet members all feel closer to him than they do to their departments. And he gives them a lot of opportunity to remember that."[14]

While the cabinet council system therefore seems to have fulfilled White House hopes and expectations during Reagan's first term, the President's second term brought with it major changes of both personnel and structure. In April 1985, the seven separate councils were eliminated, their functions absorbed into two new major policy councils: the Domestic Policy Council, chaired by Attorney General-designate Edwin Meese III, and the Economic Policy Council, headed by the new secretary of the treasury, James Baker. Although President Reagan claimed that this reorganization of the Executive Office policy apparatus reflected his continuing commitment to cabinet government, the action "was interpreted generally as a further centralizing of power in the White House."[15]

In fact, the changes made during the early stages of Reagan's second term seem to have had even more of a centralizing effect than some of their proponents had intended. As Pfiffner points out, although the "dual roles of Meese and Baker had the potential to give them major influence across the full range of domestic policy development, . . . [new chief of staff, Donald] Regan's domination of the White House policy apparatus and personnel did not allow that to happen."[16] The principals began to "go their own way," largely ignoring the cabinet council system in pursuit of policy objectives of particular concern to them. In general, White House decision making during the early phases of Reagan's second term appears to have been characterized by the kind of lack of communication and mutual distrust that came to light during and after the Iran-*contra* revelations, not to be remedied—and only partially at that—until Howard Baker replaced Regan as the President's chief of staff.

What effect Donald Regan's efforts to establish a tight, hierarchical White House organizational structure, and the subsequent (if only partial) collapse of that structure on the heels of Iran-*contra,* may have had on relations among the White House staff, the cabinet, and the "permanent bureaucracy" is difficult to gauge. On balance, however, it seems fair to conclude that earlier efforts to impart an overall "unity of purpose" to the administration were badly damaged by developments during Reagan's second term.

THE OFFICE OF MANAGEMENT AND BUDGET

As the first-term cabinet council experiment suggests, certain Reagan administration institutional innovations undertaken with a view to strengthening presidential authority over the "permanent bureaucracy" may be said to have gone the way of history. No account of developments in this area could be complete, however, that failed to take cognizance of the role of the Office of Management and Budget (OMB). And here the Reagan administration has left a mark that seems likely to endure. Although the authority of what used to be known as the Bureau of the Budget (BOB) over agency affairs has been expanding fairly steadily since it was made part of the new Executive Office of the President in 1939—its original role in supervising preparation of the executive budget having been augmented over time by the power to (among other things) clear agency legislative proposals and establish agency personnel ceilings—the Reagan years have witnessed a notable acceleration in this trend. Indeed, for better or ill (and opinions vary widely on this score), the OMB seems destined to emerge from the Reagan years as a more formidable instrument of presidential control than ever before.

Budgetary Control. Much of the OMB's prominence in the Reagan years can be attributed to David Stockman, Reagan's OMB director from 1981 to 1985. A former representative from Michigan, Stockman brought to his post an intimate familiarity with the often arcane dynamics of the congressional budget process and soon developed a deserved reputation for brilliance for his detailed grasp of domestic programs and expenditures. Convinced no less than the President himself that those expenditures had to be sharply reduced, Stockman took a number of quick and decisive steps with the assistance of White House officials and his OMB staff to restore the budget as an instrument of presidential policy.

"Whether or not as a designed administrative strategy," Frederick C. Mosher has observed, "OMB made administrative decisions on agency policies and programs during the spring of 1981 with little reference to the departments and agencies concerned."[17] The success of what Stockman would later refer to as a "divide-and-conquer" strategy—OMB and the White House imposing program and spending cuts on the President's new cabinet secretaries—was the first step in the stunning 1981 "Reagan budget juggernaut." Subsequently, through the novel use of the congressional reconciliation process, the administration succeeded in pushing through the Congress over 100 pages of changes (affecting more than 250 programs) in authorizations and appropriations in the budget for fiscal year 1982.

The "budget juggernaut" was an event of considerable significance. Among other things, it served as another object lesson for the new members of Reagan's cabinet, underscoring in no uncertain terms that whatever the nature of the President's commitment to "cabinet government," authority over departmental budgets, like authority over personnel, would not be delegated. More important, it brought about unprecedented across-the-board cuts in domestic programs and expenditures, thereby contributing significantly to the goal of reducing the federal government's role in the nation's economic and social life that President Reagan had proclaimed as central to his administration's agenda.

One should not lose sight, however, of the longer-term costs of the strategy OMB's Stockman and the White House used to achieve these results.[18] In the first place, many members of Congress regarded the Reagan/Stockman actions in 1981 as overstepping the conventional boundaries of the executive role in the budget process. They appreciated the perversity of the fact that the Budget and Impoundment Control Act of 1974, which was designed to enhance congressional control over the budget and limit that of the President, had been manipulated to achieve the opposite effect. At the least, reconciliation would henceforth no longer be acceptable as a major device for shaping presidential policy. Second, the quality of figures, assumptions, and projections on which the administration relied in 1981 left much to be desired, and the executive budget lost a good deal of credibility as a "responsible" document. Thereafter, many in Congress were simply not prepared to give the administration's (or OMB's) calculations the benefit of the doubt. For this and other reasons, every budget Reagan submitted after 1981 was promptly pronounced "dead on arrival" and almost completely ignored on Capitol Hill.

Hence, far from becoming the driving force in the budget process, after 1981 the executive budget became little more than a tentative "opening salvo" for negotiations with Congress. The systemic consequence of all this was that budgeting became a continuous, ill-defined process; in effect, "responsibility for putting together a national budget [fell] to Congress by default,"[19] but Congress, lacking the disciplinary mechanisms it would have needed to do so, was unable to respond effectively to the problem of mounting budget deficits. The Balanced Budget and Emergency Deficit Control Act of 1985, popularly known as Gramm-Rudman-Hollings, represents a last-ditch effort to tackle that problem, but the draconian solution it proposes in the event the branches are unable to agree on budgets that meet its specified yearly deficit-reduction targets—automatic, across-the-board spending cuts for defense-related and social programs alike—significantly constrains the President's flexibility and prerogatives no less than those of Congress.

Of course, there may well be, from the administration's perspective, a "silver lining" to this entire dark cloud. As one commentator has observed, "Indirectly, through the deficit, it [the Reagan administration] has changed the dialogue surrounding government from one of debating additions to the scope of government activity to a focus on how to maintain the functions and fund the programs that government has already assumed."[20] Yet, while this may indeed constitute an important Reagan "legacy," it seems fair to conclude that, despite the promising (from its point of view) start, the administration has not succeeded in its efforts to restore the budget as an instrument of presidential policy. As for OMB, Stockman's deliberate effort to "destabilize" the agency may well have been undertaken, as Allen Schick has suggested, "to enhance OMB's capacity to serve the needs and interests of the President."[21] It remains to be seen, however, whether OMB's credibility and standing have not been so compromised in the process that its capacity to effectively serve the *next* President, at least vis-à-vis Congress in the all-important budgetary arena, has not been seriously undermined.

Regulatory Review. While OMB Director Stockman's high-profile effort to "sell" the first Reagan budget and legislative economic package catapulted OMB onto the front pages of the newspapers in 1981, the agency was far from quiescent on other fronts. Within a month after the President assumed office, the administration had taken a number of important steps in an effort to bring executive agency regulatory activity more directly under presidential supervision and control than ever before, and it had become unmistakably clear that it intended OMB to play a major role in that effort.

The promulgation on 17 February 1981 of Executive Order 12291 on "Federal Regulation," which lay the groundwork for OMB's assumption of that role, represented far more than the mere continuation of a trend. To be sure, White House-level oversight mechanisms established with a view to ensuring some measure of presidential input into and control over agency regulatory decision making had become ever more elaborate in character (and ever more comprehensive in scope) since the Nixon administration initiated the process with the introduction of its "Quality of Life" reviews in 1971.[22] As noted earlier, President Carter made his distinctive contribution in this area, attempting to strengthen central regulatory clearance through the promulgation of Executive Order 12044 and the establishment of RARG (the Regulatory Analysis Review

Group). But Executive Order 12291, whose chief requirement was that all "major" agency regulatory proposals survive cost-benefit analysis, represented a departure in kind from what had come before, and it was to be followed by a second directive, Executive Order 12498 of January 1985, which further consolidated presidential control over the regulatory process. Seidman and Gilmour have captured the essence of the transformation wrought by the "Reagan revolution" in regulatory review very well:

> One result of the Nixon, Ford, and Carter measures was to broaden somewhat the President's authority over [executive agency] regulations, but it is evident that the central objective was to stem the mounting flood of regulations and to reduce the burden on the private sector. *No one had yet perceived that review of regulations would take its place with budgetary review as one of the principal management tools available to the President.*[23]

What steps brought this transformation about? In this as in other spheres, the Reagan administration moved very quickly to effect major changes in inherited institutional arrangements. The promise to eliminate burdensome and unnecessary regulations had figured as a prominent theme in Ronald Reagan's campaign, and the new President took prompt steps to begin to redeem that pledge. Two days after he assumed office, the White House announced the creation of a Task Force on Regulatory Relief, chaired by Vice-President George Bush, to review "major regulatory proposals by executive agencies" and to help formulate regulatory policy. The creation of the task force provided an early and clear signal of the Reagan administration's intention to establish a more centralized, top-down system for control of agency regulatory activity. Unlike RARG (which had included the likes of the EPA administrator), the task force membership excluded most of the key regulatory agencies. Initial members included, in addition to Vice-President Bush, Secretary of the Treasury Donald Regan, Attorney General William French Smith, Secretary of Commerce Malcolm Baldrige, OMB Director Stockman, CEA (Council of Economic Advisers) Chairman Murray Weidenbaum, and Assistant to the President for Policy Planning Martin Anderson.

The Task Force on Regulatory Relief (which was disbanded in August 1983) made its most important contribution to the Reagan regulatory program by playing a lead role in the development of Executive Order 12291. This presidential directive, whose stated purpose was "to reduce the burdens of existing and future regulations, increase agency accountability for regulatory actions, [and] provide for presidential oversight of the regulatory process," effected a number of significant changes in the procedural and substantive requirements laid down in Carter's Executive Order 12044. In essence, the new order (1) directed that, "to the extent permitted by law," all "major" rules issued by executive branch agencies survive cost-benefit analysis; and (2) authorized the director of OMB, who was charged with reviewing agency Regulatory Impact Analyses (RIAs) detailing the costs and benefits of all such rules, to delay their implementation in proposed or final form.

Considerable controversy has surrounded several of Executive Order 12291's specific provisions, particularly its cost-benefit analysis requirements, and the manner in which they have been applied. Two other preliminary points about the order's implementation warrant special emphasis, for each contributed significantly to the larger dispute engendered by the launching of the Reagan regulatory review program.

First was the administration's decision to lodge day-to-day responsibility for ensuring agency compliance with the requirements of Executive Order 12291 in the newly established Office of Information and Regulatory Affairs (OIRA) within OMB. This office had been created by the Paperwork Reduction Act of 1980, which was enacted in the waning days of the Carter Presidency. The act was passed by Congress only after steps had been taken to allay concerns about the possibility that it might be used to increase OMB's authority over the substantive policies and programs of the departments and agencies. In its report accompanying the bill, the Senate Governmental Affairs Committee noted that provisions had been added to guard against this possibility, and emphasized, with respect to OIRA, that it did "not intend that regulatory reform issues which go beyond the scope of information management and burden be assigned to the office."[24]

In view of this supposed limitation, it is more than a little ironic that the administration should have used the Paperwork Act as the jumping-off point to launch its comprehensive regulatory review program. Yet shortly after he assumed office, President Reagan abolished the Council on Wage and Price Stability (CWPS), transferring its staff to the Office of Information and Regulatory Affairs within OMB. "The result of this reorganized structure for central regulatory clearance," observed Robert Gilmour in 1983, "has been that OIRA, with 84 positions, about 15 percent of the entire OMB staff, has become the institutional czar for regulation, subject only to occasional appeals to the President's Task Force."[25]

The move to use OIRA as a comprehensive clearinghouse for regulations was almost immediately challenged on the grounds that the President had exceeded his constitutional authority in promulgating Executive Order 12291.[26] On balance, however, this objection probably took a "back seat" to another concern that appears to have loomed larger in the eyes of OMB's critics both in and out of Congress, which had to do with the large element of *secrecy* that characterized OIRA's role in the review process. This is the second important preliminary point to bear in mind in seeking to understand the controversy surrounding the Reagan regulatory review program.

The regulatory clearance process under Executive Order 12291 necessitates frequent contact between officials in OMB and the executive branch agencies whose rules are submitted to OIRA for review. Despite the fact that the Executive Order authorized the OMB director to delay publication of "major" rules until he (or the OIRA staff) was satisfied that its cost-benefit requirements had been met, the Reagan administration, at least initially, *made no provision whatsoever to enable "outsiders" to become apprised of what transpired during the course of OMB-agency negotiations over a particular rule,* that is, to discover whether or how OMB's intercession may have shaped the outcome of the rulemaking process. Moreover, while the prospect of secret communication between White House officials and agency regulation writers was disturbing enough in its own right, critics argued that the problem was compounded by the administration's failure to impose any limitations on the freedom of task force members or OIRA staff to meet "off the record" with outside private parties who might have a stake in the outcome of the review process. In effect, the administration thereby afforded regulated firms who felt that agency officials had not taken their concerns sufficiently into account an additional opportunity to make their influence felt "through the back door."

The lack of procedural safeguards in the Reagan regulatory review program also fueled controversy about the cost-benefit analytic requirements of Executive Order 12291 and how these provisions might be (or were being) applied in practice. Cost-benefit analysis is often criticized for its tendency to downplay variables that are difficult to measure, especially when the benefits of some proposed course of action (including regulatory action) may only or primarily accrue at some point in the distant future. These objections did not appear to faze top Reagan administration officials. One prominent economic adviser to the President, for example, described himself as "an advocate of more cost-benefit analysis, most importantly in health and safety matters. Though people have backed off from using it here, no special conceptual problems stand in the way."[27] Nevertheless, critics pointed to OMB's requirement that a very high 10 percent "discount rate" be used in attempting to put a price value on the future benefits of regulation as one piece of evidence that cost-benefit analysis was not being used as a neutral decision-making tool, but instead represented a "thinly disguised justification for deregulating business and industry."[28] The secrecy of the entire review process only served to reinforce that perception.

Neither the sometimes vociferous congressional criticism of its regulatory review program nor the occasional reprimands OMB received from reviewing

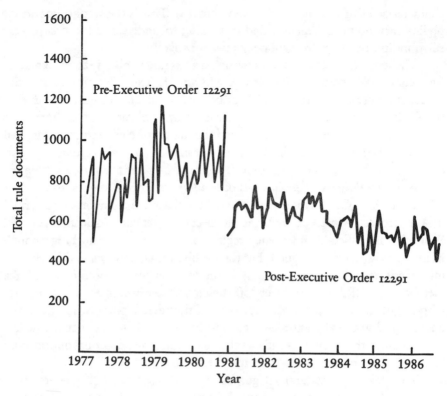

FIGURE 4.1

FEDERAL REGISTER ANALYSIS, TOTAL RULE DOCUMENTS
FEBRUARY 1977 TO DECEMBER 1986

SOURCE: Office of the Federal Register.

courts deterred the Reagan administration from aggressively implementing Executive Order 12291. By the end of Reagan's first term, it became apparent that although the vast majority of rules submitted to OIRA were "nonmajor" and cleared without much delay or controversy, the total number of rules sent to OMB for clearance had declined appreciably, indicating that the administration's efforts to reduce the overall volume of federal regulation were paying off. The period between 1981 and 1984 also witnessed a steady decline in the percentage of total rules found consistent with the Executive Order and without need for changes (from 87.3 percent in 1981 to 78.0 percent in 1984), while the percentage of those found consistent after "minor" changes increased considerably (from 4.9 percent in 1981 to 15.2 percent in 1984).[29] In short, while there was a perceptible "slowdown" in overall regulatory activity during Reagan's first term—a fact reflected in the sharp decline in the total number of rule-making documents published in the *Federal Register* (see figure 4.1)—OMB's influence over agency regulatory decision making expanded steadily over the four years.

Shortly after the 1984 election, the Reagan administration took another major step forward in its effort to centralize control over executive agency regulatory activity by promulgating Executive Order 12498, which requires each agency to develop an annual "regulatory program" to be submitted to OIRA specifying "all significant regulatory actions . . . planned or underway, including . . . the development of documents that may influence, anticipate, or could lead to the commencement of rulemaking proceedings." In a very real sense, Executive Order 12498 may be regarded as the culmination of the Reagan administration's efforts to bring the "permanent bureaucracy" firmly under direct presidential supervision and control. For each item on the annual submissions required under that order, the burden is on the agency to "explain how they are consistent with the administration's regulatory principles." If OMB decides that a proposed "prerulemaking action" (including, for example, the decision to create a task force to investigate the seriousness of certain health or safety risks) is inconsistent with the administration's regulatory principles, the agency is precluded from taking that action. And if during the year the agency decides to undertake an activity that was not originally part of the approved program, it must first seek OMB's approval. Indeed, under Executive Order 12498, *all* agency regulatory action is *automatically* stayed until OMB certifies that the action is "consisten[t] . . . with the administration's policies and priorities."

While the promulgation of Executive Order 12498 promised to place OMB even more firmly in command of the regulatory process, congressional opposition to the administration's regulatory program intensified during the President's second term. This was particularly true in the House, where, in 1986, a number of representatives led by John Dingell (D-Michigan), chairman of that chamber's Energy and Commerce Committee, prevailed on their colleagues to eliminate fiscal 1987 funding for OIRA. Although the Senate ultimately refused to go along, some concessions were wrung from the administration and OMB along the way. For example, OMB responded to congressional criticism of OIRA's "closed" review process by agreeing to adopt new procedures designed to increase public disclosure of the office's review of agency regulations under Executive Order 12291 and of agency regulatory programs under 12498.

Some senators hailed this last decision to "open up" the review process, but critics countered that the new disclosure procedures did not go far enough[30] and would do little to stymie OMB's growing authority over regulatory decision making. And in fact, despite mounting criticism in and out of Congress,

OIRA during the second term became more aggressive in reviewing agency regulations. The number of total rules found "consistent without change" under Executive Order 12291 declined an additional 9.7 percent between 1984 and 1986, while the number of those found "consistent with change" was up an additional 7.8 percent (from 15.2 percent to 22.9 percent) during the same time.[31]

In sum, OMB has emerged during the Reagan years as a very powerful instrument of "presidential management." Taken together, Executive Orders 12291 and 12498, in conjunction with the considerable authority vested in the OMB under the Paperwork Reduction Act, have provided a firm foundation on which future administrations can build. Reagan's successor may not share his particular priorities in regulatory policy, but it seems unlikely that the next President will elect to dismantle the very effective regulatory and paperwork-clearance mechanisms the Reagan administration has put in place. The establishment of these mechanisms was central to the process whereby the administration succeeded in fashioning "the most powerful budget bureau since the office was created in 1921."[32]

"Debureaucratization": Devolution and Privatization

The most direct way to diminish the federal government's role in economic and social affairs is simply to reduce the range of activities in which it is involved. The Reagan administration clearly appreciated this fact and sought to eliminate many federal domestic programs outright. This effort may be regarded as one element of a broader campaign to "debureaucratize" the federal executive establishment—that is, to place greater reliance on third parties, such as state and local governments, private firms, and nonprofit organizations to perform functions or provide services previously entrusted to the national government.

The process of consciously transferring federal responsibilities to the states and localities is referred to as *devolution*, while *privatization* refers to attempts to transfer governmental responsibilities to the private sector. The discussion that follows examines the Reagan administration's initiatives in each sphere.

DEVOLUTION

In his first inaugural address, President Reagan proclaimed that a central objective of his administration would be "to demand recognition of the distinction between the powers granted to the federal government and those reserved to the states or to the people." This statement signaled an attempt to chart a new course in intergovernmental affairs. Rather than seek to strengthen and improve the management of existing intergovernmental programs, as most earlier reformers had done, the Reagan administration set out to work a fundamental redistribution of responsibilities between the local, state, and federal governments.

In the administration's view, such a redistribution of responsibilities was necessary to redress imbalances in the federal system resulting largely from the increased reliance during the 1960s and 1970s on federal grants-in-aid to state and local governments as a preferred means for carrying out domestic programs. Much of the federal aid made available to state and local governments during this period (about half of which was earmarked for community development projects and the like, the other half for income transfer programs for individuals) enabled them to expand their traditional functions in such areas as transportation and education. Many more aid programs, however, "were designed to induce state and local governments to do what the federal government wanted done—to serve as administrative agents for federal programs and their national goals."[33]

The Reagan administration believed that this attempt to expand the scope of the national government's involvement in social and economic policy represented a serious "overreaching" of federal authority, both in the sense that it infringed on functions properly reserved to the states or localities and in the sense that many domestic programs could be run more effectively at the state or local level. It was also concerned that grants-in-aid programs had rendered the states and localities overly dependent on federal resources and unduly constrained by a host of federal requirements, and that outlays for federal aid as a whole, which nearly doubled in the 1960s and continued to expand rapidly in the 1970s, reaching an all-time high (17 percent of all federal spending) in 1978, were taking too big a "bite" out of the budget.

The Reagan intergovernmental agenda thus called for reductions in or the termination of federal aid programs wherever possible. This was to be accompanied by efforts to relax or eliminate national rules and standards that constrained the flexibility of state and local officials in using federal monies they *did* receive. Important steps toward achieving these objectives were taken with the passage of the 1981 Omnibus Reconciliation Act. This legislation achieved the first absolute reduction in federal aid outlays in several decades (from $94.8 billion in FY 1981 to $88.2 billion in FY 1982). Some sixty grant programs were simply eliminated, while funding levels for others were dramatically reduced. At the same time, seventy-seven "categorical" grant programs were consolidated into nine broader, more flexible "block" grants—the largest such conversion in history.

These early Reagan intergovernmental initiatives provoked a good deal of controversy. Although the administration sought to justify a large-scale reduction in federal assistance in part on the grounds that this "rollback" would encourage state and local governments to expand the scope of their activities, skeptics argued that Reagan was "not seeking to shift government responsibilities anywhere as much as he [was] seeking to abolish or reduce interventions he [did] not like."[34] And while grant consolidation "has long been advocated as a good technique for streamlining both federal and recipient management,"[35] the fact that many of Reagan's block-grant proposals were linked to substantial funding reductions elicited considerable protest from the recipients (i.e., state and local officials) as well as from members of Congress, many of whom traditionally have been wary of block grants, primarily out of concern that state and local officials cannot be trusted to channel funds to those regions and people most in need. Thus, while the administration was able to achieve "some remarkable legislative successes in grant consolidation and domestic expenditure reductions" in 1981,[36] it created a climate of suspicion that placed its subsequent intergovernmental reform proposals, most notably its ambitious 1982 "Federalism Initiative," in serious jeopardy.

The Federalism Initiative, which President Reagan unveiled in his 1982 State of the Union address, was the most serious attempt the administration made to "devolve" domestic program responsibilities back to the states and to clarify the allocation of functions between the state and federal governments.[37] The initiative had two major components: a "swap" (or tradeoff) component affecting the nation's three largest means-tested transfer programs, and a "turnback" component affecting approximately forty-five categorical grant programs. The "swap" component called for the federal government to assume full responsibility for Medicaid, which provides medical care for the poor and is the largest of the income transfer programs. In exchange, the states would assume complete responsibility for the AFDC (Aid to Families with Dependent Children) and food stamp programs. The "turnback" component proposed a phased withdrawal of the federal government from programs in education, community development, transportation, and social services. A Federalism Trust Fund of $28 billion would be used to fund the turnback programs during a four-year transition period, after which both the fund and special federal taxes supporting it would begin to phase out, "leaving it to the states to determine whether or not to replace lost revenues and services."[38]

Although negotiations between top administration officials and state and local government representatives on the details of the Federalism Initiative were conducted throughout 1982, it is very unlikely that whatever package they might have come up with would have received a serious hearing in Congress, which was distinctly unreceptive to the scheme. As David R. Beam has noted, the timing of the initiative's introduction did not help the administration's cause: "The turnback and tradeoff initiatives aroused hostility, in part, because they were advanced along with proposals to reduce aid outlays in a period of economic distress. The impression was created that *federalism* was nothing more than a code word for stringent expenditure cuts."[39] In any event, no agreement was reached and no legislation was ever forwarded to Congress. Nor did the administration fare much better in 1983 when it unsuccessfully proposed a revised version of the initiative (concentrating on consolidation of a number of existing grant programs into four "megablock" grants).

In the aftermath of these experiences the Reagan administration seemed to have lost much of its enthusiasm for far-reaching proposals to "debureaucratize" the federal government through the formal devolution of functions back to the states. While it continued indirectly to attempt to transfer much of the burden for domestic programs to the states and localities, for the most part the Reagan intergovernmental agenda in the President's second term shifted toward narrower and more "conventional" reform measures, such as streamlining administrative requirements for grants-in-aid (through revisions of OMB Circular A-102) and reducing federal regulatory and paperwork burdens on state and local governments.

This is not to suggest that larger questions of intergovernmental reform were entirely neglected in the second Reagan term. In 1985, for example, a Working Group on Federalism, composed largely of Justice Department officials, was established by Attorney General Meese as a subunit of the Domestic Policy Council. The attorney general described the working group's role as that of developing "a basic administration-wide rhetorical strategy for rooting basic constitutional federalism principles in Federal law and regulations."[40] It is perhaps a reflection of Meese's suggestion that it would focus as much on "maintaining theoretical consistency as on creating new policy," however, that some of the leading items on the working group's original agenda—including preparation of options for another major legislative federalism initiative—were never carried to fruition. Although the working group's efforts did yield a number of practical results (including a new Executive Order intended to reduce federal preemption of state and local regulations), the conclusion that "no large-scale devolution of federal . . . responsibilities has been accomplished"[41] seems as applicable to the second Reagan term as to the first.

PRIVATIZATION

While "debureaucratization" through devolution received relatively less emphasis after 1983 or so, the administration appears to have been responsive to conservatives who urged that "shifting government functions to the private sector" should be the "central theme" of its second-term efforts to cut the budget and reduce the size and influence of the federal executive establishment.[42] Indeed, although "privatization" had been an important part of the Reagan agenda from the outset, it was accorded an even higher priority in the President's second term.

The term *privatization* defies easy definition. It is clear, however, that the privatization "movement" has its intellectual roots in free market economic theory and "is held together by a shared belief that the public sector is too large and that many functions presently performed by government might be better assigned to private sector units [whether] directly or indirectly. . . . The private sector, it is argued, will perform these functions more efficiently and economically than they can be performed by the public sector."[43] Privatization can take two basic forms: (1) when the government simply decides to withdraw from certain activities by transferring or selling assets or programs entirely to the private sector; (2) when government places greater reliance on the private sector to *produce* services that it decides to *provide.*[44]

The contemporary appeal of privatization (both in the United States and elsewhere) is attributable to many factors, but the primary reason why privatization has assumed particular prominence on the Reagan agenda is not difficult to determine. President Reagan's victory in the 1980 election permitted leading free market economists (e.g., James C. Miller III and Murray Weidenbaum) and conservative "think tanks" (e.g., the Heritage Foundation and the Cato Institute) "to gain political and institutional influence in the federal government. No longer outsiders, the free marketeers moved rapidly to translate their theories into public policy."[45] These conservative proponents of the cause actively encouraged administration privatization efforts along *both* dimensions discussed above. As a practical matter, however, because the federal government has (for instance) never owned the telephone, airline, or automobile industries (a practice common in other countries), opportunities for "divestiture"— the outright sale or transfer to the private sector of governmental commercial enterprises—have been limited.[46] Therefore, most of the administration's privatization efforts have been geared toward affording greater opportunities for private-sector participation in the delivery of government programs.

Perhaps the most important means by which the administration has sought to advance the cause of privatization has been to insist on greater use by federal agencies of "contracting out," that is, to rely on private firms retained under contract to deliver the goods or services for which agencies have been assigned responsibility. In August 1983, OMB revised its contracting-out directive (Circular A-76), simplifying public versus private cost comparisons in a way calculated to enhance private-sector involvement. This revision of Circular A-76 drew sharp criticism (especially from federal employee union representatives) on the grounds that its relatively lax standards would permit the transfer of responsibility for public functions that were too important to be entrusted to third parties and that such a policy threatened seriously to undermine the long-term, "in-house" capacity of the federal government. For its part, OMB "argued that it was good policy to make government employees 'compete for business' with the private sector, and estimated that the government spent at least $20 billion a year in activities that could appropriately be performed by private business."[47]

The administration has actively promoted other activities under the broad rubric of privatization. It has, for example, urged increased application of user fees, whereby users of government facilities or beneficiaries of government services are assessed a charge sufficient to cover all or part of the cost of their maintenance or provision.[48] It has also advocated greater use of vouchers with a view to enabling individuals to purchase a particular service, at government expense or with government support, from either public or private sources.[49]

The privatization movement gained additional momentum in President Reagan's second term, as reflected in the establishment in September 1987 of the President's Commission on Privatization. This twelve-member body issued a report supporting earlier administration proposals to sever the federal government's financial ties to AMTRAK and to sell two Naval Petroleum Reserves (NPRs) as well as five power marketing administrations (PMAs). In addition, the privatization commission urged that serious consideration be given to turning various delivery services now controlled by the U.S. Postal Service, as well as some federal prisons, over to private contractors. It also advocated increased use of vouchers for federally subsidized housing, medical care, and schooling.

In general, the Reagan administration's privatization efforts have met with mixed results. Congress did agree to the administration's proposal to sell off CONRAIL and to the sale of some federal loans, but on the whole has been reluctant to endorse the administration's push (and that of conservative "think tanks") for more and more privatization of governmental functions.

Privatization advocates have raised important questions about whether particular functions previously assigned to federal, state, or local governments could be run more economically by private service providers. But critics of privatization challenge the notion (proffered by some) that nearly all public-sector activities are potentially amenable to being transferred to the private sector, arguing that certain "core" governmental functions (e.g., maintaining national security or public safety) ought not to be so transferred, that contracting out and other "privatization" methods or options raise serious problems in their own right, and that variables other than economic efficiency (e.g., accountability and equity) need to be factored into the decision-making equation.[50]

In the Reagan administration, the impetus toward privatization was as much directed toward cost savings as toward philosophical goals. The fact that its various privatization initiatives have appeared to many to represent little more than ad hoc attempts to reduce the budget has left the administration vulnerable to the charge that it has not given sufficient attention to developing sound principles to govern the allocation of functions between the public and private sectors. Nonetheless, it would be a serious mistake to dismiss the emphasis on privatization as nothing more than an ideological "reflex." On the contrary, this promises to represent one of the Reagan administration's more important legacies.

Management Reform: Modernizing and Economizing

Although reducing the range of activities in which the federal government was involved was a major aim of the Reagan managerial strategy, the administration was also (and perhaps equally) concerned with ensuring that the functions that remained with the federal government would be operated in the most cost efficient and effective manner possible. This was reflected in the administration's management improvement and reform initiatives, whose story breaks down into two periods, first- and second-term initiatives. The hallmarks of the first period were the establishment in September 1982 of the Cabinet Council on Management and Administration (CCMA) and the formal inauguration of the President's Management Improvement Program—"Reform '88." The midway point in the second term, early 1987, marked the beginning of the Reagan administration's final management improvement push.

FIRST-TERM INITIATIVES

The driving force behind Reform '88 was Joseph Wright, who succeeded Edwin Harper as deputy director of OMB in April 1982. During Harper's tenure, the "management side" of OMB confined its activity to building on initiatives to strengthen federal debt-collection efforts and eliminate abuse of federal travel begun under the Carter administration and providing assistance to the President's Council on Integrity and Efficiency (PCIE), which was established in March 1981 to coordinate efforts to reduce agency waste, fraud, and abuse. By absorbing these ongoing activities into Reform '88, which Wright described as an "umbrella concept" for a set of initiatives designed to reform federal management and administrative systems by the end of a second Reagan term,[51] the new deputy director undertook simultaneously to expand and focus OMB's management agenda.

There were ten initial Reform '88 objectives, aimed mostly at reducing costs and enhancing revenue collection. The ten goals were to (1) upgrade federal cash management systems; (2) increase collection of debts owed the government; (3) encourage the sale of surplus government property; (4) foster efficient and effective management and eliminate fraud and abuse through strengthening internal accounting and administrative controls; (5) identify unliquidated obligations on agency books; (6) recover funds owed agencies as a result of audits; (7) reduce nondefense workyears by 75,000 full-time equivalents from 1982 to 1984; (8) limit wasteful spending on government periodicals, pamphlets, and audiovisual products; (9) achieve significant savings through systematic reform of procurement practices (e.g., amending and making greater use of A-76 contracting-out review procedures); and (10) reduce government paperwork and thereby limit costs to individuals, private organizations, and state and local governments.[52]

While the projects of Reform '88 quickly became a centerpiece of the Reagan administration's intention to make the federal government more efficient, cost effective, and "businesslike," responsibility for forging and directing management reform efforts during the Reagan years was by no means the exclusive province of OMB. Many significant management initiatives were promoted or coordinated by two special presidential councils established during Reagan's first term. The first was the President's Council on Integrity and Efficiency which was discussed earlier. The mandate given the second council, the President's Council on Management Improvement (PCMI), established in May 1984 and consisting mostly of departmental assistant secretaries for administration, was considerably more comprehensive. The PCMI was charged to oversee and coordinate ongoing management improvement projects and to formulate additional long-range plans to promote improved management systems.

The establishment of the PCIE early in Reagan's first term provided an indication of the administration's willingness to entrust important management initiatives to groups formally operating outside OMB. This practice became clearer after September 1982 when the administration announced the creation of the Cabinet Council on Management and Administration (CCMA) under the leadership of Edwin Meese III. This was an especially noteworthy development because it provided, for the first time, an official unit in the White House responsible for the overall coordination and direction of management reform efforts, including those undertaken by OMB.

Although the establishment of the CCMA was an important event, the most visible mangement improvement initiative of Reagan's first term had its origins elsewhere. This was the President's Private Sector Survey on Cost Control (PPSSCC), better known as the Grace Commission after its chairman, J. Peter Grace. The Grace Commission was composed of task forces headed by 161 top private-sector executives. In a 47-volume report to the President issued in January 1984, the commission recommended program and management changes in 36 areas of the federal government; 2478 recommendations were made that promised savings of $424 billion over a three-year period after implementation. Dispute over the accuracy of the Grace Commission's figures and the feasibility of many of its recommendations continued unabated well into Reagan's second term.[53]

By the end of Reagan's first term, there were indications that the administration's approach to management improvement was beginning to change. Part of the reason for this change can be traced to ever expanding criticisms coming from Congress and other sources outside the executive branch. Another part may be traced to a recognition within the administration that centralization may have gone too far.

Although the administration, commenting on its first-term management initiatives, proclaimed that it had embarked on a broad program "to ensure a continued, organized emphasis on management improvement" and that Reform '88 and other measures had resulted in "substantial progress,"[54] not all observers agreed with this rosy assessment. Comptroller General Bowsher, head of the U.S. General Accounting Office (GAO), for example, suggested that the administration's record revealed the limits of a highly centralized approach to management improvement, that is, one in which principal reliance is placed on central agencies (OMB, OPM, and GSA) rather than operating agencies.[55] In its 1983 report *Revitalizing Federal Management,* the National Academy of Public Administration (NAPA) expressed a similar view, asserting that the accretion of control systems had produced a situation in which procedure overwhelmed substance. Administrative systems and increasingly centralized and detailed administrative procedures had produced a "managerial overburden" that had become a barrier to the responsiveness and cost effectiveness of government. NAPA recommended an enhancement of federal managers' roles and appropriate flexibility and discretion to allow them to provide leadership for their administrative units.[56]

Although these criticisms and recommendations were clearly at odds with the centralizing thrust of its first-term management improvement efforts, there was evidence even prior to the start of President Reagan's second term to suggest that the administration was beginning to take them to heart. This was reflected, for example, in the establishment in May 1984 of the PCMI, which symbolized the administration's willingness to take steps to "shift the center of concentration and effort for management reforms" into the hands of a few senior agency managers and supervisors, as NAPA had urged in its 1983 report.

SECOND-TERM INITIATIVES

The creation of the PCMI proved to be a precursor of a subtle shift in management emphasis. In 1986 the administration announced that continued attention would be devoted to furthering earlier initiatives like fraud prevention, payment integrity, improved cash and loan portfolio management, procurement reform, and reduction in regulatory and paperwork burden. However, new initiatives would be undertaken to improve the productivity of federal programs and the development of shared administrative support services among federal agencies with field organizations scattered around the country. This last initiative was explicitly assigned to the PCMI for development and coordination.

The final stage of the Reagan administration's management improvement efforts began in early 1987 with a reorientation of the "M side" of OMB. Recognizing that only two years remained in the President's second term, the new associate director for management, Jerry Riso, began to narrow the agency's management focus down to two priorities: (1) upgrading the financial management capacity of the departments and agencies; and (2) productivity improvements. These two developments, along with Reform '88 initiatives in areas like credit and loan management that were still under way, constitute the "final push" of the Reagan administration to modernize and economize federal management systems. The idea behind these projects was to provide enough program activity so that their momentum would carry them to completion in the next administration.

The financial management strategy was consistent with earlier Reform '88 initiatives to consolidate and move toward compatible accounting, information, and auditing systems, but was also upgraded in 1987 to head off a congressional action to create a statutory chief financial officer. Instead, by administrative action, Riso's title was changed to include the chief financial officer title. In addition, Riso was given budget examination responsibility for OPM and GSA to provide him with more political leverage over these central management agencies and within OMB. Through the annual "management review" process initiated in fiscal year 1986 and the PCMI, Riso intended to work with the assistant secretaries for management to push financial reform forward.

The second OMB initiative, productivity improvement, was linked to this process, especially the management review exercise. At first, OMB planned to involve 108 programs covering 500,000 employees and $24 billion in program spending. Its focus was on measurable outputs of government programs. In addition to cutting costs, the productivity improvement program was intended to measure improvements in services based on studies of consumer satisfaction. These objectives would be achieved by an incentive program that would reward individuals who identify areas for productivity enhancement (called "gainsharing") and the creation of "investment funds" for agencies to use as rewards for cost savings. To assure that these programs were moving forward, Riso intended to prepare a quarterly report card on a department-by-department basis as a way to motivate the assistant secretaries for management to take these initiatives seriously.

In summary, perhaps the Reagan administration's most lasting contribution to the organization and operation of the federal government will be the result of its efforts to modernize the "nuts and bolts" of management. Operating through several vehicles, the administration has focused efforts to improve how the federal government handles cash management, debt collection, real property, procurement, computer planning, travel, and other administrative overhead expenses. Although some people have charged that these efforts do not amount to management improvement in the broad sense and in reality are little more than "penny pinching" to respond to huge budget deficits, from a historical perspective one must conclude that the Reagan administration has initiated valuable, badly needed reforms in areas overlooked by previous administrations.

Reagan and the Federal Workforce

The final and probably most problematic legacy of the Reagan years has been to bring to a head some long-standing problems confronting the civil service system. Over the course of the Reagan Presidency concern has grown about a perceived erosion in the quality, morale, and effectiveness of the federal workforce. While most discussions of the civil service and its problems focus on the Senior Executive Service (SES) and equivalent levels, fragmentary and impressionistic evidence suggests that the problem goes deeper and spreads wider into the professional, technical, scientific, and administrative corps that make up the bulk of the career service.

Some of the causes for the problems surrounding the civil service can be directly attributed to the Reagan administration's efforts to reshape the size and scope of the administrative state. President Reagan has often stated his preference for less costly government, more privatization of government functions, more use of contracting out, and more tightly controlled and cost-effective operation of those functions left with government employees. This adds up to a personnel policy of a smaller, less expensive, and less autonomous workforce.

Needless to say, the Reagan agenda for the federal workforce was hardly welcomed by federal workers. But its negative implications were compounded by statements and actions of the Reagan administration's original appointee as director of the Office of Personnel Management, Donald J. Devine, who took a decidedly negative view of what he considered to be the excessive pay, benefits, and prerogatives of federal employees. During his four-year term, Devine reorganized the agency and shaped its policy priorities in ways that many critics thought "politicized" OPM and damaged the civil service. Rather than serve as an aggressive proponent of a high-quality workforce and modern human resource management, as its supporters had hoped, OPM under Devine was viewed by many as a principal agent of the Reagan administration's "war on the bureaucracy."[57] To buttress this perception, Devine's critics pointed to his tendency to engage in "bureaucrat bashing" and his advocacy of a rigid separation between political and career appointees in the policy process (i.e., political appointees should make policy decisions that career employees will carry out without question). While the criticism of the Merit Systems Protection Board (MSPB) and its independent Office of Special Counsel was less severe, it too was criticized for failing to provide adequate protection for "whistle-blowers" or to protect federal employees from merit-system abuses.

Much of the early anger of federal employees toward the Reagan administration's personnel policy focused on its efforts to change the shape and cost of the federal workforce. Immediately after taking office, President Reagan not only instituted a government-wide hiring freeze but also announced his intention to reduce federal civilian employment in nondefense agencies by nearly 100,000 people. The Carter administration had scheduled personnel cuts in its 1981 and 1982 budget projections, but Reagan promised deeper and more focused cuts in domestic agencies. Part of this strategy was in response to what Reagan regarded as dangerous reductions in defense spending. From 1970 to 1980, civilian employment in the Department of Defense (DOD) had fallen from 56 percent of total civilian employment to 41 percent. While never specifying the exact number of civilian employees to be added to DOD, Reagan proposed to increase DOD spending from 23 percent to 38 percent of the federal budget, thereby implying a significant increase in the size of DOD's civilian workforce.

The shifts in policy and budget priorities between 1981 and 1984 forced or encouraged many employees in targeted agencies to leave government service. To accommodate such shifts, several domestic agencies were forced to engage in "reduction in force" (RIF) procedures that caused more than 12,000 federal employees to lose their jobs in 1981 and 1982, several thousand others to be "bumped" down to lower-level jobs, and thousands more to leave the government voluntarily. Especially hard hit were the Departments of the Interior, Health and Human Services, Commerce, Agriculture, and Education, and some smaller agencies like the Community Services Administration and the General Services Administration (GSA).

The hiring freeze, budget cuts, and RIFs reduced the number of nonpostal domestic agency employees by 133,000 from 1981 to 1986. However, increases in the DOD, the Internal Revenue Service (IRS), the State Department, Justice, and the Veterans Administration have more than made up for the reductions. In fact, with the increase in the Postal Service of 121,000 employees during the first five years of the Reagan administration, the overall civilian workforce actually increased by nearly 5 percent, to over 3 million.

The Reagan administration's attempt to reduce the cost of the bureaucracy by changing the distribution of civilian employees from domestic agencies to the DOD was complemented by efforts to reform federal pay, retirement, and other benefits. While a number of proposals produced little in the way of legislation or concrete action, the administration did proceed on three fronts to constrain personnel-related costs. These efforts included (1) consistently resisting recommendations to raise pay for all ranks of the civil service as well as top political appointees, members of Congress, and the judiciary; (2) introducing changes in federal employee health insurance policy that reduced the government's future contributions to health insurance by several million dollars; and (3) introducing changes in the retirement system that allowed federal employees to trade off assured benefits for "portability" (i.e., the option to leave federal service with retirement benefits intact).

While constraining the costs of pay and benefits for federal employees and reshuffling the civilian workforce between domestic and defense agencies can be recognized as a coherent policy, two other Reagan personnel policies involving political appointees and the contracting out of government operations to the private sector can be understood as part of a broader strategy to control the bureaucracy and cut its size.

In its use of political appointees the Reagan administration extended a process of increasing the number of such appointees at all levels of the bureaucracy that had escalated during the Carter administration. While the increases under Reagan were not large (and were offset by decreases in the number of political appointees in the SES), the Reagan administration targeted more of its nearly 3000 political appointees for line management positions than had its predecessor. According to Patricia Ingraham, "One outcome of these increased numbers and SES flexibility [was] the creation of new management lines and systems . . . [allowing] top level political executives to bypass career managers and to rely instead upon lower level political appointees, [thereby reducing] the role and influence of career managers."[58]

The practice of bypassing top career managers for day-to-day policy advice has been called "jigsaw puzzle management." (This describes a method of using career civil servants to carry out programs while keeping them in the dark as to the overall strategy being pursued.) Although heralded by some conservatives as the best way to manage the career workforce, this management style has been widely criticized by career executives and other observers of federal program management. In 1985, 70 percent of respondents to a survey of federal career executives said that they believed the Reagan administration had failed to create conditions favorable to good management; 51 percent saw "the career/political working relationship as a deterrent to effective management."[59]

As noted earlier, one of the principal steps taken by the administration to encourage more "privatization" was its 1983 revision of OMB Circular A-76 on contracting out. Naturally, this move was greeted with anger and frustration by federal workers whose jobs might be affected and by their unions. The revision of the circular has also had mixed results because in some areas (e.g., library management and computer programming) it could not be clearly shown that contracting out would save money or assure reliable service. Furthermore, in some areas Congress passed legislation prohibiting the contracting out of functions. It is therefore no surprise that when OPM in Reagan's second term proposed a "Fed co-op" program, which would have allowed federal employees to take partial ownership of companies operating newly contracted-out functions they had previously staffed, it was met by widespread skepticism.

Another area of conflict between the Reagan administration and the federal career workforce concerns labor-management relations. In his first year in office, President Reagan successfully broke the Professional Air Traffic Controllers' Organization (PATCO) by firing striking workers. Although this was a politically popular move, it also was a harbinger of a long period of contentious relations with unions representing federal workers.

Throughout the Reagan years, federal unions often charged the administration with being "antilabor/antiunion" and with refusing to negotiate constructively with them over work rules, employee rights, and the scope of collective bargaining. In addition to opposing contracting out and privatization more generally, the unions unsuccessfully opposed the Reagan administration's introduction of drug testing in the workplace. In 1987, in the face of a presidential veto, the unions sponsored a major revision in the fifty-year-old Hatch Act, which limits the participation of federal employees in political activities. This occurred after the leaders of three large federal unions were suspended from their mostly symbolic federal jobs for endorsing candidates in the 1984 election.

IMPACTS OF THE REAGAN ADMINISTRATION'S PERSONNEL POLICIES

The Reagan administration's treatment of the federal workforce has caused several serious problems in the recruitment and retention of a high-quality workforce. At the entry level, budget cutbacks at OPM have had the direct effect of discouraging new recruits because they led to the closing of some job information centers and a stoppage in the distribution of publications intended to help potential employees find their way through the federal hiring maze. Among senior career employees, the growing "pay gap" between the public sector and the private sector and the management styles of political appointees, have taken their toll on morale and the decision to stay in or leave the federal service. A 1986 survey of all career executives who left the SES in fiscal year 1985 identified the short terms of political appointees and their lack of qualification for their jobs as important reasons for the dissatisfaction and departure of career employees.[60]

TABLE 4.1

DEPARTURES FROM THE SENIOR EXECUTIVE SERVICE
ON AN ANNUAL BASIS, 1979-86

Year	Positions Allocated	Positions Vacated during the Year	Percentage of Allocated Positions
1979	8413	390[a]	4.6
1980	8602	1185	13.8
1981	8235	1307	15.9
1982	8211	717	8.7
1983	8041	678	8.4
1984	8064	684	8.5
1985	8044	906	11.3
1986	7758	792	10.2

SOURCES: Letter from James E. Colvard, deputy director, Office of Personnel Management, to Joseph E. Ross, director of Congressional Research Service, 11 December 1986; final 1986 data supplied by OPM's Office of Executive Personnel. Reliable data on annual departures from executive ranks, prior to the creation of the SES, are not available, according to the OPM.

a. 13 July 1979 to 31 December 1979.

The size and seriousness of the present pattern of retirements is captured by table 4.1, which presents SES retirements through fiscal year 1986. The table shows that retirement rates were initially high from 1979 to 1981, then leveled off, and peaked again in 1985. Some observers have voiced a concern that a serious "brain drain" will occur if present patterns continue.

The signs of declining morale and motivation in the federal workforce and the loss of expertise and institutional memory have not gone totally unnoticed and have prompted several proposals for reshaping the civil service system. Several of these reform proposals have been directed at OPM's leadership role in installing modern methods of personnel management, human resource planning, and productivity improvement throughout the government. The CRSA promised that OPM would perform actively in these areas, and under its first director, Carter appointee Alan K. Campbell, it strengthened its capacity to foster improved personnel practices in the agencies. Under Director Devine, however, OPM reduced its staff and activities to basic personnel operations (e.g., investigations and pay and benefits recordkeeping). Lost, according to critics, was the momentum for promoting modern personnel management techniques by delegating authority to the agencies to adapt parts of the civil service system to their needs. In their view, OPM's reluctance to use its research and demonstration authority to test the feasibility of adopting human resource planning techniques found useful in the private sector has left the federal personnel system "rudderless."

In 1985, after Devine withdrew his name for reappointment to a second four-year term, he was replaced by Constance Horner. Under Horner, the OPM began to take a more constructive role in federal workforce management by rebuilding its operational capacity and allowing some degree of decentralization by approving agency requests for special pay rates. Although it has been unsuccessful in promoting a new government-wide pay plan—the Civil Service Simplification Act, which it first proposed in 1986—OPM has recently accepted (albeit with some reluctance) congressional proposals for two additional demonstration projects involving pay and benefits.

Under Director Horner's leadership, some facets of government-wide leadership for personnel improvement have slowly returned to OPM. Given the long lead times required to engage in capacity-building efforts, it is unlikely that much progress can be made toward restoring OPM's prominence in personnel management during the remainder of the Reagan years. But Horner's long-term impact may prove significant. During her time as OPM director, she has successfully changed the tone of the dialogue surrounding the federal workforce. Not only has Horner's style been far more conciliatory than her predecessor's, but she has engaged in several activities to promote the image of the federal workforce, improve federal management training, and enhance OPM's college recruiting efforts. Nevertheless, these efforts at cooling down the dialogue surrounding the administration's personnel policy have made only marginal changes in the overall picture. Late in Reagan's second term, it appears likely he will leave his successor a workforce substantially reduced in quality and morale from what he inherited.

Evaluation of the Reagan
Managerial Strategy and Legacy

Just as the Carter administration's legacy can be sorted into three categories —what to do, what to avoid, and ideas and institutional mechanisms left behind —so, too, one can undertake to assess the Reagan legacy. The most pronounced feature of the early years of the Reagan Presidency was the strong and concerted effort to secure top-down presidential control over the whole of the federal executive establishment. As we have seen, the central elements of this strategy were (1) extensive use of the appointment power to "infiltrate" the bureaucracy with appointees loyal to the President; (2) use of the cabinet council system and other interagency mechanisms to keep political appointees focused on the Reagan agenda; (3) strengthening of OMB budgetary, regulatory, and paperwork clearance powers as instruments of presidential control; and (4) continued articulation of the broad principles of "conservative" approaches to the organization and the managment of the federal government and its workforce.

The centralizing and cost-control impulses reflected in early Reagan management improvement initiatives (e.g., the establishment of the President's Council on Integrity and Efficiency and the launching of Reform '88) were instrumental in shaping the administration's entire approach to executive branch management. The emphasis on top-down control to enhance "efficiency" and "accountability" has been an important element in the administration's campaign to make the federal government more efficient and "businesslike" all along, and remains an "article of faith" among top echelons of the Reagan administration. It is important to point out, however, that Congress often has been a willing partner in these reform efforts. The legislature's receptivity to control-oriented management reforms had already been demonstrated during the Carter years, when Congress enacted such key bills as the Inspectors General Act of 1978 and the Paperwork Reduction Act of 1980. The rapid spate of additional management reform legislation passed during Reagan's first term—including the Prompt Payment Act of 1982, the Debt Collection Act of 1982, and the Single Audit Act of 1983, as well as the Federal Manager's Financial Integrity Act of 1982 and the Deficit Reduction Act of 1984—amply attests to the fact that Congress shared the administration's conviction that strong central controls were necessary to ensure that federal management systems would be kept modern and up-to-date.

Finally, it should be acknowledged that the Reagan administration's focused efforts to modernize the "nuts and bolts" of management and thereby reduce the overhead administrative expenses of government add up to some valuable changes in the way the federal government conducts its operations. The administration's successes in these low-visibility but costly management areas are likely to encourage future administrations to carry on the modernization effort as new ideas and opportunities develop.

Notwithstanding these accomplishments, which may turn out to be the Reagan administration's most lasting contribution to the organization and operation of government, it is important to recognize some of the liabilities associated with the administration's approach. In the first place, the accountability and cost-control orientation of efforts like Reform '88 reinforced an approach to management improvement that some argue is not conducive to constructive management reform. Second, the top-down approach that characterized that effort seems to have exacerbated a tendency that, in the opinion of many informed observers, has proven to be one of the main obstacles to managerial effectiveness in government, namely, the tendency for federal management to get caught up "in excessive centralization and inflexible, negative controls."[61]

This is not to say that some valuable lessons about presidential direction of the executive branch have not been learned. For example, Laurence E. Lynn, in assessing the centralization strategy, warns critics that "[f]ailure to understand the Reagan experiment in public management will mean that a valuable lesson for future administrations—administrations that may have more positive views of government—will be missed. That lesson is that loyal and competent supporters in key executive branch positions can be a potent tool of administrative leadership."[62] In Lynn's view, the importance of combining a reasonably coherent philosophy of government with (1) the institutional apparatus of OMB to give it operational meaning; (2) the appointment of appropriately skilled cabinet and subcabinet officials who share the President's vision; and (3) the subsequent delegation of authority over execution to these appointees, subject to oversight by the executive office, cannot be underestimated.

The partial "turnaround" in the Reagan managerial strategy in the President's second term, which emphasized more delegation of authority, can be attributed to two factors. First is the widespread recognition that the administration had in fact succeeded in securing firm top-down control through the use of the first two tactics Lynn described. But second, the administration began to realize that once control was well established, it could begin to "deregulate" federal management in accordance with concepts and techniques borrowed from the private sector—an emphasis that would comport very nicely both with its desire to make government more "businesslike" and with its concern to deregulate the American economy as a whole. Similarly, the tactics of devolution and privatization can also be understood as serving the Reagan administration's broader political purpose of decentralizing government responsibility.

But this strategy can give rise to serious questions about policy coordination and accountability. The Reagan administration's efforts to redeem a vision of a limited government that divests itself of functions by transferring them to the private sector, which will then drive the economy forward, has sometimes created blurred lines of control—the opposite effect of what the entire centralizing thrust presumably was designed or intended to achieve. Thus, while the administration has provided what amounts to a catalogue of management tactics ranging from user fees to shared support services, only in very few cases has it succeeded in combining them into complete systems. Meanwhile, federal managers have been left to thrash about in an environment made more complex by the very strategies the administration thought would simplify government.

The two great disasters of the Reagan years, the *Challenger* tragedy and the Iran-*contra* scandal, provide a clue to the management problem. In both cases, the government became engaged in webs of decision making and action that relied heavily on the judgment of private firms and individuals. These networks were so tangled that clear lines of accountability disappeared, and distinctions between private action and public responsibility became all but meaningless to the participants. When the political dust had settled, no one was sure who was to blame.

The high-tech, high-finance, high-risk worlds of space travel and international intrigue are only symptomatic of similar problems throughout government as it turns toward increasingly intricate organizational arrangements to conduct public business. Perhaps that is appropriate because complex problems require complex solutions. Real fiascos occur when complexity is mistaken for simplicity. And, of course, that is exactly what occurred in the *Challenger* disaster, when NASA tried to routinize a launch technology that was still evolving. Errors of similar, but one hopes less tragic, magnitude seem likely to become more common because the hybrid public/private organizations so prevalent today are eluding manageability.

Debate over the complexity of modern government calls into question the institutional capacity of the Presidency to cope with it. To what extent has the Reagan administration enhanced or depleted this capacity? On the positive side, Reagan reduced some of the complexity of governing by picking a few central objectives to guide his administration's efforts and showed future Presidents how they might use flexible instruments like cabinet councils and the Office of Presidential Personnel (OPP) to keep their programs on track. Reagan also strengthened a few key administrative mechanisms, such as regulatory review, that may prove valuable to future administrations with decidedly different policy goals. On the negative side, some critics have argued that Reagan has damaged, perhaps irreparably, two vitally important institutions that will be needed to address future problems effectively: OMB, and the senior ranks of the career civil service. In the case of OMB, the Reagan years witnessed a marked increase in the numbers and influence of political appointees at the expense of the career staff. In the view of some long-term observers of the agency, this has seriously compromised OMB's reputation for political neutrality and its institutional capacity. Lost in the process is the agency's ability to speak with authority on a broad range of policy, budget, and management issues. Similarly, by more carefully screening, placing, and directing political appointees in the upper levels of executive branch agencies and in some places encouraging (or at least tolerating) contentious relations between its appointees and career officials, the administration has succeeded in driving many of the latter into retirement. This development may deprive the next administration, and perhaps future administrations as well, of a very valuable resource and make the task of governing all the more difficult.

Indeed, in retrospect, one cannot help but wonder whether the Reagan administration's approach to seizing control of the bureaucracy by pushing aside senior career managers was necessary. Although Reagan, like Carter and several Presidents before him, harbored a deep distrust of the loyalty and responsiveness of the career civil service, there is little or no evidence to support his apparent conviction that they were impediments in the way of accomplishing his agenda.[63] More generally, we would argue that a principal failing of the Reagan administration lay in its apparent inability or unwillingness to set aside its own management strategy to take a serious look at the problem of the long-term erosion of the capacity of the federal workforce—a dubious legacy that the next administration will surely have to face.

This question becomes all the more important when viewed in conjunction with what we would suggest is the Reagan administration's most positive legacy, namely, to reshape the dialogue about the proper scope of government; the appropriate machinery of government; and the respective roles of the public, private, and nonprofit sector workforces in the service delivery process. Even though the administration has failed fully to persuade Congress or the public that its answers to these questions are the right ones, it has nonetheless succeeded in legitimizing debate over these fundamental issues in a way that assures they will remain on the public agenda for many years.

Notes

1. Ronald Randall, "Presidential Use of Management Tools: From PPB to ZBB," *Presidential Studies Quarterly* 12 (Spring 1982): 191.

2. Chester A. Newland, "A Mid-Term Appraisal—The Reagan Presidency: Limited Government and Political Administration," *Public Administration Review* 43, no. 1 (January/February 1983): 3. According to Becky Norton Dunlop, deputy director of the White House Office of Presidential Personnel, during the first Reagan term, a sixth criterion—"commitment to change"—was later added to this list. See Dunlop, "The Role of the White House Office of Presidential Personnel," in *Steering the Elephant: How Washington Works*, ed. Robert Rector and Michael Sanera (New York: Universe Books, 1987), 146.

3. G. Calvin Mackenzie, "Cabinet and Subcabinet Personnel Selecton in Reagan's First Year" (paper presented at the annual meeting of the American Political Science

Association, 1981). Quoted in James P. Pfiffner, *The Strategic Presidency: Hitting the Ground Running* (Chicago: Dorsey Press, 1988), 74.

4. Dunlop, "Role of the White House Office of Presidential Personnel," 148.

5. Quoted in Pfiffner, *The Strategic Presidency,* 84. In alluding to Schedule C appointments, James was referring to those positions at the GS-15 and below which are "excepted" from the civil service because the duties of the incumbent may involve a confidental relationship to key officials and/or advocacy of administration policy. There are some 1800 positions in all.

6. Ibid., 75.

7. Elizabeth Sanders, "The President and the Bureaucratic State," in *The Presidency and the Political System,* ed. Michael Nelson, 2d ed. (Washington, D.C.: CQ Press, 1988), 393.

8. Hugh Heclo, "One Executive Branch or Many?" in *Both Ends of the Avenue,* ed. Anthony King (Washington, D.C.: American Enterprise Institute, 1983), 42-47.

9. Newland, "The Reagan Presidency," 7.

10. Chester A. Newland, "Executive Office Policy Apparatus: Enforcing the Reagan Agenda," in *The Reagan Presidency and the Governing of America,* ed. Lester M. Salamon and Michael S. Lund (Washington, D.C.: Urban Institute, 1984), 154-55.

11. Heclo, "One Executive Branch or Many?" 46.

12. Pfiffner, *The Strategic Presidency,* 62.

13. Ibid.

14. Dick Kirschten, "Decision Making at the White House: How Well Does It Serve the President?" *National Journal,* 3 April 1982, 588.

15. Harold Seidman and Robert Gilmour, *Politics, Position, and Power: From the Positive to the Regulatory State,* 4th ed. (New York: Oxford University Press, 1986).

16. Pfiffner, *The Strategic Presidency,* 63.

17. Frederick Mosher, *A Tale of Two Agencies: A Comparative Analysis of the General Accounting Office and the Office of Management and Budget* (Baton Rouge: Louisiana State University Press, 1984), 185.

18. The account that follows draws heavily on Naomi Caiden, "Paradox, Enigma, and Ambiguity: The Strange Case of the Executive Budget and the United States Constitution," *Public Administration Review* 47, no. 1 (January/February 1987): 84-92; and Louis Fisher, "The Constitution and Presidential Budget Powers: The Modern Era" (paper presented at the State University of New York, College at Geneseo, 19 November 1987).

19. Fisher, "The Constitution and Presidential Budget Powers," 20.

20. Charles H. Levine, "The Federal Government in the Year 2000: Administrative Legacies of the Reagan Years," *Public Administration Review* 46, no. 3 (May/June 1986): 197.

21. Allen Schick, "The Budget as an Instrument of Presidential Policy," in Salamon and Lund, *The Reagan Presidency and the Governing of America,* 122.

22. For background on the regulatory review programs of Presidents Nixon, Ford, and Carter, see George C. Eads and Michael Fix, *Relief or Reform?: Reagan's Regulatory Dilemma* (Washington, D.C.: Urban Institute, 1984), 45-67.

23. Seidman and Gilmour, *Politics, Position, and Power,* 130. Italics added.

24. Senate Committee on Governmental Affairs, *Paperwork Reduction Act of 1980,* Senate Report No. 96-930, 96th Cong., 2d sess. (1980), 56.

25. Robert S. Gilmour, "Presidential Clearance of Regulation" (paper presented

to the national conference of the American Society for Public Administration, 17 April 1983), 8.

26. The constitutional arguments against the Reagan regulatory review program were first spelled out in Morton Rosenberg, "Beyond the Limits of Presidential Power: Presidential Control of Agency Rulemaking Under Executive Order 12291," *Michigan Law Review* 80 (1981): 193. For an early expression of an opposing view, see Peter L. Shane, "Presidential Regulatory Oversight and the Separation of Powers: The Constitutionality of Executive Order 12291," *Arizona Law Review* 23 (1981): 1235.

27. William A. Niskanen, Jr., quoted in Howard Ball, "Presidential Control of the Federal Bureaucracy," in *Federal Administrative Agencies,* ed. Howard Ball (Englewood Cliffs, N.J.: Prentice-Hall, 1984), 24.

28. *New York Times,* 1 November 1981, 7.

29. These figures are derived from *Regulatory Program of the United States: April 1, 1985-March 30, 1986* (Washington, D.C.: Government Printing Office, 8 August 1985).

30. The critics' chief complaints were that the procedures provided for public disclosure of only *some* of OMB's actions pursuant to the Executive Orders, and only *after* those actions had occurred and any differences between OMB and the agency had already been resolved.

31. Figures cited here are drawn from charts presented in *Regulatory Program of the United States Government, April 1, 1987-March 30, 1988, 626, 628.*

32. Sanders, "The Presidency and the Bureaucratic State," 383.

33. Donald F. Kettl, *Government by Proxy: (Mis?)Managing Government Programs* (Washington, D.C.: CQ Press, 1988), 51.

34. Hale Champion, "The Big Impacts Were Indirect," in Salamon and Lund, *The Reagan Presidency and the Governing of America,* 444.

35. David R. Beam, "New Federalism, Old Realities: The Reagan Administration and Intergovernmental Reform," in Salamon and Lund, *The Reagan Presidency and the Governing of America,* 423.

36. Ibid., 440.

37. The account that follows borrows heavily from Sandra Osbourn, "The Office of Management and Budget and Intergovernmental Management," in Senate Committee on Governmental Affairs, *Office of Management and Budget: Evolving Role and Future Issues,* Senate Print No. 99-134, 99th Cong., 2d sess. (1986), 352-53.

38. Beam, "New Federalism, Old Realities," 432.

39. Ibid., 441.

40. "Reagan Administration Federalism Group Slates Deregulation, Grants Management," *Federal Grants Management Handbook: Current Developments,* no. 85-10 (October 1985): 6.

41. Beam, "New Federalism, Old Realities," 440.

42. Stuart M. Butler, "Overview," in *Mandate for Leadership II: Continuing the Conservative Revolution,* ed. Stuart M. Butler, Michael Sanera, and W. Bruce Weinrod (Washington, D.C.: Heritage Foundation, 1985), 6-7.

43. Ronald C. Moe, "Exploring the Limits of Privatization," *Public Administration Review* 47, no. 6 (November/December 1987): 453.

44. Kettl, *Government by Proxy,* 10-11.

45. Ronald C. Moe, "Privatization: An Overview from the Perspective of Public Administration," Congressional Research Service Report No. 86-134-GOV (June 1986), 20.

46. Ibid., 23.

47. Sanders, "The President and the Bureaucratic State," 399.

48. For example, President Reagan in 1987 proposed that the Customs Service establish user fees "to totally recover costs for processing persons, aircraft, vehicles, and merchandise arriving in, or departing from, the United States. The administration estimated that $520 million in revenue would be generated from this fee alone in 1987." Moe, "Privatization: An Overview," 24.

49. During the Reagan years, vouchers have been considered as an option for "improving" local school systems and for day-care programs. Ibid., 7.

50. See generally Moe, "Exploring the Limits of Privatization"; and Kettl, *Government by Proxy*, 11-15.

51. John D.R. Cole, "Joe Wright on Reform '88," *Bureaucrat* 12, no. 2 (Summer 1983): 7.

52. Ibid., 7-9.

53. For discussions of the activities and recommendations of the Grace Commission, see Charles Goodsell, "The Grace Commission: Seeking Efficiency for the Whole People?" *Public Administration Review* 44, no. 3 (May/June 1984): 196-204; and Steven Kelman, "The Grace Commission: How Much Waste in Government?" *Public Interest*, Winter 1985, 62-82.

54. Executive Office of the President and Office of Management and Budget, *Management of the United States Government, Fiscal Year 1986* (Washington, D.C.: Government Printing Office, 1985), 9-10.

55. Charles A. Bowsher, "Building Effective Public Management," *Bureaucrat* 13, no. 4 (Winter 1984-85): 26.

56. National Academy of Public Administration, *Revitalizing Federal Management: Managers and Their Overburdened Systems* (Washington, D.C.: NAPA, 1983).

57. Murray Comarow, "The War on Civil Servants," *Bureaucrat* 10 (Winter 1981-82): 8-9.

58. Patricia W. Ingraham, "Building Bridges or Burning Them? The President, the Appointees, and the Bureaucracy," *Public Administration Review* 47, no. 5 (September/October 1987): 425.

59. Federal Executive Institute Alumni Association, *Newsletter*, no. 13 (April 1986): 1.

60. U.S. General Accounting Office, *Federal Retirement: Retirement Data for Selected Agencies*, GAO/GGD-86-123 FS (Washington, D.C.: Government Printing Office, 1986).

61. Chester A. Newland, "Federal Government Management Trends," in *Current Issues in Public Administration*, ed. Frederick S. Lane, 3d ed. (New York: St. Martin's, 1986), 431.

62. Laurence E. Lynn, Jr., "The Manager's Role in Public Management," *Bureaucrat* 13, no. 4 (Winter 1984-85): 20.

63. Joel D. Aberbach and Bert A. Rockman, "A Changing Federal Executive?" (paper presented at a meeting of the Structure of Government section, International Political Science Association, Pittsburgh, November 1986).

PART TWO

The Political Processes

5

Incomplete Realignment:
The Reagan Legacy for Parties and Elections

PAUL ALLEN BECK

In the immediate aftermath of the 1976 elections, Republican prospects seemed bleak. Republican President Gerald Ford had just been retired from office by a newcomer to national politics, a former Georgia governor, Jimmy Carter. Only a year before, Carter had been largely unknown to the American electorate and his candidacy had not been supported by many Democratic officials, in part because he seemed to be outside the party's mainstream and had campaigned as an "outsider" to Washington politics. Nonetheless, or perhaps as a consequence of being new and an outsider, he swept to the nomination on the strength of early caucus and primary victories and then managed to defeat a sitting President, albeit by slender popular and electoral vote margins.

The loss of the Presidency was only the most visible of the Republicans' problems. Other Republican candidates fared poorly in the 1976 contests, and their showings weakened the party's standing in both national and state governments. The Democrats were able to maintain their 2–1 margin over the Republicans in the House of Representatives and to increase their strength in the Senate to 61 of 100 seats (see figure 5.1). The 1976 elections saw to it that the popular branches at the national level would be unified under Democratic control for the first time since 1968.

The situation for the GOP was even bleaker in the states (see figure 5.2). The results of the 1976 elections meant that only twelve states would have Republican governors at the beginning of 1977 and that Democrats would hold more than two-thirds of the seats in the forty-nine partisan state legislatures (Nebraska's legislature is nonpartisan). The election brought a total of twenty-

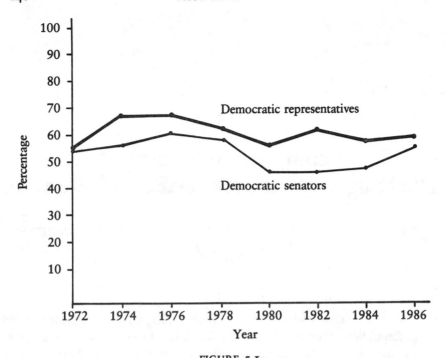

FIGURE 5.1
PARTY FORTUNES IN CONGRESS, 1972-86

nine states under full Democratic control with Democratic majorities in both houses of the legislature and a Democratic governor. Only one state was under full Republican control.

In spite of extensive efforts in 1976 to put the past behind it, the GOP saw from election returns that it had failed again to overcome electoral damage from the Watergate affair. Just twenty-seven months before, in August 1974, the Republican President elected with the greatest popular and electoral vote margin in the history of his party, Richard Nixon, had resigned his office in ignominy as he was about to be impeached by the House of Representatives—and just ahead of almost certain conviction and eviction from office by the Senate—for his role in the Watergate break-in and cover-up.[1] The November elections of 1974 had severely punished the GOP for its President's Watergate transgressions, and for the first time in years, the Democrats had emerged with more than a 2–1 margin over the Republicans in the House of Representatives and the state legislatures. The 1976 contest merely continued the electoral punishment of the party.

The Watergate affair seemed to shatter Republican dreams of a realignment of the party system that would have made their party the majority party

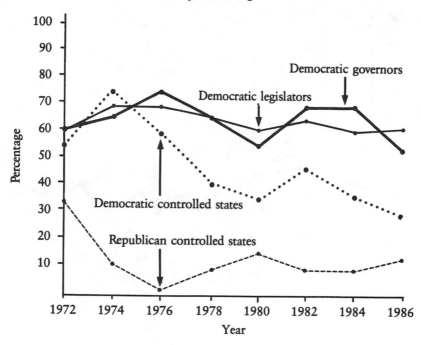

FIGURE 5.2

PARTY FORTUNES IN THE STATES, 1972-86

for many years to come. Realignments are changes in the underlying bases of the party coalitions, which have, with historical regularity, catapulted a new party into dominance. Since the New Deal realignment of the 1930s, the Republican party had suffered the status of a minority party. The troubles of the Johnson administration, especially the urban riots of the late 1960s and the Vietnam war, plus the difficulties the Democrats faced in trying to hold white southerners in the party while championing civil rights for blacks, had given the GOP new hope that the long Democratic reign was ending. The election of Richard Nixon over a divided Democratic party in 1968 and his landslide reelection in 1972 seemed to fulfill that hope. Prospects for a pro-Republican realignment seemed very bright—until Watergate.[2]

Not only did Republican candidates suffer the misfortune of post-Watergate fallout but the standing of the party was undermined as well. Most immediately, popular perceptions of the parties became more favorable to the Democrats, understandably in terms of trust but somewhat surprisingly along performance lines as well. Pollsters have regularly asked Americans which party would do a better job of handling their problems. Perhaps the best barometer of the par-

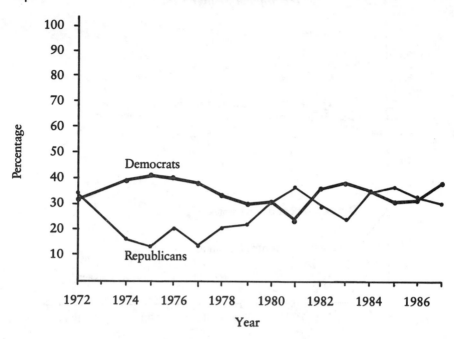

FIGURE 5.3

WHICH PARTY WOULD HANDLE MOST IMPORTANT PROBLEMS BETTER,

1972-87

SOURCE: *Gallup Report,* May 1987, 9.

ties' standing with the public is which party is viewed by the public as doing a better job handling the most important problems. By the mid-1970s, as shown in figure 5.3, the Democrats had surged to a considerable lead over the Republicans, their largest lead since 1965.

In terms of the basic partisan loyalties of the electorate, the immediate post-Watergate years tell a story of lost GOP opportunities rather than decline. Party loyalties are measured by asking people which party they think of themselves as being in or identifying with. For many years, the Democratic party had enjoyed a considerable edge in party loyalists, reflecting its status as the majority party (see figure 5.4). The number of Democrats approached 50 percent in the 1950s, for example, with Republicans falling short of enrolling even 30 percent of the electorate. The greatest Democratic advantage in recent times appeared in 1964, when more than twice as many people claimed Democratic loyalties as claimed Republican.[3] This substantial Democratic edge eroded after the mid-1960s, largely because of a growth in the number of people calling

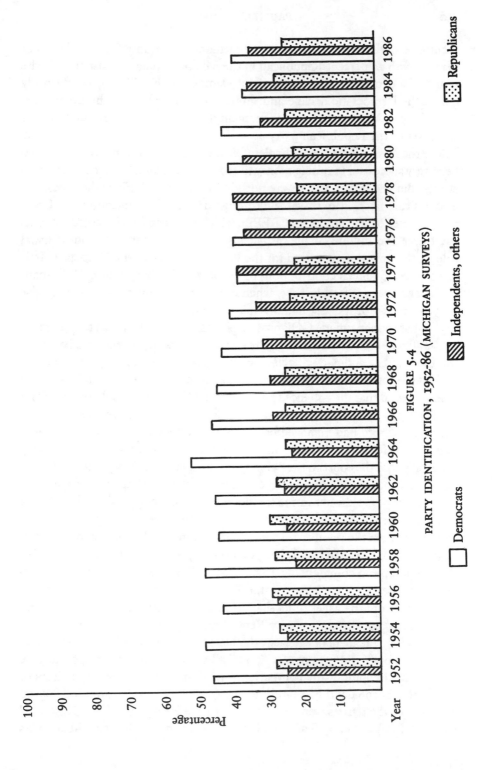

FIGURE 5.4

PARTY IDENTIFICATION, 1952-86 (MICHIGAN SURVEYS)

☐ Democrats   ▨ Independents, others   ⬚ Republicans

themselves independents. By 1972, the Democratic advantage had fallen to 41 percent with 23 percent Republican in the Michigan data, almost entirely the result of a decline in the percentage of Democrats. But Watergate effectively halted the Democratic decline and shifted the momentum to the Democrats.

The post-Watergate change in momentum is reflected in the organizational successes of the Republican party as well as in the electorate. For many years before the Nixon Presidency, the Republican National Committee (RNC) had been very successful in raising money to support its national headquarters operations. But the Nixon years were not kind to the RNC. First, the Nixon re-election campaign in 1972 was run through a parallel organization, the Committee to Reelect the President (CREEP), which raised and spent record amounts (well over $60 million) while displacing the national committee in its usual role as campaign organization for the President. Second, the Watergate affair discouraged financial contributions to the party. The low point in RNC financial health was reached in 1975, when the party committee was able to raise only $300,000 of its $2.3 million budget goal.[4]

What to many made GOP prospects seem even bleaker was the burgeoning vitality of the party's ideologically conservative wing. Some years before, in the Goldwater candidacy of 1964, conservative domination of the party had spelled electoral disaster. Based on this salient example, party moderates and liberals feared that the enhanced prospect of a GOP presidential nominee from the Right would sink the party's sagging electoral fortunes even deeper. President Gerald Ford had managed barely to head off a challenge from the Right in his quest for renomination, and his defeat in 1976 left a vacuum in party leadership that the conservatives' champion, former California governor Ronald Reagan, rushed to fill. Reagan, who had become the darling of the Right after his support of Goldwater in 1964, rebounded from his unsuccessful challenge to Ford in 1976 to emerge as the prime contender for the 1980 Republican nomination. As the 1980 presidential contest drew nearer, preferences among Republican voters for Reagan over other potential Republican nominees widened— for example, to a commanding 40 percent to 18 percent over Ford or 47 percent to 12 percent over Baker, in the December 1979 Gallup poll.

Thus, from the ashes of its shattering electoral defeats in 1974 and 1976, a more ideologically conservative Republican party seemed to be rising. The great moderate leaders of the past, the Nelson Rockefellers and Richard Nixons, were gone; and no popular "centrist" political leaders emerged to take their place. In spite of the conventional wisdom (validated by the defeats of Goldwater in 1964 and McGovern in 1972), that candidates from ideological extremes of the parties were not electable to the Presidency, the GOP seemed to embark on a course that would put forward just such a candidate as its presidential nominee. For a minority party, already beset by electoral and organizational woes, such a course of action seemed to spell disaster.

The Resurgence of the GOP

How obsolete this bleak prognosis now sounds! From a vantage point near the end of the second term of the Reagan Presidency, the first two-term Presidency since Eisenhower's in the 1950s, Republican prospects seem bright instead of bleak. The party not only has recovered from its myriad troubles of the mid-1970s, but there is renewed talk of a new realignment of American electoral politics, led by an ascendant and conservative GOP. Before exploring how one of the great reversals in American politics was accomplished, a brief review of recent changes in the standing of the party is in order.

That story begins with the problems of the Carter administration, especially rampant inflation brought on by huge increases in the price of oil and the seizure of the American embassy in Teheran by Iranian radicals, and the consequent elevation of Ronald Reagan to the Presidency. In the 1980 election the Republicans won the Senate for the first time since 1948 and cut into the Democratic margin in the House (see figure 5.1). Although a recession early in his first term cost President Reagan and his party some public support, the decline proved to be short lived. Ronald Reagan won a landslide reelection victory in 1984—with a record-breaking total of 525 electoral votes. Moreover, the GOP retained its majority in the U.S. Senate in 1984, although that majority was lost two years later when the GOP was unable to defend adequately its previous gains by holding on to the twenty-two Republican seats (out of 34) being contested. Even in the House of Representatives, where the difficulties of unseating incumbents preserved Democratic control, the Republicans were able to reduce the Democratic majority to less than 60 percent of the seats for two elections in a row for the first time in over a decade (see figure 5.1).

By the mid-1980s, Republican fortunes also had improved in the states (see figure 5.2). The Democratic margin in state legislators was reduced, although only to a still formidable 60–40 percent by 1986, and the GOP had doubled its number of governorships from twelve in 1976 to twenty-four ten years later. The 1986 elections gave a clear majority of states divided control of government, and the Democratic edge in one-party controlled states was reduced from the lopsided 29–1 in 1976 to 14–6.

The most favorable signs of Republican recovery, though, appeared in the general partisan views of the electorate, not in electoral results, however encouraging they might have been. As figure 5.3 shows, perceptions of which party would better handle the most important problems turned in a Republican direction by 1980, and these perceptions have seesawed back and forth between the parties ever since. Not since 1972, however, has the GOP been able to sustain for more than a year such a perceptual advantage.

Even more comforting to the Republicans in recent years is the distribution of party loyalties in the electorate. As can be seen from figure 5.4, the percentage of Republican loyalists has been higher in recent years than at any time since the mid-1960s; indeed, in 1984 the GOP total in the Michigan surveys surpassed the 27 percent mark for the first time since 1962. The Democratic share of the electorate declined even more precipitously—to no more than 40 percent by the mid-1980s. Based on these biennial figures, the parties were closer to parity in the 1980s than at any time in the over-forty-year history of the Michigan surveys. The Times/CBS poll found parallel differences between the parties and showed that the Democratic lead in partisanship continued to be small through 1987. Among the youngest members of the electorate, moreover, recent polls have found more Republican loyalists than Democratic.[5]

As the Reagan Presidency enters its final year and the 1988 election campaigns unfold, then, it is clear that the Republican party has risen from the ashes of defeat in the mid-1970s to become the ascendant party of the 1980s. Whatever problems now face the party—including the waning of its ideological fervor, the succession battle among its leaders and ideological factions, the difficulty of containing both social and economic conservatives in its coalition— seem trifling compared to the problems of very survival that the party faced in the mid-1970s. This GOP resurgence has occurred on Ronald Reagan's "watch." Can it be attributed to his efforts, counted as his legacy? That is the question to which we now turn.

Behind the GOP Resurgence

The most immediate contributor to the GOP resurgence undoubtedly was Jimmy Carter. Elected by a thin margin over Gerald Ford in 1976, Carter understandably might not have been an unusually popular President. Furthermore, as memories of the Watergate affair faded, it seems only natural that the GOP would recoup some of its losses of the mid-1970s. By 1978, figures 5.1 to 5.3 show a mild Republican recovery, but considering the depths to which the party had fallen, these signs were hardly cause for GOP celebration.

The collapse of the Carter Presidency in 1979 and 1980 changed that situation. To a natural Republican recovery of earlier ground was added the political fallout from the twin troubles of the final Carter years: inflation and Iran. Although these events were not sufficient effectively to undermine Carter's hold over his own party in seeking renomination, and indeed the Iran situation probably even aided him in easily turning back the Kennedy challenge, they dramatically changed the competitive position of the Democrats in the 1980 elections.

Inflation had been abnormally high during most of the 1970s, as the deferred costs of Vietnam were paid in a cheaper dollar, and the Consumer Price Index (CPI) reached 11 percent in 1974—compounding the Republicans' problems that year. But by 1979, inflation exceeded this previous decade high, reaching a CPI figure of 11.3 percent; in 1980 it rose again, to 13.5 percent as the country entered a recession. Even more precipitous was the rise in the prime interest rate, the rate banks charge their best borrowers and that indexes rates for consumer credit and home mortgage loans. From an average 6.8 percent in 1977, the first year of the Carter Presidency, the prime rate rose to 9.1 percent, 12.7 percent, and 15.3 percent, and then to a whopping 18.9 percent in 1981, before it began to drop. Such levels of inflation might bring relief to citizens of Argentina or Israel, who have experienced rates well in excess of 100 percent, but Americans are so accustomed to low inflation rates that their rise in the late 1970s forced agonizing changes in economic thinking and life styles.

Presidents and their parties typically pay a heavy price for economic troubles, whether or not they are really responsible for them, when they occur "on their watch." Carter and the Democrats bore the brunt of the blame for the inflation of the late 1970s and early 1980s, even if it was largely caused by international forces beyond their control (especially precipitous rises in the price of oil). As a result, by 1981 the historic Democratic advantage as the party of prosperity in voters' eyes had been lost: By a 13 percent margin, the Republicans now enjoyed this position.

Then, as now, Iran became a major player in the game of American politics. The turmoil caused by the overthrow of the shah in 1979 and the subsequent revolution that brought the Ayatollah Khomeini to power curtailed Iranian oil production and thereby upset the precarious balance in demand and supply, causing oil prices to surge in the late 1970s, as they had during the first "energy crisis" in 1973–74. Between March and December 1980, the price of OPEC oil doubled, going from $14 to $28 per barrel. This increased the energy bills of the energy-intensive industrialized nations. In more personal terms, oil shortages led to spiraling prices for gasoline and heating oil, and to long lines at gas pumps throughout America.

The shocks of the Iranian revolution reverberated throughout American politics in another and even more dramatic fashion. In November 1979, Iranian militants seized the American embassy in Teheran and took the staff hostage. This event haunted President Carter throughout his reelection campaign as he continually tried to gain release of the hostages by negotiating with successive leaders of the new and unstable revolutionary government and, out of despera-

tion, by launching an abortive military rescue mission in the spring of 1980.
As the presidential campaign of 1980 wore on, the Iranian hostages more and
more came to symbolize American weakness and discredit Carter's foreign policy. All of this came to a head the weekend before the presidential election,
as television's comprehensive retrospective of the hostage crisis on its first anni-
versary raised its salience for voters. Hardly an event of Carter's making, nor
one on which his leadership could reasonably be faulted, the President nonetheless suffered greatly from America's collective frustration by the Iranians.
Ironically, the hostages were released only minutes after Ronald Reagan was
sworn in as President.

Faced with an inflated economy and foreign humiliation, President Carter's
political standing plummeted as the 1980 election drew nearer. By the summer
of 1980, his Gallup poll approval rating had dropped to a record low among
modern Presidents, even below that of Richard Nixon just before the Watergate
affair drove him from the Presidency. While Carter regained some standing in
advance of the November election, still only a third of the electorate were recorded as approving the job he was doing as President in the month after the
election. Being seen by voters as closer to them than his opponent on issues
could not overcome these negative evaluations of his performance in office.[6]
The almost 10 percent margin of his loss was larger than most polls had predicted, as numerous voters made up their minds to vote Republican for President on the very weekend, perhaps even the eve, of the election.

As we saw in the Watergate affair, Presidents are too important for their
party and their fellow partisans not to affect their fate. The 1980 election contained bad news for Democratic candidates in general. The party's margin in
the House of Representatives fell to 56–44 percent, its lowest level since 1973–74
and its second lowest since the 1950s. In the Senate, more Republicans were
elected than at any time since the 1920s, and for the first time since 1952 the
Republicans became the majority party (see figure 5.1). Democratic fortunes
ebbed in the states, too, as a result of the 1980 elections, as figure 5.2 dramatizes:
Another 4 percent was chopped off their mid-1970s 2:1 advantage in state legislators. The number of Democratic governors fell to 27 (from 37 in 1976), and
only a third of the states remained under full Democratic control, in contrast
to almost three-quarters six years earlier. Clearly, the Republican resurgence
in 1980, returning the party's strength to pre-Watergate 1972 levels, was more
than anything else the legacy of the Carter Presidency.

More so than ever before, particularly abetted by the nationalizing force
of television, the Presidency is the commanding pulpit of American politics.
Especially in troubled times, as Herbert Hoover learned to his regret and Franklin Roosevelt to his party's lasting benefit, the occupant of the Oval Office has

the opportunity to affect the fortunes of his party for good or ill. Carter's troubles led the electorate to repudiate him in favor of Ronald Reagan, the champion of the conservative wing of his party. It was now up to President Reagan to make of those opportunities what he could, to try to convert Carter's legacy into his own. The conventional wisdom held that, as a conservative ideologue, Reagan would have great difficulty consolidating the short-term gains his party had made in 1980—just as it had predicted a victory of the centrist Carter over the more extreme Reagan. Again, the conventional wisdom proved wrong.

The Republican party made significant gains in the first few years of the Reagan Presidency. By 1981, more Americans perceived the Republicans than the Democrats as the party of prosperity and better able to handle the nation's most important problem—for most, the Carter-era inflation (see figure 5.3). This 1981 Republican advantage in party image of 36 to 23 percent was the largest in the thirty-six-year history of this measure in the Gallup poll. Although the subsequent recession was soon to change these images, as unemployment replaced inflation as the most important problem, an important barrier had been breached: The GOP was seen as more attractive on the economy, the issue of Democratic advantage since the Great Depression of the 1930s. By 1984, with the recession over, the Republican advantage as the party of prosperity in the public mind returned, and it has remained to this day.

But the most important gains the GOP experienced came in party identification, the most enduring indicator of a party's standing. A combination of Republican partisan gains and Democratic losses reduced the Republican disadvantage in partisanship to less than 10 percent in the Times/CBS polls of 1981 (see figure 5.5). Although the Democratic edge widened with the recession in the middle of President Reagan's first term, it was indeed auspicious for the GOP that economic troubles with their party in the White House produced such modest Republican party identification losses and Democratic gains. The ghost of Herbert Hoover, which had haunted the GOP since 1929, had been exorcised.

The Michigan and Times/CBS polls also show a noticeable decline in independents and other nonpartisans in recent years (100 percent minus the sum of partisans in figures 5.4 and 5.5). This trend reverses a long period of increasing independence that began in the mid-1960s and continued, with only the briefest interruption, until 1980. It may yet be premature to celebrate the end of a persistent decline of parties in the electorate, what scholars have called *dealignment,* but the movement of increasing numbers of voters toward party loyalties rather than away from them differentiates the 1980s from the late 1960s and 1970s.

Complementing this decline of independents have been an increase in Republican identifiers and a decrease in Democrats. Improving Republican fortunes seem to be tied directly to the Reagan Presidency. The first surge appeared at the beginning of Reagan's first term, followed by a second around the time of his landslide reelection in 1984. This second surge carried the GOP to a position of near parity with the Democrats. Even though there is considerable variation in party differences in the number of loyalists throughout the period, it is unmistakable that the Republicans have considerably narrowed the Democrats' identification advantage. Democratic gains, by contrast, have come at midterm elections, when Ronald Reagan has not been at the head of the ticket.

The obvious inference from the party identification figures is that President Reagan has been a powerful contributor to the growth of modern Republicanism. The GOP was in a good position to recoup its losses by 1980 because of the floundering Carter Presidency, and Reagan exploited this advantage. The GOP did especially well when his presence on the ballot could rally party support. As his Presidency winds down, he leaves the GOP in a far stronger position than it was immediately after Watergate and with a base of party loyalists that more closely rivals the Democrats than it has in decades. No longer can the Democrats be within striking distance of election victory by mobilizing only their loyalists, as in the 1950s. We have entered a new, more competitive era of American electoral politics.

The post-Watergate Republican resurgence, though, is built on a far firmer foundation than a popular President. Out of the Watergate doldrums came a commitment to party building, led by Republican National Committee Chairman William Brock, that has strengthened the GOP across the board in subtle yet highly important ways. On assuming the chairmanship in 1977, Brock set about to build the RNC into a powerful fund-raiser and campaign resource for Republican candidates. Brock and the RNC excelled at raising money from small contributors, as necessitated by the new campaign contribution limits, through direct-mail campaigns. A visible measure of Brock's success in these efforts can be measured by the money the RNC raised under his leadership: $34.2 million in 1977–78 and $76.2 million in 1979–80. The Democratic National Committee (DNC), by contrast, could raise only $11.3 and $15.1 million in those two election cycles.

By the 1980s, the Republican National Committee was a potent force for the recruitment of good candidates for a variety of offices, the professionalization of their campaigns, and the building of stronger grass-roots Republican organizations. The Republican congressional campaign committees enjoyed parallel successes during these years in raising money and putting it to use to support GOP candidates for the House and Senate. These efforts enabled the GOP to be an "overachiever," gaining more votes than its electoral base alone would have produced, and constituted an important investment in the future, to be recouped as the electoral environment changed. While Democratic party committees have begun to emulate the efforts of the Republicans in recent years, they have tried in vain to match their success in fund-raising, financial support for party candidates, and party building. For example, in 1985–86, the GOP committees raised $252.4 million and the Democrats only $61.8 million.[7]

Although the strengthening of the Republican party organization preceded the Reagan Presidency, its ultimate successes obviously have been heightened by a popular Republican occupant in the White House. President Reagan provided a powerful symbolic presence around which his party could rally both activists and rank and file. In contrast to the immediate post-Watergate years, when the party was in disarray and weighted down by pessimism about its electoral prospects, the Reagan success, and the Republican control of the Senate that accompanied it, generated the yeasty optimism of a party enjoying electoral momentum. The machinery put in place by William Brock could be fully exploited, as popular leadership and powerful organization symbiotically fed on one another.

Finally, the disarray of the Democratic party too has contributed materially to the post-Watergate GOP resurgence. In America's institutionalized two-party system, each party competes intensely for relative position within the American electorate, as well as for public office. Whatever weakens one party often strengthens the other, although the possibility of simultaneous demise in both parties is readily apparent in the recent period of dealignment. Democratic party successes in the post-Watergate era were very much attributable to the problems brought on the GOP by a vice-president who had to resign in office after being convicted of corruption, a President who resigned one step ahead of impeachment and almost certain conviction for his role in the Watergate affair, and a successor who pardoned him in advance for all possible crimes. But these Democratic triumphs only temporarily papered over severe long-standing problems within the Democratic party.

The basic structure of the modern Democratic party was set by the New Deal realignment of the 1930s, which came in response to the party's appeal to Catholics in nominating Al Smith in 1928, the depression beginning in 1929, and the leadership of Franklin Delano Roosevelt. This old party coalition was severely weathered by the 1980s. Voters who came of age during the 1930s, and whose partisanship was indelibly imprinted by its politics, are now in their seventies and eighties, and are rapidly passing from the scene. Replacing them, in the inexorable march of generations, are voters to whom that period and the politics it spawned seem increasingly irrelevant. Moreover, post-World War II affluence eroded the lower-status base of the Democratic coalition. Many of its most loyal members no longer look on the party as the champion of

upward mobility; they are successful, and the Democratic party's policies toward today's lower classes and blacks threaten their newfound status.

But, more than anything else, internal contradictions in the New Deal coalition itself underlie its contemporary problems. The Democratic party Franklin Roosevelt created in the 1930s combined liberal groups in the North (organized labor, the poor, religious minorities) and conservative southerners, who
could trace their Democratic roots back to the Civil War. Southern conservatism
was especially linked to preserving the role of blacks in society. Until the 1950s,
the South practiced strict segregation of the races, as a matter of social custom
and law, and preservation of that practice was central to the political identity
of many traditional members of the southern electorate, which because of voting restrictions contained very few blacks. Only as long as the issue of change
in the racial status quo was ignored could this "unholy alliance" of northern
liberals and southern conservatives be preserved.

The liberalism of the northern wing of the Democratic party ensured that
the provision of civil rights to blacks could not be ignored for long. At its 1948
presidential nominating convention, and again throughout the 1960s, the party directly addressed the issue of black rights. Each time it did so, the Democratic presidential candidate suffered defections from conservative white southern Democrats. In 1948, four southern states were carried by the candidate of
a segregationist faction of the Democratic party, Strom Thurmond, running
on the Dixiecrat party ticket. In 1964, these same states were among the five
southern states won by Republican Barry Goldwater, whose anti-civil rights
campaign appeals struck a resonant chord among white southerners.

By 1968, the desertion by conservative white southerners from the national
(they were still voting for that party in state and local elections) Democratic
coalition seemed beyond repair. Without the once-solid South, the Democrats
were no longer the majority party in the one national election America holds,
the quadrennial contest for President. The overwhelmingly Democratic loyalties
of newly enfranchised southern blacks could not compensate for the loss of
white voters. Since 1968, only one Democratic presidential candidate, southerner
Jimmy Carter, fared well in the South—and he has been the only Democrat
to win the Presidency. Carter carried ten of eleven southern states in 1976. The
Democratic candidate won only two other southern states in this period—Texas
in 1968 and Georgia (Carter's home state) in 1980. The 1980s have completed
what may have been inevitable since the Democratic party coalition was first
constructed: the death of the Democrats' majority party status in the South,
at least at the presidential level.[8]

Although the major rupture in the Democratic party was the loss of its
historically most supportive region, the South, the party has suffered other seri-

ous strains as well. The Vietnam war and the issue of America's role in the world, social issues such as crime and abortion, and policies such as busing and affirmative action to enforce black rights have been some of the issues that have intensified the conflict between liberal and moderate-conservative forces in the party. Battles over such issues have been fought publicly in presidential nominating contests since 1968, with such intensity that they undermined the nominee's chances in the general election. The Democrats have faced the electorate since the mid-1960s as a divided party.

The continuing schisms within the Democratic party have figured prominently in the GOP resurgence of the 1980s. In the aftermath of his defeat at the hands of Ronald Reagan in 1980, it is easy to forget that Jimmy Carter decisively won his other major contest that year—a challenge by the erstwhile leader of the liberal wing of his party, Senator Edward Kennedy. In 1984, Walter Mondale's candidacy was significantly undermined by his intraparty opposition, particularly Gary Hart, who depicted him as a candidate of the "special interests," one of which, organized labor, had previously been viewed by almost all Democratic candidates as a vital member of the party's coalition, not as a somehow disreputable interest. The Republicans have suffered from internal conflict as well, but they have managed to contain it. Once memories of the Watergate affair had faded, the GOP was able to exploit deep and long-standing divisions in the Democratic coalition.

It is tempting to attribute the Democrats' internal troubles to the more open intraparty conflicts brought on by changes in the presidential nominating process after 1968. The enhanced importance of primary elections, as well as more open party caucuses in the 1970s and 1980s, undoubtedly has exacerbated internal Democratic schisms by bringing them to the center stage of political campaigns and airing them for all to see. In a previous era, when the party's presidential nominee was selected by "backstage" bargaining among local and state party leaders at the national nominating convention, the usual tendency was to bridge rather than heighten divisions.[9]

The Dixiecrat successes in 1948, the Democratic voter defections to Eisenhower in the 1950s and to Goldwater in 1964, as well as the electoral problems that have plagued Democratic nominees ever since (in winning only 43 percent, 38 percent, 50 percent, 41 percent, and 41 percent of the vote, respectively, in general election contests from 1968 through 1984), suggest that the Democrats' internal schisms are rooted in the electorate, not just manufactured by nominating process rules. Studies of the party electorate's voting preferences and party loyalties (see figure 5.4) over the last several decades corroborate this inference.[10] In recent times, the party coalition assembled by Franklin Roosevelt during the New Deal years has splintered.

Identifying the Reagan Legacy

As Ronald Reagan retires from public life, he leaves behind a Republican party far stronger than the one he inherited in 1980. The party has regained the ground it lost in the aftermath of the Watergate affair and appears to be stronger in the late 1980s than it has been in decades. How much Reagan personally has contributed to the turnabout in GOP fortunes, however, is far from clear.

As we have seen, even without Reagan, several forces were working to retrieve the party from the depths to which it sank after Watergate. The twin troubles of the Carter Presidency—inflation and Iran—virtually handed the White House to the GOP in 1980, perhaps no matter who had been their candidate. Indeed, because of the conservative ideological baggage he carried, Reagan may have been less well positioned to take advantage of the anti-Carter backlash than some other GOP nominee. The party simultaneously was enjoying a growing organizational vitality, especially through the building of a grassroots donor base and a capability to aid its candidates in campaigns. Over the longer haul there has been the seemingly inexorable weakening of the Democratic party coalition—from which the Republicans, as the opposition in a two-party system, could only gain. The Watergate affair may have stalled this pro-Republican momentum only temporarily. To some degree at least, then, President Reagan inherited a party with considerable electoral opportunity. His primary accomplishment may have been the full exploitation of it to his and his party's advantage.

But this is no mean accomplishment. Political history is strewn with examples of leaders who failed to take advantage of favorable circumstances. Richard Nixon frittered away the standing he had won in a landslide victory by his deepening involvement in Watergate. Just before him, Lyndon Johnson saw his Presidency erode under the force of urban riots and Vietnam. What has distinguished Ronald Reagan has been his ability to seize the opportunities presented by an unpopular predecessor, an energized party, and a debilitated opposition. While the Iran-*contra* affair, corruption charges against high administration officials, and the October 1987 stock market decline all threaten to undermine his considerable achievements, there is good reason to believe that President Reagan will leave the White House with his party well along the way toward a partisan realignment.

The Reagan contributions to the Republican resurgence derive mostly from his leadership and the generally positive responses it has evoked from the American public. The Presidency is a powerful pulpit from which to steer the course of American politics. Presidential successes typically redound to the benefit of their party by enhancing public images of its performance capabilities. In the 1980s, in comparison to the immediate post-Watergate period, about twice as many Americans have seen the GOP as the party better able to handle the nation's most important problems, and the primary reason is the Reagan Presidency. By the mid-1980s, in fact, the Republicans had closed the party image gap with the Democrats, a gap that had been as high as 28 percent in 1975 (see figure 5.3).

Reagan's leadership has had an equally important, if more subtle, effect on the agenda of politics—the issues, controversies, even premises that structure political debate. His assault on big government put liberalism on the defensive and lent such respectability to conservative ideas that they permeated the public more deeply than ever before. The 1980s were a time of federal tax cuts, reduced growth in domestic programs, increases in defense spending, and a new surge of conservative moralism in policy making. Reagan's leadership played the major role in bringing these matters to the top of the political agenda. Ironically, even in the traditionally conservative concern for a balanced budget, which was swept aside in the early 1980s and continues to represent a major policy failure of the administration, the President's power to shape debate is illustrated: Who would have thought, before the 1980s, that today many liberal Democrats would be decrying the nation's unprecedented budget deficit or that a bipartisan consensus would emerge around the proposition that the deficit should be reduced?

The Reagan legacy is perhaps best measured by changes during the 1980s in the partisan loyalties of the electorate. The troubles of Carter and his party, as much as they may have affected the electoral fortunes of the Democrats, could not alone create greater numbers of Republican loyalists. Nor did the enhanced organizational effectiveness of the party materially affect its loyalist base; it merely improved its ability to mobilize this base and attract votes beyond it in constructing an electoral majority. Indeed, to increase its partisan strength, the GOP had to become attractive to the electorate in its own right.

We have seen from figure 5.4 that by the early 1980s, the percentage of the electorate professing Republican loyalties had regained the ground it had lost after the Watergate affair. The first GOP surge came in the early months of the first Reagan term, a time of spectacular Reagan successes with the Congress. Reagan's landslide reelection in 1984 was accompanied by additional growth in GOP loyalists. By the end of 1984, these two GOP surges had reduced the gap in party loyalists between the parties to about half what it had been little more than a decade before—and to its lowest level since reliable measurements first were available in the early 1950s. The fact that both these surges are readily linked to presidential accomplishments supports the inference that they are attributable to Ronald Reagan. Because partisan loyalties are lasting components of many Americans' political outlooks, rather than momentary

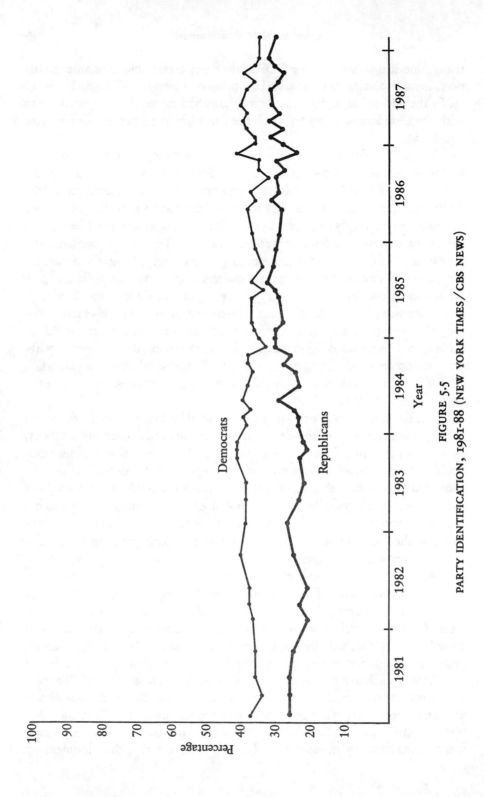

FIGURE 5.5

PARTY IDENTIFICATION, 1981-88 (NEW YORK TIMES/CBS NEWS)

responses to temporary political stimuli, the Republican gains registered in them should endure well beyond the Reagan years. This has to count as potentially the most significant Reagan legacy.

The Reagan years have promoted GOP prospects for the future in yet another important way. Eight years of conservative Republican rule have developed a new cadre of Republican party leaders. President Reagan's conservative preachings drew a new generation of ideological activists to the party and encouraged conservative activists already in it. Moreover, with the appointment of his people to some 3000 top policy-making positions in the federal government, the President created a large talent pool of now experienced and credentialed partisans from which his party can recruit for subsequent political activity. Quite consciously applying an ideological litmus test in addition to the usual party loyalty requirements, the Reagan administration has drawn into government large numbers of conservatives. This recruitment, and the grassroots activation that accompanied it, should have an impact on party politics for many years to come. An inadequate supply of good talent has been a perennial problem for the GOP, what with its historic weakness in the South and the natural aversion of conservatives to governmental careers. For the foreseeable future, this problem appears to have been solved.

Not only has the Reagan Presidency been good to his party by developing new talent, but the ideological bias in the effort has turned the GOP in a substantially more conservative direction. The once formidable liberal-moderate wing of the party has been virtually silenced during the Reagan years; its conservative wing has been emboldened. Familiar GOP candidates have refashioned their political appeals to attract more conservative support. These things are hard to gauge with any precision, but the intraparty center of gravity seems to have moved decidedly to the right. This too promises to be a durable part of the Reagan legacy, but it is potentially less propitious to a bright GOP future.

The Incomplete Realignment

The real test of the Reagan legacy, indeed the criterion Ronald Reagan might most want to invoke, is whether the partisanship gains under his leadership have constituted a pro-Republican realignment of the American electorate. A realignment occurs when there is a significant and enduring change in the party coalitions—that is, in the partisan loyalties of the electorate. Such a change would most likely displace the Democratic party from its position, since the New Deal realignment, as the dominant party in American politics.[11] Echoing a common refrain of the late 1960s and early 1970s, before the Watergate affair silenced it, many observers have called the Republican resurgence we have documented during the Reagan years "an emerging Republican realignment." If they are correct, then Ronald Reagan has left a legacy equaled by only a handful of American Presidents.

Signs of partisan realignment have abounded in the 1980s. Most conspicuously, the South has moved from a dependably Democratic to a dependably Republican region in presidential voting. Clear majorities of white southerners have consistently backed GOP presidential nominees in recent years, including 1976 and 1980 when fellow southerner Jimmy Carter was on the Democratic ticket. They flocked to the Reagan banner in 1984, giving him a full 70 percent of their vote.[12] Aside from Carter, Democratic presidential candidates have carried only one southern state (Texas by Humphrey in 1968) since the Johnson landslide in 1964. The changes in this region alone spell trouble for the Democrats because their majority status cannot be retained if they regularly lose all or most southern states.

With his conservative political philosophy dominating the political agenda, moreover, Ronald Reagan has been able to unite economic and social conservatives behind his party. Economic conservatives have been the bedrock of Republican strength throughout the twentieth century. Until lately, social conservatives, especially Protestant fundamentalists, were not especially attracted to the GOP. In the early years of the century, their natural home was the Democratic party of William Jennings Bryan, thrice Democratic nominee for President and himself a religious fundamentalist who defended the Tennessee ban on the teaching of evolution in the famous Scopes trial of the 1920s. Especially in the South, religious fundamentalists continued to prefer the Democrats during the New Deal years, when the pains of depression submerged the social conservatism of many under a populist economic liberalism. By joining together these two strains of conservatism, Reagan laid the foundation for a majority Republican party.

But past voting patterns and presidential coalition-building successes do not necessarily spell realignment. Instead, realignment requires enduring changes in the party coalitions—a lasting alteration in party loyalties, not just temporary switches in candidate preferences. The question, then, is whether the pro-Republican forces of the post-Watergate resurgence have been powerful enough to dislodge the electorate from the Democratic leanings it has held since the 1930s and then to move it significantly in a Republican direction.

This question has two separate parts, involving first the decay of Democratic loyalties and then the acquisition of Republican loyalties. Because the American political tradition offers voters a legitimate alternative to partisanship, called *independence,* a decline in the loyalist base of one party does not have to be reciprocated by growth in the other party. Two different processes, in fact, are involved: one is appropriately termed *dealignment*, symbolizing the decay of one or both existing party coalitions, and the other of course is *realignment*. Even though dealignment is likely to be followed by realignment, and even may be a necessary condition for realignment, dealignment and realignment are different political phenomena.

The evidence is undeniable that the American electorate underwent a dealignment from 1964 to 1974. Fewer members of the electorate professed Democratic or Republican party loyalties, however measured, in the years after 1965 than during the preceding decade. Among partisans, fewer claimed to be strong Democrats or Republicans. Correspondingly more Americans said that they were independents or had no preference for a party. The percentage of the electorate without either Democratic or Republican party loyalties, measured as 100 percent minus the partisan totals in figure 5.4, consequently was about 10 percent higher in 1972–78 than it had been from 1952 to 1964.[13] While both parties lost ground in this dealignment, the majority Democrats, with more to lose, suffered disproportionately more.

In the 1980s, there have been signs that this dealignment may be turning into a realignment. As can be seen in figure 5.4 and the more frequent readings of figure 5.5, the partisan share of the electorate has grown (albeit slightly and unevenly) throughout the decade. This growth has favored the GOP. Ronald Reagan has figured prominently in this movement, as new high points of Republican loyalty were achieved in the immediate aftermath of each of his two election victories—26 percent in January 1981 and 30 percent in December 1984 and January 1985 in the Times/CBS poll (figure 5.5).

Other evidence of Republican partisan gains has surfaced in some, but by no means all, of the states. Interviews with voters as they were exiting the polls on election day in 1980 and 1984 show Republican gains and Democratic losses of party identifiers in eight of nine pivotal states (California, Connecticut, Illinois, Michigan, New Jersey, New York, Pennsylvania, and Texas) and Democratic losses with no corresponding GOP gains in a ninth (Ohio). The Republican surge was particularly large in Texas, and the results of statewide polling show similarly handsome GOP gains in Florida.[14]

A similar story of Republican gains, although even less uniform, is told by changes in party registration figures. Of the twenty-five states that reported such declarations in both 1980 and 1986, the net GOP share of registered voters grew in fifteen; the net Democratic share grew in only five. The largest net Democratic gain was 4 percent, which occurred in Iowa (a 3 percent Democratic gain plus a 1 percent GOP loss). The net GOP gain exceeded this level in twelve states: Alaska (8 percent), California (5 percent), Florida (13 percent), Kansas (5 percent), Louisiana (16 percent), Nevada (7 percent), New Mexico (7 percent), North Carolina (5 percent), Oklahoma (9 percent), Oregon (6 percent), South Dakota (5 percent), and Wyoming (14 percent).

Over the longer 1972–86 period, the number of states with Republican gains (13) is almost equaled by the number with Democratic gains (9), but again the largest state gains benefited the Republicans. The largest Democratic net increase, a total of 13 percent in Maine, was exceeded by Republican increases in six states: Arizona (14 percent), Florida (20 percent), Louisiana (29 percent), Nevada (18 percent), Oklahoma (16 percent), and Wyoming (21 percent). Except for Arizona, where 1980 party registration figures were not available, these states were leaders in Republican growth in the most recent period as well.[15]

The most auspicious signs of realignment, though, came around the time of the 1984 election. Not only did Ronald Reagan appear to be the first Republican presidential candidate in over fifty years to outpoll his Democratic opponent among voters under thirty years of age, but these young voters also were more likely to claim Republican than Democratic party loyalties, again for the first time in over fifty years.[16]

In the last realignment of the American party system, the New Deal realignment of the 1930s, new voters led the way. The Democrats were successful in mobilizing into their partisan ranks overwhelmingly disproportionate numbers of young people, who had just attained voting age, and of older citizens who had not been induced to participate in previous contests. So important was this skewed mobilization for the creation of the new Democratic majority that some scholars have concluded that new voters, most of whom are young, hold the key to prospects for enduring party shifts. Lacking previous experience with electoral politics, they are more open to party recruitment and to the retention of their new loyalties for the remainder of their lives. Older voters, by contrast, may defect to opposition candidates favored by contemporary forces, but they typically return to their old habits in succeeding elections. Therefore, the recent change in the partisan behavior of young adults is especially auspicious for the GOP.[17]

Yet alongside these indicators of Republican party ascendancy are others that signal caution in trumpeting a realignment. Most ominous for the Republicans is the fact that elected officials beyond the White House remain predominantly Democratic in 1987 and 1988 (see figures 5.1 and 5.2) in spite of the party's resurgence in recent years. The Democrats still hold about 60 percent of the legislative seats at the state and national levels. Even Republican control of the Senate from 1981 through 1986, exceeding two years for the first time since the New Deal realignment, was broken in the 1986 elections.

The Republican failure to penetrate below the presidential level has been most conspicuous in the South, where Republican presidential success has been most notable. At the beginning of 1987, as has been true for more than a century, southern state legislatures were dominated by Democrats. The greatest GOP representation in either chamber of the eleven southern states was a feeble 37 percent in Tennessee's lower house. Moreover, Republicans held only 39 of 116 southern seats in the U.S. House of Representatives and 6 of 22 southern seats in the U.S. Senate. The only bright spot for the GOP in the South after the 1986 elections was that five of the eleven states now had Republican governors. What kind of realignment leaves so little imprint beyond the presidential level?

By contrast, the shock waves of previous realignments have quickly reverberated throughout the nation. Signs of the New Deal realignment, for example, appeared in congressional elections even before Roosevelt's 1932 presidential victory. In the pre-realignment 71st Congress, elected in 1928, both houses were comfortably under Republican control. By the time the dust had settled after the onset of the depression of 1929 and the Roosevelt victory in 1932, these Republican majorities had been dramatically overturned. The party lost 150 House and 21 Senate seats in the 1930 and 1932 elections! Republican ranks were thinned even further in the next two elections, which left the party with only 89 of 433 seats in the lower chamber and 16 of 96 seats in the Senate during the 75th Congress, elected in 1936.

The New Deal realignment did not sweep as quickly through state politics as previous realignments had.[18] Even so, the 1930 elections destroyed the Republican majority in governors (which they held by a margin of 30 to 18, with most of the Democrats from the South, on the eve of the elections). By 1935 only nine Republicans occupied the governor's mansions in the forty-eight states. There are no reliable data on party loyalties from that period, but party registration figures changed abruptly in many locales in the early 1930s, and by the 1940s, the Democratic party could claim more loyalists than the GOP—undoubtedly just the reverse of the situation in the 1920s.

By the standards of previous realignments, then, the 1980s fail to qualify as a realigning era. The curious dissonance in recent years between pro-Republican presidential preferences and pro-Democratic voting for Congress and in the states signifies instead an electorate that has failed to generalize its support for Republican presidential candidates and its loss of confidence in the Democratic party into broader support for the Republican party. Recent presidential coalitions, in short, are not party coalitions. Furthermore, even though the GOP can claim more self-identified party loyalists than it has enjoyed in decades, its gains remain marginal and leave the party still somewhat short of the Democratic totals. Because these gains have been based on Democratic losses and short-term rallies to a popular President, they also seem highly fragile.

Some scholars, though, have concluded that the United States has experienced a pro-Republican realignment in recent years. But theirs is a realignment devoid of meaning, based on partisan loyalties that cannot hold together across elections and thereby cease to serve as enduring guides to voting behavior. Surely no realignment has occurred if it is based on new "reconstructed partisans" who do not follow up their Republican presidential preferences by supporting candidates of the same party for other offices. Partisanship is a loyalty to a party, not to a candidate, and as such should serve as an enduring guide to voting behavior. If the politics of the 1980s greatly diminishes its role, then it is a politics of dealignment rather than realignment.[19]

What we have as the Reagan years draw to a close is an incomplete realignment—some movement toward Republican ascendancy, but no consolidation of this movement by Republican successes beyond the presidential level or in enduring partisan loyalties. That such a process has begun surely is heartening to GOP stalwarts. It has given their party powerful momentum, as important in politics as it is in sports. That the process has not yet culminated in a pro-GOP realignment when temporary conditions have been so strongly in its favor (a popular President, a fractured opposition, no foreign policy catastrophes, and real economic growth), though, does not augur well for the future of the GOP. Opportunities not seized in time may be foregone.

The principal Reagan legacy, then, is a Republican party that has recovered the ground it lost in the Watergate era and seems better positioned than at any time since the New Deal years to become the leading party in America's two-party system. Ronald Reagan's leadership, his skilled use of the opportunities provided a President for redefining political debate, is largely what has brought the GOP this far. In spite of his considerable efforts in behalf of his party, however, he has not been able to leave a more lasting imprint on the American party system. Perhaps there was not enough time for him to consolidate his party's position. Perhaps the absence of a traumatic event, something like the Great Depression, has contained the pressures for realignment-scale changes. Or perhaps, having rejected Democratic loyalties, many voters still cannot bring themselves to make a standing commitment to the GOP. Whatever the reason, it is now apparent that the Republican leaders who follow Reagan will not inherit a dominant party or a realigned party system. Instead, it will be up to them to fulfill—or break—the Reagan era promise of "an emerging Republican majority."

In this continuing quest for realignment, the Republicans enjoy several important advantages. Their national party organization is far better financed and more resourceful in campaigning than that of the Democrats. This enables them to convert close races into victories and thereby make the most of their electoral base, but it does not much affect the size of this base. GOP candidates for the 1988 presidential nomination also are more familiar and experienced than their Democratic counterparts, which may prove more advantageous this time than it did a decade earlier when Washington "outsiders" proved popular. Finally, if the economy overcomes the recent Wall Street scares, a continuation of prosperity on its "watch" should continue to benefit the GOP.

Nonetheless, the prospects for fulfillment of the realignment that seems so near depend primarily, as they always do, on presidential leadership. Ronald Reagan has carried his party up to the brink of realignment. The Twenty-second Amendment to the Constitution, if not his age, prevents him from taking the GOP any further. If Franklin Roosevelt had been similarly limited from running for a third term in 1940 and had turned over the leadership of the Democrats to John Nance Garner, Henry Wallace, or Jim Farley, might not the New Deal realignment have been derailed?

So the prospects for an emerging Republican majority depend on the ability of Reagan's successors to hold together their party's presidential coalition and then to accomplish what eluded even Reagan—the extension of that coalition to other offices or its institutionalization in GOP party loyalties. At this time, these prospects do not seem bright. It is questionable that the party can find another leader with Ronald Reagan's ability to unite social and economic conservatives with moderates in presidential politics, much less erect a grand, majoritarian coalition. A leader who is less appealing to the party's various constituencies threatens its fragile electoral base. It also is doubtful, if only because of the normal twists and turns of fate, that the economic and foreign situations can remain so favorable to the GOP. Without a new Ronald Reagan and uninterrupted good fortune, the best bet for now is that the potential pro-Republican realignment will remain incomplete and that the dealignment-style politics that have characterized the past twenty years will continue.

Notes

1. Treatments of the Watergate affair and its consequences for American politics are legion. Probably the best chronicle of the affair itself is the book by Carl Bernstein and Bob Woodward, the reporters who doggedly pieced together the story of the break-in and cover-up. See their *All the President's Men* (New York: Simon and Schuster, 1974). A detailed chronology of the affair until a few months before President Nixon's resignation, as well as transcripts from the tapes that provided the most damaging evidence against the President, appears in *The White House Transcripts* (New York: Bantam Books, 1974), 813-77.

2. For a discussion of the realignment process in general and the New Deal realignment in particular, see James L. Sundquist, *Dynamics of the Party System* (Washington,

D.C.: Brookings Institution, 1983). The Republican "realignment dream" finds its classic expression in Kevin P. Phillips, *The Emerging Republican Majority* (New Rochelle, N.Y.: Arlington House, 1969).

3. Numerous polling organizations ask a question about party loyalty or party identification. The questions and how the responses are categorized vary somewhat from organization to organization, but the distributions of party advantage rarely differ more than can be accounted for by slight differences in wording and the expected variations in samples. In discussing party loyalties in this chapter, I rely on two different surveys. The University of Michigan has measured partisanship biennially during each presidential and midterm election since 1952 using the question: "Generally speaking, do you usually think of yourself as a Republican, a Democrat, an independent, or what?" The New York Times/CBS News poll has used the Michigan question to measure partisanship on a more frequent basis since 1981, and I rely on it to follow the almost monthly ebbs and flows of partisan loyalties during the Reagan years.

4. See Leon Epstein, *Political Parties in the American Mold* (Madison: University of Wisconsin Press, 1986), 216.

5. See Helmut Norpoth, "Under Way and Here to Stay: Party Realignment in the 1980s?" *Public Opinion Quarterly* 51 (Fall 1987): 376-91, for an analysis of age-related partisanship rates using the Times/CBS data through 1985. Unpublished figures from tracking polls conducted by the Wirthlin Group into 1987 (presented by Richard Wirthlin at the 1987 American Political Science Association Meetings) show a continuing GOP partisan advantage among only the youngest members of the electorate, age 17–24.

6. See Paul R. Abramson, John H. Aldrich, and David W. Rohde, *Change and Continuity in the 1980 Elections* (Washington, D.C.: CQ Press, 1982), for a discussion of how the 1980 contest turned on negative retrospective evaluations of Carter's performance.

7. These figures on party finances come from party committee reports to the Federal Election Commission for the two-year periods up to the presidential and midterm elections. They exclude federal funds provided to the parties for running their national conventions. Funds raised by the party committees can be used to support the entire party ticket in an election, to finance various party services (e.g., public opinion polling, production of campaign ads, training), and to contribute up to $5000 per election directly to each party candidate.

8. For more comprehensive analyses of partisan changes in the South, see John R. Petrocik, "Realignment: New Party Coalitions and the Nationalization of the South," *Journal of Politics* 49 (May 1987): 347-75; and Earl Black and Merle Black, *Politics and Society in the South* (Cambridge, Mass.: Harvard University Press, 1987).

9. For discussions of the party reforms and their effects, see William J. Crotty, *Decisions for the Democrats* (Baltimore: Johns Hopkins University Press, 1978); Nelson W. Polsby, *Consequences of Party Reform* (Oxford, England: Oxford University Press, 1983); and Byron E. Shafer, *Quiet Revolution: The Struggle for the Democratic Party and the Shaping of Post-Reform Politics* (New York: Russell Sage Foundation, 1983).

10. A useful account may be found in Robert Axelrod, "Presidential Election Coalitions in 1984," *American Political Science Review* 80 (March 1986): 281-84. For more comprehensive discussions, see John R. Petrocik, *Party Coalitions* (Chicago: University of Chicago Press, 1981); and Sundquist, *Dynamics of the Party System*.

11. This is only one of several possible results. In theory, realignment requires only

a signficant change in the structure of the party coalitions, which may or may not produce a new majority party. Two other consequences of such a change might be enlargement of Democratic party dominance or the bringing of the two major parties into rough parity in terms of their numbers of loyalists. In practice, however, the dynamics of past realignments have been so powerful that they produced a new majority party. Therefore, this result is the surest indication that a realignment has occurred.

12. See Paul R. Abramson, John H. Aldrich, and David W. Rohde, *Change and Continuity in the 1984 Elections* (Washington, D.C.: CQ Press, 1986), 136, 147.

13. Scholars disagree only about the magnitude of the decline in partisanship, not the fact of a decline. A similar, but more comprehensive, story of dealignment is told in Martin P. Wattenberg, *The Decline of American Political Parties: 1952-1984* (Cambridge, Mass.: Harvard University Press, 1986); and Norman H. Nie, Sidney Verba, and John R. Petrocik, *The Changing American Voter* (Cambridge, Mass.: Harvard University Press, 1979).

14. The NBC exit poll results are reported in Laurily K. Epstein, "The Changing Structure of Party Identification," *PS* 18 (Winter 1985): 48-52. Exit polls record only the loyalties of voters, and consequently their results can be affected by the turnout differentials between party supporters that often arise in landslide elections. Thus, one must be cautious in generalizing these results to the entire state electorate. For Florida results based upon the full electorate, see Paul Allen Beck, "Realignment Begins? The Republican Surge in Florida," *American Politics Quarterly* 10 (October 1982): 421-38. More recent surveys show continuing GOP gains in Florida through 1987.

15. For a variety of reasons, especially the need to register only when voting for the first time in a particular place, party registration changes usually lag way behind party identification changes. The party registration figures reported here were taken from Michael Barone and Grant Ujifusa, *The Almanac of American Politics,* published most recently by the *National Journal* in Washington, D.C. They are based on the final registration figures for presidential and midterm elections in each state. Because many states do not have party registration, and two states in 1986 did not require any formal registration at all, figures cannot be supplied for all states, thus limiting the utility of party registration data for tracing the realignment phenomenon nationwide.

16. See Thomas E. Cavanagh and James L. Sundquist, "The New Two-Party System," in *The New Direction in American Politics,* ed. John E. Chubb and Paul E. Peterson (Washington, D.C.: Brookings Institution, 1985), 48-49, in addition to the materials cited in note 5.

17. For an expanded treatment of the role of new voters in the realignment process, see Paul Allen Beck, "A Socialization Theory of Partisan Realignment," in *The Politics of Future Citizens,* ed. Richard Niemi (San Francisco: Jossey-Bass, 1974), 199-219.

18. For an excellent description of the delayed effects of the New Deal realignment in the states, see Sundquist, *Dynamics of the Party System,* chaps. 10-12.

19. Martin P. Wattenberg refers to it as a "hollow realignment"—hollow in the sense that party and candidates are no longer strongly linked. See his "The Hollow Realignment: Partisan Change in a Candidate-Centered Era," *Public Opinion Quarterly* 51 (Spring 1987): 58-74. Everett C. Ladd sees recent years as a realigning period with dealignment features, resulting in a two-tiered electoral system that is Republican at the presidential level and Democratic below. See his "On Mandates, Realignments, and the 1984 Presidential Election," *Political Science Quarterly* 100 (Spring 1985): 1-25.

6

The Reagan Presidency and American Public Opinion

JAMES W. CEASER

Ask any political observer today how President Reagan will be remembered in the future, and you will probably hear about his special relationship with the American people. After all, common journalistic descriptions of Ronald Reagan to this point have focused on his public image and his capacity for popular persuasion. He has repeatedly been referred to as the "great communicator" and, for as long as the label would stick, the "Teflon President."

This chapter is about the Reagan Presidency and American public opinion. But it does not assume that Ronald Reagan will leave his most significant legacy in the sphere of public relations. There are at least two reasons to treat claims of this kind with caution. First, although the President's reputation as a "great communicator" has some basis in reality, it has been built up largely to serve political ends. Friends of the President have latched on to the phrase to puff up his reputation, but it has been repeated with much greater success by the President's political enemies. To pick an example almost at random, the Yale economist James Tobin has argued that only Reagan's "smooth performances on television" explain how this "simplistic ideologue" could put over on the American people his fraudulent economic program.[1] In Tobin's view, the "great communicator" is in reality a "great manipulator."

Second, it is doubtful whether being temporarily popular or persuasive with the public constitutes a claim to a significant legacy. A "strategic" perspective on the study of the Presidency holds that any Presidency should be evaluated from the viewpoint of its overall ends or goals. The efficacy of various ways of using power is then judged in the light of how each promotes the achievement of those goals. In this view, an independent treatment of presidential popularity is of scant interest. Indeed, even the value of popular approval is an open question, for its pursuit in the short term might not always promote the President's broader objectives. There are times when a popular President may be unable to accomplish much and, conversely, times when an unpopular President can move things in the direction of his goals.[2]

Reagan's basic goals have been far more ambitious than those of most Presidents. Put in the simplest terms, Reagan has sought, on the domestic side, to shrink the size of government; in national security and foreign affairs, his aim has been to put the United States on guard and ready to engage, through various means, in a struggle against communism. For Reagan, achieving these goals is not simply a matter of having government do (or not do) certain things. It is also a matter of changing how people *think* about the role of government and about the mission of the United States in the world. Public opinion at this deeper level is known as a "public philosophy," and shaping a new philosophy has been one of Reagan's fundamental goals.

It is necessary, accordingly, to keep distinct the different senses of the term *public opinion*. In its ordinary applications in the study of the Presidency, public opinion refers to the general level of approval for the President and popular support for specific policies, programs, or actions. In a "strategic" perspective, these forms of opinion are treated as means, not ends. In a less frequent application, public opinion refers to the deeper beliefs of a public philosophy, a change in which can constitute a goal or an end of presidential governance. This has clearly been the case with the Reagan administration.

The Reagan Presidency and the "Failed Presidency" Model

In contrast to the strategic perspective sketched above, a different view of the importance of presidential popularity in recent years has enjoyed great influence. When Ronald Reagan was elected President, many observers had come to think that a President's approval rating had intrinsic significance as a measure of the legitimacy of his administration. By itself, such a belief, being only a belief, might be dismissed as inconsequential. But the Presidency today operates in an environment in which a community of analysts dissects every movement in the polls and then disseminates to the public a report on the President's status. This self-consciousness about a President's public standing has created expectations that have an impact of their own.

In 1981, professional Presidency watchers in journalism and academia were instructing Americans to view a modern Presidency as a single-act tragedy.

Under this model, a President comes to office with a generous measure of public support and goodwill. But at a certain point, through an inevitable misstep or misjudgment, the President's support begins to erode. Like an ancient Chinese emperor whose "mandate from heaven" is revoked, the President—with the Presidency watchers interpreting the opinion polls—loses the level of public confidence he needs to be effective. His Presidency is then solemnly pronounced "finished," "over," or "dead." Nothing remains but a sad denouement, whether it be forced resignation (Nixon), withdrawal (Johnson), or certain defeat in the next election (Ford and Carter).

This model, although based on recent experience, has an appeal of its own for Presidency watchers. Aside from its promise of a crisis, which is always exciting to journalists and academics, the model has the advantage of encapsulating the story of failure into a simple plot in which the unfolding of each Presidency respects the classic dramatic unities of time, place, and action.[3]

No wonder, then, that the Reagan Presidency has proven so great a disappointment to America's Presidency watchers. Not only has it not failed in the way the model predicted—although certainly not for want of repeated efforts by analysts to make it conform—but it has repeatedly violated the dramatic rule of a single plot. Instead of a simple story of up, down, and out, the Reagan Presidency has been characterized by fluctuating fortunes, alternating seasons of despair with periods of strong support. (In this respect, it seems to follow more the rule than the exception of two-term Presidencies in American history.) Whatever legacy the Reagan administration may ultimately leave on the Presidency or the nation, it should have a salutary effect on the study of the Presidency, laying to rest a model that has been both perverse and simplistic.

The President's Approval Rating

The Reagan Presidency, as gauged by its standing in public opinion, has gone through six different periods: *takeoff*, which ran from the inauguration until the autumn of the first year; *decline*, which, paralleling the recession, lasted until the summer of 1983; *restoration*, which ran from the summer of 1983 until after Reagan's reelection; *anointment*, which continued until the initial revelations of Iran-*contra*; *debacle*, which followed the Iran-*contra* affair and ended in the early fall of 1987; and *equilibrium*, which began with the signing of the INF treaty at the Reagan-Gorbachev summit in December 1987.

The six periods are defined by reference to an index of presidential approval based on the simple survey question, "Do you approve/disapprove of the way (name of President) is handling his job as President?" This rating may be considered a function of the public's assessment of three interrelated factors:

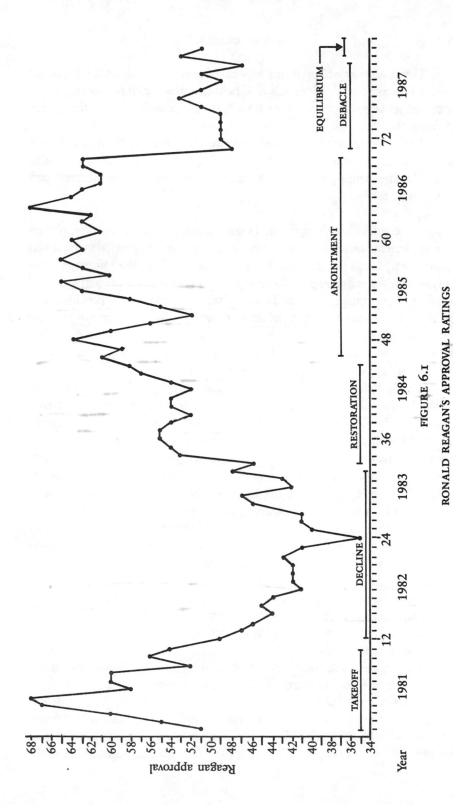

FIGURE 6.1

RONALD REAGAN'S APPROVAL RATINGS

QUESTION: DO YOU APPROVE OR DISAPPROVE OF THE WAY RONALD REAGAN IS HANDLING HIS JOB?

1. The condition of important aspects of reality for which the President is held partly responsible (domestic well-being, consisting of economic performance and social justice; international well-being, consisting of security, peace, and respect).

2. The performance of the President and the administration in the tasks of governing (e.g., Can the administration get things done? Is it free of scandal?).

3. The President's persona or character (Is the President competent, caring, decisive, etc.?).[4]

Social scientists have long debated what influences weigh on people in making assessments of this kind. Without entering here into the tangled metaphysics of perception, let us say that public opinion is based on the following commonly recognized influences. In the first place, people see, feel, experience, and interpret things on their own. For example, when people see workers lose their jobs and read newspaper reports of an increase in business failures, they draw conclusions about the dire condition of the economy. Or when a candidate appears confused and incoherent in a television debate, people form or alter their impression about that candidate's persona.

Second, public opinion rests on interpretations supplied by certain "speakers" who have regular access to the public, among them the President, his spokesmen, leading "official" opponents, opinion makers, commentators, and news analysts. Such speakers might interpret matters to say, for example, that the economy, though performing poorly, is now actually showing signs of strength; or that a posture of toughness (or, alternatively, one of conciliation) toward the Soviet Union is needed to bring it to the bargaining table. Such supplied interpretations are needed or are offered because what people see for themselves is not always complete or clear enough to establish for them a definitive meaning, and because experience has shown that the conclusions people draw are susceptible to being altered or changed by external arguments.

Finally, opinion rests on manufactured images, moods, and impressions, again supplied by certain speakers, often in this case "professionals" of public opinion and public relations. Here the effort is virtually to create something on top of "reality." For example, a President's staff may suggest a presidential trip abroad in order to display the President as a "statesman." Or a President's foes may engage in a calculated campaign of innuendo and phased revelations designed to create doubts about the President's integrity.

When it comes to the Presidency, the public is constantly bombarded by such interpretations and images. Certain speakers are recognized as "interested participants," such as the President's spokesmen or opposition party leaders, who naturally want to depict things in a light favorable or unfavorable to the

President. Others are nominally "objective analysts," who comment not only on what is going on in the world but also on the rhetorical strategies of the President and his opponents. All these speakers are constantly interacting with one another, attempting to anticipate and take into account what others will be doing. The object, especially among interested participants, is to have one's interpretation or image prevail over those supplied by other speakers. This constant and today highly self-conscious interaction can be called the *dialogue* on the public Presidency.

Does this dialogue on interpretations and images really matter? Or is it people's direct experience with the world that counts most? In the contemporary study of the Presidency, two opposing schools define the poles of thought on this matter. According to one school, what counts are real-world conditions, understood almost exclusively in terms of economic performance. Indeed, for this school there is no need even to speak of perception; the President's support score can be predicted directly from the "short run fluctuations in prices, income, and employment."[5] For the other school, what counts is perception, and among perceptions not people's own immediate grasp of reality but interpretations and images supplied by various speakers. Everything is a battle of rhetoric and "spin" control, and the world that people "see" is composed of a set of more or less fictitious symbols.[6]

The position taken here lies somewhere between these two schools. Real-world conditions (as perceived) generally count the most, and to this extent the second school's view of manipulated reality is exaggerated. But the relevant conditions by which people judge a President are not always economic, as an event like the Iran-*contra* affair shows. Moreover, interpretations and images not only have an effect on the President's approval score but, more important, help determine how well a President is able to enlist support for his goals.

Period One: Takeoff

Takeoff is the period that begins with the inauguration, runs through the spring and summer when President Reagan's approval rating increased, and ends in the autumn of 1981 when his rating falls below the point at which he began. During this period, the Reagan administration outlined and pushed through its economic program of tax cuts and reductions in anticipated domestic spending—the so-called Reagan Revolution.

Mention of the administration's economic program puts before us the central item that drove the President's approval rating during the first term. In fact, there is probably no Presidency in modern history in which the public's judgment was based less on sophisticated public relations strategies and more on an observable and tangible test. After the initial decisions about the economic program had been made, the fate of the Reagan Presidency in the first term rested very much on two questions (admittedly subject to interpretation): (1) Would Reagan stick with the program? and (2) Would its consequences in the end prove positive or negative?

President Reagan's relations with the public during this period of takeoff were unusual in two respects. First, even though Ronald Reagan had defeated his opponents, Jimmy Carter and John Anderson, in one of the nation's largest electoral vote landslides, his approval rating on assuming office was lower than that for any other modern President. The opposition that developed to his economic program cannot account for this initial low rating, for polls were taken before the program was proposed to the public. True enough, Reagan's percentage of the popular vote in 1980 (50.7 percent) was not very impressive, but it was larger than Jimmy Carter's in 1976 (50.1 percent), Richard Nixon's in 1968 (43.2 percent) and John Kennedy's in 1960 (49.8 percent). Yet each of these Presidents seemed to enjoy a far greater initial approval rating.

The other unusual aspect of this takeoff period is that President Reagan managed to generate significant additional support and then to hold it for a time. Other Presidents have seen their support either remain steady or decline. Thus, although President Reagan's approval rating during this early period is generally lower than for his predecessors, his curve is more favorable. He did not sit back and enjoy a honeymoon, but gambled the (limited) affection he had, using the first period to put his relationship with the American public on a newly constructed foundation. This immediately polarized opinion, solidifying an opposition, but also winning him an increased constituency.

One can only speculate on why President Reagan's initial approval rating was lower than that of his predecessors. One reason may well have been that Ronald Reagan was the least centrist candidate to have been elected President in this century. Other candidates who, like Reagan, have been more or less consciously associated with a movement and wing of their party (e.g., William Jennings Bryan, Barry Goldwater, and George McGovern) were defeated in the general election. Moreover, Reagan was probably the only person in this century to be elected who proposed a definite break with the prevailing "public philosophy."[7] As a result, probably far fewer people than usual were disposed to surrender themselves to Reagan in a presidential honeymoon.

Another reason undoubtedly lies in the hostile attitude toward Ronald Reagan that existed (and still exists) among America's intelligentsia. This group has a powerful "trickle down" effect on public opinion by virtue of its capacity to reach and influence segments of the public through articles, books, and solicited expert analysis. And one thing is certain: Ronald Reagan suffered from the blind contempt of intellectuals almost as much as John F. Kennedy had once enjoyed their unreflective adulation. For the intelligentsia, the idea that Reagan might be elected President was inconceivable. As Nicholas von Hoffman explained, it was "humiliating to think of this unlettered, self-assured bumpkin being our President."[8] If intellectuals hated Ronald Reagan less than they did Richard Nixon, it was because they dismissed Reagan more readily.

One fact about Reagan, above all others, constituted a grave offense to the intelligentsia: his background as a Hollywood actor. For some reason, an acting career was treated as an occupational disqualification for the Presidency. There was, perhaps, a subtle instrumental quality to this obsession. Reagan's background could be used to "explain" or concede his skill at communicating with the American people—a skill that intellectuals lionized when they found it in Franklin Roosevelt or John Kennedy—and yet cast doubt on its being positive or authentic in Reagan's case.

When, contrary to the intellectuals' expectations, Reagan was elected, the prospect that he might actually succeed was more than impossible. It was *unacceptable*. A measure of the prevalence of this attitude was the frequency with which intellectuals, one year into the Reagan Presidency, were still reminding themselves of the "insight" that Reagan might not be quite as inept as they thought. The belief in Reagan's incompetence, though comforting, began working to Reagan's advantage. As von Hoffman noted, "We make it easier for him by underestimating him."[9]

To the extent that Ronald Reagan *was* taken seriously by intellectuals, he was regarded as anachronistic and dangerous. Reagan's views were depicted as outside the mainstream, well beyond what polite company was prepared to accept as respectable conservatism. His ideas on domestic politics were treated as a throwback to Calvin Coolidge on one day and to Herbert Hoover on the next. On international affairs, he was likened to John Foster Dulles, the champion of the cold war, only in far more dangerous times.

Not surprisingly, this assessment of Reagan was shared by a large part of the journalistic community, whose views generally parallel those of the intelligentsia. Yet, by most accounts, Reagan did not initially receive an unusually hostile press, and it was often charged that he was given a "free ride." Two opinions prevalent at the time among members of the fourth estate help account for this possible restraint relative to their real sentiments. First, many journalists believed they had played—and were perceived to have played—a key role in bringing down the previous two or three administrations. They were reluctant to put themselves in this position again, not merely from concern for the stability of the republic but from fear of a reaction against the press. Second, many in the press corps were convinced that Reagan was so incompetent and out of touch with reality that the administration would quickly fail of its own accord, without the need of the press to supply a gentle adversarial nudge.

Let us now turn to why Reagan was able to improve his standing with the public during this period, making use of the three factors cited that help account for the President's approval score. Usually the most important determinant is the public's assessment of the conditions of reality. Yet this factor does not operate in the initial period in the usual way or with the usual force. Indeed, what makes the initial period unique is that the real-world situation is not held against the new President, especially if he has replaced a President from the other party. Conditions are the responsibility of the previous administration—hence the inverted rhetorical situation that sometimes occurs in this period in which the President stresses how bad things are, while his foes say how good they are.

Even though a new President is not held accountable for what is going on, there is nevertheless a set of perceived conditions that form the context in which he operates. With interest rates and inflation running at an unprecedentedly high level at this time, the American people saw the economic situation in dire terms, amounting to a feeling of genuine crisis. No doubt this resulted in part from the fact that the main economic problem was acute inflation, an evil that breeds an almost universal uncertainty. But it went beyond this. The 1970s had witnessed a collapse of many of the major precepts of macroeconomic theory. As the consequences of this collapse filtered down to the level of mass politics, they were expressed in terms of a growing feeling, endorsed by many politicians, that basic economic problems were beyond political control. This sentiment, bordering on fatalism, spilled over to views about the capacity and efficacy of the political system, which at the time was experiencing difficulties of its own. Government, it was thought, could do nothing; the system was permanently stalemated.

Ronald Reagan had run for the Presidency against this general view, which he attributed to the prevailing liberal public philosophy. And in no small measure his victory was a result of his aligning the Republican party with the fundamental American belief in the possibility of progress. Yet Reagan's election obviously did no more than provide a glimmer of hope in the prevailing mood of pessimism. On assuming office, the administration did not seek to downplay or deny the severity of the economic situation, but to confirm and embrace it, making a crisis the central perceived reality. Some Reagan strategists had suggested declaring an "economic Dunkirk"; Reagan stopped just short, telling Americans in his first television address, "We're in the worst economic mess since the Great Depression."[10]

Reagan "used" this crisis to establish a test, not only of his economic theories, but of his general political views as well. The economic crisis, he argued, reflected a misguided public philosophy regarding the proper role of the federal government. Many had come to expect too much of the federal government, to look to it for policies of positive action to cope with all the major areas of societal activity and to resolve every social problem: "Just conceiving of a program to help someone somewhere was itself reason enough to pass a law and appropriate money. . . . Congress had more solutions than the country had problems."[11]

This policy-making state, Reagan contended, would not work. It extracted too great a share of the national wealth, creating a drag on the real sources of economic growth; it produced an attitude of dependency on the federal government that in the public realm inhibited activity by citizens at the state and local levels and in the private realm stifled entrepreneurial creativity. It produced ineffective government by loading too much on a political structure never designed to be used for extensive social planning. To succeed, government had to attempt less in the way of programs and policies. It had to retrench and simplify.

Yet Reagan's call for less policy making was decidedly not a plea for less political responsibility. To the contrary, Reagan asserted that the economic crisis was resolvable by the decisions of elected officials. At a time when many had been attempting to decouple political responsibility from economic performance, Reagan emphasized their intimate connection, making the state of the economy the centerpiece and test of his whole philosophy of government. He mortgaged the political to the economic because, for him, the economic crisis itself reflected—indeed was part and parcel of—a crisis in political theory.

A President operating strategically is interested in instruments that will help him achieve his objectives. General public approval is widely thought to be one such tool. But other forms of public opinion are more strategically effective because they can translate more readily into usable levers. In particular, a public conviction that there is a crisis, especially at a time when the President is not responsible for it but is newly armed to master the situation, is one of the best aids to strong leadership.

It is here that mention must be made of the Reagan mandate. For certain commentators, it is important to establish the precise policies people favored at the moment they voted in November 1980. After analyzing postelection polls, the political scientist James Q. Wilson was undoubtedly correct in concluding that "when [Reagan] took office the only mandate he had was to be different from his predecessor."[12] Yet, as Charles Jones has pointed out, if the focus is on presidential leadership, it no longer matters what the mandate was, but how it is interpreted at the time a President wants to make use of it. It is the contemporaneous interpretation of the mandate that counts most. As House Speaker Thomas P. ("Tip") O'Neill conceded, "The record *shows* there was no mandate, but Congress thinks there's one and is acting in that manner."[13] In the end, even this interpretation of the mandate was made in the light of the economic crisis Reagan had defined.

Was there magic or brilliance in the administration's actions? If so, it certainly did not consist in creating something from nothing. Ronald Reagan's speeches did not make the crisis of 1981. John Kennedy, scarcely the inferior to Reagan as a communicator, could not stop talking of a crisis after his election in 1961. But he was hard pressed to say exactly what the nature of that crisis was or to persuade Americans that one existed. Words cannot a reality make. What Reagan can be credited for—and this is no small part of political prudence—is taking advantage of an existing opportunity. In the parlance of Shakespeare, "There is a tide in the affairs of men which, taken at the flood, leads on to fortune." In the parlance of contemporary policy analysts, there is a "window" which, when left ajar, may be thrust open and everything pushed through it. This is the strategy the administration employed.

The second factor that accounts for the President's support score is the public's assessment of the performance of the President and the administration. Contrary to the many predictions of ineptitude, the administration initially proved to be highly skilled in proposing and then pushing through its domestic program of budget and tax cuts. Some critics attempted to give the credit to the President's advisers rather than the President, who was only recognized for his excellent speechmaking performances. Still, the President could not help but derive some benefit from this situation.

This assessment of skill was all the more striking in light of the widespread belief that the government was stalemated. The administration showed that decisive action was possible, a point expressed in the unusual banner headlines in newspapers at the time proclaiming a policy "revolution." Whatever people might have thought of the revolution's economic consequences (some believed it reckless) or its immediate impact on their lives (many argued that it sought to resolve the nation's economic problems at the expense of the poor), there could be no question that the political initiative lay with the President. For a time, this kept many Reagan opponents uncertain and astounded, occupied in watching the results.

The final factor is the public assessment of the President's persona, or his personal qualities. Students of presidential character have provided lists of the important attributes for which a President may be praised or blamed, including honesty, piety, compassion, competence, vision, and strength. Some of these qualities have never been much at issue in Reagan's case. What is of interest here are the attributes that have been emphasized in the public debate, either by the President's detractors or supporters.

The President's critics have emphasized three negative aspects of his persona. The first is a lack of compassion and an indifference to the poor and underprivileged. Although often directed at the administration's policies, this charge has frequently spilled over into an attack on the President's character.

The second criticism has charged that Reagan is doctrinaire, rigid, and ideological. For many, being a "right-wing conservative" is synonymous with being doctrinaire. But it becomes a charge of inadequacy of character when used to suggest an incapacity to see facts as they are or to make the necessary accommodations that are part of the art of governing.

Finally, Ronald Reagan has been said to lack the intellect and energy to run the government. Not to put too fine a point on it, he is incompetent. A polite way of making this criticism was to refer to the "age issue." Ronald Reagan is old today—he is seventy-seven at this writing—but we are apt to forget that he was already widely discounted as too old when he ran for the Presidency in 1976. The age issue, however, was most important for what it was intended to suggest about the President's other inadequacies. It was not that Ronald Reagan chose to run the government with a hands-off or laid-back style; it was that he lacked the intelligence to do anything more. He had to be programmed by his aides, told what to say and how to proceed. His administration was a cue card or puppet Presidency.

The aspects of persona that worked in Reagan's favor were, first, his "common touch." Ronald Reagan in many respects possesses the model American personality: open, likeable, devoid of presumption. Even those who hate him have trouble truly disliking him. (Only once in his fifty-four films did he play a villain, and the movie was a complete flop.) Reagan has the knack, as Eisenhower did, not to offend by pomposity, yet never to disgrace by an affected populism.

A second character attribute for which Reagan was admired was his honest dedication to his basic political convictions. Even those who feared or hated these convictions seemed to accept that they were honestly held. Reagan was seldom accused by his opponents of simple opportunism or of being a mere "politician." To his followers, this conviction made Reagan a leader of vision, clearsighted in what he wanted to do with government.

A final favorable character attribute was the impression Reagan gave of strength, decisiveness, and toughness as a leader. Of the personal qualities measured in the 1980 presidential campaign, strong leadership was the aspect on which Reagan scored best in comparison to Jimmy Carter.[14] While this result was conceivably as much a reflection on Carter as on Reagan, as time went on Reagan as President was able to demonstrate these qualities on his own. It is clear that decisiveness is in tension with, although not exactly the opposite of, incompetence, and some of the major battles over Reagan's persona during his Presidency focused on the conflict between these two qualities. Reagan's decisiveness, when it proved effective, pushed charges of incompetence into the background. If people recognized his lapses, they saw them as largely irrelevant to his being a good leader and even as a sign of an endearing detachment. By contrast, when Reagan's fortunes were low, charges of incompetence loomed much larger and nearly overwhelmed his reputation for decisiveness.

Developments during the takeoff period served on balance to enhance the President's standing. True, the Reagan economic program fueled charges of a lack of compassion, and it was widely rumored that he dozed at cabinet meetings. But three events clearly contributed to a more positive assessment of his persona.

The first was the assassination attempt in March 1981, which very nearly took the President's life. This tragic event gave Reagan the admiration that goes to those who, like decorated soldiers, have sacrificed for their country. Lacking a war record, Reagan never enjoyed this kind of acclaim. His rise in national politics was based on his advocacy of certain political views, which did nothing to win him the esteem of those who did not share his beliefs. The assassination attempt changed this. A bond formed between the American people and Ronald Reagan that went beyond partisanship. For many, Reagan went into the hospital a Republican and emerged a President. He had, moreover, acted with such undeniable warmth and grace under pressure that David Broder of the *Washington Post* wrote, "In the hours after his own life was threatened, he elevated those appealing human qualities to the level of legend." The memory of Reagan in the hospital, Broder went on, would make it impossible for anyone to "portray Reagan as a cruel or callous or heartless man."[15]

Next was the enactment, already noted, of Reagan's economic program. A President is never so much admired as when he is successful. The resulting impression of Reagan as a strong and decisive leader, buoyed by the frequent comparisons in the media of Reagan to Franklin Roosevelt, made charges of incompetence appear ungenerous and carping.

Finally, there was the President's action in the PATCO strike in August, when the administration fired and refused to rehire air traffic controllers who had walked out in an illegal strike. This event was crucial in forming a lasting image of the President's toughness. The situation was tailor-made for presidential action. Still, given the prevailing view of government's incapacity to act, few thought that a President could resolve the situation quickly. The display of firmness and resolution left David Broder satisfied and amazed: "The message is getting around: don't mess with this guy. Whatever gets in his way, he tries to break."[16] Another *Post* commentator, Haynes Johnson, also came away with the conclusion that Reagan was a strong leader, perhaps too strong: "He was firm, he was decisive . . . [but] a dash of compassion, a display of a generosity of spirit, are also welcome, but absent now." Johnson wondered, as Soviet leaders must have, "how he will respond if faced with a direct, and dangerous, foreign challenge."[17]

A "strategic" assessment of Reagan's "public Presidency" in the takeoff period must evaluate how effectively the administration used public opinion to achieve its goals. Reagan's economic program, on its own terms, constituted an important step toward his goal of a more limited role for the federal government. The public perception of a crisis served as a powerful lever in pressuring Congress to accept his program, as did Reagan's specific appeals on behalf of his legislation. In this sense the President used public opinion strategically to achieve his ends. Furthermore, setting forth the case for the economic program provided Reagan with an ideal platform to articulate his domestic public philosophy and set it up as a reality test for future events. Even if people did not accept his views, they now knew the direction of his thoughts.

The seeds of a major public opinion controversy that would plague the rest of Reagan's Presidency were sown during this period. Reagan set forth his major premise of limited government, to be achieved by tax cuts and spending reductions. But, for fear of losing the main point, he did not insist on a minor premise that would force spending cuts into reasonable balance with overall government revenues. The door was thus left open to a President and a public opinion that could tolerate large deficits.

Finally, even though Reagan launched a major defense buildup, he did little to articulate the foreign policy component of his public philosophy. Although it may have been wise to focus the public's limited attention on domestic affairs, there was still a price to be paid. Foreign policy lay outside the "Reagan Revolution," a dimension unto itself. In contrast to his economic program, he established no real-world test to prove the validity of his view of international relations.

Period Two: Decline

The period of decline began in the autumn of 1981 when President Reagan's approval rating fell below the initial point from which he had engineered his takeoff. By the spring of 1982, more people disapproved than approved of his job performance, and by the midterm election, Reagan stood lower than any

President at a similar time since Truman. After the election, his approval rating fell still further, reaching its nadir in the winter of 1983 at an anemic 35 percent approval score. Not until late in the summer of 1983 did Reagan enjoy a genuine recovery of public confidence.

A statistical portrait does not begin to convey the depth of the President's difficulties. From the euphoria of the days of the Reagan Revolution, with its expectations of an ideological sea change and a political realignment, the drop was dramatic. By the summer of 1982, many analysts concluded that another single-term Presidency was all but inevitable. It was widely predicted that Reagan would not seek a second term, largely to save himself from acute embarrassment. Hypothetical match-ups for the presidential election showed Reagan to be in serious trouble, trailing, for example, Senator Edward Kennedy.[18] By January 1983, the "failed Presidency model" was being invoked in full force. For the *New York Times,* in a lead editorial entitled "The Failing Presidency," the point was expressed with a powerful olfactory metaphor: "The stench of failure hangs over Ronald Reagan's White House."[19] Not to be outdone, David Broder wrote: "What we are witnessing this January is not the mid-point in the Reagan Presidency, but its phase out. Reaganism, it's becoming increasingly clear, was a one-year phenomenon."[20] "Phase out," "failure," "end"—a myriad of such terms could be found in the analyses of Presidency watchers of the day.

The President's decline can be accounted for, first, by the public's assessment of the conditions of reality. The overwhelming fact was the onset, beginning in mid-1981, of what would turn out to be the deepest economic recession in decades. A downturn of this magnitude would have caused difficulty for any President, but it was all the more damaging to President Reagan because of his predictions of immediate success. Indeed, the President hoped that the passage of his program would itself produce a surge in economic confidence, a position that led him in the late summer of 1981 to play cheerleader to the economy's flagging prospect: "I hope the people on Wall Street will pay attention to the people on Main Street. If they do, they will see there is a rising tide of confidence in the future of America."

The facts began to speak otherwise. And as they did so, there was a rapid drop in public confidence in the President's economic program, and the administration became increasingly vulnerable on the so-called fairness issue. From the outset, when critics had attacked the social justice of Reagan's program in relation to the poor and disadvantaged, his response had been that "a rising tide lifts all boats" and that a strong economy was the best welfare program. That "welfare" program was now clearly in jeopardy.

The public's assessment of conditions, we have said, is a function of what people see, feel, and experience for themselves, and of interpretations and images supplied by recognized speakers. On questions of economic performance, people's own experiences will weigh very heavily, for here people have direct contact with the essential facts. Interpretations, if they are to have any plausibility, must begin from a set of conditions that people recognize, even when a speaker attempts to convince people that conditions are not as they appear.

When a President is in this rhetorical situation, especially when he can plausibly be held accountable for the prevailing conditions, he will, at a minimum, suffer the fate of becoming one voice among many, losing his usual position as the nation's principal speaker. After all, when reality appears to differ from the President's portrayal, the public is likely to give greater attention to interpretations by "objective" analysts and by the President's opponents. At a certain point, if conditions continue blatantly to confute the administration's interpretation, a President not only loses the initiative with the public but risks the destruction of his credibility as well. Even though it is the perceived reality of conditions more than rhetorical joustings that determine approval ratings, a President's performance under such trying circumstances affects his capacity to recover support.

President Reagan's response to the new economic conditions was threefold. First, he began to concede, as of November 1981, that there was a recession, but he predicted a turnaround by the first half of 1982. When the turnaround did not occur, he was reduced to repeating the same predictions, constantly moving back the moment of recovery. By December 1982, he was saying, "I am convinced this coming year, 1983, is going to see a definite upturn."[21]

His second response was to attempt to draw a "balanced picture" of the economy, pointing to the reduction in inflation and interest rates. But this argument left the impression that these positive developments resulted from the recession and might vanish with a recovery. Moreover, enduring a recession to squeeze out inflation—the so-called old-time religion—had never been a part of the new supply-side theories of economics that Reagan had been propounding.

Finally, President Reagan argued that the basic responsibility for the recession lay not with his program but with the misguided theories and practices of the previous era of liberalism. Problems that had their origin in years of wrong-headed policies could not be solved overnight. This argument evidently had at least some resonance, as a majority throughout 1982 continued to believe that while the economic program was not working in the short run, it nevertheless would prove itself in the long run.[22] This glimmer of support, referred to as the public's "pool of patience," was a source of wonderment, even to some of the President's aides. The steep decline the President experienced in January 1983 may have been a sign that the pool was drying up, ironically just as the first indications of a recovery were about to appear.

In this troubled time, the President's general strategy hardly served to make him look very effective, and the rhetorical initiative lay almost entirely with the President's foes and the nominally objective Presidency watchers. The derisive term "Reaganomics" now made its appearance and became synonymous with all the injustice and misery his enemies attributed to his economic policies.

Was there, however, a silver lining for the President in the unceasing torrent of criticism? Perhaps. Attributing the recession fully to Reaganomics meant that for whatever happened afterward, the President could take credit. If it had been Reagan's recession, it would be his recovery. Only one fact could have prevented this: if the President had seemed to abandon his program. While he did allow certain modifications, amounting to a midcourse correction, it was always the original program that was seen to be in effect. Reagan stuck to his program, not only during the 1982 congressional campaign with its theme of "staying the course," but afterward as well. By January, there was tremendous pressure to abandon it, from both inside and outside the administration. According to Martin Plissner, the political director of CBS News: "In holding on to the tax cut and defense increases, Reagan has set himself against not only the Democratic but much of the Republican leadership in Congress as well as the private convictions of many people in his own White House." The *New York Times* intoned: "All factions share an obligation to force the President to lead in devising a new and credible plan for recovery."[23] The *Times*'s alternative plan was based on a sharp cut in military spending and a cancellation of the last phase of the tax cut, positions that the polls now showed had the support of the American public.[24]

People's assessment of the conditions of foreign affairs during the period of decline was no more favorable than their assessment of domestic affairs. The only solace to the administration may have been that the problems seemed slightly more removed. Foreign affairs, except in times of war or crisis, are further from people's immediate daily experience than economic matters. It follows, in analyzing public opinion in this area, that more weight must be given to the influence of interpretations and images supplied by the various speakers in the dialogue on the public Presidency.

Two powerful interpretive paradigms of foreign affairs were at work in the public arena when Ronald Reagan took office. Each found expression in the views of distinct groups, but both could be seen operating, as conflicting tendencies, in the minds of most Americans. On one side, there was a belief that the United States had recently lost power, respect, and prestige in the world, a condition epitomized by the national humiliation of the Iranian seizure of hostages in 1979. More broadly, it was held that the Soviet threat to our security was growing and that our foreign policy had to show more firmness and a greater readiness to employ military force and to support its use by America's allies.

The other view harkened back to the peace movements of the previous decade. In stark contrast to the position described above, this view saw the disposition to use military force as what was morally wrong in American foreign policy and what was likely to lead the United States into war. This combined appeal to morality and fear undergirded the opposition to a "hard-line" approach. But in contrast to the spirit that prevailed in the peace movements of the 1960s and 1970s, the peace advocates of the 1980s seldom preached that the United States was the *fundamental* source of wrong in the world. Curiously, this less moralistic posture put a greater onus on the United States in its relationship with the Soviet Union, for as the more enlightened and mature of the two superpowers, America had to make allowances for Soviet short-sightedness.

President Reagan sought, as part of his anticipated change of America's public philosophy, to move national public opinion toward the first view. As he would later put it, "Military force, either direct or indirect, must remain an available part of America's foreign policy . . . we will not return to the days of defeatism, decline, and despair."[25] But he quickly met resistance on two fronts.

First, in seeking aid for the government of El Salvador in its war against leftist rebels, Reagan ran into a maelstrom of criticism. Assistance to El Salvador became the focal point in 1981 and 1982 for opposition to the administration's alleged "belligerence" in the conduct of foreign affairs. Reagan's critics warned that our involvement in El Salvador (and later Nicaragua) would lead to "another Vietnam." Administration officials complained of an enervating Vietnam syndrome, but despite repeated attempts, President Reagan could never establish in the public mind a firm consensus in favor of significant military support for anticommunist forces in Central America. Indeed, years later—this time in relationship to aid for the *contras* in Nicaragua—President Reagan was still struggling to win the same argument, and his inability to carry the day was an important part of the background to the Iran-*contra* affair of 1986-87.[26]

The second area of opposition was to Reagan's nuclear arms position. Reagan argued that a nuclear build-up was a precondition for any future program of control. The old criticism that Reagan was an inflexible cold warrior reappeared in the charge that his policy might lead the United States into a nuclear war. A new mass movement spread across Western Europe and the United States, calling for an immediate freeze on nuclear armaments. It was the most powerful grass-roots movement of the past decade. The *New York Times* columnist Tom Wicker described it as an "instrument for mobilizing the millions of Americans profoundly disturbed at what they consider the likely prospect of nuclear war, and for bringing their pressures to bear on [the] administration's strategic policy."[27]

President Reagan opposed an immediate nuclear freeze, but the idea gained increasing support among the people and in Congress. Reagan sought to take the initiative in a speech in which he called for the elimination of all intermediate range nuclear missiles in Europe—the zero-option plan. (This proposal became the basis for the INF Treaty signed at the Washington summit in December 1987.) At the time, however, the President's opponents in the freeze movement found the President's plan both implausible and inadequate. Senator Edward Kennedy accused the President of practicing "voodoo arms control"; Paul Warnke, writing in the New York Times, argued that "a rigid insistence on the zero option is not likely to bring reductions in the Soviet nuclear threat [but rather] bring suspicion that America is not serious in controlling nuclear arms."[28]

Finding himself ever more on the defensive on the issues of Central America and nuclear arms, Reagan nevertheless pressed on in his warnings against the threats, moral and physical, posed by communism. Near the end of the period of decline, Reagan uttered what was perhaps the most controversial phrase of any of his speeches. In an address to the National Association of Evangelicals on 8 March 1983, Reagan urged religious leaders to avoid a moral posture of indifference between the two superpowers and to pay heed to "the facts of history and the aggressive impulses of an evil empire." For the mention of an "evil empire"—taken from George Lucas's Star Wars—Reagan was widely condemned for injecting a theological moralism into politics.

The second general factor that accounts for the approval rating is the public's assessment of the performance of the President and his administration. The period of decline opened with many questioning the administration's once-vaunted skill and professionalism in handling policy formulation. The first indication of difficulty came at the end of the summer of 1981 when the administration, shortly after the passage of the originial economic program, came back to ask Congress for more cuts, thus conceding that its projections had been incorrect. Even though the President eventually would prevail again in the legislative arena, the immediate impact of introducing the second plan was to erode the perception of executive competence.

Far more damaging were the revelations of David Stockman in November 1981. Stockman, the young director of the Office of Management and Budget, had been the mastermind behind much of the economic program, winning an inordinate amount of credit from those who had an interest in promoting the notion that the President was a mere figurehead. Stockman's national reputation was such that what he said could not be lightly dismissed. In a series of interviews with *Washington Post* reporter William Greider, Stockman revealed that the economic projections of the Reagan program were based on figures "cooked" to produce the desired results. The tax plan, he implied, was devised chiefly to help the wealthy.[29]

As the administration's aura of skill and professionalism began to wear off, so too did Reagan's reputation as the "great communicator." The political scientist Fred Greenstein, writing in the *New York Times,* observed that "Reagan, the rhetorical paragon fluently following his teleprompter . . . has a lot to learn about being persuasive from Dwight David Eisenhower, who is remembered for bumbling public utterances. . . . Ike at mid-term had 68 percent approval, Ronald Reagan, 41 percent."[30] Critics who had attributed Reagan's success to his rhetoric were now content to attribute his failures to his policies.

By the time of Black January, the attacks on the administration's performance were scathing. According to Anthony Lewis, "Two years into the Reagan Presidency, Americans are beginning to suspect the awful truth: they have a government incompetent to govern, an Administration spotted with fools and rogues . . . [engaged in a] pattern of evasion and ineptitude."[31] According to David Broder, "Less and less an effort is made to pretend that Ronald Reagan is managing . . . decisions on a day by day basis. . . . [He is] probably the most detached President that has served in that office in a long, long time."[32]

These columnists, although clearly expressing their own views, were also reporting a consensus within the press corps. The press reported that the President had lost command not only of Congress but of his own administration as well. This view was accepted by a majority in the nation; a striking 56 percent agreed with the statement that Reagan was "losing control of what's going on in his administration."[33]

The criticisms of the administration spilled over into attacks on the President's character and persona. The President was accused of lacking compassion. A question posed to him at a news conference in March 1982 repeated the charge of the "rich man's President" in connection with a vacation trip to Barbados. Yet the sharpest attacks by far were reserved for Nancy Reagan. One can dip almost at random into the press of the day and find such items as the 24 March 1982 cover of the *New Republic,* which depicted Mrs. Reagan with the headline "Let Them Eat Cake." The implications of such coverage were that the Reagans and their friends were living it up at the White House, at Camp David, and at the Santa Barbara ranch, while America's poor suffered from the budget cuts the President had ordered in his "War on the Poor."

A second attack focused on the dimension of ideological inflexibility. According to Anthony Lewis, Americans "have a President frozen in ideological fantasy-land. . . . Rigidity is a large part of the explanation. . . . The denial of reality immobilizes him. . . ."[34] David Broder added that Reagan's sole concern was "how the measures they [his advisers] were recommending could be reconciled with his promises of 1980-81 and the simplistic rhetoric of his thirty years on the conservative banquet circuit."[35]

The portrayal of the President-in-fantasy-land image was also meant to add fuel to the old charge that Reagan was incompetent and ill equipped to run his administration. Yet there was a slight problem with this criticism. The original incompetence charge had been that the President could not think without direction from his staff and thus, puppetlike, had to follow his advisers. (This image was the one that detractors emphasized when things seemed to be going well, for it minimized the personal credit that might accrue to the President.) Now the charge was that Reagan stubbornly refused to do what his advisers wanted and insisted they follow him. (This was obviously the preferred line of attack when things were going poorly, for it maximized the blame that could be attributed to the President.) However effective the fantasy-land charge proved to be at the time, it nonetheless prepared the ground for a reversal, by leaving the impression that the President in his own curious way was running the show. Depicted as a kind of Don Quixote, madly tilting at windmills, Reagan was his own man with his own vision of the world. And what if the windmills turned out to be giants?[36]

A strategic assessment of Reagan's relation to the American public in the period of decline may challenge conventional views of the value of presidential popularity. Even though Reagan was at his low point, with failed-Presidency rhetoric echoing all around him, it does not follow that, from a strategic standpoint, he lost much. On the domestic side, he neither proposed nor needed important new programs to promote his basic goals. Thus, even if one accepts the (questionable) assumption that a high level of public approval is needed to win support for a major new program, the value of popularity is far less when no new initiatives are needed. A minimal level of popular support—which Reagan nearly lost—may be helpful in warding off the threat of having one's opponents impose an alternative agenda, but a high approval rate in a period such as this may be a luxury a President can do without.

In foreign affairs, greater presidential popularity might have been of some help to Reagan in achieving more assistance for El Salvador and for moving the nation toward his basic goal of establishing the foreign policy tenets of his public philosophy. Yet even in later periods, when Reagan enjoyed a high approval rating, he has never been able to establish a broad consensus for his Central American policies. Nor can personal popularity enable a President to alter beliefs on matters of public philosophy without any accompanying demonstration in the real world.

This is the period when Reagan's prowess as the great communicator came under the most intense questioning. And yet from a strategic perspective this may be the period when his speechmaking proved most valuable in promoting his goals, even if it served to help drive down his overall approval rating. One usually associates the "great communicator" epithet with a picture of the President scoring a smashing victory aided by speeches that command the public's adherence. Yet no amount of rhetoric, it seemed, could then have produced such a victory, given the existing state of the public mind. The real danger for Reagan during this period was that he would have been forced by opposition to abandon El Salvador and yield to the demands of the nuclear freeze movement. His speeches were one component of a strategy to help stave off these defeats. He pitted his rhetoric against the prevailing tide of public opinion, and if he did not win, neither was he compelled to abandon his broader objectives.

Period Three: Restoration

The period of restoration began in the summer of 1983 when, for the first time in more than a year, as many Americans approved as disapproved of President Reagan's performance. By the fall of 1983, this renewed level of support was being regularly confirmed in the polls. Reagan ended the year with an approval rating of over 50 percent, as high as it had been since the end of his takeoff period. He maintained this level through the campaign and until after his reelection.

Statistically, this was a period of restoration; morally, it was a period of vindication. As the economy improved, Reagan was in a position to claim "I told you so," without necessarily having to say it. The entire dialogue on the Presidency underwent a stunning reversal, which had been prepared for in part by the rhetorical strategies of the previous period. Reagan emerged as a statesman of vision, while his opponents found themselves more and more on the defensive, wedded to a pessimism increasingly at odds with the mood of the American people.

As in the previous period, the public's assessment of the performance of the economy had the greatest impact on the President's approval score. In early 1983, economic indices began to show signs of an upturn, and by the end of June, Reagan modestly declared that the nation was "making headway against the crisis we inherited." Now it was the President who reminded the public that he had stood fast against demands to cancel the third year of the tax cut.[37]

The improvement in the economy became apparent in the fall of 1983, and the public attitude toward Reagan's handling of the economy underwent a sudden change. Just as suddenly, the President's general approval rating improved.[38]

Now it was the President's opponents who faced the uphill task of trying to convince the public that economic conditions were not what they seemed to be, or what they could or should be. Their efforts at interpretation, which continued throughout the election campaign, included some of the following arguments: that the recovery was nonexistent; that the poor and unemployed were still bearing an unacceptable burden; that we were far behind where we would have been without the recession; that the huge deficits would abort the recovery; that the recovery, if it existed, owed nothing to Reagan's bizarre economic theories, but could be explained in more traditional terms; and finally that, to the extent there was a recovery, it was due to the midcourse correction of 1982 forced on the President. While charges of "unfairness" continued to resonate, the other arguments proved less convincing, increasingly so as the recovery gained momentum.

Reagan's vindication on his economic policy, at least as far as the public was concerned, came in the 1984 election. In explaining the results of the election, Gallup put it this way: "Reagan backers this year cited his economic policies as their main reason for choosing him."[39]

The public's assessment of foreign affairs also underwent a change that worked in Reagan's favor. Two events helped turn the tide. The first was the Soviet attack on Korean Air Line flight 007 in September 1983. The effect of this attack was to render less implausible Reagan's characterization of the Soviet Union as an "evil empire." In contrast to the nuclear arms race, for which critics could somehow hold the President responsible, the shooting down of the KAL could not be placed at Reagan's doorstep. Reagan characterized the tragedy as the product of leaders "who reject our ideals and who disregard individual rights and the value of human life."[40] A majority of American (54 percent) saw the destruction of the plane as "typical Soviet behavior."[41]

The KAL tragedy was followed by Reagan's decision to send U.S. troops to the island of Grenada. The sight of American soldiers being welcomed by frightened U.S. medical students on the island and by a grateful local population made a powerful impression on the American populace. Unlike the dismal scenes of the Vietnam war, here was a visible example showing that the use of military force was not always evil or unwelcome. Reagan saw the invasion as a potential catalyst for transforming American public opinion in foreign affairs, putting an end to the Vietnam syndrome. "Under this administration," Reagan told an audience in South Carolina, "this nation is through with hand-wringing." Hopes for a lasting transformation were misplaced, but there is no doubt that the Grenada invasion gave the Reagan administration's general view of foreign policy a much needed boost. The American people approved of the President's decision, the more so as time went on and criticisms became fewer and less strident.[42]

Along with the public's positive assessment of the prevailing conditions in the economy and foreign affairs, there emerged in 1984 an almost euphoric interpretation of the nature of the times. This interpretation, in large part the result of a spontaneous conclusion drawn by people from their own encounter with events, was encouraged by the President and his public relations strategists. The character of this period cannot be grasped without considering this new mood.

President Reagan's personal restoration was accompanied by a remarkable transformation in the public's level of confidence. Gallup polls had for several years been measuring how satisfied people felt with the way things were going in the United States. The percentage of Americans expressing satisfaction stood at 33 percent shortly after Reagan's inauguration in 1981 and in the mid-20s throughout 1982. By August of 1983, when the period of restoration began, 35 percent were satisfied, and by February 1984, the figure soared to 50 percent. As Seymour Martin Lipset wrote: "The cynicism about politics that so marked the Johnson, Nixon, Ford, Carter, and early Reagan years seems almost like a bad memory. Magazine after magazine, newspaper and TV stories emphasize a rebirth of patriotism, of belief in the nation."[43]

Not only did Reagan, as President, benefit from this change, but he could also claim a special credit for it. More than anyone else, he had bet on America, even when his optimism had become an object of ridicule and when others were prepared to surrender to a more modest view of America's possibilities. Reagan's vision had triumphed. In the glossy PR theme for the 1984 campaign it was "Morning Again in America."

Indeed, America was "back." Hardly a television commercial was made that did not in some way celebrate America. It was a period of an exuberant, if somewhat infantile, patriotism of celebration of the triumphs in Grenada and at the Olympic games in Los Angeles. Never mind that the deeds did not always quite measure up to the words, that the Grenada invasion had defeated no great army and that the Olympic victories had taken place without Soviet competition. After years of frustration and humiliation, none of this mattered. It was Ronald Reagan, apple pie, and the American dream. Unable to resist this powerful tide of feeling good about America, the Democratic party at the final session of its national convention had each person in the hall wave a small American flag. But somehow everyone could sense that, for the moment, it was Ronald Reagan's banner.

The next factor—the performance of the President and the administration —also worked on balance to the President's advantage. Although there were few important legislative victories, neither were there the outright embarrassments that marked the last period. The decision to place troops in Lebanon may have been ill considered, but the President proved flexible enough to cut his losses by eventually withdrawing the American contingent. The administration's hesitancy and vacillation was counterbalanced by the decisive action in Grenada.

With all these successes, the image of Reagan's relationship to his own administration began to change. The President was now seen to be stronger than his advisers. The cause of the administration's success was not them, but him. True, he was laid back and had an easy management style. But now he was seen in the ultimate sense to be in charge, admittedly in his own loose way.

The final factor that helps explain the President's approval score is the public's assessment of his persona. The period of restoration is instructive in illustrating the significance of persona because of the close scrutiny it receives during an election campaign.

First, it is evident that certain aspects of character are decidedly more important than others. Ronald Reagan, although managing to avoid the impression of outright contempt for the poor, never fared well on the attribute of personal compassion. His opponent, Walter Mondale, scored far better than the President on this point. Yet on the attribute of strength, Reagan was the clear favorite.[44] It would appear that even in the modern age, when compassion has figured so prominently in American political rhetoric (especially for Democrats), it does not count nearly so much in people's final judgment as decisiveness as a leader. Indeed, there is probably a grain of truth in some of the "pop psychology" later used to explain the election result. Ronald Reagan was the tough cowboy; Walter Mondale was the caring and sensitive man of compassion. In the end, the Americans preferred the "tougher" candidate.

Second, it is clear that assessments of a President's persona are colored by people's judgments of real-world conditions and by presidential performance. This is true because the attributes that loom largest in assessing character, such as decisiveness and competence, are certain to be influenced by a President's record in running the country. The same attributes somehow appear different in a President according to whether conditions turn out well or poorly—a fact that differentiates the assessments of the President's persona from that of other presidential candidates. It follows that since success in managing affairs can "improve" a President's character, a shrewd President must be willing to sacrifice a good reputation on character attributes that, although judged praiseworthy in themselves, do not help him achieve effective results. This is why a President will find it useful to be feared even before he is loved.[45]

Finally, even though an incumbent's record colors the perception of his persona, his character nevertheless manifests itself independently of his record. The presidential debates of 1984, which were showcases for the candidates' personae, illustrate this point. Before the debates, Reagan enjoyed a great advantage on the dimension of strong leadership, but a stumbling and incoherent performance in the first debate immediately rekindled the "age" issue and provided fuel for Mondale's charge that Reagan had been providing "leadership by amnesia." Reagan's critics now attempted selectively to uncouple his record from his persona, arguing that his successes were the result of good fortune or the advice of others. It took a comeback of sorts by Reagan in the second debate to quiet these doubts and allow the previous view of his character to reassert itself.[46]

A strategic assessment of Reagan's use of public opinion during the restoration period must take into account the context of the ensuing presidential election. In this setting, presidential approval becomes almost an end in itself, as no further objectives can be accomplished without being reelected. A President must cash in and take care that not too much approval is risked for long-term objectives at the expense of short-term support. By this criterion, Reagan's relationship with the American public at this time was managed effectively.

Nevertheless, the President was criticized, more often by supporters than opponents, for running a glossy election campaign based too much on vindication and personal popularity. The campaign, it was said, abandoned a strategic perspective. Not enough emphasis was placed on a harder, partisan appeal that might have laid the groundwork for a program in the years to come. True, Reagan made tax reform a key issue (and would later carry through on it), but he made little headway in establishing a consensus for resolving the budget deficit on his terms. In the President's defense, it may have been thought that a truly stunning victory would allow him to dictate terms after the election.

Period Four: Anointment

The anointment period began with Reagan's reelection and continued until the fall of 1986, with the initial revelation of the Iran-*contra* affair. The period of anointment represents a continuation of the positive trend of the past year and a half. But President Reagan's approval rating now clearly moves up a notch, to over 60 percent, with the exception of a three-month dip, associated with the controversial visit to Bitburg.

The public's attitude toward Reagan also changes. What was once a hypothesis (Reagan is back) is now a given. Ronald Reagan is identified with the Presidency as perhaps no other President in recent times. By the middle of his

fifth year in office, he is the most well-respected President at a comparable period since polling began, well surpassing Dwight Eisenhower. He is "King Reagan." And in the style of monarchies, while one may attack the ministers and
the policies of the government, the person of the king remains inviolate. This
"rule" was respected even more by Reagan's detractors than his defenders. Detractors discovered that the best way to neutralize Reagan's influence was not
to dispute his benevolence. People might love Ronald Reagan, but that implied
nothing about his policies.

Reagan's anointment was helped by a continuation of good times. According to *U.S. News and World Report,* "Poll after poll reflects the overall sense
of well-being, a high plateau in public opinion that has existed since 1984."
Two opinion analysts summed up the public's assessment of prevailing conditions. Wrote the Democratic pollster Peter Hart: "There's no sense of imminent danger, either from abroad or from any possible economic collapse." According to Seymour Martin Lipset, "People feel good about Reagan, and they
want to hear that the positive trends will continue. To them, Reagan is Dr.
Good News."[47]

And good news there was—for the most part. The economy continued
its steady growth. Yet there was dislocation in traditional manufacturing sectors and, by the end of 1985, a severe recession in farm states and oil states.
(This sectional recession was a key factor in the Republican's disastrous loss
of the Senate in the 1986 midterm elections.) The major economic problem,
however, was an abstract one: the huge federal budget deficit. It was a problem
that all politicians talked about and most citizens condemned. But, unlike earlier problems, such as inflation or unemployment, the deficit had no tangible
results that people could directly experience. The budget deficit was a statistic
interpreted by various speakers to be responsible for almost any economic ill
that appeared on the scene, from a dollar that was too strong (the complaint
in 1983) to a dollar that was too weak (the complaint in 1986).

In foreign affairs, there were no major crises during the period of anointment and nothing to remind one of the mass nuclear freeze movement in 1982
and 1983. The first Reagan summit with a Soviet leader, which took place in
Geneva at the end of 1985, led to hopes for serious arms control negotiations
and quieted opponents in the peace movement camp. Indeed, in the United
States the hysterical fear of nuclear war that marked the previous years van-
ished almost as quickly as it had appeared.[48] Anti-Reagan crusades now turned
their attention to attempting to establish U.S. responsibility for apartheid in
South Africa and the Marcos dictatorship in the Philippines.

Reagan also showed a continued willingness to use military force—as a
means now for dealing with terrorism. In April 1986 Reagan ordered an attack

on military targets in Libya in response to Libyan-sponsored terrorist acts. Critics branded Reagan a trigger-happy "Rambo" and predicted the raid would invite additional terrorist attacks. But the American public gave the President its decisive support, with 77 percent indicating approval.[49] Later in the summer, air power was used to force the landing of a plane carrying terrorists who had brutally slain an American citizen, Leon Klinghoffer. Reagan's tough warning to terrorists was, "You can run, but you can't hide." Nevertheless, Reagan had not always toed such an unyielding line. A year earlier, in July 1985, the administration was willing in effect to trade Palestinian prisoners held in Israel for the release of a planeload of Americans on TWA flight 847.

The period of anointment continued the positive, upbeat mood of the previous year. The celebration of America's "return" still ran strong, although somewhat in the vein of a party continuing too long. For those who had found the patriotism of 1984 offensive, that of 1985 must have appeared downright obnoxious. Distressed viewers of the film *Red Dawn* now had to suffer through a series of new Sylvester Stallone movies.

The performance of the President and the administration during this period began on a sour note. Shortly after the inauguration, Reagan agreed to visit a war cemetery in West Germany where some Nazi SS members had been buried. The preparations for the visit had been handled with no forethought given to this problem. What was to have been a triumphant state visit turned into a highly damaging incident, although one from which the President was able quickly to recover.

In his relationship with Congress, Reagan was unable in the aftermath of the election to force quick attention to the centerpiece of his domestic legislative program: tax reform. Indeed, no sooner was he firmly fixed in the stratosphere of 60 percent approval ratings than numerous stories in the media depicted Reagan as a lame duck, unable to control the legislative agenda. Some of this talk amounted to no more than a whispering campaign designed to diminish the President's reputation. But there was a measure of truth in the claim that Reagan in 1985 was in no way able to focus the nation's attention as he did in 1981, when he had a much lower approval rating.

The "problem" did not reflect a lack of skill on the part of the administration. Rather, tax reform was not the kind of issue that riveted the public's attention. As Thomas Mann said, "I've yet to see evidence of a groundswell for it out in the country—or even any real interest." Austin Ranney added that tax reform is "a very hard issue for the President to take to the country. It's very complicated. . . ."[50] In the end, more than a year later, Reagan got his tax reform bill, and for a few days he was once again hailed as the great master of the legislative process in a way reminiscent of the days after the Reagan Revolution. Yet, despite the possible historical significance of the bill, even after it passed, polls indicated that it never really made a big impression on public opinion.[51]

A final event that bore curiously on presidential performance was the second Reagan-Gorbachev summit, which took place in Iceland just before the 1986 election. Without going into details, at the close of the summit it appeared that the President and his advisers were caught wholly off guard by the meeting and indeed had made a serious tactical error in even agreeing to it. Initial reactions indicated that the event would prove the occasion for a new round of charges of presidential incompetence and an administration adrift. Sensing this possibility, the President, in an effort to snatch victory from the jaws of defeat, immediately moved to declare the meeting a great success. As no immediate, tangible results flowed from the summit, it was one of those events in which public perceptions are peculiarly susceptible to the "spin" interpretations of various speakers. And the President's version won, at least on the surface. The public's judgment of the Iceland summit shows one of the few pure uses of a high approval rating. A President in a weaker position would almost surely have been further weakened and placed on the defensive. A high approval rating entitles a President to a slight benefit of the doubt and is thus a modest insurance policy against a certain kind of stumble. But as the Iran arms affair shortly would show, not all stumbles are equal.

A strategic analysis of Reagan's "public Presidency" during the period of anointment indicates some of the assets and some of the limitations of public opinion as an instrument of power. Although Reagan's personal popularity was at an all-time high, it did not, as noted, translate into a capacity to drive the legislative agenda. Yet it does not follow that Reagan made poor use of his popularity, for in a strategic understanding of presidential power, the object is not to dominate the legislative agenda for its own sake but to move the legislative process in a direction important for one's goals. The major item that promoted Reagan's goal, tax reform, was not amenable to being pushed in a dramatic fashion by means of public persuasion and mobilization. This was all the more true because mobilization in 1985 and 1986 was not taking place, as in 1981, in the context of a perceived national crisis.

This analysis points up the limitations of a high approval rating and public persuasion as instruments of leadership. From a strategic perspective, however, the existence of such limits has no moral or normative connotations. There is no intrinsic reason for preferring public persuasion as a lever of power to other instruments, especially when those other instruments may be just as effective. While some celebrate the leadership model of a "rhetorical Presidency" in which the President attempts to govern principally by swaying public opinion through speechmaking, other analysts have questioned not just the short-term efficacy of this model in many circumstances, but also its consequences, when employed indiscriminately, for the well-being of the political system.[52] Besides, talk about limits should not obscure the fact that Reagan did get his tax bill and that his public standing and efforts at mobilization were an important part of his success.

In respect to his other goals, the period of anointment was one mostly of treading water. Unable to persuade Congress or the public of the need for large domestic budget cuts, Reagan "accepted" the huge deficits and left the resolution of the problem for another day. If there would be any progress in resolving this problem under Reagan's Presidency, it would not be by means of a dramatic act of opinion mobilization on behalf of either budget cuts or higher taxes, but by decisions made by "insider" politics. In foreign affairs, Reagan diminished the strength of the reflexive reaction against the use of military force by showing it could be employed effectively in some cases. But he had not really moved the nation to his policies on Central America, and he remained where he had always been: hanging on.

Period Five: Debacle

The autumn of 1986 began poorly for Ronald Reagan. Following the Iceland summit, which was less than a stunning success, Reagan embarked on his last election campaign, and despite the heavy investment of his personal prestige, Republicans lost control of the Senate. These setbacks were minor, however, compared to the bombshell that rocked the nation in late November. In two successive revelations, it was learned that, with the President's approval, the United States had sold weapons to Iran and that, allegedly without the President's knowledge, some of the proceeds had been diverted by National Security Council officials to assist the *contras*.

Following these revelations, the President's approval rating tumbled dramatically, from 67 percent to 46 percent in one month.[53] His approval rating remained around the 50 percent mark for months. But, as everyone could sense, it was a "weak" 50 percent. As the President's chief of staff, Howard Baker, would later admit, there was for a long time a question of whether the administration would survive. Indeed, the issue hung at least partly in the balance for some nine months, as congressional hearings dragged on to see if there was a "smoking gun." Did the President approve the *contra* aid diversion? The Iran-*contra* affair did not really end until about August 1987 when the congressional hearings concluded and the public suddenly lost interest in the whole matter.

For Ronald Reagan, the magic had gone out of his relationship with the American public. Ignoring his previous status as "King" Reagan, critics mounted a campaign in December and January for an official public apology by the President. Casuists in the press then debated at length whether Reagan's various concessions met the rigorous standard for a true apology. The demand that the President appear, as it were, in sackcloth and ashes was made on the grounds that only such an act of contrition would allow the nation to get beyond the affair. In reality, the aim was to make the President a weaker figure and reduce his influence on the public.

Public reaction to the Iran-*contra* affair cannot be understood without recalling that it was actually two affairs wrapped up in one. It consisted of the Iran arms sale, widely judged to be stupid, although not illegal, and the *contra* aid diversion, widely considered illegal, but not altogether stupid. The combination of these two blunders, with its peculiar marriage in the public mind of the stupid and the illegal, gave this affair its special force. President Reagan could be ridiculed for allowing the United States to be duped by the Ayatollah at the same time that the administration could be vilified for a zealous anticommunism that led to a "secret government" outside normal constitutional channels.

What we know today as a presidential "affair" is a special case in the dialogue on the public Presidency. During an affair, the President is rhetorically disarmed and the initiative lies with his critics and with "objective" analysts. A presidential affair emerges from a blunder, impropriety, or illegality, plus a possible cover-up, which is charged to the President or to high administration officials and which puts the Presidency on the defensive in the eyes of the nation. Many would add that an affair must also unfold so that what occurred and why it occurred are not thought to be known in full, opening the door to a steady stream of revelations (the "dribble-out" effect). The mere charge of "yet another" revelation works to the detriment of the President by calling into question the very premise of candor. (This is why the power of the media seems to increase in proportion as the President's approval declines.) Once the momentum of an affair is under way, the best a President can hope for, other than a blunder by his accusers, is that, having made all the requisite gestures of contrition, his public spanking will be administered quickly.

The principal factor that accounts for presidential support—the public's assessment of the conditions of reality—played no role whatsoever in the President's decline in support. Nothing in the major conditions of the economy changed for the worse; and although some argued that the threat of terrorism had markedly increased, this was more an abstract proposition than a felt reality. If nothing about the Iran-*contra* affair had ever become public, Reagan's period of anointment would have continued without interruption.

The fall of the President's approval rating was therefore wholly a function of the public's assessments of his performance and the closely related aspects of the President's persona. On the dimension of performance, the administration suffered, so to speak, quadruply: (1) from the original revelations; (2) from the way the revelations were handled, with intense public disagreement among administration officials about what had happened; (3) from the report of the President's appointed commission, soundly criticizing the President's management style and lending official sanction to the old charges of a "puppet Presidency"; and (4) from the televised congressional hearings in the summer, which publicly aired the infighting, deception, and mismanagement in the administration.

The Iran-*contra* affair proved a field day for critics who had chafed under Reagan's apparent successes during the previous two periods. Some of the nation's leading Presidency watchers joined in. A highly reputed political scientist, James David Barber, observed (speaking of himself): "This critic of Reagan, who has been such through all these years when political science conferences one after another puffed him up, this one is not laughing. This one is not out with 'I told you so.' This one is seriously concerned that the government of the United States fails to work effectively for peace and justice and liberty out there in the real world."[54] Arthur Schlesinger, Jr., was more direct. The administration was "incoherent, incompetent, duplicitous, and dedicated to rash mindless policies."[55]

These judgments of Reagan's performance naturally affected assessments of the President's persona. For the first time in his Presidency, doubts arose concerning the President's honesty. A majority believed Reagan lied about his knowledge of the diversion of aid to the *contras,* although a majority continued to believe that the President had more integrity than most people in public life.[56] Far more important, the affair displayed a President who, especially in the aftermath of the event, looked weak, unaware of what was going on, and unable to get a hold on events. This image struck at the core of what had always been the greatest asset in Reagan's persona: his strength as a leader. Imperceptibly, the "Rambo" image faded. (Coincidentally, there were no occasions during this period for Reagan to wield a stick.)

There are curious dimensions to the affair that reveal some of the general aspects of persona. First, the affair again demonstrates that certain character traits are far more important than others in promoting a good reputation. From all accounts, Reagan's sympathy for the hostage families played a large role in his consenting to the arms deal. And yet, although previously critics had attacked him for excessive militarism and inflexibility in international affairs, hardly anyone now gave him credit for his compassion or applauded at least his inclination to follow something other than a "hard-line" approach.

Second, the affair shows the degree to which character and persona are colored by the outcome of events. A fair reading of the Iran arms decision indicates that Reagan demonstrated unusual decisiveness, acting on his own view over the repeated objections of his secretary of state and secretary of defense. Yet because the scheme ended in failure, his decisiveness never formed even the slightest part of the picture that issued from the event. All that emerged was a general impression of incompetence. Indeed, in place of complaints that Reagan was not "in charge" of his administration, critics now took to wondering how a President could ignore the advice of his principal advisers. The fact that character judgments are bound up so closely with the outcome of events lends some support to Machiavelli's extreme formulation that, if successful, "the means will always be judged honorable and praised by everyone, for the people are always taken . . . by the outcome."[57]

A strategic assessment of Reagan's public Presidency during the period of debacle must take into account that a time of crisis such as this creates its own goal: survival. Opponents of the President were seeking to mobilize opinion to weaken the President, if not destroy him. As the dynamics of a "pure" presidential affair came into play, the President inevitably lost the rhetorical initiative. Despite repeated suggestions that he do something to put the affair behind him, there may have been far less he could have done rhetorically than people imagined. Without any real-world crisis to turn events, the President could only wait for matters to run their course.

During the period of debacle, the President did not lose as much as one might think. With the tax bill behind him, there were no new major domestic initiatives on the table. In foreign affairs, Iran-*contra* had the curious effect of "confirming" the administration's "hard-line" view by making the public less inclined to treat matters of hostages apart from concerns of the national interest. But Reagan's general loss of prestige as a leader created difficulties for him in foreign affairs, where he sought to act against the views of his opponents. The narrow thread on which his policy in Central America hung continued to be stretched still more.

Period Six: Equilibrium

By the fall of 1987, the Iran-*contra* affair ended, and the President recaptured a degree of public approval. Yet, in contrast to his comeback after the period of decline, he could not turn the events of Iran-*contra* to his advantage. Now, all he could hope for was that matters would be forgotten or put in perspective and that he would recover in some measure the initiative as a speaker. This Reagan was able to do with the signing of the INF treaty in Washington in

December 1987, which put him in the posture of statesman and peacemaker on the grand stage of East-West relations. Once widely depicted as the "evil emperor" whose uncompromising stance compelled the formation of peace movements in the United States and Western Europe, he was now the benevolent figure whose foresight disarmed them. Once decried as the only recent American President not to meet his Soviet counterpart, he was now the leader who had held the most summits and who had put U.S.-Soviet relations on their most normal footing.

Clearly, the Ronald Reagan of this period was a different figure, presenting a less formidable and softer image. As people began to look back on the whole of his Presidency, he was viewed in a far more charitable light than during the Iran-*contra* affair. A certain respect for the President reemerged, and, as in the period of anointment, some critics found that a gentler treatment of his character served their ends, especially as he would soon be stepping down.

From a strategic perspective, the period of equilibrium leaves, at this writing, as many questions as answers. In the final year of any Presidency, little can or should be expected by way of new domestic initiatives that rely on public mobilization. The public simply is not inclined to accord this kind of license to an administration in its final year. In foreign affairs, there is much the President could do and wanted to do—ratification of the INF treaty, the negotiation of a possible long-range missile agreement, a withdrawal of the Soviet Union from Afghanistan, and a favorable resolution of the civil war in Nicaragua. But as important as the outcome to these specific policies in foreign affairs is the broader general "lesson" to be learned. Will Reagan manage to teach that it is only by holding firm and applying pressure that one achieves results? Or will others seize the initiative and teach that it is only by conciliation and concession that the nation can have peace?

Conclusion

This chapter has treated President Reagan's relationship to the public in strategic terms, focusing on how his approval ratings and rhetorical skills may have helped him to achieve his broader substantive goals, including a change in the nation's public philosophy. A strategic approach does not deny that a President may seek instrumental objectives, such as reelection, nor does it insist that every presidential action be viewed in strategic terms. Part of a President's job is managing the shop, which means he must cope with discrete problems that may be only very indirectly related to basic objectives. Nevertheless, our most famous, if not always our greatest, Presidents have gone beyond responding to events and have sought to move the nation in a new and broad direction.

President Reagan certainly fits this category, and his Presidency is especially well suited to a strategic analysis because of its self-conscious understanding that it wanted to change the nation's agenda and alter its public philosophy. How well did it succeed?

Previous efforts to alter the nation's public philosophy have all relied on a restored or renewed political party to serve as the institutional vessel to carry the new ideas. In attempting to construct a political base for his public philosophy, Reagan too had hoped to lead a grand political realignment in which the Republicans would emerge as the nation's dominant party. The result, after seven years, is still uncertain. The Republicans' early hopes of capturing the House of Representatives have been relegated to the long term, and the immediate question is whether they can recapture the Senate. In terms of partisan identification, however, Republicans have gained some ground on the Democrats, though they still trail by a small margin; and, taking account of the tenuous character of many Democratic identifiers, many observers detect a slight Republican advantage on the level of presidential voting. Yet this striving for partisan position has been taking place in an era in which, because of the importance voters assign to individual candidates, the value or worth of partisan attachments is far less than in the past.

When it comes to the substance of his public philosophy, it is clear that Reagan has succeeded for the moment in making his program the "base" of American political discourse. Just as candidates once defined their position by reference to the New Deal, they now define themselves by reference to the Reagan Revolution. For those who have argued that the only way to a positive legacy is through an expanded role for the fedral government in domestic affairs, Reagan's stewardship has demonstrated that it is possible for the American public to entertain a more modest view of what the government should do. If this view becomes established and endures for the next generation, President Reagan, like President Andrew Jackson, will leave a positive legacy by taking a negative stance on an increased role for the federal government in American society.

In international affairs, the final year of President Reagan's tenure will do much to fix his legacy. The conservative movement that the President led to power was attractive to many Americans for its promises of resolve and firmness in dealing with the Soviet Union. Yet many believed that a conservative President would be incapable of taking advantage of any possibilities for developing a strategic relationship with the Soviets, and this belief remained a major point of vulnerability for the President through the 1984 presidential campaign. For the short term, the President leaves his party in the enviable position of being able to claim both a greater firmness *and* a greater capacity to deal with

the Soviets. Yet what this political triumph means for the structure of underlying opinion remains unknown, and some conservatives worry that it may sap
the vigor of popular distrust of communism and of the long-range intentions
of the Soviet Union.

To return from the deeper level of public philosophy to the surface level
of presidential approval, it is worth emphasizing how little approval ratings
have to do with any lasting judgment of presidential performance. A President's
legacy derives from his accomplishments or failures, and no President will be
long remembered for having an average approval rating of more than 60 percent, nor quickly forgotten for having an average lower than 45 percent. As an
instrument of presidential power, a high approval rating has some value as a
reminder to others of the potential "cost" they might have to pay in opposing
a popular President. Yet it is important to remember that an approval rating is
a lag, rather than a lead, indicator. What determines the score will be the public's assessment of conditions, performance, and persona. An astute President
should accordingly be prepared in most cases to sacrifice his standing today,
if by doing so he can affect positively the future assessment of these factors.

What impresses anyone looking at presidential approval scores is their remarkable variability. Journalists may worship at the altar of approval ratings,
but they are apt to discover that they have placed their faith in a fickle god.
Almost nothing in a high support score tends to ensure that it will remain high,
just as almost nothing in a low score means it will stay low. For Presidents
this conclusion is at once humbling and hopeful. On the stage of presidential
politics, it is never over until it is over, and it is never finished until it is done.

Notes

1. James Tobin, "Reaganomics in Retrospect," in *The Reagan Revolution,* ed. B.B.
Kymlicka and Jean V. Matthews (Chicago: Dorsey Press, 1988), 103.

2. For a discussion of the "strategic" concept in the study of the Presidency, see
Erwin C. Hargrove and Michael Nelson, *Presidents, Politics, and Policy* (Baltimore: Johns
Hopkins University Press, 1984).

3. For a full treatment of the "failed Presidency" model by one of its most devoted
adherents, see Theodore J. Lowi, "Ronald Reagan—Revolutionary?" in *The Reagan Presidency and the Governing of America,* ed. Lester M. Salamon and Michael S. Lund (Washington, D.C.: Urban Institute, 1984), 47.

4. These categories are obviously not airtight, and aspects of one spill over into
aspects of the others. They are used merely as convenient categories for analysis.

5. D. Roderick Kiewiet and Douglas Rivers, "The Economic Basis of Reagan's Appeal," in *The New Direction in American Politics,* ed. John E. Chubb and Paul E. Peterson
(Washington, D.C.: Brookings Institution, 1985), 88.

6. This view can be derived from Murray Edelman's *Political Language: Words
That Succeed and Policies That Fail* (New York: Academic Press, 1977), 43-49.

7. In 1932, Franklin Roosevelt ran for the Presidency on a fairly moderate platform. It was not until 1936 that he used a presidential campaign to articulate his new public philosophy. The one who comes closest to Reagan, in the sense of articulating an alternative public philosophy prior to being elected, was Woodrow Wilson in 1912.

8. Nicholas von Hoffman, "Contra Reaganum," *Harper's,* May 1982.

9. Ibid.

10. From Reagan's presidential address, 18 February 1981.

11. Speech of 2 March 1981, *Public Papers of the Presidents, Ronald Reagan, 1981* (Washington, D.C.: Government Printing Office, 1982), 177.

12. *American Spectator,* March 1982.

13. *Wall Street Journal,* 27 April 1984.

14. Sixty-one percent of the American people saw Reagan as having "the strong leadership qualities the nation needs," as against 18 percent for President Carter. See *Public Opinion,* February/March 1981, 47.

15. David Broder, *Washington Post,* 1 April 1981, A21.

16. *Washington Post,* 9 August 1981, E7.

17. Ibid., A3.

18. *Gallup Poll Index,* May 1982, 30.

19. *New York Times,* 9 January 1983, E22.

20. David Broder, *Washington Post,* 12 January 1983, A19.

21. From comments of 23 December 1982, *Congressional Quarterly,* 3167.

22. In CBS/New York Times poll, January 1983, 56 percent of the public disapproved of Reagan's handling of the economy, and only 21 percent thought economic conditions were getting better. Nevertheless, 56 percent had faith that Reagan's economic program would eventually work.

23. *New York Times,* 9 January 1983, E22.

24. By a 2 to 1 margin, Americans favored cutting defense spending to balance the budget; by the same margin, they favored foregoing the next 10 percent income tax cut to balance the budget. CBS/New York Times poll, 16 January 1983.

25. *Newsweek,* 16 April 1984, 24.

26. The exact degree of public support for Reagan's policies in Central America has been hotly disputed, with the amount of support varying with the situation and the phrasing of the questions. While the degree of opposition to the President's policies has sometimes been exaggerated, no one can say that he was ever able to establish anything approaching the consensus he sought. Aid for El Salvador eventually became less controversial after the election of José Napoleon Duarte as president, but the struggle for public support was reproduced on the question of assistance for the Nicaraguan *contras.* See Everett C. Ladd, "Where the Public Stands on Nicaragua," *Public Opinion,* September/October 1987.

27. *New York Times,* 2 April 1982, 35.

28. *New York Times,* 26 January 1983, A23.

29. Stockman had given these interviews out of a curious need to unburden himself. After the interviews appeared in print, many demanded that Stockman be replaced. The President, however, stood by him, an act of loyalty that Stockman later would repay, after resigning from the administration, by signing a lucrative contract for a memoir attacking the administration.

30. *New York Times,* 29 January 1983, A23.

31. *New York Times,* 6 January 1983, A26.

32. *Washington Post,* 12 January 1983, A19.

33. CBS/New York Times poll, 16-19 January 1983.

34. *New York Times,* 6 January 1983, A26.

35. *Washington Post,* 12 January 1983, A19.

36. At his low point of approval in 1983, 60 percent of the public still saw Ronald Reagan as someone who "offers a vision of where he wants to lead the country." CBS/New York Times poll, 16-19 January.

37. *Congressional Quarterly,* 28 June 1983, 1371.

38. Polls from 1983 show the following percentages:

	Handling of the Economy				Handling of the Presidency		
	App.	Dis.	No opin.		App.	Dis.	No opin.
14-17 January	29	64	7	28-31 January	35	56	9
19-22 August	37	54	7	19-22 August	43	46	11
18-21 November	48	46	6	18-21 November	53	37	10

39. *Gallup Report,* November 1984, 10.

40. *U.S. News and World Report,* 3 October 1983, 22.

41. CBS/New York Times poll, 14 September 1983.

42. Americans approved of Reagan's decision to send the troops to Grenada by a margin of 55 percent to 31 percent in the aftermath of the President's explanation in a television address on 27 October. The Grenada invasion came the same week as a terrorist attack on the U.S. Marine base in Lebanon. CBS/New York Times poll, 27 October 1983.

43. *Public Opinion,* April/May 1985, 7.

44. In the CBS/New York Times poll of 9 October 1984, comparing the personal qualities of Reagan and Mondale, 75 percent of the respondents thought of Reagan as a "strong leader" compared to only 44 percent for Mondale. By contrast, 70 percent saw Mondale as one who "cares about people like you" compared to 56 percent for Reagan.

45. This conclusion is adapted from Machiavelli's *The Prince,* in which he also observes: "[A prince] must not mind incurring the scandal of those vices without which it would be difficult to save the state."

46. The judgment on the first debate was more one-sided than any presidential debate held thus far. Three days after the debate, 66 percent found Mondale the winner, compared to 17 percent for Reagan, with 10 percent judging the outcome a tie. For the second debate, 41 percent thought Reagan the winner, 38 percent Mondale, and 16 percent a tie. CBS/New York Times poll, 9 and 21 October 1984.

47. *U.S. News and World Report,* 13 January 1986, 77.

48. The number of Americans citing nuclear war as the most important problem facing the nation dropped dramatically from the preelection years 1982-84 to 1986. See CBS/New York Times polls of May 1982 and September 1984, and September/October 1986.

49. CBS/New York Times poll, 15 April 1986.

50. *Newsweek,* 10 June 1985, 23.

51. CBS/New York Times poll, September-October 1986.

52. See Jeffrey Tulis, *The Rhetorical Presidency* (Princeton: Princeton University Press, 1987); and Samuel Kernell, *Going Public* (Washington, D.C.: CQ Press, 1986).

53. The figures here are taken from CBS/New York Times poll, not Gallup, because Gallup conducted no poll of presidential approval in October.

54. "Reagan, Iran, and the Presidency," *American Spectator,* April 1987, 18.

55. *Maryland Law Review,* Fall 1987.

56. CBS/New York Times poll, 30 November 1986.

57. Machiavelli, *The Prince,* chap. 18.

PART THREE

The Public Policies

7

Lower Taxes, More Spending, and Budget Deficits

PAUL E. PETERSON
and
MARK ROM

When Ronald Reagan assumed the Presidency, he had three major policy objectives: to reduce the size of government; to reestablish a low-inflation, growth-oriented economy; and to rebuild America's defenses. Drawing on supply-side ideas about economic growth, President Reagan claimed that to accomplish the first goal would be to gain the second. Reducing the size of government would lower tax burdens on workers and investors. Since they would keep for their private use a larger share of their earnings, they would have a greater incentive to work and invest. Gains in productivity would occur more quickly, and economic growth would be stimulated. Inflation would be controlled by the increased availability of capital and labor that came with lowered taxes; the Federal Reserve Board would help by slowing down growth in the supply of money. Reagan was also determined to strengthen America's claim as the world's greatest military power. To do this, he planned to make defense his top budget priority.

Reagan's policies were bold and original. The largest tax reduction in U.S. history was to take place as defense spending increased by 20 percent. Reagan believed this could be done in part because dramatic, across-the-board cuts in nearly all domestic programs would reverse the long-standing propensity of government expenditures to grow. In addition, supply-siders claimed, the tax cuts could actually *increase* government revenues. Cutting taxes, by greatly stimulating the economy, would produce so much additional income that the *amount* paid by taxpayers would go up, even though the *rate* or percentage they paid was declining.[1]

Although President Reagan's stunning electoral mandate was reinforced by a Republican majority in the Senate, his ideas were so unusual and controversial that Congress was expected to modify them substantially. It was anticipated that moderate Republicans would unite with Democrats to alter presidential proposals in the Senate and that the sizable Democratic majority in the House would put up even stiffer resistance. Instead, Congress received the Reagan ideas in the spring of 1981 with alacrity. The country had wearied of years of rising inflation, falling rates of productivity, economic stagnation, and rising taxes. The Iranian hostage crisis symbolized President Jimmy Carter's inability to control the nation's direction amid poorly understood economic and political currents. Reagan's ability to survive with pluck and courage a presidential assassination attempt just three months after his inauguration induced a rush of popular support that overwhelmed remaining congressional opposition to his policies. Within seven months of his inauguration, Reagan was putting into place all three key components of his political agenda: tax cuts, reduced domestic spending, and an increased commitment to defense. Meanwhile, the Federal Reserve Board was rigorously tightening the nation's money supply in the hope that inflation would quickly diminish.

As dramatic as Reagan's successes were in his first year, they were not followed up by comparable domestic policy successes during the remainder of his administration. With the exception of the Tax Reform Act of 1986, a landmark piece of legislation that established a new standard for setting tax policy, Reagan spent the remainder of his term fighting an increasingly animated congressional opposition. The deterioration in the President's political fortunes in 1982 coincided with the onset of the deepest recession in fifty years. Although the President blamed the economic misfortune on "decades of economic mismanagement," the public did not hold Reagan entirely blameless.[2] His popularity declined steadily throughout 1982, and the Democrats regained twenty-six seats in the House of Representatives that year.

After the economy began to recover (in the spring of 1983), the President's popularity revived and Reagan acquired the immunity from public criticism that won for him the accolade of the "Teflon President." But for all the President's political popularity, he was unable to regain the legislative initiative he had in 1981. The domestic policy debate became a stalemate between a President determined to retain the victories he had achieved and a Congress determined to keep him from advancing further.

Budgetary debates dominated the prolonged period of legislative-executive confrontation. Because tax cuts did not increase government revenues, as supply-siders had hoped, the continuing increase in expenditures generated extraordinarily large fiscal deficits. The President pointed to these deficits as the reason for cutting existing domestic programs ever more sharply and avoiding putting new ones into place. Blaming the deficits on the President's tax cut and military build-up, Democrats tried to hold back military increases, raise new revenues, and keep domestic programs intact. Meanwhile, policy analysts argued that the deficits hindered domestic business investment and contributed to the rapidly deteriorating U.S. balance of trade in international markets.[3] Because deficits became the central domestic issue of the Reagan administration, we first describe their magnitude, next show how they were induced by the tax cut of 1981, then describe the way in which they shaped the debate over domestic and military expenditure. We conclude with an assessment of the long-term economic impact of the deficit politics of the 1980s.

The Deficits

By any measure, Reagan's deficits surpassed those of any President since Franklin Roosevelt. For the first six years of the Reagan administration, deficits averaged $161 billion each year (see figure 7.1 on page 216), compared to an annual average since 1950 of just $28 billion.[4] Interest payments on the growing national debt increased rapidly both because the amount of borrowed money had more than doubled in seven short years and because interest rates were much higher than in earlier decades. By 1986, the cost of financing the debt was nearly $120 billion compared to $60 billion in 1980 and $30 billion in 1970. It took 3.25 percent of the gross national product (GNP) to finance the national debt in 1986, compared to 2 percent in 1980 and 1.4 percent in 1970 (see figure 7.2 on page 217).

The deficits were so large that they dominated public discourse over domestic policy. As both President and Congress accused the other of fiscal irresponsibility, two senators, Phil Gramm (R-Texas) and Warren Rudman (R-New Hampshire), proposed in 1985 an innovation in governmental policy making that dramatized the extent to which deficits had become the all-consuming legislative issue. The senators proposed a bill (popularly called "Gramm-Rudman") that would automatically reduce deficits by ever increasing amounts over a five-year period. According to their original proposals, if the deficit was expected to be above a specified amount, each and every program would be reduced proportionately to bring the overall deficit down to the required level. The General Accounting Office (GAO) was charged with the responsibility of calculating how large the program cuts would have to be in order to reach Gramm-Rudman targets.

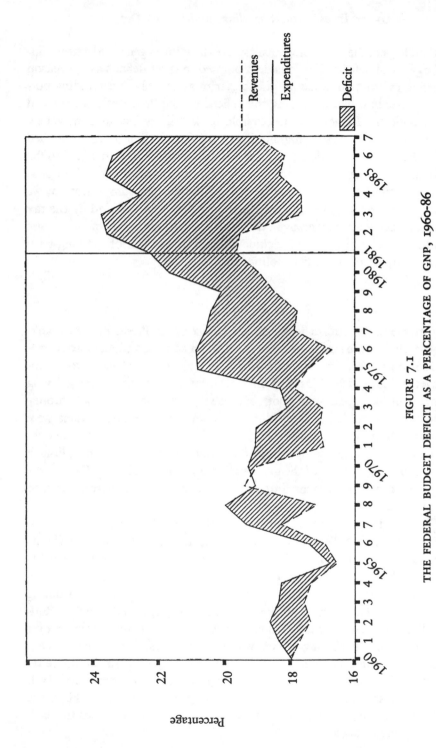

FIGURE 7.1

THE FEDERAL BUDGET DEFICIT AS A PERCENTAGE OF GNP, 1960-86

SOURCE: Figures compiled from *The Economic Report of the President, 1987* (Washington, D.C.: Government Printing Office, 1988), tables B.1, B.76.

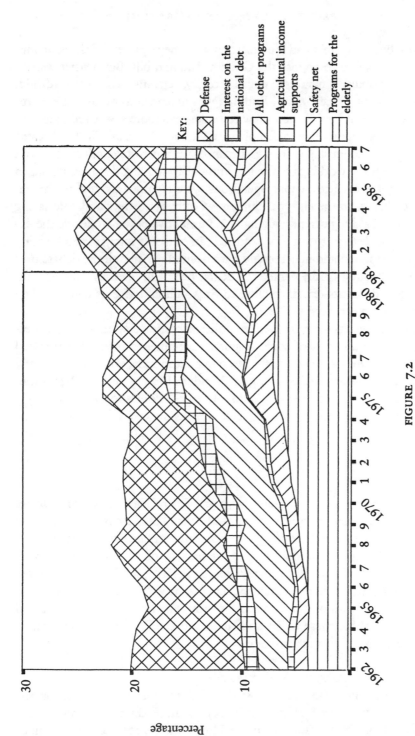

FIGURE 7.2

FEDERAL GOVERNMENT EXPENDITURES AS A PECENTAGE OF GNP, 1962–85

KEY:

Defense

Interest on the national debt

All other programs

Agricultural income supports

Safety net

Programs for the elderly

SOURCE: Figures compiled from *Budget of the United States, Fiscal Year 1989* (Washington, D.C.: Government Printing Office, 1988), tables 3.1 and 3.3.

Since both Congress and the President said they wanted deficit reduction, neither could afford to oppose the Gramm-Rudman bill. But neither wanted cuts in such popular programs as social security, veterans' pensions, Medicaid, and food stamps. Once Gramm-Rudman was amended to exempt these programs from cuts, it became necessary to make even more severe reductions in remaining programs in order to comply with Gramm-Rudman. The law became known as the "doomsday machine" because, were it to take effect, it would greatly disrupt the workings of the government by making deep reductions in funds for many agencies whose operations were regarded as vital to the nation's well-being. In the end, the Supreme Court saved the day by declaring unconstitutional the provision giving GAO executive power to decide the exact amount of cuts that would be required (an outcome many of those voting for the bill expected and may secretly have desired).[5] After all the debate over Gramm-Rudman, it hardly dented the deficit problem;[6] even by 1988, the annual projected deficits remained close to $145 billion, twice as high as when Reagan came into office.[7]

Since the deficits were the focus of political controversy, their origins necessarily became a matter of some dispute. According to most congressional Democrats, the major cause was the steep tax cut in 1981, which permanently reduced federal revenues. According to President Reagan and his Republican supporters, the major cause was the failure to cut domestic spending deeply enough. As we shall see, there is considerable evidence for both sides of the argument.

Tax Policy

Reagan's tax reforms were in many ways among the least consistent policies of his administration. In 1981 he proposed sharp cuts in business taxes and in the taxes of higher-income groups in order to stimulate investment and economic growth. But within four years of the passage of this landmark piece of tax legislation, the Economic Recovery Tax Act (ERTA), the President proposed tax reform that would eliminate tax shelters for the well-to-do and impose major new tax liabilities on the corporate sector. The one thing that remained constant throughout these twists and turns was the President's commitment to a lower personal income tax rate.

THE ECONOMIC RECOVERY TAX ACT (ERTA)

Reagan's $162 billion tax cut in 1981 dwarfed any that had occurred in the postwar era (Ford's $22.8 billion cut in 1975 taking a distant second place).[8] At first, the Democratic leadership in the House and Senate attempted to moderate the tax-cutting fever by proposing a modest, one-year cut aimed at low-income groups. When it became evident that the President could easily overwhelm this proposal with his three-year cut in personal income taxes plus additional cuts in corporate taxes, capital gains taxes, and taxes on investment income, the Democrats, not to be outdone, produced their three-year proposal. Although the Democrats' proposed cuts in personal income rates were somewhat less than the President's, they proposed their own set of tax breaks and loopholes for investors and corporations. In a shrewd political maneuver that nonetheless seemed consistent with his conservative philosophy, President Reagan incorporated into his proposal most of the tax cuts the Democrats had suggested. With both public support and business backing, the President put together a House coalition of Republicans and boll-weevil[9] Democrats that proved irresistible. With a Republican majority in firm control of the Senate, ERTA sailed through Congress within eight months of Inauguration Day. As finally passed, ERTA's major features included a 23 percent reduction in personal income taxes, a cut in the highest marginal tax rate from 70 to 50 percent, a cut in the capital gains tax from 28 percent to 20 percent, and major cuts in business taxes, mainly by allowing businesses to speed the depreciation of their assets (e.g., buildings, machinery, and vehicles).

The cuts in personal income taxes had a permanency unlike that of any tax bill Congress had previously passed because Congress accepted the President's proposal to index tax brackets to the inflation rate. In the past, individuals were pushed into higher tax brackets and thus paid a higher percentage of their income in taxes whenever their income rose in step with inflation. In other words, a person's tax rates could increase even though his or her real income—the amount of goods and services that it could purchase—remained unchanged. To offset the gradual shifting of individuals to higher tax brackets, Congress had in the postwar period "cut taxes" modestly on eleven different occasions in order to keep inflation-induced tax increases from becoming too burdensome.[10]

This approach to tax policy formation had a definite political appeal because tax increases occurred silently with inflation, filling government coffers with new revenues without any explicit action by Congress. Tax "cuts" could be enacted with great fanfare and enthusiasm because they usually did little more than partially offset quietly occurring "bracket creep." If the tax cuts turned out to be excessive, yielding a shortfall in government revenues, this created no permanent problem. Gradually, individuals would shift into higher tax brackets, revenues would increase, and deficits would slowly disappear.

Reagan's tax-indexation plan transformed this politically pleasant world of bracket creep and tax cut. It was applauded by policy analysts because it meant that any new tax increase had to be explicitly enacted by Congress. As incomes rose with inflation, tax brackets were adjusted. Individuals would no longer pay a higher percentage of their income in taxes just because inflation was occurring. Persons would be taxed more, and the government would receive more revenues, only if Congress passed and the President signed a law raising taxes. But as sensible as tax indexation seemed to policy analysts, it meant that political leaders could no longer solve the problem of fiscal deficits by quietly waiting for revenues to increase little by little each year as individuals shifted into higher tax brackets. The problem of how to collect more revenues, which had once solved itself, became the dominating political issue of the 1980s.

TAX POLICY AFTER ERTA

After the passage of ERTA, tax policies during the Reagan years veered in a new direction. In an administration that prided itself on its ideological coherence, intellectual consistency, and commitment to principle, it was remarkable that within five years of ERTA's passage President Reagan would sign a bill (the Tax Reform Act of 1986, or TRA) that not only eliminated most tax shelters, corporate loopholes, and other tax preferences but also removed many low-income households from the tax rolls and shifted the incidence of taxation from individuals to corporations.

Although ERTA and TRA ostensibly had the same goal—to enhance economic growth—their methods for accomplishing it were entirely different. ERTA gave tax breaks to corporations and wealthy individuals in order to spur business investment. It reduced the marginal rate on high-income taxpayers to encourage them to be more productive and to invest their money in a growing economy. According to one estimate, the highest-income groups received as much as 26 percent more in take-home personal income as a result of ERTA tax cuts.[11] ERTA did much less for low-income taxpayers.

The Tax Reform Act of 1986 enunciated a startlingly different conservative philosophy. Economic growth would be encouraged by taxing all income uniformly regardless of the way in which it was earned. Tax preferences for certain kinds of economic activity were to be eliminated because they distorted the choices individuals were making in the marketplace. Tax shelters for the rich only encouraged them to pour money into potentially wasteful activities. Because high taxes on low-income households discouraged members from working, the personal deduction would be nearly doubled, removing an estimated 4.3 million low-income families from the tax rolls.[12]

Not only were the poor among the big winners in 1986, but business groups that had done well in 1981 proved to be big losers. The incidence of taxation shifted heavily from individuals to corporations; their taxes were expected to just about double, from $60 to $120 billion between 1985 and 1987. High income households that had used tax shelters to reduce their apparent earnings could no longer dodge their tax liabilities. Stockholders who realized capital gains on their investments would now pay as much as 33 percent on their profits.

The change in Reagan's policy was dictated in part by the change in the political situation. By 1986, Democrats were once again firmly in control of the House of Representatives, and no change in the tax law could be pushed through over liberal objections. But this change in partisan politics was less important than Reagan's commitment to a tax reform that would lower personal tax rates. He pushed recalcitrant Republicans to support his reform initiatives, and he declared its passage one of the proudest achievements of his administration.

Two factors seem to account for the decisive shift in Reagan's tax policy. First, rising deficits made it clear that no further revenue losses could be contemplated. On the contrary, Congress decided in 1982 and again in 1984 to help reduce the deficit by withdrawing some of the most egregious of the 1981 tax concessions, including the bizarre provision that allowed corporations to sell their business losses to other corporations (who could then count the loss as a tax deduction). Loophole closing, in fact, was becoming an increasingly popular device by which Congress, with the President's acquiescence, was "enhancing" federal revenues without increasing the personal income tax rate. Second, the President became convinced that the tax rate on individuals could be further reduced if loophole closing was carried to its logical conclusion—the uniform treatment of all income. Already, ERTA had reduced the top marginal tax rates from 78 to 50 percent; tax reform would bring these rates down to 33 percent without any loss in revenues to the federal government if loopholes were plugged. The President appreciated the political appeal of lower marginal rates; like many others, he felt that high marginal tax rates were a major infringement on individual liberties as well as a deterrent to economic growth. With the issue posed in these terms, he was willing to sacrifice a lot: business tax preferences, favorable treatment of capital gains, and tax shelters for the rich. Nothing justifies Reagan's claim to populist conservatism as clearly as does his 1986 tax reform.

The tax reform of 1986 did not revive government revenues, however. Tax brackets remained indexed, and government revenues were expected neither to increase or decrease as a result of the legislation. Thus the net effect of Reagan's policies on revenues and fiscal deficits was shaped primarily by the 1981 tax. Figure 7.1 places this tax cut in historical perspective. It shows that, except for a brief period around 1970, federal revenues as a percentage of the nation's GNP had hovered around 18 percent ever since 1960. Beginning in the late 1970s, however, federal revenues as a percentage of GNP began to climb steadily, from 18 percent in 1978 to 20 percent by 1981, the year that the Reagan administration took office.[13] These increases were the result of bracket creep. Had the old tax law remained on the books, revenues as a percentage of GNP would have continued to climb. The Reagan tax cut of 1981 reversed this trend by reducing revenue flows to about the average level since 1960.

Two interpretations of these trends are possible. Reagan administration officials emphasize the continuity of their revenue policies with the past. They point out that the United States has always resisted revenue flows that exceed 19 percent of GNP during peacetime and explain that the tax cut of 1981 was not so much a cut as a refusal to allow inflation to impose a tax increase on the American public. Critics point out that no arbitrary number represents the "correct" amount of taxes that government should collect and justify tax increases by showing that the need for both domestic and defense programs has gradually increased. To evaluate these spending "needs," we turn now to Reagan's expenditure policies.

Reagan's Spending Policies

Reagan's first-year tax successes were matched by his accomplishments in achieving his spending goals of cutting government and rebuilding defense. Less than a month after Reagan took office in 1981, his budget chief, Director of the Office of Management and Budget David Stockman, presented Congress with a budget for fiscal year 1982 proposing $7.2 billion more in defense spending and $41.4 billion less in nondefense spending than President Carter had requested. Stockman's strategy was to push Reagan's budget through Congress as quickly as possible, while the Democrats were still demoralized by the election and confused about their own goals. "Early victories were necessary in order to cow the opposition and stampede as many members of Congress as possible onto the winning bandwagon."[14]

As with taxes, the Democratic leadership in the House of Representatives proposed an alternate plan that made much smaller changes (only $15.8 billion in cuts) than the Reagan plan. As with taxes, Reagan took control of the legislative process by putting all his proposals in one large package and by appealing for support directly to the people through a televised address in which he warned that if his budget was not passed, an "economic calamity of tremendous proportions" would result.[15] Through deft maneuvering, Stockman was able to push this budget quickly as a unified whole through Congress by late July 1981. The Omnibus Budget Reconciliation Act (OBRA) gave the President what he wanted. Virtually all of his defense requests were approved, as were $35 billion in cuts in nondefense programs.

This was the largest spending policy success that the President was to have with Congress. Even in late 1981, when the President requested an additional $13 billion in cuts, Congress gave him only $4 billion. By 1982, congressional majorities believed government spending on domestic programs had been cut enough, and budgetary issues engendered a political dogfight. President Reagan blamed the budget deficit on Congress (especially the Democratically controlled House of Representatives), which he said refused to cut back unnecessary domestic programs. Democratic leaders in Congress responded by accusing the President of gutting the revenue base of the government in the name of supply-side economics and of insisting on wasteful defense spending at the expense of the elderly, farmers, the poor, and the disadvantaged. At the same time, the Democrats hesitated to come out too strongly in favor of a tax increase or against some increases in spending on the military for fear that they would be labeled the "tax and spend" party or "soft" on defense. The partisan debate over these fiscal issues was so intense that outcomes were typically settled in one grand appropriation bill—rather than a number of separate bills, as had traditionally been the case—passed at the end of the year when all parties were forced to find a way of compromising their differences in order to keep the government running.

The net results of these controversies can be seen in figure 7.2, which places expenditures under Reagan in historical perspective. Between 1960 and 1986, federal expenditures increased from about 18 percent of GNP to 24 percent. The increase was not a steady one because both wars and recessions placed temporary burdens on the federal fisc. Military spending induced by the Vietnam war generated a higher level of spending in the late 1960s, recession pushed federal costs up in the mid-1970s, and the recession of 1981-82 pushed the expenditure rate to an all-time high. But while these cyclical forces affected budget growth, they do not disguise the long-term trends also evident in the graph. After each new peak is realized, the valley to which it falls is higher than the preceding one. By 1986, there is no longer even a valley, as federal expenditures remain as high after the economic recovery as they were in the depths of the recession.

The increases in expenditures were not uniform across programs. The biggest gains were in defense and in financing the rapidly growing national debt. On the domestic side, program areas that were key to the partisan struggle (programs for the elderly, farmers, and the poor) survived with surprising resilience Reagan's commitment to reduce the size of government. But programs having relatively minor significance for the debate between the parties were gutted.

THE ELDERLY

The clearest domestic winners during the Reagan era, as in earlier decades, were the elderly. In fact, the growth in pensions and medical insurance since 1965 has been so great that one cannot understand the forces shaping federal fiscal policy without first coming to terms with this basic fact.[16] This growth has been steady, continuous, and substantial. Between 1965 and 1970, programs grew by $43 billion; between 1975 and 1980, they grew by $56 billion; and between 1980 and 1985, they grew by another $56 billion. Expenditure growth under Reagan has thus been as great it was under Carter or during the Great Society years. Furthermore, the increase in the cost of programs for the elderly basically offset all other cuts in domestic programs.

The rising cost of these programs reflected both political choices and demographic shifts. Congress made key decisions in the 1950s and 1960s to include more and more members of the workforce under social security, to provide a system of comprehensive medical insurance to the elderly (Medicare), and to broaden definitions of eligibility for disability assistance. Besides bringing more people into these retirement programs, policy makers also indexed benefit levels to keep pace with increases in the cost of living. Some programs were indexed in such a way that they grew faster than the overall rate of inflation: The cost of medical services since the passing of Medicare increased at a rate 32 percent greater than the general price level.[17] Meanwhile, the size of the population over the age of sixty-five grew from less than 17 million in 1960 to about 26 million in 1984.

Federal policy has unequivocally helped the aged. As benefits have gone up and more people have become eligible for these programs, the percentage of persons over the age of sixty-five living in poverty has declined. Nearly a quarter of the elderly were poor in the 1970s; today, that number has been cut in half. Life expectancy has steadily risen for both men and women since 1970, and it is expected to continue to grow. Improvements in life expectancy seem related to improved income support and medical assistance to the elderly.[18]

Because benefits were spread broadly and deeply, the Reagan administration faced serious problems regarding social security; the mismatch between taxes and benefits was driving the program's fund into deficit in the early 1980s. To resolve the crisis, a bipartisan commission moved to cut benefits—but only a little, and mainly for future retirees—while expanding taxes in the short run. As part of the bipartisan agreement reached in 1982, benefit increases tied to the cost of living were delayed for six months and the age of retirement was scheduled to rise gradually from age sixty-five to sixty-seven in the next few decades. The federal government also began regulating medical costs under Medicare more closely. Regarding taxes, the bipartisan agreement advanced the dates at which social security taxes increased, raised the self-employment tax, taxed half the benefits of higher-income recipients, and required federal workers and all workers in nonprofit institutions to contribute to the social security system.[19] Later, the price paid for Medicare insurance was increased.

As a result of these decisions, social security taxes became the one source of federal revenue that continually grew during the Reagan years. Whereas social security taxes accounted for but 31 percent of federal revenues in 1980, by 1987 they constituted 36 percent—an increase from $157 billion to about $300 billion.[20] Although the costs of programs for the elderly grew during the Reagan years, increased taxes and fee charges ensured that social security would remain self-financing. Indeed, by 1987, the social security system was running an annual surplus of $20 billion, leading the American Association of Retired Persons (AARP) to complain that social security taxes were being used to finance the huge deficits in the remainder of the federal budget. Decisions with respect to the elderly ran contrary to the general philosophy of the Reagan administration. Program cuts were small, so expenditures climbed almost as steeply as they had in the past. Taxes were raised to cover the increased costs.

These deviations from Reagan's conservative philosophy appeared to have been dictated by practical politics. Reagan had once proposed putting social security on a voluntary basis, and that suggestion haunted Reagan in every one of his subsequent political campaigns. Gerald Ford had used it effectively against him in the 1976 primary contests for the Republican nomination, and the Democrats used it in both presidential races and as an argument for keeping a Democratic Congress. In his first budget message, Reagan did propose social security cuts, but even a Republican-controlled Senate immediately passed (by a 96–0 vote) a resolution confirming its commitment to existing benefits. The administration quickly retreated, and only minor adjustments were made in social security even at a time when the Reagan administration was at the height of its budget-cutting powers.[21] After the bipartisan agreement on social security in 1982, Reagan insisted that the issue be kept off the table in all budget-balancing discussions. From time to time, both Republican and Democratic members of Congress suggested making modest changes in social security policy (waiving the cost-of-living increase for one or more years; taxing a higher percentage of social security benefits; charging higher fees for Medicare, etc.), but both Reagan and party leaders remained adamantly opposed to cuts in retirement programs. As a result, their costs continued to grow.

THE NEEDY AND THE SAFETY NET

The federal government established a number of social programs during the New Deal, and later during the Great Society of the 1970s, as a "safety net" providing a minimum level of support for what are often referred to as the "truly needy." Several major programs make up the safety net. Supplemental Security Income (SSI) provides cash assistance to those with low incomes who are aged, blind, or disabled. Aid to Families with Dependent Children (AFDC) provides cash assistance to families in which a parent is absent, incapacitated, or (in some states) unemployed. Food stamps are given to the poor without regard to family status for purchasing groceries at retail stores. Medicaid pays the medical bills incurred by recipients of SSI and AFDC. Between 1965 and 1980, these programs grew in real dollar terms at an average rate of $3.5 billion a year.

Reagan had long been critical of many of these programs as wasteful and destructive of individual incentives to work. For example, during his first presidential campaign he had campaigned against welfare abuses, telling an anecdote about a woman in Chicago whose "tax-free cash income (from the government) is over $150,000."[22] Thus he might have been expected to unleash a full-scale attack against these programs. At least as David Stockman saw it, "The Reagan Revolution . . . required a full frontal assault on the American welfare state. . . . Accordingly, forty years' worth of promises, subventions, entitlements, and safety nets issued by the federal government . . . would have to be scrapped or drastically modified."[23]

Nonetheless, programs aimed at the poor, the needy, and the handicapped were spared major reductions during the Reagan years. Indeed, the cost of these programs reached new highs in 1982 when the recession forced more people to turn to welfare for subsistence. After this date, the size of the programs fell, but even in 1986, at the height of the economic recovery, their real cost was only slightly less than in 1980.

The intensity of partisan disputes over fiscal matters once again helps account for the surprising durability of these programs in an era when minorities and the poor were often said to be without friends in high office. To counter Democratic charges that he was trying to balance the budget on the backs of the poor, President Reagan promised to maintain the "safety net" for those who had fallen on hard times. But the President also said that he did not want to encourage dependency on federal largess, and he made a number of efforts to reduce the federal role in welfare. In 1981 he was able to secure from Congress changes in the requirements governing eligibility for cash assistance given to poor families with dependent children, 1 percent cuts in food stamps plus a delay in inflation adjustments, and substantial reductions in low-income housing programs. The President also proposed, in 1982, to shift fiscal and policy responsibility for welfare from the federal government to the states, and in 1987 he suggested that states be given more flexibility in the administration of their programs. The President also proposed to cap Medicaid expenditures, as well as cut and deregulate education programs for the handicapped and for children from low-income families.[24]

But although the President was able to check the growth of safety-net programs, he was not able really to cut them back; the outcome was to stabilize the programs as they had evolved by 1980. Except for marginal changes made in 1981, a Democratically controlled House and a combination of Democrats and moderate Republicans in the Senate fought vigorously to sustain safety-net programs, exempting most of them even from the automatic cuts required by Gramm-Rudman. Presidential vetoes were seldom threatened and never used on these programs because the President was vulnerable to charges that he lacked sympathy for the plight of the poor. Democrats were unable to expand the safety net, but the Reagan administration, despite its concern that federal programs were making the poor too dependent on government handouts, could not reduce them or change their design.

FARMERS

In yet a third income-support program, farm subsidies, the Reagan administration was largely unsuccessful in cutting government spending. Although the federal government has a long history of supporting farmers, farm subsidies exploded in the 1980s. The farm economy, and farmer incomes, had boomed during the 1970s as foreign markets for U.S. grain grew an average of 10 percent per year. Exports and incomes slumped sharply in the 1980s, however, as a result of a rising dollar, increased production in other parts of the world, and slower demand from countries already heavily in debt. Real farm-sector earnings dropped from an average of $21 billion between 1970 and 1974 to $12 billion between 1980 and 1984.[25]

The foundation of federal agriculture policy was a system of price supports in which the government set a minimum price for many farm products. If market prices fell below the minimum price, the government would buy the farmers' products. During the 1970s, the government's minimum price rose. As long as prices were generally rising, this did not cost the government very much, because farmers were selling most of their products on the open market. As prices began to fall in the 1980s, however, the government was forced to assume a huge burden; suddenly its minimum guaranteed price became the best price available, and the government was faced with buying billions of dollars worth of crops. Federal farm programs looked like they would become increasingly expensive.

The Reagan administration was no fan of these programs. "The worst nonsense of all in the budget, of course, was farm subsidies," said David Stockman, the President's key budget adviser.[26] Consistent with this view, Reagan's initial budget proposals virtually eliminated all farm subsidy programs. These plans went exactly nowhere. Republicans could not ignore their strong supporters on the farms in the small towns of the Midwest, and the rural bias of the Senate ensured that the claims of these constituents were well represented in Congress. Seeing the farm crisis as a weak point in the Republican political armor, Democrats resisted all attempts to hurt "the family farmer."

Bipartisan support for new farm legislation was readily mobilized, and a new farm bill, continuing liberal subsidies, was passed in 1985. It attempted to reduce surplus production (to cut government-held stocks) while supporting farm income. While eliminating the yearly increases in price supports that had been occurring since 1975, it retained the price-support system and otherwise merely extended production limits and trade incentives.[27] Even with these concessions to rural America, the Republicans in 1986 lost Senate seats in such farm states as North Dakota, South Dakota, Alabama, Georgia, and North Carolina. Meanwhile, federal spending on farm income support increased from $2.6 billion in 1974 (the low point in the last three decades) to $26 billion in 1986. In the end, the President lost both control of the Senate and his battle to reduce the size of farm programs.

IRON TRIANGLES ON THE DEFENSIVE

The Reagan administration was more successful in cutting other domestic programs. These programs are so varied that it is difficult to state comprehensively which interests were hurt. But as can be seen in figure 7.3, the slashed programs included those in energy, environment, transportation, housing, law enforcement, general scientific research, health education, employment training, and aid to state and local governments. The share of the budget for these and other domestic programs fell from 24 percent in 1980 to a startlingly low 15 percent in 1988.

Both a Republican administration and Democrats in Congress were willing to sacrifice these programs in order to make some small progress toward deficit reduction. Although each program had its specialized constituency fighting to keep its piece of the federal pie, a congressional subcommittee that traditionally could be counted on to protect its funding, and a federal agency willing to defend its "turf," these programs did not feature prominently in the strategic calculations of party leaders in Congress and the White House. In the battle over fiscal deficits, they were the big losers.[28]

Ironically, some of the biggest losers were program favorites of previous Republican Presidents Nixon and Ford. General revenue sharing, the community development block grant, aid to desegregating school districts, and education-

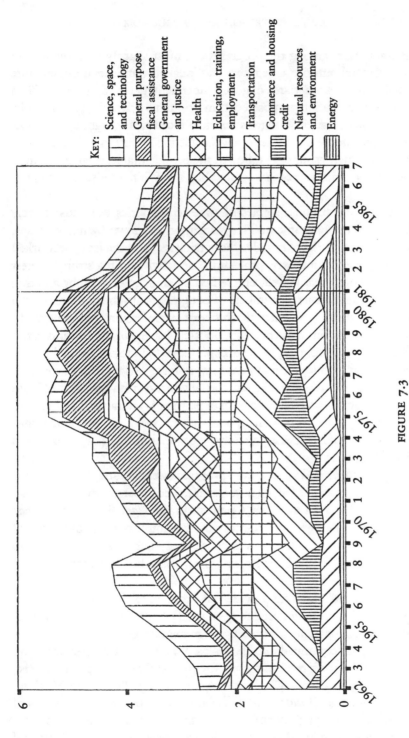

FIGURE 7.3

DOMESTIC DISCRETIONARY PROGRAMS AS A PERCENTAGE OF GNP, 1962–86

KEY:
- Science, space, and technology
- General purpose fiscal assistance
- General government and justice
- Health
- Education, training, employment
- Transportation
- Commerce and housing credit
- Natural resources and environment
- Energy

SOURCE: Figures compiled from *Budget of the United States, Fiscal Year 1989* (Washington, D.C.: Government Printing Office, 1988), table 3.3.

al block grants were among the programs cut most sharply or eliminated.[29] As a result, general-purpose aid to state and local governments dropped more dramatically than any other area of government activity (see figure 7.3). When the Reagan administration proposed cuts in programs originally sponsored by Republicans, Democrats in Congress had few incentives to fight on their behalf. Unlike the intense resistance to any suggestion of cuts in aid to the poor or the elderly, Congress not only followed the presidential lead but sometimes made even deeper cuts in these programs than the White House had suggested.[30]

One of the institutional staples of American politics was thus severely wounded during the Reagan era. This institution is known by many names: the vested interests, the iron triangle, "holy trinities," and the issue network.[31] It consists of a specific industry, profession, or activity with a strong interest in a particular policy that is well represented by an aggressive lobby and that has built close connections to members of congressional subcommittees (who often come from districts in which the industry or profession is concentrated). The lobby also maintains close ties with political leaders of the administrative agency managing the program, who are expected to fight for its gradual expansion. Agency, subcommittee, and interest group form a triangle that works together in a nonpartisan manner to counter any threat from the White House or the congressional leadership. Program expansion is guaranteed by quiet insider negotiation, partisan neutrality, and the cultivation of key influentials. Funding sometimes continues long after the original purpose of the program is fulfilled or forgotten.

During the 1960s and 1970s, these programs were among the rapidly expanding components of the federal government. Their cost grew from less than 3 percent of GNP in 1962 to nearly 6 percent in 1980 (see figure 7.3 on page 229). Many considered them the quintessential example of government out of control. Government grew and grew because the system was well designed to meet the demands of special interests, no matter what the cost to the American taxpayer.[32]

The "impact aid" program provides an excellent example of this institutional nexus.[33] This program, originally enacted during World War II to assist school districts dramatically affected by large military concentrations mobilized by the war, has continued into the 1980s. Wherever federal personnel live or work, a school district receives money for every child of a federal employee, military or civilian, attending a local school. School districts in Virginia, Maryland, California, Florida, and Texas are among the major recipients of this federal aid, even though it remains to be shown just how they are in more need of federal help than other school districts. Indeed, many are better off because the federal installation in their district generates economic activity that helps sustain the tax base of the local district.

Over the years, Presidents have generally sought to reduce the size of the impact-aid program. As President Kennedy observed when he reluctantly signed a law keeping this program alive in 1961:

> . . . undesirable is the continuation for two more years of the current aid-to-impact-areas program, which gives more money to more schools for more years than either logic or economy can justify. This Administration recommended a reduction in the cost of this program, an increase in its eligibility requirements and local participation, its extension for only one year instead of two, and its eventual absorption in a general aid-to-education program. The rejection of all these requirements highlights the air of utter inconsistency which surrounds this program.[34]

In spite of presidential resistance over the years, the legislation remained popular in Congress, which was lobbied assiduously by the National Association of Impacted Districts. Over 4000 school districts, located in virtually every congressional district, became beneficiaries of the program as program eligibility was gradually extended.[35] In 1956, for example, children of military personnel on active duty away from home were made eligible; in 1958, restrictions on monies to larger school districts were eased, Indian children became eligible, and any child with a parent in federal employ was counted for purposes of aid distribution. In 1963, Washington, D.C., schools became beneficiaries; in 1965, construction assistance was made available to areas suffering a "major disaster"; in 1967, the definition of "minimum school facilities" was broadened; in 1970, children living in federally subsidized, low-rent housing were included in the program. In 1974, and again in 1978, Congress attempted to organize these changes into a systematic statement on eligibility, which in the end further extended the benefits and introduced new complexities into eligibility requirements.

All these complex, continuing extensions of eligibility by Congress helped sustain legislative support for the law. As shown in table 7.1, Congress has appropriated hundreds of millions of dollars more for impact aid than the President requested in every year since 1970. But impact aid was one of the major casualties of the Reagan era. Its budget was cut from nearly $1.4 billion a year in the early 1970s to just over $600 million in the mid-1980s. As strenuously as the affected school districts tried, they were able to keep only 60 percent of the funding they had received in the late 1970s. Instead, the elementary and secondary education dollar was concentrated on programs for the poor and the handicapped, which actually increased in size between 1980 and 1985.[36]

The shrinking of the impact-aid program is just one example of the shift in power away from the iron triangles of agency, subcommittee, and interest

TABLE 7.1

THE IMPACT-AID PROGRAM

Fiscal Year	Budget Requested by the Administration (in millions)	Amount Appropriated by the Congress (in millions)
1970-74	$808.1	$1379.0
1975-78	489.6	1050.5
1981-84	373.3	571.7
1985-87	436.6	611.0

SOURCES: *Congressional Quarterly Almanac* (1969), 547; (1970), 261; (1971), 205; (1972), 874; (1973), 157; (1974), 110; (1975), 785; (1976), 791; (1977), 297-98; (1978), 106; (1979), 237; (1980), 225; (1981), 501; (1982), 252; (1983), 505; (1984), 422; (1985), 335; (1986), 200. See also *Budget of the U.S. Government, Fiscal Year 1988* (Washington, D.C.: Government Printing Office, 1987), 4-77; and *Education Week*, 26 January 1988.

group on the one side, to party leaders and central decision makers on the other. The shift has occurred in both the executive and legislative branches.

Within the executive branch, power over both budgetary and regulatory questions has shifted from the agencies and the departments to the Office of Management and Budget (OMB) and the White House staff.[37] Although agencies still prepare preliminary budgets, these are now severely scrutinized by OMB examiners, who not only look for soft spots in agency proposals but are prepared to make massive reductions in order to meet the President's cost-cutting fiscal objectives. The new power of OMB is also signaled by its energetic review of all agency regulatory proposals. The politicized use of OMB power is indicated by the fact that key positions in OMB are no longer held by program analysts, known for their technical expertise, but by fiscal analysts, whose main concern is the President's overall budgetary targets.[38]

Centralizing forces are also apparent within Congress. In part this reflects the increasing prominence of the new budget committees, which are responsible for establishing overall fiscal targets and are less closely connected to specialized interests than the old appropriations subcommittees had become. In addition, the budget has become such a crucial area of partisan debate that appropriations are now typically settled in a year-end set of negotiations among party leaders more concerned with achieving certain deficit-reduction targets than responding to specialized constituencies.[39] In this highly politicized context, the only groups that can exercise effective political muscle are those that have become the focal point of the two-party debate. In this context, the elderly, the needy, and farmers do surprisingly well. Institutionalized special interests take a beating.

No one would mistake the Congresses of the 1980s for a highly centralized body; legislators still have ample incentives and resources to go their own way on many less visible issues. But both the President and Congress have demonstrated that they are able to make fairly radical policy changes and are not captive to forces limiting them to minor, incremental adjustments. Reagan in 1981 was able to achieve large tax cuts and a substantial reordering of spending priorities. In 1986, Congress, with Reagan's support, was able to pass sweeping tax reform that stripped many tax breaks from special interests while providing a simpler, fairer tax system. Few would have predicted that either event would come to pass.

GUNS AND BUTTER

Although Reagan succeeded in cutting grants to state and local governments and other domestic programs, these reductions barely offset the increases in expenditure for the elderly, farmers, and safety-net programs. Overall, domestic federal expenditures as a percentage of GNP remained roughly the same from the beginning to the end of the Reagan administration. Given this stalemate on domestic spending (and the increased cost of financing the public debt, which was taking 2 percent more of GNP than it did in pre-Reagan years), the only way that Reagan's commitment to increased military strength could be realized was by increasing the overall rate of federal expenditure.

After a Vietnam war peak in 1968 (at $219 billion in 1982 dollars), real defense spending fell steadily throughout the 1970s. In 1980, only 5 percent of GNP was used for defense, the smallest amount since immediately after World War II. The composition of defense spending also shifted, away from weapons development and procurement and toward personnel and operations. Although President Carter had proposed and received modest increases in defense budgets every year he was in office, Reagan's defense proposals far exceeded Carter's. Reagan firmly held to the position that the only way to negotiate with the Soviet Union was by having a powerful military; he advocated peace through strength. Iran's ability to take U.S. embassy personnel hostage and taunt the United States for its inability to do anything about it (taunts emphasized by the humiliating failure of an attempted rescue) drove home this point to the American public.

The perception of American military weakness became so convincing that Reagan was able to push through Congress virtually all his initial defense proposals, which constituted the largest peacetime defense build-up in history. The politics of the matter initially were simple. Republicans in Congress tended to favor defense spending; at any rate, they supported their popular President. After a decade of reducing real military expenditures, Democrats knew they were vulnerable to charges of being "soft" on defense, and so they more-or-less willingly followed Reagan on this issue. Real spending on defense increased by 17 percent in Reagan's first year in office. But congressional willingness to fund a continued steep growth in defense expenditures in the face of huge budget deficits waned noticeably in Reagan's second term. The outcome looks different depending on the way it is measured. As a percentage of GNP, defense costs rose only to 7 percent, still short of the 10 percent level of the Vietnam era (see figure 7.2); but in real dollar terms, defense expenditures climbed well above their Vietnam war high.

The debate between the President and Congress seemed to hinge on whether spending would emphasize "guns" or "butter." Congress regularly reduced the President's proposed defense appropriations by an amount more or less equal to the amount by which they increased his domestic proposals. In this way, Congress was able to keep the deficit from rising above the level indicated in the President's original budget.[40]

The President threatened to veto efforts to shift his budget priorities from defense to domestic objectives. Congress countered by refusing to appropriate the defense budget until domestic appropriations had been approved. Since neither side wanted to give the other a tactical advantage, both defense and domestic appropriations came to be included in one large piece of legislation passed at the close of the fiscal year. If the President vetoed the bill, he could not obtain the increased defense appropriations he sought. If he signed the bill, he accepted higher domestic expenditures than he wanted. After using a threatened veto to win the best compromise he could get, the President was forced to accept major congressional modifications to his budgetary proposals. By 1988, the President was so frustrated by this procedure that in his State of the Union address he promised to veto any unified spending bill passed at the end of a legislative session.

In the end, the country got both guns and butter (see figure 7.2). The great growth in domestic expenditure that had occurred in the 1970s remained at the same high level it had reached by 1980. The increase in defense costs came in addition to, not instead of, domestic programs. These decisions meant that in the absence of additional revenues, large deficits were inevitable. As the public debt escalated, the increased costs of financing it further fueled the growth of federal expenditures. Far from cutting the size of the federal government, Reagan presided over its increase to new heights.

Economic Consequences

Thus far, three of Reagan's policy objectives—reducing government, rebuilding defense, and rejuvenating the economy—seem at least partially to have been met. Certainly the growth in taxes has been halted, and Reagan has gained the largest increase in peacetime defense spending. Reagan supporters also point with pride to the longest sustained economic recovery in peacetime since the Great Depression. After an initial, sharp recession in late 1981 and 1982, the economy has grown steadily from the spring of 1983 until mid 1988, a recovery that has exceeded the average postwar recovery by two years. More people are employed than ever before, and hourly earnings have increased. Unemployment rates have fallen from over 10 percent to about 6 percent. Corporate profits have risen, and the stock market (even after its October 1987 crash) has more than doubled. All of this has been achieved without renewing rampant inflation.

If prolonged economic growth, low inflation, and declining unemployment seem to herald a major triumph, this has hardly hushed the critics of what George Bush, in a widely quoted phrase, once identified as Reagan's "voodoo economics." Reagan's tax cuts have not brought about the surge in revenues he hoped would pay for his defense build-up. Instead, combined with increased interest payments and no reduction in domestic costs, the policy changes have led to huge deficits. The recovery of the 1980s, it is asserted, rests on tenuous footing because these deficits have been financed by public borrowing on a scale previously unheard of in times of peace and economic prosperity.

The effect of budget deficits on the economy depends on where the government borrows the money to finance them. Government can borrow from three sources: domestic savers, foreign investors, and itself. When the government "borrows" from itself, it basically "creates" money to pay its debts. Although this may seem a most politically attractive way to finance the deficits, this kind of borrowing is inflationary. The Federal Reserve Board, supported by the Reagan administration, consequently avoided this technique in the early years of the administration. Instead, the government mainly financed its deficits by borrowing from domestic savers and foreign investors. In doing so, it increased the competition for capital, increasing real (inflation adjusted) interest rates.

Heavy government borrowing, and the increased interest rates it produces, has adversely affected the economy in several ways. First, it has soaked up much of the pool of domestic savings. The net national savings rate (private savings minus government borrowing) has fallen from an average of 7.5 percent of GNP in the 1960s to 6.9 percent in the 1970s to 2.8 percent in the 1980s.[41] As the government borrows more to finance its deficits, less is available at greater cost for business investment. Inasmuch as business investment is necessary for future economic growth, federal deficits can hinder that growth.

Second, by increasing the real rate of interest, deficits have attracted foreign investment to the United States. Ever since World War I, the United States has invested more around the world than it has borrowed. But as fiscal deficits have mounted, Americans have invested less abroad, while foreigners have found U.S. investments attractive. In 1986, the United States became the world's largest debtor nation.[42] Interest payments on this debt, instead of remaining in this country for future investment, have flowed abroad.

Finally, even though foreign investment helped supply the especially strong demand for credit within the United States (and thus helped prevent real interest rates from rising even higher), the increase in foreign investment in the United States caused the value of the dollar to increase dramatically. Between 1980 and 1985, the value of the dollar (vis-à-vis its major trading partners) rose by 50 percent. This increase temporarily helped the purchasing power of U.S. consumers by making imports cheaper, contributing to the economic prosperity of the 1980s. But the increase made it difficult for U.S. producers to sell their goods abroad, and the U.S. trade balance (exports minus imports) fell precipitously. In figure 7.4 one can see that in the 1980s, U.S. imports have kept rising at the same rate they had moved upward in earlier decades, but exports have leveled off and actually declined, leaving an increasingly large trade deficit.

The dollar's value peaked in 1985; since then, the dollar has steadily declined so that in 1988 it is worth about what it was worth in 1979. But the trade deficit has not shrunk. Although foreign products are no longer the bargains they were during Reagan's early years, foreign competitors, by establishing sales outlets, winning consumer loyalty, and sacrificing some of their profits, have secured an apparently enduring position in the U.S. market, thereby keeping trade deficits at record-breaking levels. Should these deficits continue they will injure the country's economy in the same ways that heavy foreign borrowing does: Funds, and jobs, will continue to flow out of the country.

The Reagan Legacy

The President's supporters believe that Reagan's policies have brought a new morning of prosperity to America. His critics look at the same policies and see a disaster waiting to happen. Which is it? Neither, entirely. Reagan's legacy is more complex than either side might care to admit.

The good news is that in most respects the American political system seems to have worked. This view is not a popular one with either those who reject Reagan's policies or those who object to Congress's unwillingness to adopt them in full. But even critics must admit that a determined President was able to accomplish many of his stated goals. Reagan gained the largest increase in peacetime defense spending, a step he felt was necessary in order for the country to regain its position as the world's preeminent military power. Reagan cut tax rates sharply and dramatically altered the income tax system, policies to which his administration was also deeply committed. Reagan sheared back a great number of domestic programs, thus carrying out in good part his promises

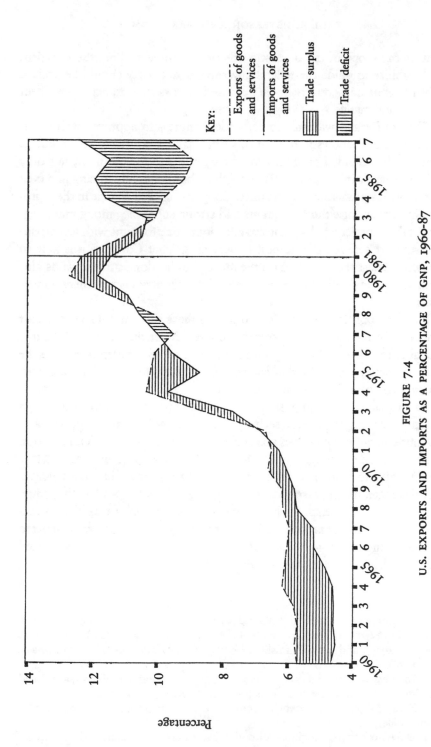

FIGURE 7.4

U.S. EXPORTS AND IMPORTS AS A PERCENTAGE OF GNP, 1960-87

KEY:

- - - - Exports of goods and services

———— Imports of goods and services

Trade surplus

Trade deficit

SOURCE: Figures compiled from *Survey of Current Business*, tables 4.1 and 4.2, various issues.

to reduce the scope of the domestic side of government. That the President had the ability to guide the federal government decisively should be praised by both liberals and conservatives, because it shows that an active President can effectuate change.

Though Reagan was able to persuade Congress to approve much of his defense, tax, and domestic programs, Congress was no mere rubber stamp. It tenaciously defended programs for the elderly and for the poor, not only rejecting Reagan's initial proposals to cut them but eventually forcing him even to withdraw proposals along these lines. Congress blocked change in these programs in part because these programs had strong suppport among many segments of the American public. Meanwhile, domestic programs with less broad-based support suffered the deepest budget cuts. That Congress was able to successfully resist the President on the most popular domestic programs also demonstrates the political responsiveness of the country's governmental institutions.

But if the political system worked well in these ways, it did so at the cost of creating fiscal deficits unprecedented in size. Under the circumstances it is reasonable to ask why little significant action has been taken to reduce the deficit. The answer must be that current officeholders have a greater commitment to goals other than deficit reduction.

As long as the President resists any increase in personal income taxes, cuts in defense, or changes in social security policy, and as long as Congress maintains entitlements and preserves safety nets, scant progress on deficit reduction will be made. But there is no need for this deadlock to be permanent. It is not impossible to imagine a President and Congress, operating in a changed political climate, mixing tax increases and military "build-downs" with gradual reductions in entitlements. Such a strategy seems especially feasible, given a President with a fresh mandate and a Congress that is more centrally directed than before. Indeed, deficit reduction may be one of the first issues addressed once the stalemate of the Reagan years is broken.

Notes

1. Explanations of supply-side philosophy by prominent advocates include Arthur Laffer and Jan Seymour, *The Economics of the Tax Revolt* (New York: Harcourt Brace Jovanovich, 1979); and Jude Wanniski, *The Way the World Works* (New York: Basic Books, 1978).

2. For Reagan's opinions about the causes of the economic problems, see David A. Stockman, *The Triumph of Politics* (New York: Avon, 1986), 162.

3. Henry Aaron et al., *Economic Choices 1987* (Washington, D.C.: Brookings Institution, 1986), 22.

4. Unless otherwise specified, all dollar figures are in constant dollars (1982).

5. The President himself said that he thought the bill was unconstitutional on the day he signed it, and his solicitor general argued before the Supreme Court against its constitutionality. A year later, a weaker version of Gramm-Rudman was passed, and its provisions took effect for a short period in October 1987.

6. The law was later passed without the automatic GAO provision and did not take effect for a couple of months. But without the GAO provision providing automatic cuts in the absence of congressional action, it lost much of its "doomsday" quality.

7. *Congressional Quarterly*, 6 February 1988.

8. This was the expected change in revenue per year in current dollars after the policies had taken full effect. Joseph A. Pechman, *Federal Tax Policy*, 5th ed. (Washington, D.C.: Brookings Institution, 1987), 40-41.

9. The boll weevil infests the cotton plant and has long been a concern of southern politicians. The term is now used to refer to southern Democrats who break with their party leaders on issues thought to be of particular importance to the South.

10. Pechman, *Federal Tax Policy*, 40-41.

11. Douglas Hibbs, *American Political Economy* (Cambridge, Mass.: Harvard University Press, 1987), 311.

12. Office of the President, *Economic Report of the President, 1987* (Washington, D.C.: Government Printing Office, 1987), 85.

13. Data on federal expenditures, revenues, and deficits are presented as a percentage of GNP because this allows meaningful comparisons over time. When presented in this form, we control for changes in the size of the U.S. economy.

14. James P. Pfiffner, "The Reagan Budget Juggernaut," in *The President and Economic Policymaking*, ed. James P. Pfiffner (Philadelphia: Institute for Human Studies, 1986), 111; see also Stockman, *Triumph of Politics*.

15. Pfiffner, "Reagan Budget," 113.

16. The largest programs in this category are social security, pensions for veterans and federal employees, and Medicare.

17. Social security faced similar problems. As inflation raised wages of employees, they became eligible for higher benefit levels. When they retired, cost-of-living adjustments raised their benefits a second time. In 1977 Congress changed the law to eliminate this quirk for those retiring after 1979. See Kent Weaver, *Automatic Government: The Politics of Indexation* (Washington, D.C.: Brookings Institution, 1988).

18. The rate of gain in life expectancy was much greater after 1970 than in the two previous decades. On data and discussion of these issues, see Gary Burtless, ed., *Work, Health and Income among the Elderly* (Washington, D.C.: Brookings Institution, 1986).

19. The story of how this bipartisan agreement was realized is well told in Paul Light, *Artful Work: Politics of Social Security Reform* (New York: Random House, 1985).

20. Historical Tables, *Budget of the United States Government, 1988* (Washington, D.C.: Government Printing Office, 1987), table 2.1(2).

21. Gary Freeman, "Presidents, Pensions, and Fiscal Policy," in Pfiffner, *President and Economic Policymaking*, 151-53.

22. *New York Times*, 15 February 1976. Cited in Mark Green and Gail MacColl, *Reagan's Reign of Error* (New York: Pantheon, 1987), 85.

23. Stockman, *Triumph of Politics*, 9.

24. Paul E. Peterson, Barry G. Rabe, and Kenneth K. Wong, *When Federalism Works* (Washington, D.C.: Brookings Institution, 1986), 222-24.

25. Gary L. Benjamin, "The Financial Stress in Agriculture," *Economic Perspectives* (Federal Reserve Bank of Chicago), November/December 1985, 3-16.

26. Stockman, *Triumph of Politics,* 166.

27. Raymond E. Owens, "An Overview of Agricultural Policy . . . Past, Present, and Future," *Economic Review* (Federal Reserve Bank of Richmond), May/June 1987, 39-50.

28. The story of how these cuts affected five agencies is well told by Irene Rubin, *Shrinking the Federal Government* (White Plains, N.Y.: Longman, 1985).

29. The effects of these cuts on local governments were much less than many had expected. See George E. Peterson and Carol W. Lewis, eds., *Reagan and the Cities* (Washington, D.C.: Urban Institute, 1986).

30. Peterson, Rabe, and Wong, *When Federalism Works,* chap. 9.

31. The literature on this well-researched topic is vast. For examples, see Hugh Heclo, *A Government of Strangers* (Washington, D.C.: Brookings Institution, 1977); V.O. Key, Jr., *Politics, Parties and Pressure Groups,* 5th ed. (New York: Crowell, 1964); Harold Seidman and Robert Gilmour, *Politics, Position and Power: From the Positive to the Regulatory State,* 4th ed. (New York: Oxford University Press, 1986); and Andrew McFarland, *Common Cause* (Chatham, N.J.: Chatham House, 1984).

32. See Morris P. Fiorina, *Congress: Keystone of the Washington Establishment* (New Haven: Yale University Press, 1977); and Allan H. Meltzer and Scott O. Richard, "Why Government Grows (and Grows) in a Democracy," *Public Interest* 52 (Summer 1978): 111-18.

33. The following three paragraphs are adapted from Paul E. Peterson, "Background Paper," in *Making the Grade, Report of the Twentieth Century Fund Task Force on Federal Elementary and Secondary Education Policy* (New York: Twentieth Century Fund, 1983), 77-78.

34. *Congressional Quarterly Almanac* (Washington, D.C.: CQ Press, 1961), 243.

35. U.S. Office of Education, "Administration of Public Laws 81-874 and 81-875," *Annual Report of the Commissioner of Education, Fiscal Year 1978* (Washington, D.C.: Government Printing Office, 1979), 23.

36. Peterson, Rabe, and Wong, *When Federalism Works,* 39-40.

37. Terry Moe, "The Politicized Presidency," in *The New Direction in American Politics,* ed. John E. Chubb and Paul E. Peterson (Washington, D.C.: Brookings Institution, 1985), 235-74.

38. Hugh Heclo, "Executive Budget Making," in *Federal Budget Policy in the 1980s,* ed. Gregory Mills and John Palmer (Washington, D.C.: Urban Institute, 1984), 255-91.

39. Allen Schick, *Crisis in the Budget Process: Exercising Political Choice* (Washington, D.C.: American Enterprise Institute, 1986), 32-40.

40. Paul E. Peterson, "The Politics of Deficits," in Chubb and Peterson, *New Direction in American Politics,* 365-98.

41. Aaron et al., *Economic Choices,* 23.

42. Ralph Bryant, *International Financial Intermediation* (Washington, D.C.: Brookings Institution, 1987), 39.

8

Reagan and the World:
An "Awesome Stubbornness"

I. M. DESTLER

"The secret of Ronald Reagan's success," wrote William Schneider in 1986, "is his ability to have his cake and eat it too. He defines his program in bold, uncompromising terms, and then proceeds to play the cautious, moderate politician, bargaining for the best deal he can get. Throughout his Presidency, Reagan's failure to carry out the most controversial elements of his program has saved him politically. . . ."[1]

With the December 1987 Reagan-Gorbachev summit and the signing of the treaty eliminating medium and shorter-range nuclear arms, this sort of interpretation has become standard concerning Reagan as foreign policy President. Extreme in rhetoric but moderate in action, conclude many relieved liberals; a "useful idiot for Soviet propaganda," cry critics from the Far Right.[2] Both see the President as driven by experience and pragmatism from resonant right-wing rhetoric to safe (or nefarious) mainstream practice.

On many issues, this has clearly happened. China policy offers an early example. Taiwan was seeking in 1981 to purchase the FX fighter plane; the People's Republic threatened a downgrading of relations if such a sale was made, or indeed unless the United States set a date for terminating all arms sales to Taiwan. Reagan's heart and right-wing constituency clearly lay with the anticommunist island regime, but he twice sacrificed ideology to *realpolitik;* first deciding not to sell the FX, then stating officially in August 1982 the U.S. intention "to reduce gradually its sales of arms to Taiwan." The way was then open to the further development of normalization, to the benefit of the People's Republic, the United States, and quite possibly Taiwan as well.[3]

In international economic relations, the Reagan administration started out spurning international economic coordination, especially over exchange rates. But beginning in 1985, domestic protectionist pressures drove it to lead an ambitious effort by "Group of Five" finance ministers to get the dollar down and the trade balance right—the sort of action that many mainstream economists had been urging for years.[4]

The public at large was particularly anxious about whether Reagan would send American forces into battle; this was reflected in general public opinion polls and in the intense negative reaction to early administration bellicosity over El Salvador. But in the actual use of armed force, the President proved quite cautious. Only tiny Grenada was subject to presidentially ordered U.S. military intervention, under circumstances of governmental breakdown that minimized domestic and international opposition and maximized prospects for success. Nicaragua has been the target of the *contras* and countless Reagan speeches, but not the U.S. Marines.

On covert intelligence activities, Reagan (and his late Central Intelligence Agency [CIA] director, William Casey) sought secret operations as a means to toughen foreign policy without the risks—and domestic political costs—of direct military action. But although they worked persistently to elude congressional controls, as the Iran-*contra* embroglio illustrated, that same embroglio forced the President to promise close consultation with Congress, as Jimmy Carter had before him.

There were also occasions where Congress quite simply overrode Reagan: on sanctions toward South Africa, on selected arms control and weapons development issues, and sometimes on aid to *contra* forces in Nicaragua.

Last, and certainly not least, the President's hosting of Gorbachev, head of the "evil empire," resembled the Nixon-Ford "détente" policy, against which *candidate* Ronald Reagan had railed, with considerable effect, in the 1976 and 1980 Republican primaries.

Certainly the recent foreign policy record has not been one of "Reagan *uber alles*." Like previous Presidents, this one has learned that chief executives simply *do not* and *cannot* dictate foreign policy the way that *some* constitutional interpreters suggest they should.[5]

Hence it is hardly surprising that on most issues, over his first seven years as President, Ronald Reagan *did* move to the center. So did his predecessors. Yet on several very important issues where he was deeply and personally committed, Ronald Reagan hung tough. He stood fast on the budget, thus perpetuating American trade and payments deficits. He did so on strategic arms control and particularly his Strategic Defense Initiative (SDI). He did so on support of the *contras* in Central America. And he did so, until the scandal broke, on selling arms to Iran in connection with his effort to win release of Americans held hostage in Lebanon, despite the passionate opposition of Secretary of State George Shultz and Secretary of Defense Caspar Weinberger.

His stubbornness mattered. By holding to his position on these issues, Ronald Reagan changed the position of the United States in the world, leaving it significantly different from the way he found it.

Put another way, Ronald Reagan has certainly been a pragmatist, but the goals to which he has proved most committed have typically *not* been centrist. As President, he has been able to use his leverage to block actions inconsistent with his goals and to move the range of possible outcomes in his preferred direction. On the budget. On SDI. On Central America. And, albeit abortively, on Iran arms sales.

In particular, Reagan has exploited the autonomy of the modern American President: his capacity to set the public agenda; his day-to-day operational leeway on issues where executive agencies have the action; his effective veto over compromises that involve a sharing of pain. Reagan's policy persistence, his personal stubbornness—these have been what made his foreign policy regime distinctive. And they are what this chapter examines.

The Political Base for Stubbornness

To make his personal mark on American foreign policy, Ronald Reagan needed a strong domestic base. It would have been best to have enthusiastic majority support for his specific, hard-line positions, but this was rarely present. Reagan's core constituency on the Right, of course, was more than happy to place SDI ahead of arms control, or to see Central America primarily as an arena for ideological combat. But such viewpoints were seldom shared by most American citizens. Without such broader backing, support by the Right alone was a distinctly mixed blessing, since actions enthusiastically endorsed by that constituency were likely, almost by definition, to provoke opposition from the Left and Center.

Another potential source of political strength, highlighted in the work of Richard Neustadt, is professional reputation. As Neustadt reminds us in his classic *Presidential Power,* the Washington policy community is constantly watching the President and his key aides, evaluating and reevaluating their standing and skills. If these are highly rated, members of this community, meaning the other Washington policy players, are more willing to grant the administration leeway on specific issues, and more wary of risking direct challenges.

But Washingtonians' attitudes toward the Reagan regime have been ambivalent. There has been enormous respect for, and not a little fear of, the President's public political skills. His capacity to evoke broadly shared public values in support of his initiatives has been widely admired; his readiness to label Democrats as taxers, or warn anti-*contra* congressmen that *they* will be held accountable for any spread of communism in Central America if they beat him on a crucial vote—these have made other policy players think twice about going all-out on these issues. Through such public advocacy, Reagan bought both time and acquiescence for his positions.

But the administration's reputation for policy competence has not been at all high regarding either individuals or the broader policy-making system. The Tower Board investigating what it labeled "the Iran-*contra* affair" found "a flawed process" and "a failure of responsibility" on the part of every senior policy player from Ronald Reagan down.[6] Just as devastating, perhaps, is that one searches their report in vain for offsetting praise of the administration's policy making on other issues. The board's members—former Senator John Tower, former Secretary of State Edmund S. Muskie, and former national security assistant Brent Scowcroft—had watched and worked with the administration on numerous issues since Reagan entered office. Had they been favorably impressed during earlier encounters, they would surely have found some way to say so. The fact that they said nothing positive about the President, his people, or their policy-making system suggests a more sweeping critique.

Certain administration officials have frequently commanded bipartisan respect: Secretary of the Treasury James Baker III and Secretary of State George P. Shultz come to mind. But the leadership at the CIA, the National Security Council (NSC), and the Defense Department did not, at least until the departure of the late William Casey from the first and the appointment of Frank Carlucci to direct the second and (then) the third.

The political base Reagan did gain, through the central years of his administration, was broad public backing. This was not support for specific foreign policy positions and initiatives; it was wide approval of his performance as President. This approval coalesced at the end of 1983, was reflected in his landslide reelection in 1984, and rose to even higher levels in 1985 and 1986.

From January 1981 onward, the first two questions in the New York Times/ CBS News public opinion poll were these:

1. Do you approve or disapprove of the way Ronald Reagan is handling his job as President?

2. Do you approve or disapprove of the way Ronald Reagan is handling foreign policy?

In Reagan's first two and three-quarter years, the responses could not have been all that encouraging to the White House. Approval numbers on the first question ran in the 60s and 50s during the honeymoon year of 1981, but dropped to the 41–47 range thereafter. These levels were generally *below* those of Reagan's predecessors at comparable stages of their Presidencies.

For question 2, Reagan's results were worse: The average foreign policy approval rating was 51 percent in 1981 and just 41 percent from January 1982 through September 1983.

Such public ambivalence is not hard to explain. Most important, no doubt, was the downturn of the economy, which plunged into severe recession by early 1982 and dropped the President's *economic* policy approval ratings into the 30s! But there were also foreign policy-based reasons for popular skepticism. Reagan himself neglected foreign policy in his initial years, giving overwhelming priority to winning congressional approval of his economic program. The only international matter getting serious presidential attention in 1981 was an unpopular arms sale to Saudi Arabia, where Reagan's personal intercession was necessary to avert a congressional veto.

Reagan's White House aides, meanwhile, were waging intermittent battles with Secretary of State Alexander Haig. And both Reagan and Haig were showing a penchant for careless public speculation on matters nuclear—about "exchange of tactical weapons against troops in the field" or "demonstration" detonation of a nuclear device at times of crisis—fueling anxieties just where the President had been particularly vulnerable, on whether he might involve the nation in war.

In late 1983, however, Reagan's job approval ratings jumped back above 50 percent. And they remained there for three years. What brought this about? The most important general cause, no doubt, was improvement in the economy —at mid-year, the unemployment rate began a steady decline, from 10.1 percent in June 1983 to 7.2 percent eighteen months later. But the administration action that directly preceded the jump in Reagan's public standing was the successful use of U.S. forces in October 1983 to overturn the divided, embattled Marxist regime on the tiny island of Grenada. The rationale and pretext for the action was to protect American lives. Its popularity soared when U.S. medical students rescued by the mission kissed the ground on their return to the United States. It stayed high when the Grenadians themselves welcomed the action, and Reagan therefore was able to bring the troops back home before Christmas.

In any event, the percentage of Americans approving of "the way Ronald Reagan is handling his job as President" jumped from 46 in September 1983 to 58 in late November. It held in the mid-50s through the election year of 1984, encouraged by economic resurgence, but also by Reagan's diminished public vulnerability on issues of war. At the State Department, the cautious George

Shultz had replaced the contentious Haig. At the Pentagon, military build-up had allayed anxieties about Soviet "superiority." That nation's continuing leadership turnover, combined with the shoot-down of Korean Air Lines flight 007, had softened criticisms of Reagan's first-term failure to negotiate effectively with Moscow. For no one on the other end of the hot line seemed to stay around long enough to establish a working relationship!

After Reagan's forty-nine-state reelection victory, his popularity jumped again, to a higher plateau. The job approval rating reached 65 percent in January 1985. After a dip that spring, the rating returned to the 60s in July and remained there through October 1986, when it was 67 percent.

It plunged to 46 percent a month later, with the Iran-*contra* revelations, the "sharpest one-month drop ever recorded by a public opinion poll in measuring approval of presidential job performance."[7] And it has generally remained in the 40s and low 50s thereafter; even the December 1987 summit with Gorbachev brought just a one-month boost in Reagan's approval rating.

Foreign policy events seem to have triggered two of the three major turns in Ronald Reagan's job approval ratings. (The third, the plunge in early 1982, was presumably triggered by the recession.) More important for our purposes is not what foreign policy actions did for the Reagan Presidency, but what the popular base Reagan maintained in 1984–86 enabled the President to do vis-à-vis the world. For while his foreign policy ratings (question 2) generally ran lower than his overall job rating, save the short-lived peak of 76 percent following the bombing of Libya in April 1986, it was general public support that gave him political strength—and day-to-day leeway—on foreign policy issues.

Reagan employed this leeway on issues to which he gave particular priority:

1. Reaganomics—tax reduction above all
2. Arms control and the Strategic Defense Initiative
3. Central America and the *contra* war against the Sandinista regime
4. Securing release of U.S. citizens held hostage in Lebanon.

On each of these issues save the last, Reagan's policy priorities were established *before* his surge in public standing. The economic package was legislated in 1981; his public presidential commitments to SDI and the Nicaraguan *contras* date from early 1983. But persistence in these commitments through the high-water years made the difference. Each of these deserves separate treatment.

Reaganomics and the Legacy of Debt

"America Is Back." "It's Morning Again in America." The slogans captured a deep Reaganite aspiration: to bring about a resurgence of U.S. strength and pride and global standing. And the administration clearly accomplished some strengthening of American military forces, through unprecedented peacetime increases in the defense budget.

It is likely, however, that a more durable legacy of the Reagan years will be an erosion of American strength, a result of mortgaging the economic base that underlies both domestic living standards and international power.

To make this point requires a review of well-known history and a detour into the international side of macroeconomics. The basic, inescapable starting point is that the Reagan administration won enactment, beginning in 1981, of major income tax cuts and defense spending increases. These were the primary forces driving the U.S. budget deficit from an average of $63 billion in fiscal years 1978 through 1981 to an average of $207 billion in fiscal years 1983 through 1986.[8]

Since the U.S. private savings rate was low (and declining), for government to borrow such funds on domestic capital markets would have squeezed private investment and pushed interest rates through the ceiling. But there could be an escape from this squeeze if substantial private capital was available from abroad. In the short run, it was: Japanese and Europeans, with home demand sluggish, were eager to invest in American assets, so eager that investment money flowing into the United States bid the value of the dollar up sharply in 1982–85. This produced huge trade deficits, exceeding $100 billion from 1984 onward. The net annual accrual of debt was measured by the global U.S. current account deficit, which shot up from $46 to $106 to $118 to $141 billion in the years 1983 through 1986.

No nation had ever borrowed from foreigners at this rate. And such debt must be financed, if not always repaid. Through borrowing, therefore, the United States incurred substantial—and growing—obligations to send interest payments overseas. By Reagan's last year, relatively optimistic projections saw the nation becoming a *net* international debtor to the tune of $1 trillion by some time in 1992. This compared to a net creditor position of $141 billion in 1981. If the average interest rate were 8 percent, each additional $100 billion of net borrowing would require an additional annual debt service payment of $8 billion to foreign creditors. And this burden would continue indefinitely, unless and until the United States began paying back its debt by running *surpluses* on its international trade accounts.[9]

International borrowing is not always bad. In the short run, it is a means to balance accounts. Over the longer term, borrowed money can make possible a higher level of investment, leading to greater future production in the borrowing nation. Thus citizens of a debtor nation might be better off even *after* meeting interest payments. Unfortunately, this was not the case for Americans.

Private investment in the 1980s in the United States was not notably different from that of previous periods. Instead, what the unprecedented inflow of foreign money *was* financing was a private and public consumption binge: a trade deficit (Americans consuming $150 billion a year more than they were producing); lower tax rates without lower levels of federal spending.

Over time, foreign confidence eroded, as overseas investors increasingly doubted the American capacity to continue on this course and the American will to change it. So the inflow of foreign private funds fell off sharply in 1987, the dollar fell recurrently, and only massive dollar buying by foreign central banks kept it from falling still further.[10]

By the end of 1987, the United States was in a policy bind with no easy exit in the short term and a debt-financing burden in the long term. Yet leaders still resisted drastic attacks on the budget deficit, notwithstanding the enactment of the Gramm-Rudman-Hollings legislation in 1985, which ostensibly required regular spending cuts, and notwithstanding a one-shot improvement of $70 billion in fiscal year 1987 resulting from the phasing in of tax reform. The stock market plunge of October 1987 brought the Reagan administration and congressional leaders together for new budget negotiations, but the results were, by the consensus of leading world economists, "grossly inadequate," since "the agreed 'cuts' would leave the structural deficit in FY 1989 no lower than its present level [$150-160 billion]."[11]

The budget impasse is bemoaned universally, and the standard villain in many accounts is "the Congress." Yet while majorities of the House and Senate certainly did vote for Reagan's tax cuts and defense spending increases in the early 1980s, neither initiated them. Senate Majority Leader Howard Baker signaled his skepticism by labeling tax cuts a "riverboat gamble!" And leadership in tackling the budget imbalance has come, since 1981, from Capitol Hill, not from 1600 Pennsylvania Avenue.

In the spring of 1985, for example, Senate Republican leaders were bold enough to put on the table all the major elements of the needed budget compromise. The President would agree to tax increases, an issue where he held Democrats hostage; the Democrats in turn would agree to reduce the growth of social security payments, the issue on which Republicans were most vulnerable. Defense and other spending would be further pruned, with the balance here again reflecting a compromise between the two parties. For several years, a Bipartisan Budget Coalition, headed by Peter G. Peterson, has been making the case for just such a compromise and suggesting what its components might be.

But for such a package to become a reality in the American system, the White House must play a central role in putting it together and pressing for its enactment. And this Ronald Reagan has refused to allow. His White House shot down Senate Republicans' 1985 compromise (as did Democratic House leaders). The White House has put forward no realistic alternative, constitutional amendment proposals notwithstanding.

In Reagan's first term, some members of his administration did conspire with leaders of the Congress to slow the increase in defense budgets and augment tax revenues. Had they not, the deficit might well have exceeded $300 billion. But for major change, they needed the protection of doing it *with* the President. And this protection Ronald Reagan has consistently, persistently, failed to provide. As David Stockman put it in the final paragraph of his book: "The American economy and government have literally been taken hostage by the awesome stubbornness of the nation's fortieth President."[12] Reagan's agreement to hold the fall 1987 negotiations represented a modest tactical adjustment in the wake of the stock market crash; Reagan had made similar adjustments in 1982 and 1984 when he felt vulnerable politically. But the "stubbornness" persisted. The President yielded little of substance, the agreement produced only marginal budget changes, and the deficit persisted.

This stubbornness made enormously more difficult the administration's fight against trade protectionism. The budget deficit was the trade deficit's prime cause, but legislators were tempted to blame the latter on unfair foreign import barriers and to legislate retaliation. Hence both houses passed a complex, potentially very restrictive trade bill in 1987; Senate and House conferees removed its worst features, but Reagan's veto left the administration with no bargaining authority in ongoing trade talks. Presidential stubbornness has also made it far harder for Treasury Secretary Baker in his adroit, widely admired effort to enhance economic policy coordination among advanced industrial nations. How was he to get Germans and Japanese to stimulate their economies, buy more U.S. goods, and help avert a global economic slowdown when he did not even hold the card (reducing the U.S. budget deficit) they most wanted him to play?

Arms Control and the Strategic Defense Initiative

If economic policy is one area where Reagan has clearly affected America's global position — albeit not, for the longer term, in a direction he intended — strategic weapons policy is clearly a second. Here, as in economic policy, Reagan's desire to make major changes was articulated before he came to office. He had denounced the "fatally flawed" SALT II treaty completed by Jimmy Carter (and begun by Richard Nixon, Gerald Ford, and Henry Kissinger). For Reagan, demonstration "to the Soviet leadership that we are determined to compete," meaning "the possibility of an arms race," was a prerequisite to negotiating agreements more favorable to U.S. interests.

So the administration took leave of its predecessor's arms control posture, and took more than a year to adopt a negotiating position of its own. An arms build-up to redress Soviet "superiority" came first. By the end of 1981, Reagan did propose the "zero option" for eliminating all intermediate weapons from Europe—those the Soviet Union already had in place, and those the West was planning to deploy. This was followed in spring 1982 by the administration's START (Strategic Arms Reduction Talks) position, which called for sharp cuts in long-range strategic weapons, particularly on the Soviet side. Neither proposal led to serious negotiations. And neither was really intended to.

The administration did promise in 1982 to "refrain from actions which undercut" SALT II "as long as the Soviet Union promises equal restraint," and it held to this policy until late 1986. It also adopted in 1983, under congressional pressure, a more realistic strategic arms negotiating position, as a "gang of six" senators and representatives, speaking for centrists who held the balance of power, made this their price for approval of the MX missile. But with the Soviet shoot-down of a Korean commercial airline that overflew Soviet air space on 1 September 1983, Moscow's international reputation declined, and so therefore did pressure on Reagan to negotiate on arms. And with the closely bunched deaths of Soviet leaders Leonid Brezhnev (November 1982), Yuri Andropov (February 1984), and Konstantin U. Chernenko (March 1985), there seemed no one very durable in Moscow to negotiate with anyway!

During this period, however, Reagan further complicated the arms control picture by endorsing development of a sweeping new system of defense against nuclear attack. On 23 March 1983, at the conclusion of a television address scheduled to shore up support for his defense budget, the President evoked a vision of developments in defensive military technology that would render nuclear weapons "impotent and obsolete." Such an idea had never before been taken seriously by a President or anyone close to him. But from 1983 forward, this notion—the Strategic Defense Initiative (SDI) to its supporters, "star wars" to its critics—became a centerpiece, often *the* centerpiece, of the President's nuclear arms policies and the arms control debate.

The idea was simple and appealing: If one *could* design a leakproof defense against nuclear attack, the "balance of terror" would be history. The unappealing strategy of basing security on the capacity for overwhelming nuclear retaliation would become passé.

But no one but the President considered this at all possible in the foreseeable future. There were enormous technical obstacles, and even if these were overcome, there was the likelihood that future changes in offensive weapons technology could overwhelm the new defense system. And until Reagan's dream *was* feasible, it could cause enormous complications. Existing arms balances and control arrangements were built on the balance of terror, on what specialists labeled "mutual assured destruction"(MAD). If one side made major strides *toward* an effective defense against incoming missiles, this would threaten that balance. For the side making the defensive breakthrough could conceivably find it rational to strike the other side first, confident that its antimissile "shield" could destroy most of the (diminished) missile force that came in retaliation. Thus neither side could tolerate the other's developing such a system alone. Recognition of this principle had led, in fact, to the Anti-Ballistic Missile (ABM) treaty signed and ratified in 1972, which sharply restricted the testing and deployment of ABM systems.

Certainly the Soviet Union was unlikely to agree to destroy half of its nuclear warheads—the administration's central strategic arms reduction proposal—if SDI would threaten the effectiveness of those that remained. For all these reasons, "the future of [Ronald Reagan's] Strategic Defense Initiative" became, in the words of four prominent critics, "the most important question of nuclear arms competition and arms control on the national agenda since 1972."[13] These four establishment luminaries—McGeorge Bundy, George Kennan, Robert McNamara, and Gerard Smith—saw "star wars" as incompatible with serious arms control. So did some arms control adversaries, who saw *promoting* SDI as a convenient way of undercutting future agreements. At the same time, if the Soviets were as concerned about the system as they declared themselves to be, it might prove a formidable bargaining chip were the administration willing to trade it away or accept constraints on its development.

Ronald Reagan may not have understood these implications, but he stuck with his idea, and his commitment—or willfulness—made it everybody else's concern also. SDI joined the list of cherished right-wing causes. Its critics numbered not just the four "liberal" establishment luminaries quoted, but also Richard Nixon's secretary of defense, James Schlesinger, and most important of all, Sam Nunn of Georgia, the senate's most respected defense specialist, who became Armed Services Committee chairman with the Democrats' recapture of the Senate in 1986.

What they criticized was not the idea of a strategic defense program involving research; new technologies were developing, they needed to be examined, and the Soviet Union was clearly active in this area. Rather, it was the President's resistance to what they saw as practical compromises. To clear the way for SDI testing, the administration put forward in 1985 a radical reinterpretation of the 1972 ABM treaty, suddenly claiming that—contrary to what almost everyone thought at the time—the secret record of negotiations leading to that treaty indicated that it did *not* prohibit testing of defensive systems based on futuristic technology. Most involved in its negotiation disagreed; so did Nunn, who reviewed the record himself and gave a major Senate speech rebutting this interpretation. The general furor forced the administration to retreat; it would not, for the present, act on this radical interpretation. But the President remained inflexible about negotiating limits on SDI testing and deployment, even though the system was proving to be a potent bargaining chip with the Soviets, and even though technical compromise was available that could preserve the program through Reagan's watch and years beyond.

Reagan's priority was exhibited in its most extreme form at the Reykjavik summit of October 1986. The President and Gorbachev seemingly agreed at one point to eliminate all strategic offensive arms by 1996. But then the President backed away from any agreement because, in the words of the astonished James Schlesinger, he was "unprepared to compromise on outside-the-laboratory testing of SDI."

> In Western strategy the nuclear deterrent remains the ultimate and indispensable reality. Yet at Reykjavik the President was prepared to negotiate it away almost heedlessly. By contrast, the Strategic Defense Initiative was treated and continues to be treated as if it were already a reality ("the key to a world without nuclear weapons"), instead of a collection of technical experiments and distant hopes.[14]

On the issue of intermediate nuclear forces, however, Reagan's persistence paid dividends. The "zero option" proposing elimination of all such weapons from European soil had long been regarded as nonnegotiable, since it would require asymmetric Soviet concessions. Indeed, it was originally proposed for frankly propagandistic purposes by the *bête noire* for arms control, Assistant Secretary of Defense Richard Perle.[15]

But Reagan persisted with it as a substantive stance, Gorbachev was seeking to break out of past policy binds, and the result was a treaty, signed in Washington in December 1987, providing for destruction of all such weapons, and shorter-range weapons as well. Here a U.S. build-up was followed by Soviet readiness to dismantle weapons long in place, just as Reagan campaign rhetoric had suggested! Once the treaty was ratified by the Senate and entered into force, the Russians would have to destroy, within three years, 1752 missiles, compared to 867 missiles destroyed by the United States. And as the Senate began hearings on the INF treaty, arms negotiators were laboring over a START accord. The target here was completion in time for a springtime summit in Moscow.

The INF pact had its critics. Some, like Senator Jesse Helms (R-North Carolina), would have found objectionable *any* pact the Soviet Union would agree to. Others, like General Bernard Rogers, the former NATO commander, and Henry Kissinger, the former secretary of state, feared that removal of all American intermediate nuclear forces form Europe would cast doubt on the overall U.S. nuclear umbrella and render NATO more vulnerable to conventional force imbalance. There were also those who feared that the President might repeat Reykjavik in the follow-on strategic pact, making dangerous concessions on existing deterrent forces to protect his "star wars" dream that might never be.

The SDI issue also became intertwined with INF ratification. Nunn, with an eye to the ABM treaty interpretation flap, insisted that the administation must declare its testimony on the pending INF treaty to be "authoritative" and hence legally binding. After weeks of negotiations, Nunn and Senate Majority Leader Robert Byrd (D-West Virginia) extracted a letter from Shultz giving them most of what they wanted. Their position was reinforced when the Senate Foreign Relations Committee conditioned its favorable recommendation on a proviso asserting the constitutional authority of the Senate to insist on holding to the interpretation of the treaty agreed to at the time of ratification: The President could not alter this later without Senate approval. Nunn was also proposing to add a proviso that the treaty covered futuristic weapons! While ostensibly applying only to the INF pact, both were clearly aimed at undercutting the administration's reinterpretation of the ABM treaty.

Yet on the positive side, with the INF pact concluded and U.S.-Soviet agreement already reached on many features of a strategic arms accord, the Reagan record on arms control stood a real chance of proving historic. If it did, who but quibblers would dwell on the administration's erratic route to getting there? And might not Ronald Reagan's policy stubbornness be judged at least partly responsible for the impressive result?

Central America and the Contras—and Iran Arms Sales

If the President's persistence made its mark on U.S. international economic relations and redefined the strategic dialogue, it also generated American political dramas on two matters whose centrality to U.S. interests was far less obvious: the "*contra* war" against the Sandinista government of Nicaragua, and the plight of Americans held hostage in the chaotic land of Lebanon. As revealed to an astonished public in November 1986, the two matters became intertwined in a truly bizarre fashion during Reagan's second term. Administration officials used arms sales to Iran, channeled through a quasi-private group labeled "the Enterprise," as means to influence the hostages' Shiite captors and then diverted some of the profits from these sales to help finance the Nicaraguan insurgency.

Central America was a prominent subject of American foreign policy during the Carter administration, with the negotiation and ratification of the Panama treaties in 1977–78, the Sandinista overthrow of the Somoza tyranny in

Nicaragua a year later, and the rise of civil conflict in El Salvador. Haig's State Department gave priority and visibility to El Salvador from the start, as a place to "draw the line" against leftist revolutions backed by Havana and Moscow. But mail poured in against U.S. military involvement, and the White House took its distance from the issue in 1981 and 1982.

Political controversy also had a more durable effect, by increasing the appeal of covert operations. Through these, the administration could hope to avoid, or at least dilute and defer, the requirement of obtaining domestic backing. So the same President who was publicly downplaying the Central American conflict signed in December 1981 an intelligence finding authorizing covert U.S. aid to forces seeking to overthrow the Sandinista government.

The political respite proved short-lived. The operation remained "covert" for less than a year, when a November 1982 *Newsweek* cover story exposed the program's existence and many of its details. The House Intelligence Committee grew concerned about the operation, and its chairman, Edward Boland (D-Massachusetts), won enactment of legislation in December 1982 prohibiting provision of "military equipment, military training or advice, or other support for military activities, *for the purpose of* overthrowing the government of Nicaragua or provoking a military exchange between Nicaragua and Honduras" (italics added). This compromise, later labeled "Boland I," was "based more on semantics than substance,"[16] as the congressional Iran-*contra* committees would note. The administration had not declared such a "purpose"; its stated aim was not to overthrow the Sandinista regime but to impede arms shipments from Nicaragua to El Salvador. (Later rationales were to force Managua to negotiate with its neighbors, and to adopt internal democratic reforms.) And Boland I's weakness reflected congressional divisions: Both House and Senate were split on the issue, but the senior body, under Republican control, generally supported the administration in showdown votes.

House concern was partly an echo of public sentiment, as polls showed consistent opposition to deepening U.S. military or paramilitary involvement in the region. The President might therefore have taken Boland I as a political warning and moderated his objectives. But in the months that followed, he did the exact opposite: He toughened his stand and went public. He called for increased aid to El Salvador. He made the Central American conflict a personal presidential crusade by addressing a joint session of Congress in April 1983. Pointing to both El Salvador and Nicaragua, he sounded a not-so-muted political warning to his policy critics, asking, "Who among us would wish to bear responsibility for failing to meet our shared obligation," for "stand[ing] by passively while the people of Central America are delivered to totalitarianism and we ourselves are left vulnerable to new dangers?" Another signal of a toughening administration line was the ouster of the regional assistant secretary of state, Thomas Enders, a conservative pragmatist who had been trying to put together a compromise policy toward the region.

Congress became more obliging on aid to El Salvador, one reason being the election of respected Christian Democrat José Napoleon Duarte as that country's president in May 1984. But opposition to *contra* aid intensified. Congress limited it to $24 million for fiscal year 1984; the administration nonetheless expanded the operation as it sought, unsuccessfully, to get the spending cap lifted; its cause was undercut by revelation in April 1984 of direct U.S. involvement in mining Nicaraguan harbors and by the charge of Senate Intelligence Committee Chairman Barry Goldwater (R-Arizona) that the CIA Director, William Casey, had deceived his committee about this operation. Finally, in October 1984, Congress enacted a general prohibition, Boland II:

> During fiscal year 1985, no funds available to the Central Intelligence Agency, the Department of Defense, or any other agency or entity involved in intelligence activities may be obligated or expended for the purpose or which would have the effect of supporting, directly or indirectly, military or paramilitary operations in Nicaragua by any nation, group, organization, movement or individual.[17]

Boland II did not prove to be the last congressional words on the subject. By August 1985, Reagan was able to sign into law a measure authorizing $27 million in humanitarian aid to the *contras*. And the following year, Congress voted $100 million, some of which could be spent for weapons. These retreats from Boland II were in response to continued White House pressure, as Ronald Reagan hammered away, publicly and privately, in behalf of the Nicaraguan "freedom fighters." But for the twelve-month period of October 1984–September 1985 the administration was statutorily barred, by any reasonable reading of the law, from *any* actions in support of that cause.[18]

But the President persevered, making it clear that he wanted the *contras* kept together while he worked to get Congress to change its mind. A then-obscure, middle-level NSC staff official, Lieutenant Colonel Oliver North, became the in-house entrepreneur raising funds at home and abroad, directing logistics, working the regional politics. Undertaking such an effort in the face of explicit statutory prohibition raises the broader question whether a President's aides can, in practice, carry out a personal, quasi-private foreign policy outside the law, in defiance of public constraints. And if North's testimony to the congressional committees is to be believed, this was precisely what senior officials, including CIA Director Casey, had in mind: "to create a worldwide private covert operation organization [The Enterprise], with significant financial resources,"[19] and thereby free themselves from democratic constraints entirely.

North also became the point man for another now-famous administration initiative: the use of arms sales to the Ayatollah Khomeni's Iran as a vehicle to gain release of Americans held hostage in Lebanon. Here, too, the impetus clearly came from the President, who developed a deep personal concern about these citizens' fate and wanted to do something about it, if one will forgive the use of a familiar pun, "in the worst possible way." Here, too, a private network was employed. Here, too, laws were bent and broken; for example, an explicit decision was made *not* to inform any members of Congress, the requirements of the Intelligence Oversight Act of 1980 notwithstanding. And here, unlike on *contra* aid, the President met strong resistance *within* his administration, as Secretary of State Shultz and Secretary of Defense Weinberger denounced the effort as undercutting the "no compromise with terrorists" policy with which the administration and Reagan personally were deeply identified.

If clandestine pursuit of this goal did not undercut the antiterrorism policy, exposure in November 1986 certainly did. Even more searing was the damage to the President's public standing, suggested quantitatively by a 21-point drop in his approval ratings in December 1986 and qualitatively by the comment of one Reagan appointee: "It's like suddenly learning that John Wayne had secretly been selling liquor and firearms to the Indians."[20] The President's antiterrorism policy was in shambles, as was his "Rambo" reputation. And the juicy tidbit served up by Attorney General Meese in November—that North and national security assistant John Poindexter had diverted profits from the sale to the Nicaraguan *contra* cause—opened up a broad investigation of administration operations on *that* issue. This exposed White House deviation from the governing statutes and contributed to a new congressional repudiation of *contra* aid in February 1988.

The Uses of Stubbornness

Ronald Reagan has been an unusually popular President, at least during his middle years. He has used his general popularity to pursue noncentrist objectives, goals not supported by the broad public that likes him personally: an unbalanced budget policy, SDI, *contra* aid, shipping arms to Iran.

He did not get all he wanted on any of these issues. But he got a lot, for a long time. How? Why?

His success has not, by any available evidence, been the product of a coherent, sophisticated vision of the world. Reagan is no geo-strategist in the Nixon mold, nor is any senior official in his administration. And if one credits Stockman's account, the President's capacity to connect budgetary specifics to broader goals and relationships is extraordinarily limited.

Did Reagan's administration compensate for lack of intellectual sophistication through competent, effective policy-making institutions? The answer here seems to be no; his has seemed, for the most part, the very opposite of a coherent, purposive foreign policy administration. Consider these points:

☐ No previous President has had *six* national security assistants, the first driven from office in a furor over two Japanese watches, the second with no pre-Reagan foreign policy background whatsoever, and the third and fourth perpetrator-victims of the singular Iran-*contra* fiasco.

☐ In prior years, it was under the *strong* national security assistants—Henry Kissinger above all—that the NSC crossed the line from coordinating to operating. Under Reagan, an assistant generally viewed as weak and narrow, John Poindexter, presided over the most egregious abuse of the NSC's role since the council's creation in 1947.

☐ Reagan has been blessed with a committed, durable secretary of state. But George Shultz's effectiveness has ebbed and flowed with the shifting staff scene at the White House. And none of Shultz's predecessors ever cited chapter and verse in open congressional hearings, *while in office,* of their *inability* to sway the President on a central policy issue like the Iran arms sales.

☐ In sum, over Reagan's seven-plus years, the longest presidential service since Dwight Eisenhower's, no clear system for foreign policy management has emerged. Arms control policy was dominated in the first term by an assistant secretary of defense, Richard Perle. Shultz gained a central role on that issue thereafter, with the help of national security assistant Robert McFarlane, but Shultz was cut out of Iran policy—and lied to repeatedly, it appears—by McFarlane's successor.

☐ The key reason for the lack of coherent process, by all accounts, has been the thinness of the President's personal engagement in specific issues. The Tower Board found this the central flaw on Iran-*contra*: Reagan "did not seem aware of the way in which the operation was implemented and the full consequences of U.S. participation"; "at no time did he insist upon accountability and performance review."[21]

Yet this same detached President dominated policy, as both Poindexter and Shultz were to testify. Reagan may not have grasped, or cared about, the details; he may not have faced the contradictions; but *his* priorities, *his* values were being pursued. It was Ronald Reagan who blocked serious budget compromise through his "awesome stubbornness." It was Ronald Reagan who made SDI central to the strategic debate. It was Ronald Reagan who kept *contra* aid going. It was Ronald Reagan who pushed dealings with Iran in order to get American citizens out of captivity.

Why did he do it? He had declared in his campaign days that there were often "simple answers" to questions; they just weren't "*easy* answers." His stubbornness in office on each of these issues reflected a simple conviction, pushed far beyond what most others would consider its proportionate usefulness. Persistence in these goals reflected *Ronald Reagan*'s values, what he came to care about most deeply in the course of his Presidency.

How did he do it? There is no evidence that he mastered in any detail either the substance or the politics of these issues. There is no evidence that he even had much *interest* in their substance or their politics. What Reagan did understand and exploit, in an exceptionally effective manner, were his own assets as President. He understood his own strengths, and the strengths of his position. He used the presidential pulpit to shape debate. He exploited the autonomy of his office to get *his* officials moving in desired directions. And he employed the President's effective veto over policy solutions to resist compromises that other players—Robert Dole on the budget, Sam Nunn on defense—saw as necessary and reasonable.

As the most skilled public speaker to occupy the oval office since Franklin Roosevelt, Ronald Reagan knew how to define his goals in phrases that found resonance with the broad public. Time and again he would characterize the budget issue as a raising-taxes issue, positioning himself clearly against it and putting Democrats (and Senate Republicans) on the political defensive. And while his position on SDI never attained the same broad support, his depiction of a future shield, an escape from the nuclear dilemma through technology, was very "American" in its quest for utopia through scientific advance.

Also important was Reagan's use of presidential autonomy. On supporting the *contras* and dealing with Iran, he employed the day-to-day operational leeway that Presidents are granted, and the staff and quasi-staff agencies responsive particularly to him: the NSC, but also the CIA. It is difficult, in the short run, for congressional or executive branch critics to counter the President's use of these agencies, for they respond overwhelmingly to him, it is generally agreed that they *should* respond to him, and their power flows and ebbs according to his satisfaction with their response. And at its roots, this autonomy comes from the Presidency's constitutional separation from the legislative branch.

Closely linked to this autonomy, equally dependent on the President's separate power base, was his *effective veto* over constructive resolutions on major policy issues. Ronald Reagan seems to have understood and exploited this best of all. On the budget, on arms control, on Central America, he realized that no durable domestic agreement on policy was attainable without him; he could gain leverage, therefore, by *not* playing the game by others' rules. He could hold out, articulate *his* strategic vision year after year, push for aid to his freedom fighters year after year, recognizing that whatever others thought of his stances now, they would need presidential involvement in any resolution later and might just move closer to his position in order to get it. He could play his own game without being cut out of theirs.

The approach depended, of course, on reasonably high standing with the public. When that standing fell, Reagan had to compromise more—on budget substance during the recession of 1982 and after the crash of 1987, on senior staff personnel and processes after the revelations of November 1986. Howard Baker and Frank Carlucci and William Webster were not *his* people; Caspar Weinberger and William Clark and William Casey had been. After-the-fiasco understandings on reporting intelligence activities to Congress were not his style; ad hoc operations known only to a narrow circle apparently were. With the winding down of the Reagan administration, we are likely to see more of the former and fewer of the latter.

But while Ronald Reagan had broad political backing, his approach worked for him. It moved policy in his preferred directions. The Reagan formula on foreign policy was his formula on policy generally: Take a simple position founded on principle, give voice to it repeatedly, adhere to it stubbornly, and let others—executive branch subordinates, members of Congress, American citizens, foreigners—do the adjusting. Let them fill in the details; let them deal with the consequences. Let them worry about internal consistency. He would push the values *he* thought were important.

If it worked for Ronald Reagan, was it helpful to America? On balance, the answer from this corner is no. If one believes in squeezing the nondefense public sector, and that doing so is worth running a huge trade deficit and accumulating substantial international debt, and tilting the political debate to make tax increases and social security constraints much more difficult for American politicians, one *might* justify the results of Reaganomics. Otherwise, it is very hard to do so.[22] It is even harder to find any redeeming value in the Iran arms escapade.

On aid to the *contras,* history could end up recording a connection between the pressure it put on the Sandinistas and the external accommodation and internal democratization they seemed to be moving toward, grudgingly, with the Arias peace plan framework in late 1987 and early 1988. But this must be weighed against the earlier contribution of *contra* aid to legitimizing repression by that regime and militarizing the Central American conflict.

One is left, then, with arms control, and on this history could prove very much kinder to Ronald Reagan. It is hard to find, even in retrospect, an inevitable logical connection between an arms control stand initially taken, in part, to prevent or postpone serious negotiation and a negotiating result very close to that stand. Yet this is what Reagan accomplished on intermediate weapons and could well accomplish on strategic arms, if he softens his stubbornness on SDI. In any case, that program is likely to recede, in successor administrations, to the status of the research and limited testing program it was before the President made it something more.

If the President does achieve the *big* arms control breakthrough, important causes will doubtless lie elsewhere—above all in Gorbachev's freeing up of Soviet policy across a range of issues. And any strategic arms accord will face far tougher Senate scrutiny than the INF pact. Still, without Reagan's persistence, Gorbachev would not have had to move as far to reach arms accords. And so, presumably, he would not have done so.

For Reagan's fellow citizens, then, there may be some important policy gains from his stubbornness. But the overall balance appears negative. So also does the political legacy. For Ronald Reagan has demonstrated that a President can be successful politically and influential substantively by willfully recasting the policy debate, ignoring the chorus of critics who felt it was wrong to be playing "let's pretend" on the federal budget or dreaming our way out of the dilemmas of the nuclear age.

Notes

1. William Schneider, " 'Rambo' and Reality: Having It Both Ways," in *Eagle Resurgent? The Reagan Era in American Foreign Policy,* ed. Kenneth A. Oye, Robert J. Lieber, and Donald Rothchild (Boston: Little, Brown, 1987), 70. The volume was completed before the Iran-*contra* revelations.

2. Howard Phillips, president of the Conservative Caucus, quoted in *Washington Post,* 5 December 1987.

3. I.M. Destler, "The Evolution of Reagan Foreign Policy," in *The Reagan Presidency,* ed. Fred I. Greenstein (Baltimore: Johns Hopkins University Press, 1983), esp. 131-35.

4. For chapter and verse on that effort, see Yoichi Funabashi, *Managing the Dollar: From the Plaza to the Louvre* (Washington, D.C.: Institute for International Economics, 1988). For how the previous neglect helped precipitate a trade policy crisis, see I.M. Destler, *American Trade Politics: System Under Stress* (Washington, D.C.: Institute for International Economics and New York: Twentieth Century Fund, 1986), esp. chap. 5.

5. For example, Presidential Counselor [and future Attorney General] Edwin Meese III declared in April 1983: "It is the responsibility of the President to conduct foreign policy; limits on that by the Congress are improper as far as I'm concerned." *Washington Post,* 15 April 1983.

6. *Report of the President's Special Review Board,* 26 February 1987.

7. *New York Times,* 2 December 1986.

8. Calculated from U.S. Congress, Joint Economic Committee, *Economic Indicators,* November 1987, 32.

9. For a full analysis, see C. Fred Bergsten and Shafiqul Islam with C. Randall

Henning, *The United States as a Debtor Country* (Washington, D.C.: Institute for International Economics, forthcoming).

10. Stephen Marris, *Deficits and the Dollar: The World Economy at Risk,* updated edition (Washington, D.C.: Institute for International Economics, 1987), xxvii-xxxi.

11. "Resolving the Global Economic Crisis: After Wall Street: A Statement by Thirty-Three Economists from Thirteen Countries" (Washington, D.C.: Institute for International Economics, Special Report 6, December 1987), 7.

12. David A. Stockman, *The Triumph of Politics: The Inside Story of the Reagan Revolution* (New York: Avon Books, 1987), 458.

13. McGeorge Bundy, George F. Kennan, Robert S. McNamara, and Gerard Smith, "The President's Choice: Star Wars or Arms Control," *Foreign Affairs,* Winter 1984/85, 264.

14. James Schlesinger, "Reykjavik and Revelations: A Turn of the Tide?" in *America and the World, 1986,* ed. William G. Hyland (New York: Council on Foreign Relations, 1987), 433, 434.

15. See Alexander Haig, *Caveat: Reagan, Realism, and Foreign Policy* (New York: Macmilan, 1984), chap. 11; and Strobe Talbott, *Deadly Gambits: The Reagan Administration and the Stalemate in Nuclear Arms Control* (New York: Knopf, 1984), chap. 3.

16. *Report of the Congressional Committees Investigating the Iran-Contra Affair,* S. Rept. 100-216, H. Rept. 100-433, November 1987, 31.

17. Ibid., 41.

18. Administration defenders have developed, after the fact, an ingenious but unpersuasive argument that the National Security Council staff was not covered by the prohibition, notwithstanding its very deep "involvement" in the intelligence activities that were the amendment's target. See the Iran-*contra* committee minority report, endorsed by all six House Republican members on the committee and two of its five Senate Republicans. Ibid., 489-99. For the majority view, see 395-407.

19. Ibid., 331.

20. Quoted in Schlesinger, "Reykjavik and Revelations," 441.

21. *Report of the President's Special Review Board,* IV-10.

22. For the most comprehensive critique, by an old-style conservative, see Peter G. Peterson, "The Morning After," *Atlantic,* October 1987, 43-69.

PART FOUR

Two Perspectives

9

The View from Europe

ANTHONY KING
and
DAVID SANDERS

During most of Ronald Reagan's Presidency, the majority of the American people have held him in high esteem. They like him personally; and although there were doubts in 1981-82 and again following the Iran-*contra* affair, he is widely given credit in the United States for restoring the health of the American economy and for enhancing American power and prestige around the world. The view of him from Europe, as we see in this chapter, is rather more complicated.

Reagan and the Leaders of Europe

The leaders of the world's leading industrial nations increasingly constitute a kind of informal club. Far more than before World War II, when meetings between heads of government were relatively rare, presidents and prime ministers of countries like the United States, France, Great Britain, West Germany, Japan, and Canada nowadays write to one another, talk on the telephone to one another, and meet together face-to-face—either bilaterally or in larger gatherings such as the regular economic summits. The telephone and the jet airplane have created a new international intimacy. In the 1970s, President Valéry Giscard d'Estaing of France and Chancellor Helmut Schmidt of West Germany became close personal friends. So did American President Jimmy Carter and Britain's then prime minister, James Callaghan. Sometimes in recent years, the leaders of different countries have had better working relationships with one another than with their political colleagues back home.

The quality of the personal relationships among the world's political leaders is important. They increasingly find themselves making decisions together on interest rates and exchange rates, on arms control and defense, on the deployment of advanced nuclear weapons systems. For any one leader, the ideal qualities in another leader are honesty, predictability, a willingness to compromise and see others' points of view, and the ability to deliver politically: It is no use making an agreement with the leader of another country if that leader is then unable to win his own cabinet's or legislature's assent to the agreement. When Jimmy Carter suddenly canceled America's neutron bomb project in 1978, his international reputation for reliability suffered. When he was unable to persuade the Senate to ratify the Salt II treaty with the Soviet Union in 1980, his reputation for being able to deliver politically likewise suffered.

Given that global interdependence means a degree of personal interdependence among the world's top leaders, it is not surprising that they spend a good deal of time thinking—and talking—about one another. Like the members of any small club, they are undoubtedly intrigued by one another's personalities; but they also have a professional need to know whether President X or Prime Minister Y is intelligent, has good judgment, et cetera. They engage therefore in a continuous process of sizing one another up. It is probably one of the more enjoyable things they do, involving, among other things, a mixture of good gossip and amateur psychology.

What did Europe's political leaders make of Ronald Reagan? This is a hard question to answer because top political leaders are obviously not in the business of talking about one another in public. One negative remark about the wrong person at the wrong time could cause disaster, or at least unnecessary ill will. Discretion is the name of the game. Nevertheless, it is possible to piece together, from newspaper and television reports and personal observation, a reasonably accurate picture of European leaders' views of Ronald Reagan.

Their overall view of him was probably one of puzzlement. They did not know quite what to make of him. Most Europeans have a fairly clear idea of what a top political leader ought to be like. He (or she) should have had long experience of national politics and government. He (or she) should probably have served in a number of cabinet-level posts before achieving the top office. He (or she) should probably have had some experience of international affairs and should, ideally, speak at least one foreign language. He (or she) should behave with a certain *gravitas,* a certain dignity, in private as well as in public. The average European's stereotype of a top political leader probably corresponds roughly to the average American's stereotype of a well-established, successful Wall Street investment banker.

But Ronald Reagan, unlike most of his predecessors stretching back to Franklin D. Roosevelt and Herbert Hoover, did not correspond to this stereotype. He was an ex-actor, an ex-professional after-dinner speaker. He had no direct experience of national government before becoming President; and he had no experience of international politics. He spoke no foreign language. He commenced meetings with foreign leaders, not with a solemn handshake and perhaps a few reminiscences about previous encounters between their nations' heads of government, but by telling jokes, occasionally in somewhat doubtful taste. And this folksiness in private was, of course, matched by his public folksiness. Watching Ronald Reagan on television celebrating his birthday, blowing up balloons, or professing his undying love for Nancy, European politicians were known to cringe with embarrassment. Reagan appeared to want to be "one of the boys." Europeans thought this a strange ambition: He ought to want to be one of the men.

European political leaders, confronted by Ronald Reagan, suffered, in short, from considerable culture shock. They also suffered from doubts about Reagan's ability, his personal capacity. Reagan was undoubtedly a man with strong views, and those views frequently (indeed more often than not) coincided with the views of his allies on the other side of the Atlantic; during most of Reagan's Presidency, the governments of most major European nations were quite conservative in their ideological orientation. Yet at the same time it was hard to take Ronald Reagan, as a politician, altogether seriously. He was not very bright; his strong opinions were evidently secondhand; he did not seem to know very much about economics or world affairs; he often came to meetings hopelessly badly briefed. It was reported that, at the Reykjavik summit with Mikhail Gorbachev, Reagan had been visibly startled by the volume of documentation that the Soviet leader had brought with him. "You seem to have a lot of papers," Reagan had said apprehensively. Many in Europe suspected that, if Reagan had had the same amount of papers, he would not have read them; or, if he had read them, he would not have understood them.

This was a part—a large part—of the view of Reagan that most European leaders had in their minds. But it was not the only part. European leaders' puzzlement arose out of the fact that, even if they did not take Reagan seriously, the American people certainly did; and more important, it was clear that Reagan's two terms in the White House could not, in any reasonable way, be accounted a failure. On the contrary, they had many of the hallmarks of an outstanding success.

European leaders could hardly fail to be impressed by the fact that despite his inexperience of national government, Reagan had been triumphantly elected to the Presidency in 1980 and even more triumphantly reelected four years later.

His hold on the American people's affections remained strong even when he himself stumbled or his policies failed. There was, to be sure, a good deal of chaos in and around the Reagan White House; but European leaders were used to that: It was often difficult to find out, and always had been, whether American foreign policy was made by the President, his national security adviser, the secretary of state, the defense secretary, or Congress (or indeed whether America had a coherent foreign policy at all). The Reagan White House operation seemed no worse managed than many of his predecessors' had been; and his relations with Congress, although sometimes difficult, never degenerated into the kind of institutionalized hostility that developed under (to take the extreme case) Richard Nixon. Under Reagan, the American system of government "worked," in a way it had often not worked under Nixon, Ford, and Carter.

Reagan's policies seemed, on the whole, to work too. The American economy grew at a reasonable rate; unemployment fell; inflation was checked. Europeans were dismayed by the growth of America's budget deficit and were very worried about its accumulating effects on their own economies and on the world economy; but, interestingly, they did not seem disposed to blame the deficit on Reagan personally. From afar, it seemed fair to apportion the blame more or less equally among the President, the Congress, and the American people. In foreign affairs, Reagan's policies also seemed to have been broadly successful. Europeans, like Americans, could point to specific instances of failure: in Lebanon, probably in Nicaragua, and certainly over the arms-for-Iran deal. But the central point was that, despite Reagan's ignorance of foreign affairs and his often belligerent-sounding rhetoric, nothing too awful happened in the world. World peace was maintained. Major wars did not break out in the Middle East or Central America. Relations with the Soviet Union did not become too strained. The Soviets were not able to take advantage of Reagan's ignorance and inexperience to make strategic (or even tactical) gains.[1] On the contrary, it looked in early 1988 as though President Reagan's final year in office might well be crowned by further arms agreements and the opening of a whole new era in superpower relations.

The European view of Reagan was thus somewhat schizoid. On the one hand, European leaders viewed him with a degree of contempt; on the other, they could not deny—and, in most cases, did not wish to deny—that the Reagan Presidency had been, on balance, a success. These two views were not fused in any way; nor were the evident contradictions between them resolved. They simply existed side by side. Most European leaders remained slightly mystified by Reagan, not knowing how to reconcile his ignorance and gaucherie with his evident success as a political leader in the American context. It may be that this slight mystification, coupled with the American President's wholly un-

European political style, had the effect of causing at least some top European leaders to feel less close to the United States than they had in the past. Reagan's America, more than Eisenhower's, Kennedy's, or even Nixon's, was alien, "other," an allied country but a country apart.

A further point may be of interest. Among the informal club of Western political leaders, no two members were closer during the 1980s than Ronald Reagan, who was elected President toward the end of 1980, and Margaret Thatcher, who had taken office as prime minister of Great Britain somewhat earlier, in May 1979. The two had close ideological affinities; they liked each other personally; and they were supportive of one another, privately as well as publicly. Yet, paradoxically, had Reagan been a British politician, he probably would never have been appointed to Thatcher's cabinet or administration; or, if he had been, he would not have survived for more than a few months.

The reasons are twofold. In the first place, Margaret Thatcher is a very hard worker and expects everyone around her to be the same. She reads everything she can lay her hands on, sits up far into the night with her official papers, and often knows more about her colleagues' business than they know themselves. She briefs herself; she expects others to brief themselves—and woe betide those who do not. The phrase "I'm sorry, I misspoke," used more than once or twice, would be a passport out of any Thatcher administration; so would a penchant for taking afternoon naps or extended holidays on a California ranch. Reagan, if he were a British politician, would be altogether too laid back for Margaret Thatcher's taste. The second reason why Reagan would not succeed in a Thatcher administration is that, Mrs. Thatcher, although fond of the President personally, is as aware as anyone else of his intellectual limitations. "Poor dear," she once said in an unguarded moment to a British civil servant, "there's nothing between his ears."[2]

This, then, was what European leaders made of—and failed to make of—Ronald Reagan. What were the views of Europe's peoples?

Reagan and the Peoples of Europe

A serious problem confronts any attempt to describe the reactions of the peoples of Europe to Reagan. Surprising though it may seem, very little opinion-poll evidence was ever collected on a Europe-wide basis with the specific purpose of assessing how Europeans viewed the President. Despite this general paucity of crossnational evidence, however, poll data over time are available for certain countries.[3]

Since 1981, for example, the British Gallup poll has asked respondents: "Do you think Mr. Reagan is or is not proving a good President of the United

TABLE 9.1

INDEX OF REAGAN'S APPROVAL RATINGS IN BRITAIN, 1981-87

Question asked: "Do you think Mr. Reagan is or is not proving a good President of the United States?" (Percent saying "is proving" minus percent saying "is not proving")

1981	1982	1983	1984	1985	1986	1987
−4	−31	−32	−23	−6	−12	−29

NOTE: The polls were not conducted on a regular basis. The figures reported are averages for each year. The score for 1981 is averaged from two separate polls; for 1982, from three polls; for 1983, five polls; for 1984, four polls; for 1985, three polls; for 1986, seven polls; and for 1987, seven polls.

SOURCE: *Gallup Political Index,* 1981-87.

States?" Table 9.1 reports the results obtained from subtracting the percentage of those saying "not proving" from the percentage saying "is proving." It shows that, having begun with a mildly negative rating of −4 in 1981, Reagan's popularity in Britain plummeted to −31 during 1982. A recovery followed in 1984–85, but by 1987 the President's rating (−29) was again falling back toward the low level of 1982–83. While it is difficult to establish the precise causes of these variations over time, it seems likely that the initial decline was not unconnected with Reagan's apparent hesitancy in supporting Britain during the 1982 Falklands crisis. Similarly, with the U.S. role in the Falklands War largely forgotten, the recovery followed the triumphant reelections of Mrs. Thatcher in 1983 and Reagan in 1984. The subsequent decline seems to have occurred in the wake of the Libyan crisis and the Iran-*contra* affair of 1986–87.

The findings reported in table 9.1, however, are limited in the sense that they describe movements in public opinion only in Britain, not in Europe as a whole. Fortunately, several studies during the 1980s did seek to capture European mass attitudes toward the United States as a world power. A European Community (EC) poll conducted in April 1982, for example, asked samples of people from each of the main EC countries questions concerning their confidence in the United States. As table 9.2 indicates, although the responses varied from country to country, the overall response was not particularly favorable to the United States. Some 45 percent of all respondents had either "not very much confidence" or "no confidence at all" in America's ability to "deal responsibly with world problems." Fully 65 percent believed that the United States took little or no account of their own country's views in matters concerning their country's security; and 55 percent thought that during the previous year U.S. policies and actions had increased the risk of war. This last response, referring roughly to Reagan's first year in office, indicated quite a high level of European dissatisfaction with U.S. foreign policy at that time.

TABLE 9.2
EUROPEAN PERCEPTIONS OF THE UNITED STATES, APRIL 1982[a]

Question	France	West Germany	Italy	Britain	Average
In general, how much confidence do you have in the ability of the United States to deal responsibly with world problems? (percent answering "not very much" or "none at all")	45	45	39	53	45
When the United States makes decisions that affect the security of [our country], how much do you think it takes [our country's] views into account? (percent answering "a little" or "not at all")	77	56	66	68	65
On balance, do you think that U.S. policies and actions during the past year have done more to promote peace or more to increase the risk of war? (percent answering "more to increase the risk of war")	50	46	52	70	55

SOURCES: *Eurobarometer* 17 (April 1982); ICPSR Study 9024.

a. "Don't know" and "not applicable" excluded from percentage base.

At first sight, these negative responses to American policy look grim; but there are two good reasons for supposing that the results need to be interpreted cautiously. First, the British responses—the most negative on both the "confidence" and "risk of war" questions—were probably distorted by the EC survey's timing. The survey went into the field in April 1982, after the Argentinian invasion of the Falkland Islands at the end of March but before the Reagan administration had publicly expressed its support for Mrs. Thatcher's declared intention to repossess the islands by force. The survey for that reason was conducted at a time when anti-American sentiment in Britain was at an unusually high level. The second reason for treating the findings in table 9.2 cautiously is that they could be taken to indicate European displeasure with Reagan only if they could be compared with similar findings from before Reagan became President. But no such data are available. It is therefore not possible to assess how far the 1982 survey actually measured dissatisfaction with Reagan and how far it reflected a more generalized, long-term dissatisfaction with the United States.

TABLE 9.3

EUROPEAN PERCEPTIONS OF ECONOMIC RELATIONS WITH THE UNITED STATES,
1979-85[a] (IN PERCENT)

	France	Belgium	Netherlands	West Germany	Italy	Britain	Average
April 1979 pro-U.S. response[b]	27	44	59	58	53	62	51
October 1985 pro-U.S. response[c]	31	32	59	47	59	47	46

a. "Don't know" and "not applicable" excluded from percentage base.
b. Percentage of respondents who believe that the United States seeks to cooperate with Western Europe for mutual economic advantage. SOURCE: *Eurobarometer* 11 (April 1979); ICPSR Study 7752.
c. Percentage of respondents who believe that the United States has been "fairly" or "very" cooperative in trying to resolve economic problems with their country. SOURCE: *Eurobarometer* 24 (October 1985); ICPSR Study 8513.

Fortunately, some comparisons can be made between European attitudes to the United States both before and after Reagan's election, making it possible to determine how far European attitudes changed during Reagan's two terms and, accordingly, to assess the impact that his personality and policies appear to have had on Western European publics.

One field in which Reagan's occupancy of the White House did not seem to make much difference was with regard to economic cooperation between Europe and the United States. In 1979, a *Eurobarometer* poll asked respondents whether they thought the United States sought to cooperate economically with Western Europe or whether they believed that the United States sought to gain unfair advantages for itself or even to dominate the European economies. As table 9.3 shows, over half the 1979 respondents (51 percent) took the more benign view of American intentions, believing that U.S. policy aimed at achieving cooperation with Western Europe for the purpose of mutual benefit. Although this particular question was not asked in subsequent *Eurobarometer* polls, a comparable question was asked in 1985. As table 9.3 shows, 45 percent of respondents in this later poll—conducted four years after Reagan came to office—believed that in "trying to resolve economic problems with their country" the U.S. administration had been either "fairly" or "very" cooperative. Despite the variations in question wording, it seems likely that the responses in 1979 and 1985 both reflected general European perceptions of the effects of U.S. economic policy on Europe; and a fall of only five percentage points (from 51 percent to 46 percent) suggests that the Reagan administration's foreign economic policy, although it produced some dissatisfaction in certain countries, in general had only a marginally adverse effect.

A second field in which the Reagan Presidency did not seem to affect European public attitudes was fear of war. The vigorous anticommunist rhetoric of the early Reagan years might have been expected to set alarm bells ringing in Western European pubs and cafés. In the early 1980s there were indeed indications that European fears about the likelihood of world war were growing. A *Eurobarometer* poll in October 1981, for example, found that 25 percent of respondents believed that there was a greater than 50 percent probability of a world war occurring in the next ten years, compared with only 15 percent four years before.

TABLE 9.4

EUROPEAN PERCEPTIONS OF THE LIKELIHOOD OF WAR, 1971-86

Percentage thinking world war is likely
(greater than 50% probability) within next 5-10 years

	France	Belgium	Netherlands	West Germany	Italy	Britain	Average
July 1971	12	8	11	11	13	—	11
October/November 1977	14	21	17	13	14	13	15
April 1980	42	33	24	25	32	39	32
October 1981	25	32	20	32	18	21	25
October 1982	20	20	19	19	14	17	18
October 1983	24	17	13	18	18	17	18
October 1984	13	16	21	14	12	12	13
October 1985	11	12	10	12	11	10	11
October 1986	11	16	6	12	11	10	11

SOURCES: For 1971-85, *Eurobarometer: Public Opinion in the European Community*, no. 22 (Brussels: Commission of the European Communities, December 1984), 11; for 1985-86, *Eurobarometer: Public Opinion in the European Community*, no. 26 (Brussels: Commission of the European Communities, December 1986), 18.

These figures might be taken to indicate that Reagan's rhetoric had begun to affect European attitudes. In fact the increased European "war fear" of the early 1980s was not the consequence of anything Reagan said or did. As table 9.4 indicates, the increased fear of war in Europe dates from at least April 1980, nine months before the new President took office. This was when Carter was still in the White House and when the West as a whole was still coming to terms with the Sandinista victory in Nicaragua in June 1979, the Soviet invasion of Afghanistan in December 1979, and the toppling of the shah of Iran in January 1979. Not surprisingly, "war fear" in Europe was still at a relatively high level in 1981 (average 25 percent), but this had little or nothing to do with

President Reagan's anticommunist belligerence. It simply reflected the aftermath of the heightened East-West tensions of 1979-80—a natural consequence of the tendency of "war fear" to dissipate only gradually over time. By October 1986, European fears of an imminent war had fallen back to the levels of the early 1970s. Reagan's vigorous anti-Soviet stance had not produced catastrophe, and European publics had altered their perceptions accordingly.

With regard to economic cooperation and the imminence—or nonimminence—of war, Reagan's effect on European attitudes appears to have been minimal. The same cannot be said of European perceptions in the one area that, in the long run, probably matters most: general European predispositions toward the United States. Here the news is less good from the American point of view. In October 1978, respondents in the "big four" Western European countries—France, West Germany, Italy, and Britain—were asked to say whether they had a relatively "favorable" or a relatively "unfavorable" opinion of the United States. Even among the French—traditionally regarded as the most anti-American people in Western Europe—pro-Washington sentiment was remarkably high, with 79 percent of the sample recording a favorable opinion of the United States (see table 9.5). The Italians (84 percent favorable) and the British (83 percent favorable) were even more well-disposed toward their Atlantic ally. And in West Germany fully 97 percent of respondents were favorable toward the United States.

By April 1982, however, barely fifteen months after Reagan had taken office, the picture had changed considerably—and for the worse. As table 9.5 shows, the average "favorable" score of the European "big four" fell from 86 percent in 1978 to 69 percent in April 1982. Even taking into account the temporarily

TABLE 9.5

EUROPEAN GENERAL OPINIONS OF THE UNITED STATES, 1978-85[a]

(IN PERCENT)

	France	West Germany	Italy	Britain	Average
October 1978 pro-U.S. response[b]	79	97	84	83	86
April 1982 pro-U.S. response[c]	69	75	71	63	69
October 1985 pro-U.S. response[d]	72	80	81	72	76

a. "Don't know" and "not applicable" excluded from the percentage base.
b. Percentage of respondents saying they have a "favorable opinion" of the United States. SOURCE: Eurobarometer 10A (October-November 1978); ICPSR Study 7807.
c. Percentage of respondents saying they have a "somewhat" or a "very" favorable opinion of the United States. SOURCE: Eurobarometer 17 (April 1982); ICPSR Study 9023.
d. Percentage of respondents saying they have a "fairly good" opinion of the United States. SOURCE: Eurobarometer 24 (October 1985); ICPSR Study 8513.

high level of anti-American sentiment in Britain referred to above (the proportion of Britons with a favorable opinion of the United States dropped from 83 percent in 1978 to 63 percent in 1982), the overall fall constituted a serious decline in the reservoir of goodwill that the United States had built up in Western Europe over the previous forty years. As table 9.5 also indicates, by April 1985 the proportion of British respondents with a good opinion of the United States had risen well above its Falklands-inspired low-point of 63 percent and reverted to a more typical score of 72 percent. This increase in turn served to raise the "big four" European average to 76 percent. Nevertheless, even with this recovery, the United States in the mid 1980s was still far less well regarded in Europe than it had been in 1978, before Reagan's election.

TABLE 9.6

EUROPEAN PERCEPTIONS OF THE TRUSTWORTHINESS OF AMERICANS, 1980-82

Percentage of respondents saying that Americans
are either "fairly" or "very" trustworthy[a]

	France	Belgium	Netherlands	West Germany	Italy	Britain	Average
October 1980	58	75	79	82	73	80	75
April 1982	58	46	57	73	57	76	61

SOURCES: *Eurobarometer* 14 (October 1980); ICPSR Study 7958. *Eurobarometer* 17 (April 1982); ICPSR Study 9023.

a. "Don't know" and "not applicable" excluded from the percentage base.

Table 9.6 points in the same direction. Immediately before Reagan's victory in November 1980, the *Eurobarometer* asked respondents in six countries how "trustworthy" they thought Americans were. Although the French, as ever, proved somewhat suspicious (only 58 percent found Americans trustworthy), the average for Europe as a whole was high, with some 75 percent of respondents saying that Americans were either "fairly" or "very" trustworthy. After fifteen months of the Reagan administration, however, perceptions had changed. Although the French and the British (despite the Falklands) were constant in their opinions, the Belgians, the Dutch, the Germans, and the Italians were far less trusting than they had been in the late 1970s. Indeed, the average pro-American response across Western Europe dropped from 75 percent in 1978 to 61 percent in 1982. While this latter figure may possibly have recovered somewhat since 1983 (data are lacking), the overall pattern of change suggests that Reagan's Presidency has been associated with a quite rapid decline in Western Europeans' "affective" attachments to the United States. Europe not only developed a less favorable opinion of the United States after Reagan achieved office; it also became significantly less trusting in its attitude toward the American people.

But did all this really matter? There are two reasons why one might suppose that it did not. First, as we have seen, although Europeans in the late 1980s were on average less favorably disposed toward the United States than they were before 1981, Reagan's Presidency does not seem to have had much impact on European fears about American economic dominance in Europe or the imminence of war. Second, and more crucially, it is possible that mass opinions about foreign countries simply do not have much effect on nations' actual foreign policy decisions: Experience suggests that, in the short run at least, political leaders in most Western democracies are perfectly happy to ignore fluctuations in public opinion in order to pursue whatever policies they consider to be the most appropriate to their nation's needs. Popular perceptions scarcely enter into the decision calculus.

That said, it seems unlikely that public opinion can be wholly ignored in the long term. Given the high level of mistrust of the Soviet Union among European publics,[4] for example, it is virtually inconceivable that any contemporary Western European leader (assuming that he or she wanted to) could enter into a close political relationship with the Soviet bloc without risking a serious loss of domestic support. By the same token, from Europe's point of view the maintenance of close relations between Washington and Western European governments almost certainly requires that mass attitudes in Europe remain broadly sympathetic toward the United States. A serious long-run decline in Europeans' affective attachment to the United States could prejudice the future stability of Euro-American relations.

The reason is simple. Western European publics have always entertained some suspicions of the "real" intentions of the United States toward Europe. There has always been a feeling—most frequently articulated by the political left—that the American forces stationed permanently in West Germany are there primarily to ensure that, in the event of hostilities breaking out between East and West, Europe (rather than the continental United States) will become the battlefield. For most of the postwar period, these fears have been submerged beneath a general affection for both the United States and the American people. But, partly as a result of Europe's distaste for Reagan's new cold war rhetoric and partly because of cynicism about the President's intellectual capacities, the Reagan years appear to have led to a weakening of that affection.

Of course, if the process of weakening goes no further, the strategic partnership between Western Europe and the United States will be unaffected. Indeed, the recent Reagan-Gorbachev accords on nuclear disarmament may well restore the United States to its favored place in European hearts and minds.

But if the Reagan years have initiated a longer-term decline in Europe's affective commitment to the United States, then the consequences could be serious. A continuing decline in European perceptions of American trustworthiness could presage a long-term weakening of Western Europe's commitment to NATO. This would in turn have profound implications, not only for Western Europeans, but for American defense and foreign policy worldwide.

Reaganism and Thatcherism

We remarked earlier on the close ideological affinities between Ronald Reagan and the British prime minister, Margaret Thatcher; and before we move on to consider the impact that Reagan has already had on the continuing relationship between the United States and its allies in Europe, it is worth pausing to look more closely at the phenomena of "Reaganism" and "Thatcherism." How similar, in fact, are these two political and economic approaches?

It is easy to see why the two are so closely associated in many people's minds. Not only do Ronald Reagan and Margaret Thatcher like each other personally and constantly pay tribute to one another, but if one listened only to their rhetoric one might suppose that they were virtually identical political twins. Both are conventional moralists, opposed to the "permissive society." Both are (or were) resolutely anti-Soviet. Both are patriots, not to say superpatriots. Both believe in the paramount importance of national defense. Both are old-fashioned economic individualists, believing in private enterprise and the market economy. Each of them claims to be opposed to high levels of government spending. Both of them claim to be opposed to high levels of taxation. When Reagan said during the 1980 election campaign, "Government isn't the solution to the problem, government *is* the problem," he was using a phrase that might well have been used by Mrs. Thatcher.

And, of course, there have been some similarities in their actual behavior. Neither, for example, has seriously sought to reimpose a Victorian (or even a 1950s) code of morality in the 1980s; and both have taken their countries a considerable distance down the parallel roads of economic deregulation and privatization (with the United States leading in the former case, Great Britain in the latter). But there have also been profound differences in their countries' actual behavior while Ronald Reagan and Margaret Thatcher have been in office, and two, in particular, are worth noting.

In the field of foreign affairs, although both Reagan and Mrs. Thatcher came in time to take an increasingly pragmatic view of the Soviet Union, Mrs. Thatcher in general proved the tougher international operator of the two. Reagan, as the saying went in Washington, tended to "speak loudly but carry a limp noodle." Mrs. Thatcher also spoke loudly, but carried as big a stick as Britain, in its relatively straitened economic circumstances, could afford. Despite his rhetoric, Reagan showed himself throughout his Presidency to be somewhat conflict averse. He appeared reluctant either to raise his voice in international forums or to send U.S. forces into action (as distinct from reviewing them on parade). There were notable exceptions, of course—the invasion of Grenada, the raid on Libya, the deployment of U.S. naval forces in the Persian Gulf—but they were exceptions. More typical of Reagan's approach were his withdrawal of U.S. marines from the Lebanon when they were seriously threatened and his (or his administration's) willingness to bargain for the release of Americans held hostage by Iranian-backed terrorists.

Mrs. Thatcher, by contrast, seemed positively to relish conflict, not merely with her country's adversaries but with its putative friends. She fought with Britain's European Community partners over Britain's contribution to the EC budget. She fought with Britain's fellow members of the Commonwealth over the imposition—or, rather, nonimposition—of economic sanctions on South Africa. Most famously, she fought Argentina over sovereignty of the Falkland Islands. Unlike Reagan, she would have no dealings with people whom she regarded as terrorists, even when, as in 1987-88, one of the people they were holding hostage was a prominent Englishman, the archbishop of Canterbury's special envoy, Terry Waite. For better or worse, Mrs. Thatcher's tough rhetoric was matched, much more often than not, by tough behavior. She consistently out-Reaganed Reagan.

But it was in the field of economic policy that Reaganism and Thatcherism, in practice, most radically diverged. Indeed, anyone who was familiar with the course of economic policy in the United States and Britain during the 1980s, but who at the same time knew nothing of the two countries' politics, would never have dreamed that the two countries were governed during these years by leaders professing similar economic ideals.

Margaret Thatcher and Ronald Reagan differed in one particular right from the outset. Mrs. Thatcher never believed in "supply-side economics." The supply-siders claimed that big tax cuts were, in effect, an alternative to big cuts in government spending. Substantial tax cuts, the supply-siders alleged, would lead to greatly increased rates of economic growth, and this increased growth in itself would result in such large increases in tax revenues that there would be no difficulty in paying for existing, or even expanded, government programs. Mrs. Thatcher, like many in the United States, was skeptical. First, it was by no means certain that big tax cuts would automatically lead to big increases in economic growth, at least in the short term. Second, many government programs were intrinsically undesirable and economically inefficient. Third, and for Mrs. Thatcher decisive, immediate tax cuts without corresponding (or even greater) spending cuts would be almost certain to lead to growing budget deficits, vast increases in government borrowing, high interest rates, and inflation. Mrs. Thatcher was, and remains, an orthodox fiscal conservative, preoccupied with the problem of inflation and the need to balance the government budget.

Whatever the rights and wrongs of the original supply-side debate, the Thatcher and Reagan administrations have pursued fundamentally different economic strategies. Mrs. Thatcher's policy has been to cut government spending and, if that has not proved possible, to raise revenues in order to prevent runaway growth in the budget deficit (known in British parlance as the "public sector borrowing requirement"). Reagan's policy has been to cut government spending and, if that has not proved possible, to continue with tax cuts nevertheless—in the hope that, sooner or later, the economic growth promised by supply-side economics would accelerate rapidly enough to catch up with the budget deficit and eliminate it. Since both countries have, overall, failed to cut their levels of public spending since 1980, this has meant in practice that Mrs. Thatcher has reluctantly acquiesced in tax increases in Britain, while Reagan has almost invariably been opposed to them in the United States (partly, to be sure, as a weapon to be used in his running battles with Congress over budgetary policy, but partly also on grounds of economic doctrine).

TABLE 9.7

GENERAL GOVERNMENT FINANCIAL BALANCES: SURPLUS OR DEFICIT
AS PERCENTAGE OF NOMINAL GNP/GDP

	1982	1983	1984	1985	1986	1987[a]
United States	−4.6	−5.2	−4.5	−4.9	−4.8	−3.4
Great Britain	−2.8	−2.8	−3.1	−2.4	−2.3	−2.1

SOURCE: *OECD Economic Outlook* 42 (December 1987): 23.
a. OECD projection.

An indication of the results of these two strategies, in terms of the two countries' national budget deficits, is given in table 9.7. Relevant OECD figures are not available for 1980 and 1981; but since 1982, as can be seen, the U.S. deficit as a percentage of gross domestic product has always been much larger than the British—in two years out of the six shown, more than twice as large. The Thatcher era in Britain has been characterized by a sternly orthodox, deflationary fiscal strategy, while the Reagan era in the United States has witnessed the growth of budget deficits that are, by any measure, given the size of the U.S. economy, among the largest in human history. Someone ignorant of the life and sayings of Ronald Reagan could be forgiven for supposing that the United States in the 1980s had been in the hands of a Keynesian who had been allowed to run amok or some kind of Far Left extremist. In fact, the table, in which the figure given for 1987 is merely an OECD projection, understates the difference between the two countries: In 1987-88, Great Britain achieved a substantial budget *surplus,* and an even larger surplus was forecast for 1988-89.[5]

But this is an aside. The most important questions about Reagan's Presidency, as seen from Europe, concern the development of America's relationship with its European NATO allies and the changes in America's world role as a superpower. To these we now turn.

Europe, the Third World, and the Strategic Defense Initiative

We noted earlier that Western European politicians were somewhat puzzled by both Reagan's leadership style and his domestic political success. With the possible exception of Margaret Thatcher, they were also puzzled by the strength of the anticommunist sentiment that permeated his public foreign policy statements. They could understand why Americans had been alarmed by the 1979-80 developments in Nicaragua, Afghanistan, and Iran; but in general they regarded the President's anticommunist rhetoric and his apparent belief that the Soviets had created an ever-expanding "evil empire" as somewhat simpleminded.

During the 1960s and 1970s Western Europe, as part of détente, had developed an extensive network of economic contacts with the Soviet bloc; and, as a result, Western European leaders had become much more familiar with the countries of Eastern Europe. While they remained suspicious of the long-term intentions of the Warsaw Pact, they found it hard to believe that the "Soviet Empire" possessed either the will or, more particularly, the capacity to extend itself further—either inside or outside Europe.

Moreover, as the costly Soviet war in Afghanistan dragged on during the 1980s, the general European belief that the Soviets were already strategically overextended was reinforced. The Soviet Union was certainly large and undoubtedly ambitious. But it was also impoverished. Did it really threaten the strategic interests of the West—as well as world peace—to quite the extent that Ronald Reagan seemed to believe? The leaders of Western Europe were far from convinced that the situation was as ominous as it was being portrayed in Washington. In their view, provided that the West maintained an unaggressive but determined defensive posture toward the East, the accommodation between

NATO and the Warsaw Pact that had been in place since the late 1950s could continue into the indefinite future.

Bearing in mind this divergence of views between the United States and most of Western Europe as to the character of the Soviet threat, what impact did Reagan's foreign policies have on Europe? In order to answer this question, it is necessary to distinguish between Reaganism's effects on the situation in the European theater itself and its effects on developments in the Third World and in American defense policy generally. As we shall see, the Reagan administration's foreign policy strategy, while having only a marginal impact on the former, had more substantial consequences with regard to the latter.

REAGAN'S FOREIGN POLICY IN THE EUROPEAN THEATER

Ever since 1949, the cornerstone of American foreign policy toward Europe has been the North Atlantic Treaty alliance (NATO). Yet, although the alliance has for almost forty years proved successful in deterring Soviet aggression in Western Europe, neither the Europeans nor the Americans have ever been entirely happy with it. The Europeans are content to have their own defense partly subsidized by the American taxpayer but have always been wary of the possibility that the massive U.S. military presence in Western Europe has been somehow eroding their national sovereignty. The Americans, for their part, willingly assist in European efforts to contain communism but have been increasingly irritated by Europeans' reluctance to bear the full costs of their own defense. Even before Reagan took office, the NATO alliance was experiencing internal tensions over the size of member states' financial contributions and over European fears that the United States was, to an unacceptable degree, dominating alliance strategy. Although Reagan's Presidency did little or nothing to resolve these problems, his performance in this regard was probably neither better nor worse than that of his predecessors. Short of a complete American withdrawal from Western Europe, the problems just mentioned were probably largely insoluble in any case.[6]

With regard to the other major issues that confronted NATO during the 1980s, the impact of the Reagan Presidency was also minimal. The key decision affecting NATO's military strategy for the 1980s—the deployment of nuclear-armed cruise and Pershing II missiles in Britain, West Germany, Belgium, and Italy—had already been taken in December 1979, over a year before Reagan took office. Notwithstanding the domestic resistances that the implementation of the new strategy initially encountered in Europe, the deployment went ahead on schedule. In pursuing the deployment policy, President Reagan was not doing anything innovative or unusual. He was merely acting as any of his predecessors would have acted in the same circumstances: adhering to the terms of a formal agreement entered into by a previous administration. Reagan or no Reagan, the deployments would have occurred.

One of the huge ironies of the Reagan years was, of course, that, having deployed cruise and Pershing missiles in Europe in the early 1980s, the administration subsequently went to such great lengths to negotiate them away under the terms of the 1987 INF treaty (the payoff being that the Soviets also dismantled their European theater intermediate range missiles). Nevertheless, although Reagan rightly sought to gain domestic political credit for signing the INF agreement, the treaty itself was not primarily the consequence of the earlier pursuit of "Reaganite" policies. On the contrary, many people in Europe believed that what really produced the agreement was the changed climate of opinion in the Soviet Union, leading to the rise of Gorbachev. It was this changed climate that produced a more conciliatory posture on the part of the Soviets; and it was this more cooperative attitude that, in turn, made possible an agreement. In the view of most European policy makers, the INF agreement was less the result of resolute Reaganite anticommunism and more the result of the autonomous changes that had been taking place in Soviet society and the Soviet economy. Reagan had simply benefited from a change in Soviet strategy that had itself been motivated by a mood of increasing liberalization at home and guarded conciliation abroad.

Yet, regardless of who had "really" been responsible for the INF treaty, the European members of NATO in 1988 looked set to end the Reagan era in more or less the same military-strategic posture as they had begun it. There were still tensions within the alliance, but they had been there since NATO's inception, and they were not noticeably worse (or better) in 1988 than they had been eight years earlier. NATO's internal cohesion had not changed appreciably, and the alliance's broad deterrent strategy, consisting of American and European conventional forces in West Germany backed up by the extended American nuclear deterrent, was still in place. Thus, inside the European theater, Reagan's impact, despite his belligerent language, was limited. The same could not be said of his impact outside Europe. In this context, the "Reagan effect" was greater, and there was consequently more cause for concern in Europe.

REAGAN'S FOREIGN POLICY OUTSIDE THE EUROPEAN THEATER

Viewed from Western Europe, Reagan's extra-European policy during the 1980s was dominated by two major issues: the way in which the United States dealt with threats to Western interests in the Third World and the implications for Western Europe's security of the Strategic Defense Initiative (SDI).

The Reagan administration's general policy toward the Third World was far bolder than that of its immediate predecessors. This greater boldness arose primarily from Reagan's simple *realpolitik* analysis of the world situation. In his view, the major threat to the West's global strategic interests was the Soviet Union's grand design for world domination. On this analysis, any country that sought to distance itself from the United States—militarily, politically, or economically—was an automatic candidate for inclusion in the Soviet hegemonic sphere. On entering office, therefore, Reagan made it clear that the hesitancy of the Ford and Carter years, generated in part by the disastrous Vietnam experience, was over. The Reagan White House would vigorously defend the West's strategic interests throughout the Third World. The sequence of "losses" that had begun with South Vietnam, Laos, and Kampuchea in 1974, and which had continued with Ethiopia in 1974-75, Angola and Mozambique in 1975, Afghanistan in 1977-78, Nicaragua in 1979, and Iran in 1980, would not be allowed to continue.

The result of this assertive new Reaganite posture—in addition to the provision of U.S. support for the Nicaraguan *contras* and the Afghan *mujahadeen*—was a series of U.S. interventions in various Third World theaters. In September 1983, an American peacekeeping force, supported by smaller contingents from Britain, Italy, and France, was despatched to Lebanon in order to cover the Israeli retreat from Beirut. In October 1983, a mainly American force intervened in Grenada to remove a badly divided Marxist government from office and restore a democratic constitution to the island. In April 1986, following a long campaign of Libyan support for terrorism in various parts of the world, U.S. warplanes undertook a "reprisal raid" against selected targets in Tripoli and Benghazi. And in August 1987, U.S. warships were sent into the Persian Gulf to protect Western shipping from Iranian attack.

As far as Reagan was concerned, these actions were all necessary to defend the strategic interests of the West as a whole. Yet, if the President expected universal approval from his allies, he was disappointed. Although he could always rely on the firm support of Margaret Thatcher (who was even prepared to overlook the fact that during the Grenada affair she had not been consulted over the invasion of a fellow member of the Commonwealth), the other European allies were equivocal. The French and Italians had been prepared to lend their initial support to the multinational force in Lebanon, partly because of their long-standing historical interest in the country and partly because the stated function of the force had been a peacekeeping one; but, as events unfolded, they began to suspect that the force's real purpose was simply to relieve the pressure in Beirut so as to make it easier for the Israelis to maintain their military hold over southern Lebanon and that the multinational force was not in Beirut to "keep the peace" but to serve the interests of American-Israeli strategy. Similarly, over Grenada, the Europeans were inclined to view the American intervention not as "nipping Soviet expansionism in the bud" but more as a case of American bullying, of the United States imposing its own preferences on a small and helpless neighbor. American backing for the Nicaraguan *contras* was viewed in Europe with some hostility, but also with head-scratching: Even allowing for Nicaragua's physical proximity to the United States, Europeans found it hard to understand why the Reagan administration, at the head of a rich nation of 240 million, was getting so worked up about developments in a desperately poor nation of little more than 3 million. News of Nicaragua seldom made the front pages of Europe's newspapers.

With regard to the bombing raid on Libya, European opinion was more disquieted. Tripoli was much closer to the capitals of Western Europe than it was to Washington. And, regardless of the impression given in Steven Spielberg's movie *Back to the Future,* there were far more Libyans at large in Europe than there were in the United States. Whatever President Reagan intended when he bombed Colonel Qadafi, it would be Europe that would pay the price in terms of any terrorist reprisals. As the months passed, however, and the expected reprisals failed to materialize, Europe's leaders began to recognize that perhaps Reagan's approach to "the Libyan mad dog" had been appropriate after all. Yet they remained skeptical as to whether this modern equivalent of nineteenth-century gunboat diplomacy could be successfully employed again in the labyrinth of the Middle East. It was for this reason that they greeted President Reagan's decision to escalate the Gulf naval confrontation with Iran with some consternation. There was no telling where this new strategy might lead the United States itself or what knock-on effects it might have on Europe, especially since the underlying purposes of American policy were not entirely clear.

For Western Europeans, then, the new spirit of adventurism that characterized Reagan's Third World policy was a mixed blessing. On the one hand, they were delighted that someone was doing something to challenge communist expansionism and stamp on international terrorism. On the other, they were suspicious that challenging communism also meant violating the sovereignty of small nations and that efforts to suppress terrorism might merely provide a pretext for further terrorist outrages. Yet, even in their ambivalence, they were not united. Margaret Thatcher, who not only shared Reagan's *realpolitik* view of the world but was also indebted to him for his support during the 1982 Falklands campaign, consistently provided strong backing for Reagan's global strategy. Continental Europeans, however, were more reserved. They feared that if they were to offer their public support to the United States they would damage their carefully cultivated relations with a large number of Third World regimes, especially in the Middle East. As a result, they distanced themselves from both U.S. policy and that of Mrs. Thatcher.

This divergence of Western European opinion over President Reagan's Third World policy had important consequences for the European Community itself. It had been hoped in the late 1970s that the development of a common European foreign policy would help restore the momentum of European integration, a momentum that in the early 1970s had faltered. Crucially, the divisions over Lebanon, Grenada, Libya, and the Gulf acted as powerful constraints on the growth of this common policy. Accordingly, they had the indirect effect of dampening the efforts of the more ardent Europeanists to revive the integration process.

One other aspect of Reagan's policy outside Europe requires brief consideration: SDI. Despite the President's optimistic initial portrayal of "Star Wars" as a defensive weapons system that would render the whole Western world safe from nuclear attack, his claims were interpreted in Europe from the outset as meaning that the system would offer a means of protecting only the continental United States. The widespread belief that the "umbrella" could not possibly be extended to cover Western Europe caused considerable alarm in European capitals. Secure in their nuclear-proof, continent-wide astrodome, the Americans might be tempted to contemplate the (previously) unthinkable: the fighting of a nuclear war with the USSR. All too aware of the devastating consequences that this kind of encounter would have on the Eurasian land mass, the Europeans (as ever, with the exception, at least in public, of Mrs. Thatcher) were horrified. Their worst fears were only allayed as it became clear, first, that the necessary technology for SDI still required extensive development, and, second, that for the foreseeable future any operational SDI system would probably offer only a "point defense" of important U.S. military targets rather than a blanket defense of the entire North American population. In these circumstances, the American people would remain just as vulnerable to nuclear war as the Europeans, a fact that would presumably inhibit any American temptation to believe that the United States could fight a nuclear war and emerge from it relatively unscathed.

All this said, SDI disturbed the Europeans. They were surprised by Reagan's simple-seeming belief that, with appropriate funding, American scientists could solve the enormous technical problems involved in the construction and deployment of such a gargantuan system. They did not believe his suggestion that, once the system had been perfected, it would be offered to the Soviets as a vehicle for universal defense and, by implication, universal peace and security. In particular, they could not square this latter proposition with the President's continuing belief—articulated again as late as December 1987—that the Soviet Union was an evil empire bent on the West's destruction. If the President's Third World policy had merely stimulated Europeans' ambivalence and division, his SDI policy had caused them to worry not only about the judgment of the man whose finger was on the nuclear trigger but also about the long-term basis of their own security. Fortunately, President Reagan himself was ineligible for a third term. But one question in the minds of Western European governments was whether his successor would persevere with his beloved SDI project. If SDI did remain the policy of the post-Reagan administration, it would undoubtedly represent a central problem in European-American relations into the indefinite future.

The impact, then, of Reagan's foreign and defense policies was mixed. With the notable exception of Margaret Thatcher, European leaders found his language and rhetoric alarming. They found his analysis of world events simplistic. In their view, it underemphasized the importance of indigenous changes in the Third World and overemphasized both the power and the malevolence of the Soviet Union. Inside the European theater, none of this mattered too much. NATO's agreed strategy had been firmly in place before Reagan took office, and he did little to change it. Outside Europe, things were different. Reagan's Third World strategy met with strong approval in Britain, but was treated with suspicion elsewhere. The main consequence of these varied responses was that the disagreements they engendered among the Europeans themselves put a brake on emerging attempts to build a common European foreign policy. The Strategic Defense Initiative was the source of greatest long-term concern for the Europeans. They were not convinced that it could ever offer the kind of immunity from nuclear attack for which the President longed. They were extremely worried about the damaging implications that SDI might have for the strategic balance that had kept the peace in Europe for forty years. They simply did not know what the Reagan legacy in this context might be.

Conclusion

Ronald Reagan came to the White House in January 1981 with the ambition of making America "walk tall" again in the world. In the early months of 1988, there were few signs—certainly in Europe—that he had achieved this ambition. In the first place, most Europeans had never shared Reagan's belief that American prestige in the world needed to be restored. They had viewed American setbacks, such as the seizure of the U.S. embassy hostages in Iran, as being the result of bad luck or specific miscalculation, not as the result of America's having, in some profound way, lost its way in the world. President Carter, so widely reviled in the United States, had been quite well regarded overseas.

Second, very few people outside the United States believed in 1988 that America was actually walking taller in the world than it had been at the time of Reagan's election. Reagan appeared, rightly or wrongly, to be a man of limited abilities, with an infirm grasp of the realities of the world situation. His policies, as over SDI and the deployment of American warships in the Persian Gulf, frequently seemed both confused and dangerous. Europeans, at least, found Reagan perplexing rather than imposing, a man to inspire caution rather than confidence. He was certainly not esteemed in the way that men like Truman, Eisenhower, Kennedy, and Nixon (in the field of foreign affairs) had been esteemed. Many in Europe remained puzzled that such a man had ever been elected to the U.S. Presidency.

Still, as we noted toward the beginning of this chapter, nothing too awful happened while Reagan was in the White House. World war did not break out. NATO did not disintegrate. In the long term, much would depend on the evolution of the SDI program and on whether America's trade and budget deficits, which Reagan did so little to curb, brought on a major world recession. Otherwise, Reagan's Presidency was regarded in Europe as having been, on the whole, a nonevent.

Notes

1. One caveat perhaps needs to be entered to this statement. There was, in connection with the negotiations that led up to the 1987 INF agreement, a good deal of nervousness in Europe lest the Reagan administration weaken Western European security by depriving NATO of needed nuclear firepower while leaving the Soviets with an overwhelming superiority in conventional and chemical weapons; and even after the treaty had been signed at the Gorbachev-Reagan summit, a few voices were still to be heard claiming that Reagan had been too trusting and had negotiated away too much. But such voices were in a small minority. Most European leaders, privately as well as publicly, welcomed both the INF deal and the improved superpower relations that had made it possible.

2. Quoted in Peter Jenkins, *Mrs. Thatcher's Revolution: The Ending of the Socialist Era* (London: Jonathan Cape, 1987), 210.

3. For reviews of existing findings, see Ivor Crewe, "Why the British Don't Like Us Anymore," *Public Opinion,* March/April 1987, 51-56; Werner J. Feld and John K. Wildgen, *NATO and Atlantic Defense: Perceptions and Illusions* (New York: Praeger, 1982); and Andrew Ziegler, Jr., "The Structure of West European Attitudes towards Atlantic Cooperation: Implications for the Western Alliance," *British Journal of Political Science* 17 (October 1987): 457-77.

4. In a Eurobarometer poll conducted in 1982, for example, only 17 percent of respondents across Europe found the Russians to be either "fairly" or "very" trustworthy. See *Eurobarometer* 17 (April 1982). ICPSR Study 9023.

5. The London *Economist* of 24 October 1987 headed a discussion of conservative economics in the 1980s "Lord Wishful, Lady Rigorous" and observed (p. 21): "Ronald Reagan and Margaret Thatcher claim to have rewritten the rules of economic policy during the 1980s. They see themselves as leaders of the same conservative revolution.

Comparing their policies, you would hardly guess it. . . ." See also a special issue entitled "The Conservative Revolution," *Economic Policy* 5 (October 1987).

6. For recent analyses of these problems, see Evan Luard, "Western Europe and the Reagan Doctrine," *International Affairs* 63 (Autumn 1987): 563-74; Phil Williams, "The Limits of American Power: From Nixon to Reagan," *International Affairs* 63 (Autumn 1987): 575-87; Charles Williams Maynes, "America's Chance," *Foreign Policy,* Fall 1987, 88-99; Jonathan Dean, "Military Security in Europe," *Foreign Affairs* 66 (Fall 1987): 22-40; Barry Buzan, "Common Security, Non-provocative Defence and the Future of Western Europe," *Review of International Studies* 13 (October 1987): 265-80.

10

President Reagan as a Political Strategist

Aaron Wildavsky

When I speak of politicians as strategists, I mean (1) that they have a vision, a broad sense of direction toward which they wish the nation to move; and (2) that they use effective and creative (nonobvious) means in pursuing these ends. Nothing is implied about the desirability of the directions chosen, for then politicians could be strategists only by being in accord with the preferences of the analyst. But I do mean to rule out nondemocratic means and ends, for one of the major tasks of a strategist is to work by persuasion rather than coercion. The more a politician alters prevailing policies and expectations concerning behavior while moving events in the desired direction, that movement and direction being compatible with democratic norms, the better the strategist.

There is a difference between being fact smart and being strategy smart. Jimmy Carter was fact smart. Unfortunately for him,[1] but fortunately for Ronald Reagan, the Presidency does not depend on memory for facts. The short-answer theory of the Presidency—that President is best who would score highest on a short-answer test—leaves a lot to be desired.

President Reagan's disinterest in, and misstatement of, facts about many aspects of public policy have led some observers to characterize him as dumb.[2] His flouting of the conventional wisdom on such issues as deficits has led others to dismiss him as obtuse. The fact that he keeps besting them deeply discomforts his policy opponents. Even then, they seek explanations outside of Ronald Reagan's strategic abilities. They denigrate the public, to whose low mentality the boob in the White House appeals. Or they upgrade his communication skills, damning with faint praise by suggesting he possesses some ineffable essence that exudes persuasiveness. Amiability as a substitute for understanding is the farthest his critics will go in alloting their limited supply of credit. The thesis of this chapter, by contrast, is that President Reagan is a superb political strategist.

Getting the Democrats to Support Republican Issues

The extraordinary character of the 1984 presidential campaign provides ample evidence of the profound effect that Ronald Reagan has had on national political debate. His steadfast support of across-the-board tax cuts in the face of immense pressure from established opinion led his Democratic party opponent, Walter Mondale, to make the achievement of a balanced budget into a positive moral virtue. Thus a Republican issue that, given its diffuse nature, never served that party well, became the mainstay of Democratic speeches and advertisements. At one stroke the Democratic party denied its traditional (and mostly successful) recourse to spending to create employment; it also obligated itself to keep the revenues it can raise from new taxes to reduce the deficit. The presidential campaign reduced the Democratic party issue—fairness—to a price tag of $30 billion, the additional sums Mondale would have spent on social welfare. If this 3 percent of total spending was all fairness amounted to, the remaining 97 percent was thereby blessed as "fair." Even if he had lost the election, Ronald Reagan would have won the battle over future domestic policy.

If Mondale was so smart and Reagan so dumb, why did the Democrats campaign on Republican issues? Surely the sanctity of the Constitution—due to President Reagan's support of constitutional amendments on budget limits, abortion, and prayer—and budget balance are not the issues the party of government intervention would choose to present itself. Virtually nothing was heard from the Democratic party about social welfare. Hardly a peep sounded in regard to a massive jobs program. That undoubtedly was the President's fault, for he shifted the entire debate in an economically conservative direction.

Domestic Policy Leadership

Denigration of the President has led Democrats to underestimate his policy guidance. For Ronald Reagan has integrated public policy with political support so as to provide creative policy leadership.

Ronald Reagan is the first President since Herbert Hoover (although, considering his activist temperament, Calvin Coolidge might be better) to favor

limited government at home. Pursuing his aim of restricting the reach and reducing the resources available to the federal government, Reagan helped cut
income taxes across the board dramatically, reducing the highest bracket from
70 to under 35 percent. His acceptance of historically high deficits, in an effort
to use resource scarcity to depress domestic spending still further, is eloquent
testimony to his singleminded devotion to decreasing the size of the domestic
government compared to the size of the economy.

Rumor has it that the President is so dumb that he cannot understand
complex tax questions. Presumably that is why we hear little or nothing about
raising taxes but a great deal about cutting spending. Shaping the congressional
agenda so that the major debate is whether defense or domestic programs should
be cut the most, even though this is not entirely to the President's liking, represents a substantial strategic success.

Ronald Reagan has succeeded in coordinating domestic policy. Every official in Washington is aware of what the President wants—less. When there
are conflicts, the goal of reducing the size of government wins out.

Even when the President's ostensible aim is not achieved, his adherence
to priorities provides a sense of direction. Reagan's initiative on restructuring
the federal system, for instance, failed for a number of reasons, including his
unwillingness to come up with the cash to cover the transition. Nevertheless,
the budget cuts have had a similar effect. For, as Richard Nathan's studies of
the responses show, a number of state governments have elected to fill in the
spending gap.[3] Perforce, state governments are exercising greater responsibility.

Emphasis on individual policies underestimates the accomplishments of
the first Reagan administration. There may, for instance, be less deregulation
than you or I or, indeed, the President would wish. Consideration of such matters, important as they are, however, does not begin to exhaust the moral influence of the President's devotion to more limited government. For there is an
extensive and persuasive (yet unrecorded) influence on individual behavior that
weans people from dependence on government. My favorite overheard conversation, in Berkeley no less, goes like this: "It would be a great idea to do such
and such. Wonderful. Let's get a government grant. Yeah. Oh, well, with Reagan around that's impossible. Do you suppose we could sell the service and
do this ourselves?" Though the uncoordinated efforts of millions of people moving to take care of themselves are not heard at a single time and place, so they
are not recorded as events, they add up to a transformation of expectations,
and, therefore, of practice in a self-reliant direction.

The sheer strategic brilliance of getting the opposing candidate to adopt
your major theme of limited government through a born-again commitment

to budget balance, while using the current imbalance as the only effective ceiling on spending the nation has known for a half century, has blinded Democrats to the policy genius of Ronald Reagan. He may not be that great a communicator, since Democrats have missed how badly he has outmaneuvered them, but he has provided both policy leadership and a political strategy to go with it.

The Do-Good Game

Democrats believe in using other people's money to support causes they deem desirable. "Doing good" requires at least a modest increment of resources over the prior year; this way, most everyone gets a little and a few receive a lot. "Tax and spend," as the slogan went, adding only "elect and elect," was in truth their motto. Ronald Reagan has changed all that. It is not so much that he led the drive for tax cuts (although he did) but that he prevented the substantial tax increases necessary to play the do-good game—you support my good cause and I'll support yours, as long as no one has to take less.

Before Reagan, the federal government's tax take was approximately 19 percent of gross national product. Now it is just about the same. How can this be with big marginal cuts in income tax rates? The built-in tax increases passed on by earlier governments—social security above all but also bracket creep and "windfall" energy taxes—have kept the overall federal tax rate constant. Had nothing changed, the tax take would have risen to about 23 percent, the 4 percent difference making up most of the entire deficit. It could be argued, to be sure, that Democrats could not have gotten away with such a substantial increase in the tax take, but I believe that without a visible increase in the income tax, they would have done (or, more precisely, failed to undo) exactly that. The crucial clue here is the dog that didn't bark; the missing factor for the Democrats is the tax increases that would have gone into effect automatically that they did not get to spend.

President Reagan has appropriated tax cuts (his good cause) that would otherwise have been available to Democrats for their favorite causes. With one blow, the President wiped out a decade of incremental increases in spending the Democrats would have used to smooth their way. These "it might have beens" are the saddest words as far as the mainline, liberal, left-of-center Democrats, the bulk of the party activists, are concerned.

Look at the deficit as a political strategy. Democrats need to justify a modest deficit either as a fiscal stimulant or as a response to pressing social problems. In the past, Republicans simply rejected deficits, proposing lower spending and higher taxes to fill the gap. To the extent that they follow Reagan's strategy, however, Republicans now prefer to keep marginal tax rates low, and hence economic incentives strong. They follow their President in arguing that if taxes are increased, "they (the liberals) will only spend it." Every time it looks like the Democrats might lower the deficit sufficiently to do good as they see it, Reaganite Republicans will counter with tax cuts so that taxpayers can do good as they see it. Indeed, instead of knee-jerk budget balancing, the Republican party of the future may view a declining deficit as an invitation to cut taxes still further.

Indeed, *if* (it is a big supposition) Ronald Reagan's successor is a Republican who continues to starve liberal Democrats of revenue, the Democratic party may well self-destruct. The reason Democrats have so little to say (observe the vigor of conservative versus liberal publications) is that they literally do not have the money to say it with. Allow them their spending increments and, *voila!* they would have plenty to talk about. In short, it is not a nonexistent decline in intellectual capacities but the lack of food for thought—namely, the money to spend on good causes—that makes modern Democrats appear dumb.

Keeping the Party Together

Ronald Reagan enjoys unparalleled supremacy within the Republican party because he is a perfect exemplar of its two main tendencies: social conservatism and what used to be called economic liberalism (i.e., reliance on free markets). To retain this position he must lend support to both wings of his party. But not, I hasten to add, at the same time. For if the two wings have to decide whether government should restrict individual choice, they would soon be at each other's collective throats. So far the President has managed to sidestep this conflict. One way has been to separate the two wings in time. Social issues have been stressed at election time and economic issues in between. Another way has been to separate the combatants in space. This separation may be accomplished through local option or by shifting the arena via proposals for constitutional amendments. Had the President not papered over the potential cracks in his party coalition, there would not now be talk about the possibility of party realignment.

The existence of a party realignment is a restrospective judgment. From the vantage point of today, there is only a large presidential victory not accompanied by corresponding change in congressional seats. Tomorrow remains to realize itself. What can be said is (1) that the 1984 election offered voters big policy choices; and (2) that President Reagan continues to pursue a distinctive strategy that (3) *could* rally extensive support in the future.

The election policy equation (as suggested by Alex Mintz) may be written as

$$revenue + deficit = defense + domestic\ expenditure$$

The candidates filled in the policy equation in assymetrical ways:

Mondale	+	−	=	−	+
Reagan	−	+	=	+	−

In the past, as the party of responsible finance, Republicans would try to cut spending and deficits; generally they were successful at neither. Under Reagan, they have abandoned the tasks at which they failed in the past in favor of others that are easier to accomplish.

So far, the Democratic party appears poised to campaign on two issues in 1988: taxes and defense. Everyone knows that tax increases do not constitute the best election promises. But by 1988, I expect, Democratic stultification with their inability to support deserving people will grow beyond their bounds of toleration. For them, politics is good causes; without money to fund them, politics lacks all point. Anger at President Reagan justifies being against the large deficits that he is for. Thus the Democratic party's campaign will not so much emphasize higher taxes as lower deficits.

Because the President has set booby traps for them, Democrats will have to propose straight, out-and-out tax increases. The first "trap" was the passage of tax indexing, which, until now, has resulted in higher revenues without higher tax rates as inflation pushed taxpayers into higher brackets. The second "trap" is in the flat (more accurately, a broad-based, low-rate income) tax. Of course, if rates are to be lowered, tax preferences must be reduced. The point is that with far fewer preferences, each increase in tax rates will be far more visible. After all, since the promise of tax reform is to reduce rates, it will be even more difficult than in the past to raise them. Given that rates cannot be raised, moreover, the only way to increase revenues is by cutting preferences. By joining preference cuts to rate cuts, the tax reform limits the reduction of preferences as a revenue-raising technique. Thus Ronald Reagan has deprived Democrats of their previously most potent instruments of public policy. Democrats therefore will have to make the argument implicit in their party's preferences: Higher progressive taxes are necessary in order to support social programs. Since most of the people have most of the money, tax increases will have to cover the broad middle masses. That, as Republicans have discovered, is not necessarily the most popular path.

The President as Intervenor of Last Resort

Ronald Reagan has not only altered trends in public policy, he has also transformed the role of President. Indeed, his alteration of the presidential role may be Reagan's most significant contribution. Until Reagan's time, it had been assumed that the breadth of presidential decision making would expand with the scope of government. The invention of presidential machinery to reach into other institutions (congressional liaison; mass media; officials for contact with mayors, governors, racial, ethnic, and religious groups) had resulted in making the concerns of external institutions part of those in the White House. But Reagan has changed roles and confounded expectations. He has chosen to reinterpret leadership not to mean what it meant before. Instead of the Presidency being the institution of "first resort," stepping in to solve problems, real and alleged, as soon as (perhaps sooner than) they manifested themselves, in Reagan's time the Presidency has become the institution of "last resort," entering the fray only when others abdicated. And not always then.

There are, of course, other things the President would like than smaller domestic government, but these are secondary, not primary. Thus the President is not nearly as conflicted about the use of his personal resources because his priorities are clear. The contrast with the mobilization regime of President Kennedy, or the restless opportunism of President Nixon, or the harmonization of government actors under President Ford, or the managerial style of President Carter, all of whom had long lists of priorities, even if they altered them frequently, could hardly be greater. It may be that steering in a single important direction, so as to get part of the way, will become more attractive than steering in different (Richard Nixon) or too many (John Kennedy or Jimmy Carter) directions or just emphasizing implementation (Gerald Ford) of existing programs.

Among the many criticisms raised about President Reagan, there is one especially relevant to him as a strategist: He is allegedly run by his staff. My observations are different. From his days as governor of California onward, Ronald Reagan, following his own understanding of how he might best use his talents, has deliberately structured his staff so that he would (1) make the critical choices; and (2) save his time.

There is evidence on Reagan's use of staff. In a book that can be described either as generally critical (because of the President's lapses) or disparagingly admiring (because of his undoubted successes), Laurence I. Barrett reveals that the President is quite capable of reining in his staff. Here, for instance, is an adviser who reported that the President not only rejected advice that three large tax reductions in a row might be too much but insisted that his preferences be respected.

> You look at all the stories being published about backing and filling and they give
> the impression that Reagan was changing back and forth. That's wrong. The peo-
> ple around him were changing, or some of us were. We were having doubts, and
> the news coverage reflected that. Reagan hardly moved at all. At one meeting Rea-
> gan got a little impatient with us. He said, "Listen, you guys are talking to each
> other and no one is asking me what I think. I'm sticking with it. . . ."[4]

It deserves to be emphasized that the President resisted not merely advice from
his own staff, including an ever-insistent David Stockman, but also from most
of the nation's vocal economists and business spokesmen. Without these cuts,
I might add, there would have been no distinctiveness to the President's program and no real reason for electing him rather than any other person.

I am reminded of the insightful discussion of the pluses and minuses of
removing a subordinate that takes place in James Gould Cozzens' fine novel
(set in the air force), *Guard of Honor*. The man has many shortcomings, but
these are known. His associates have learned how to take them into account.
A new man might well be more talented, but his hidden defects would, for
a time, remain unknown, and his colleagues would have to invest time and
effort in discovering them.

In exactly this sense, President Reagan has an investment in his staff. His
reluctance to fire is based on his investment in them as well as a realization
that everyone makes mistakes. When they arranged among themselves to swap
places, James Baker going to the Treasury, Donald Regan to the White House,
the President swiftly ratified their choice. Is this passive behavior? Or is this
a wise realization that weeks of search were unlikely to provide a chief of staff
who was necessarily better and about whom he would certainly have known
a good deal less?

Has the Iran-*contra* affair, widely portrayed as the result of a passive, dis-
engaged President, altered my judgment of Reagan as an active President?[5]

President Reagan was not misled by his advisers. He is the politician. He
is the one above all others who should have anticipated the near-universal revul-
sion to sending arms to Iran. "Iranamok" is an act of commission by a President who was continually interested in what was happening and asked far more
questions about the hostage situation than might have been expected. It was
not that the policy was good but its execution flawed, as the President said,
but that using arms shipments to penetrate Iran was a bad idea from the beginning. Bad policy makes bad politics; indeed, bad politics is part of bad policy.
Being critical makes it all the more important to criticize presidential behavior
for the right reasons.

President Reagan's fall from grace is not a result of inattention but of over-
reaction. My guess is that with two years to go, he tried too hard to control

events. The Danilov affair (where the planes carrying him out of the USSR and a Soviet spy out of the United States nearly passed each other) cost Reagan dearly in credibility. Yet the Soviets would have had to release the American reporter in order to continue their "peace offensive" in Europe. The escort service in the Persian Gulf must be the least cost-effective policy in recent history. What these and similar events have in common with the Iran-*contra* affair is that they were unnecessary. Had President Reagan slept through these events, as alleged, he would still be the most popular second-term President in recent times. Alas, impatience is not only a fault of the young.

Fusing Personal Style and Policy Preferences

Changes in the role of the Presidency and in the expectations surrounding it help explain one of the mysteries about President Reagan's public standing. Following upon a series of apparently discredited or unpopular Presidencies (how they will look in retrospect is another matter), President Reagan is seemingly immune to the vicissitudes of fortune. He makes errors of fact with apparent impunity. Failing policies (e.g., Lebanon) leave him apparently untouched. Even the Iran-*contra* affair has not prevented him from leading, as his arms control agreement shows. The pall that hung over Nixon's or Carter's last year stubbornly refuses, despite what critics consider substantial provocation, to settle on him. Why not?

Attention has been focused on the President's personal constitution (a charm that makes him difficult to hate) rather than on the changes he has wrought in the institutional constitution. Although Reagan reads a prepared speech well, one would have thought the first presidential debate of 1984 and numerous press conferences disposed of him as a "great communicator." The emphasis on this inexplicable skill, however, does obscure the need to talk about the substance of what he does and how he does it, that is, his strategic capacity.

I think personality and role work together; indeed, the fit is so close (limited government propounded by a man who likes to work limited hours) that it has deflected attention from the radical change in practices. A President such as Jimmy Carter, who expects to have enacted a series of substantial changes in policy based on his personal study of them, naturally reinforces expectations that he will do as advertised. A President who preaches self-reliance to the citizenry does not have to work as hard or know as much about public policies the government should not have or to provide help for people who should look after themselves. Role and responsibility are related.

Presidents not only make policies, policies make Presidents. Ronald Reagan has arisen as a political force in response to policies promulgated by the Democratic party. His strategic creativity (apart from appropriating Democratic symbols such as Franklin Roosevelt and Harry Truman) lies in crafting responses to take advantage of Democratic weaknesses.

When the Federalists struggled with the Antifederalists over whether the Constitution would replace the Articles of Confederation, Alexander Hamilton and James Madison turned the tide of opinion by reversing the direction of the political argument. Localism, which had been seen as the source of republican virtue, became parochialism, a source of special interests. The national government, then regarded as corrupting public virtue by introducing artificial inequality into public life, became the source of disinterested wisdom. Whether or not Ronald Reagan has realigned the electorate, he has reversed the arguments by which political action is justified; he has succeeded in taking the tag of "special interests" away from "the plutocrats" and pinning it onto the Democrats.

An intuitive understanding of the variety of views in American political life, and how to transcend them, is a rare gift. In one area, at least—tax reform—I think Ronald Reagan has this gift. Since it would be out of place here to give my reasons for believing that the heart of American exceptionalism lies in the belief that liberty and equality are (or can be made to be) compatible,[6] let us just take this for an assumption. The recent history of tax reform, meaning essentially a broader-based income tax with fewer and smaller tax preferences, is full of ups and downs. After Ronald Reagan made it a major feature of his second term (not that others, like Senator Bill Bradley [D-New Jersey] and Representative Richard Gephardt [D-Missouri], had not pushed the idea to little avail before), he worked hard to make it popular, but with mixed success. Every time the President and tax reform were counted out, however, he and it have bounced back. Why?[7]

The three major American cultures—individualism, egalitarianism, and hierarchy—are rendered compatible in one piece of legislation. People of low income either pay no taxes or pay less. Some businesses pay more but the individuals in them pay much lower marginal rates and the reduction of tax preferences is promoted as increasing incentives. All the while, higher deductions for children reduce somewhat the cost of larger families. Observe that the President defends the reform on the grounds it is fair, will spur economic incentives, and is good for the family. These terms are contemporary code words for greater equality of condition (fairness), greater equality of opportunity (incentives), and greater hierarchical order (the family). Obviously, Reagan saw something in this issue others did not see.

The fact that such a radical change passed, whereas it had before been considered near hopeless or even utopian, speaks to the President's willingness to go out on a limb for an apparent loser that he felt would eventually gain support. And the fact that tax reform makes it difficult to raise income tax rates in the near future, thereby holding down spending, will not, from Reagan's point of view, hurt either.

No leader is perfect, and Ronald Reagan is no exception. Anyone can think of problems that remain unresolved. The decisive movement of blacks into the Democratic party, for instance, is not only bad for democracy, it is also a barrier to the potential emergence of a Republican majority able to capture not only the Presidency but also both houses of Congress. Should Mexican Americans also become overwhelmingly Democrat, the Republicans might forever remain a minority party. It may be that there is an undercurrent of Republican support among blacks and Mexican Americans based on individualism and family values. If so, not enough has been done to make manifest the administration's identification with these people, even if it cannot accede to those among them who view larger government as the main solution to existing problems.

By showing that the Presidency can still be a powerful office, Ronald Reagan may have strengthened more than his own office. In a poll of academics who specialize in the Presidency, the *National Journal* noted that these observers gave Reagan credit for "his success in . . . reviving trust and confidence in an institution that in the post-Vietnam era had been perceived as being unworkable."[8] As Seymour Martin Lipset points out, ". . . it is ironic that the President's successes . . . have greatly increased faith in governmental institutions, while they have done little to reduce the high level of distrust of private power. . . ."[9] Irony, like unanticipated consequences, is the stuff of life. Strategic success may be a double-edged accomplishment.

But I think not. The President's vision is made up of social conservatism as well as economic liberalism (i.e., limited government). He believes in institutions, and he believes they should be effective in doing the jobs his political philosophy deems appropriate for them.

Foreign Policy

In regard to foreign and defense policy, the President has provided only partial leadership. He wants more for defense, but more for *what* remains unclear. Instead of being guided by a single, overarching framework, he is faced with innumerable smaller decisions that, like Lebanon, often turn out badly. Instead of managing internal conflict, as he does domestically because he knows what he wants, the President lacks a doctrine from which he can give guidance.

The United States lacks support for its foreign policy. European opinion is aghast. American opinion is skeptical. It takes a vast effort to get tiny sums for Central America. The opinion that the United States is the aggressor re-

mains widespread among its elites. The gap between rhetoric and action—
two minor interventions amid the continual need to deny bellicosity—bothers
friend and foe alike.

In sum, the consent necessary to maintain foreign and defense policy has
not been secured. Should a time of trouble arise, therefore, no one can say
whether even the most modest use of force would be sustainable nor the least
adverse consequence supportable. Among all the contenders for the Democratic
party nomination for President, for instance, there is not one that agreed on
the desirability of using force except under conditions—no serious Soviet objection, completely containable consequences, high moral stature of allies—
that cannot be met. Yet the forces in society these candidates represent (for
the Democrats are still the majority party) will remain in Congress and country when the election is over. Nor does one have to go to Democrats to find
opposition to foreign military involvements. The conditions laid out by former
Secretary of Defense Caspar Weinberger—massive public support, overwhelming
superiority, absolution in advance for defeat, an open-ended commitment to
do whatever it takes—are no less impossible. Leaving behind a legacy of opposition to foreign and defense policies in a democratic nation cannot be regarded as a success.

When he came into office, Ronald Reagan had long since decided to break
with the prevailing doctrine of enhanced governmental intervention by trying
to implement a rival doctrine of free-market economics. In regard to defense
and foreign policy, however, he did not challenge the direction of existing policies. The United States remained the democratic pillar of a bipolar world in
which containment of communism was its major responsibility. Thus the United
States remained the decision maker of first resort, undertaking to act first whether or not its allies went along. The President was faced with a continuing stream
of decisions concerning intervention without substantial support either from
his own people or his nation's allies. The choices were ambiguous; the results,
tenuous; the willingness of elites and citizens to support drawn-out endeavors,
dubious.

There is a blatant mismatch between public support and the missions assigned to the armed forces. The task of the Reagan administration, therefore,
is to reduce the disparity by increasing domestic support and decreasing the
need for it.

"Star Wars" as a Political Strategy

The President has begun to meet one of the requirements of leadership in the
international arena: forging a connection between defense and foreign policy.

The rationale of his Strategic Defense Initiative ("Star Wars" to aficionados) goes beyond whether it will be possible to stop a significant proportion of Soviet missiles in their early or mid-launch phase. For the very idea of defense challenges the conventional wisdom that there is no defense. Instead of promising to reach arms agreements that, at best, would still leave the world subject to mass destruction, Reagan promises to render these weapons far less destructive.

Question: Why is the United States spending so much money on defense? *Answer:* to defend the United States, its allies, even its foes against nuclear attack. The President now has part of a defense policy that he can explain to his people. Suppose it fails? At worst, the nation will have developed conventional antiballistic missiles that do work and that will make its land-based missiles less vulnerable to attack. But the President still needs to know where he wants the nation to go with a defense-oriented strategy. The emphasis on near-zero reduction in nuclear weapons is such a strategy.

Ronald Reagan has radically restructured American foreign policy. Before Reagan, the U.S. government was unable to convince its people or its allies to support a policy aptly called MAD (Mutual Assured Destruction). Now public support for the INF treaty and European recognition of its need for American nuclear defense are overwhelming. By pursuing a policy of vast reductions in nuclear weapons, coupled with strategic defense, the United States is on its way to achieving the two requisites of a successful policy—national defense coupled with public support.

What about conservative opposition? It is small and will get smaller because it cannot show how to get public support for the defense it wants. What about liberal opposition to the Strategic Defense Initiative? It will increase until new reductions in nuclear forces are agreed on. As the momentum of reduction in nuclear forces grows, while the limitations of inspection are clarified, however, more and more people will want defense against cheating. Both ground and space-based defense will then come back into vogue. So will European and Asian self-defense, not through American importuning but through their adjustment to a world in which less risk of nuclear war may mean greater risk of nonnuclear but hardly conventional conflict. Through all this change, the diminution of past fears and their replacement with hopefully less cataclysmic new ones, President Reagan's policies will have led the way.

It would be nice if, in addition to his ability to put government on creative paths, President Reagan was better at remembering facts. Who has not wanted to cut the eyes out of the potato of life? Yet if President Reagan represented our conventional view of how a President should act, he might not be the kind of person who didn't know that tax reform was impossible or that going down to very low levels of nuclear weapons was unfeasible.

A Meteoric Leader in
an Antileadership System

What has Reagan wrought, in sum, that justifies the sobriquet "strategist"? He has devised appropriate means for keeping his party together. He has provided policy guidance (with the exception noted) to coordinate the farflung efforts of his administration. He has integrated his personality with his policy positions and his administrative style. He has altered expectations, at least in domestic policy, from government as the intervenor of first resort to intervenor of last resort so as to suit his policy preferences. No other postwar President redirected both domestic and foreign policy in his desired direction while gaining reelection and keeping his party united.

In critical areas of policy, the President has shaped the congressional agenda to his liking. Although he cannot control outcomes, not being all-powerful, he has been able to keep items, such as income tax increases, off the agenda and to keep those he wants discussed, such as cuts in domestic spending, at the forefront of concern. He has exposed the weaknesses of his opponents; the deficit has deprived them of the opportunity to keep supporting their constituencies. Indeed, he has, so to speak, converted them to a Republican doctrine, budget balance, that will make their political lives much more difficult. Nor was this easy. Confronted with the necessity of giving up not only his tax cuts but all that this implied in terms of his vision of limited domestic government and incurring large deficits in view of his party's historical opposition to them, Ronald Reagan chose limited government. And unless there are drastic economic changes, the large, tax-led deficits he helped create have not been noticeably harmful. Reagan has also begun to enunciate a rationale for a defense-led, low-level, nuclear weapons policy that combines domestic support with protection of the nation. Yet, to his critics, this is not enough.

A good part of the objections to Reagan's style comes from those who think that Presidents should have many more preferences and should intervene far more directly to achieve them. They must wish someone else was President because their advice would be suitable only for a different person. This is the essence, I take it, of James D. Barber's characterization of Reagan as a "passive-positive" President, that is, someone who is upbeat but reactive rather than proactive. I think not. The difference in appraisal really boils down to whether having many preferences, and therefore, priorities, will get Presidents further in advancing their objectives than having very few. In today's political context, where the call for the exertion of leadership is followed immediately by efforts to tear it down, the risk of having a big agenda is big stultification. I see no reason to tie Ronald Reagan to a mode of behavior that has not worked for his immediate predecessors.

Whether by accident or design, Ronald Reagan's political style fits well with the opportunities and constraints offered by the American national political system in the 1980s. The constraints are not only structural—the separation of powers, checks and balances, federalism—which usually operate to restrict what chief executives can do on their own. Hierarchy, the expectation that authority inheres in formal position, has historically been weak in America. Nor are these constraints entirely political, his Republican party being a large minority in the Senate (where Reaganite conservatives are but one faction), and a distinct minority in the House of Representatives. All this means is that the President has to bargain. Nothing new here.

On top of his party's minority status, the President faces a political milieu both desirous and distrusting of leadership. Were this not so, it would be difficult to explain the series of failed Presidents who preceded him. When we look at the social movements that have risen as Presidents have fallen, with but two interconnected exceptions—the antiabortionists and Protestant fundamentalists such as the Moral Majority—they are devoted to greater equality of condition. The civil rights movement, the women's movement, gay rights, children's rights, gray power, and more, are avowedly devoted to diminishing differences between groups of people. The point here is that authority is a form of inequality, for it would allow some people to decide for others. Viewing the Presidency as part and parcel of American social life, it is not so surprising that it has been buffeted (the higher the rank, the stronger the winds) by fierce political storms.

Were these critical currents directed against individual officeholders, they might more easily be withstood. But they are not. It is the political system itself, not a policy or a politician or a party, that is held to blame or, to use the current code, that is deemed unfair. System blame has grown to epidemic proportions. When groups of leaders were asked by Sidney Verba and Gary Orren whether poverty in America was the fault of the poor or the system, for instance, 86 percent of black leaders, 76 percent of feminists, 68 percent of Democrats, 50 percent of media, and 44 percent of intellectuals blamed the system.[10] No wonder Democratic as well as Republican Presidents have been held in disrepute!

Presidents are elected for fixed terms and given large constitutional and legislative responsibilities. They cannot appear only at ceremonial occasions, following the national consensus on policies where it exists and returning to obscurity when conflict threatens.

What, then, are our poor Presidents to do when the same people who urge government to do much more simultaneously blame the system that has to do it? Efforts to provide across-the-board guidance on a panoply of problems fail, a la Jimmy Carter, because they become the simultaneous focus of criticism of those who believe the government has taken on too much and those who believe it has not done enough because the system from which decisions stem is fatally flawed. Similarly, it is not partisan bias that afflicts the media but the disposition to system blame that leads its practitioners to excoriate politicians. The severe reaction to the Iran-*contra* episode has only strengthened my conviction that the Presidency is situated within an antileadership system. President John F. Kennedy, for instance, after taking responsibility for the Bay of Pigs, was able to shut off all efforts to make him talk about it in public.

Nevertheless, amid the continuous casting of blame, the demand for presidential leadership continues unabated. Whether the subject is deficits, social security, disarmament, trade, tax reform, immigration, or whatever, there is no substitute for the President. Hence Presidents are tempted into action only to discover that whatever they do is not what they were somehow supposed to have done.

Enter Ronald Reagan. By undertaking a very few major initiatives, with widespread consequences, he is seen as a positive leader. By reserving his imprimatur for only the matters he considers most vital, he makes an infrequent target. By disclaiming intimate factual knowledge of specifics, he reduces the expectation that the President is responsible for whatever is disliked. And when the complaints that the President has provided insufficient leadership rise to a crescendo, he may notice, along with us observers, that the demand to do more in the future does not decline (indeed, it may well be enhanced) just because he has refused to rise to the bait before.

Were the United States a country in which authority inhered in position, Presidents could emulate Jimmy Carter by emitting constant calls for action. But it is not; and they should not. While no one can look back from a future that is yet to unfold, so we cannot yet know how successful President Reagan will be in changing the vision of America through the long-run alteration of ideas, he is providing about as much direction as the existing American antileadership system can support. For what he does not attempt, as well as for what he does, President Reagan is the appropriate leader for his time.

Notes

1. See Jack Knott and Aaron Wildavsky, "Jimmy Carter's Theory of Governing," *Wilson Quarterly,* Winter 1977, 49-67.

2. President Abraham Lincoln, often viewed as a paradigm of seriousness, allocated his time predominantly to war and union. A lot got left out. In a distinguished series of essays on Lincoln, David Donald observes:

Less than any other major American President did Lincoln control or even influence the Congress. Noting that many of the Civil War congressman were his seniors and humbly declaring "that many of you have more experience than I, in the conduct of public affairs," Lincoln bowed not merely to the will but to the caprice of the legislators. . . . The President had remarkably little connection with the legislation passed during the Civil War. He proposed few specific laws to Congress: his bill for compensated emancipation is notably exceptional. He exerted little influence in securing the adoption of bills that were introduced. In some of the most significant legislation enacted during his administration Lincoln showed little interest. The laws providing for the construction of a Pacific railroad, for the creation of the Department of Agriculture, for the importation of "contract laborers" from Europe, for the tariff protection of American manufacturers, and for the establishment of land-grant colleges had little connection with Lincoln aside from his formal approval of them. That approval was usually granted without hesitation. Less than any other important American President did Lincoln use his veto power. . . . Lincoln was also ineffectual in controlling the executive departments of the government. He and his cabinet never formed a unified administration. (David Donald, *Lincoln Reconsidered: Essays on the Civil War Era* [New York: Random House, 1956], 191-93.)

3. Richard P. Nathan and Fred C. Doolittle, "The Untold Story of Reagan's 'New Federalism,'" *Public Interest,* no. 77 (Fall 1984): 96-105.

4. Laurence I. Barrett, *Gambling with History: Ronald Reagan in the White House* (New York: Penguin, 1984), 133.

5. See my "What the Hell Is Going On? Reagan, Iran, and the Presidency," (with a reply by James David Barber), *American Spectator* 20, no. 4 (April 1987): 14-18.

6. See my "The Three Cultures: Explaining Anomalies in the American Welfare State," *Public Interest,* no. 69 (Fall 1982): 45-58; "Industrial Policies in American Political Cultures," in *The Politics of Industrial Policy,* ed. Claude E. Barfield and William A. Schambra (Washington, D.C: American Enterprise Institute, 1986), 15-32; and "The Party of Government, the Party of Opposition, and the Party of Balance: An American View of the Consequences of the 1980 Election," in *The American Elections of 1980,* ed. Austin Ranney (Washington, D.C.: American Enterprise Institute, 1981), 329-50.

8. Dom Bonafede, "Presidential Scholars Expect History to Treat the Reagan Presidency Kindly," *National Journal* 17, no. 14 (6 April 1985): 743-47.

9. Seymour Martin Lipset, "The Confidence Gap: Down but Not Out" (typescript, April 1985).

10. Sidney Verba and Gary R. Orren, *Equality in America: The View from the Top* (Cambridge, Mass.: Harvard University Press, 1985), 74.

Index

About the Contributors

CHARLES O. JONES is the Glenn B. and Cleone Orr Hawkins Professor of Political Science at the University of Wisconsin-Madison.

BERT A. ROCKMAN is professor of political science and research professor in the University Center for International Studies at the University of Pittsburgh.

DAVID M. O'BRIEN is an associate professor of government at the University of Virginia.

PETER M. BENDA is an assistant professor of government at the University of Virginia.

CHARLES H. LEVINE is a Distinguished Professor of Government and Public Administration at The American University.

PAUL ALLEN BECK is professor of political science at Ohio State University.

JAMES W. CEASER is professor of government at the University of Virginia.

PAUL E. PETERSON is professor of government at Harvard University.

MARK ROM is a research assistant at The Brookings Institution.

I.M. DESTLER is a professor in the School of Public Affairs at the University of Maryland, College Park.

ANTHONY KING is pro-vice-chancellor and professor of government at the University of Essex.

DAVID SANDERS is a lecturer in government at the University of Essex.

AARON WILDAVSKY is professor of political science at the University of California at Berkeley.